McCARTHYISM
VS. CLINTON JENCKS

McCARTHYISM
VS. CLINTON JENCKS

RAYMOND CABALLERO

FOREWORD BY MICHAEL E. TIGAR

UNIVERSITY OF OKLAHOMA PRESS : NORMAN

Publication of this book is made possible through the generosity of Edith Kenney Gaylord.

Library of Congress Cataloging-in-Publication Data

Names: Caballero, Raymond, 1942–, author.
Title: McCarthyism vs. Clinton Jencks / Raymond Caballero ; Foreword by Michael E. Tigar.
Description: Norman, Oklahoma : University of Oklahoma Press, 2019. | Includes bibliographical references and index.
Identifiers: LCCN 2019000824 | ISBN 978-0-8061-6397-0 (pbk. : alk. paper)
Subjects: LCSH: Jencks, Clinton E., 1918–2005—Trials, litigation, etc. | Trials (Political crimes and offenses)—United States—History—20th century. | United States. Supreme Court—History—20th century. | Political persecution—United States—History—20th century. | Labor movement—Political activity—Southwestern States. | Strikes and lockouts—Zinc mining—New Mexico. | Civil rights—United States—Cases.
Classification: LCC KF224.J45 C33 2019 | DDC 345.73/0231—dc23
LC record available at https://lccn.loc.gov/2019000824

The paper in this book meets the guidelines for permanence and durability of the Committee on Production Guidelines for Book Longevity of the Council on Library Resources, Inc. ∞

CONTENTS

List of Illustrations   vii
Foreword, by Michael E. Tigar   ix

Introduction   3
1. Clinton Edward Jencks   10
2. Grant County, New Mexico   19
3. Red Scares and Anticommunism   25
4. Clinton Jencks and Local 890, 1947–1950   42
5. Empire Zinc Strike   51
6. *Salt of the Earth*   70
7. *United States v. Clinton E. Jencks*   86
8. The Jencks Trial Personalities   93
9. Clinton Jencks on Trial   105
10. *False Witness*: Matusow's Confessional   124
11. Questionable Witnesses and the Motion for New Trial   133
12. The Court of Appeals   145
13. The Supreme Court   151
14. FBI Files and the Reverend J. W. Ford   167
15. FBI Files and Harvey Marshall Matusow   178
16. Clinton Jencks after the Trial   188
17. Some Observations   195

Notes   209
Bibliography   275
Acknowledgments   293
Index   295

ILLUSTRATIONS

FIGURES

Mochida family	6
Clinton and Virginia Jencks	15
FBI director J. Edgar Hoover	29
U.S. senator Joseph R. McCarthy	39
Picket line, Empire Zinc strike	56
Strikebreakers taunting pickets	57
Leslie Goforth, Grant County sheriff	57
Local 890 leadership in jail	63
Nathan Witt, Maurice Travis, Clinton Jencks, Cipriano Montoya, and David Serna	63
Herbert Biberman and *Salt of the Earth* film crew	81
Jencks family	90
U.S. district judge R. Ewing Thomason	94
John T. McTernan	99
Jencks at federal courthouse in El Paso	109
Harvey M. Matusow	127
Herblock cartoon	135
Associate Justice William J. Brennan Jr.	159
John V. Lindsay	175

MAPS

Southwest New Mexico	17
Grant County, New Mexico	20

FOREWORD

IN THIS BOOK, Raymond Caballero has given us a compelling, eloquent, and timely history of Clinton Jencks's life and work. When Clint died in December 2005, I wrote this in memoriam:

> I met Clint Jencks in about 1959 when I was an undergraduate at Berkeley. He was getting his Ph.D. and was the teaching assistant in economics for our section. I knew of his history and was honored to get to know him. We spent many hours together talking about labor history and his own life. As a teacher, he was inspiring. He put basic economics into historical and political context. He led volunteer reading group sessions outside of class.
>
> More than all that, we became political allies. He inspired me to read more deeply and greatly influenced my own passage into the field of human rights in a national and international context. My father, who was a union leader, had died when I was 14, and I looked up to Clint as though he were my father.
>
> In 1962–63, when I was a journalist in London (taking a year between undergraduate school and law school), Clint came and stayed with me for a time. He was working on his Ph.D. thesis, studying the working

conditions of miners in the United Kingdom and Poland as well as the United States. Eventually, he got that Ph.D. and went to teach at San Diego.

My memory of him is that he embodied soft-spoken courage and integrity. He spoke no more than he could defend, but what he knew and could and would defend was the most basic of human truths. He lived and exhibited this greatness of character in so many ways. His contribution to human dignity is immeasurable.

Lawyers who represent the accused in federal court say "the Jencks Act" and the "Jencks case" every day of their working lives. For those of us privileged to know Clint and his story, we say it with a mental picture of this great man. And now when I say it, I will (as at this moment) have an ever-renewing sense of our great loss.

Clint's role as leader of the miners' union during intense labor struggles in New Mexico and Arizona gives us an example of courage, and will give valuable counsel to this generation of those who campaign for worker rights. In my latest book, I have discussed the revival of labor organizing campaigns that are community-based and focused on the wages and working conditions of the most marginalized and disadvantaged workers.

The centerpiece of this book is the fascinating discussion of the events that led to and followed from *Jencks v. United States*, decided in 1957. In the antiprogressive hysteria of the 1950s, it was inevitable that Jencks would be a target of hostile government action. The House Committee on Un-American Activities, the Subversive Activities Control Board, and the department that calls itself "Justice" had a stable of witnesses, serial perjurers who were ready to swear that somebody had been at a meeting, paid dues, or uttered dissenting remarks. When Jencks was accused of falsely swearing he was not a member of the Communist Party, several of these witnesses were called upon.

As almost everybody knows, cross-examination is the essential tool for uncovering falsehood. Indeed, we read in Proverbs 18:17: "He that is first in his own cause seemeth just, but his neighbor cometh and searcheth him." This precious right is nearly worthless unless the cross-examiner has access to the lying witness's prior statements, given before the government purchased the perjury with threats or reward. The Supreme Court's Jencks decision upheld that right of access, and a Congressional statute codified it in "the Jencks Act."

In the Supreme Court, the government lawyers surely knew that basic fairness would likely win the day. So they portrayed the issue as one of "national security," daring the justices to unlock the box containing truth for fear that state secrets might be inside as well. The Court reminded them of its 1953 ruling that "judicial control over the evidence in a case cannot be abdicated to the caprice of executive officers." And Judge Learned Hand had said in 1950: "Few weapons in the arsenal of freedom are more useful than the power to compel a government to disclose the evidence on which it seeks to forfeit the liberty of its citizens."

So here is another way that Clinton Jencks's life and work can instruct us. We hear the old and tired, perennially renewed government cry of "national security" again in our time, and with the same insistence that the government be allowed to intrude on basic rights. And the answer must be the same: insistence on judicial power to rein in the Executive Branch, an insistence that found an early champion in Chief Justice John Marshall.

At the beginning of this foreword, I remarked that when I met Clinton Jencks I already knew of his history. Valuable episodes in that history are chronicled in the film *Salt of the Earth*, in which he played a leading role as the labor leader that he was. When you have read the book you hold in your hand, you will probably want to look up the film and come to know Clinton Jencks even better. Certainly, Raymond Caballero has done us a great service by writing this introduction to Clint.

Michael E. Tigar

McCARTHYISM
VS. CLINTON JENCKS

INTRODUCTION

FRIENDS AND FAMILY GATHERED in December 2005 for the funeral of Clinton Edward Jencks, a kind, respected, and beloved emeritus economics professor and decorated World War II veteran. A convert, he received Jewish rites and was honored at a large memorial event. The man whose life they celebrated had also been a Communist, a convicted felon, a militant and reviled union organizer, and a rabble-rouser. He was a civil rights activist notorious for having led Mexican American miners in a strike famous for having wives and mothers replace men on the picket line. The strike was memorialized in *Salt of the Earth,* a boycotted film made by blacklisted Hollywood Communists. In these and other events, Jencks experienced many variations of McCarthyism's repression, including his 1954 conviction in a stridently anti-Communist Texas court, a judgment the U.S. Supreme Court reversed in a landmark decision.

■

In the early 1950s, millions of Americans feared a Soviet nuclear attack and the domestic Communist threat. Maps depicted the growing Communist danger as a menacing red ink blot devouring nation after nation. U.S. senator Joseph R. McCarthy warned us about treacherous Soviet spies working inside our government with complicit high-ranking fellow travelers approving their presence. News publications revealed secret Communist cells undermining our nation and our way of life. On television's *I Led Three Lives,* advertising executive Herbert Philbrick, an intrepid American counterspy, penetrated a secret Communist cell for the FBI. Weekly, the telegenic Catholic bishop Fulton J. Sheen highlighted communism's evils. Bringing the threat closer to home, public service announcements encouraged us to join the Ground Observer Corps and Operation Skywatch to help the U.S. Air Force detect and identify Soviet bombers flying over us en route to deliver their nuclear payload and the likely end of the Western world. Air raid sirens wailed during periodic tests, and air raid shelters appeared everywhere, reminding everyone of the peril.

Elementary schools drilled students on how to prevent their incineration in an atomic blast by bending down and holding their heads. The nuns at parochial schools contributed to students' fears in warning that the Blessed Virgin had given the children at Fatima three messages, including one about communism so dreadful that it could not be revealed until 1960. Fatima's terrible third secret helped the anti-Communist Catholic Church install fascist dictatorships in Spain and Portugal, oppressive regimes that lasted more than a generation. For decades at Mass, Catholics had been praying for Russia's conversion. That pervasive fear generated a hatred of Communists and the Soviets such that Joseph Stalin seemed to replace Satan. The FBI became the nation's protector as it shifted its well-burnished image from combating tommy gun-armed bank robbers to exposing Communist spies and subversives, with J. Edgar Hoover becoming a national St. Michael.

Most Americans had no idea how the national terror over communism affected those who had joined the American Communist Party or those who were suspected subversives, because those individuals had been stripped of their humanity, rendering them utterly contemptuous. Americans erred in assuming that it was illegal to be a Communist or that Party members were not entitled to the law's protection. It was much later that many came to realize that they had also taken part in that era's national hysteria, adding their share of fear and hatred.

■

On a cold, windy, and overcast March 4, 1933, the president of the United States stood on the podium before the U.S. Capitol, eased up to the lectern, and addressed an anxious America in his first inaugural address. Franklin

Delano Roosevelt came to power in the nation's darkest hour, a time when many Americans, perhaps most, had lost hope, and when the nation seemed incapable of righting its moribund economy. As the irrepressible new president addressed the nation, he attempted to revive its better instincts, its inner strength, and the spirit he was convinced had always been there. Along with calls to action and for driving the "money changers" from the temple of government, he uttered the words that would thereafter define his persona. "This great Nation will endure as it *has* endured," he said with determined mien and voice, "will revive and will prosper." And then in the next sentence, to underscore the drama in the historic words to follow, FDR paused after "is," a word he stretched with rising intonation as he continued, "So first of all, let me assert my firm belief that *the only thing we have to fear iiis—fear itself*—nameless, unreasoning, unjustified terror which paralyzes needed efforts to convert retreat into advance."[1]

That was a wise observation spoken by a leader who understood fear and the paralysis and evil it could produce. But in the years following, FDR sometimes forgot his own words, such as two months after Pearl Harbor when he ordered, without evidence or due process, the immediate arrest, internment, and dispossession of more than 100,000 West Coast Japanese—newborns to the aged, men and women, citizens and noncitizens alike.[2] The suspicion was that these people were more loyal to the Japanese emperor than to America, and because there was no way to determine their allegiance, the operating presumption would be that they were disloyal and would collude with the empire, making their internment a military necessity. It was an order based on an unreasoning fear pushed along by racism. Years later, universal criticism of that presidential order underscored the wisdom of FDR's own earlier admonition.

Fear is a natural response to a threat. It was unreasoning and unjustified fear that Roosevelt had warned against. The Japanese Empire was a deadly, dangerous menace to America and should have been feared, but there was no basis for distrusting all but a handful of America's Japanese. In the *Korematsu* case,[3] the Supreme Court upheld FDR's internment order and sanctioned its clear violation of Japanese Americans' constitutional rights. The Supreme Court did so with the help of the solicitor general, who violated his office's traditional obligation of candor to the Court in withholding a key Naval Intelligence report noting that U.S. Japanese were not a general security risk and could be screened individually. The solicitor was also aware that there was no study showing the contrary, making baseless his "military necessity" argument. The withheld Ringle report's conclusion was that the

Members of the Mochida family awaiting evacuation bus. Hayward, California, May 1942. *Photograph by Dorothea Lange. Bancroft Library, University of California at Berkeley.*

"entire 'Japanese Problem' [had] been magnified out of its true proportion, largely because of the physical characteristics of the people."[4] In the mid-1980s, after the Ringle report and its concealment surfaced in the *Hohri* case, the District of Columbia Court of Appeals held that "the suppression of the Ringle report and the absence of countervailing data suggest that the Justice Department misled the Supreme Court when it argued that 'military necessity' justified a mass evacuation of Japanese-American citizens."[5] Years later, a former acting solicitor general noted that even when the line-attorney handling the internment cases suggested to the solicitor general that withholding the Ringle report would be close to "suppression of evidence," the wartime solicitor general concealed the report. Yet despite insistence by Justice Department lawyers writing the briefs that the Ringle report be divulged and that "military necessity" be dealt with honestly, in the brief the government filed, the Court was not so advised, and at the oral argument, the solicitor general maintained that there was nothing to detract from the government's assertion that the internment was a military necessity.[6]

The Japanese internment would not be the last time that Americans, again overcome with unreasoning fear, would confuse a true external threat with an exaggerated domestic risk, nor would it be the last time that the solicitor general would intentionally mislead the Supreme Court of the United States.

■

From the late 1940s and into the 1960s, the same unreasoning and unjustified fear gripped America once more. With the Cold War and the possibility of a nuclear holocaust, Americans' initial anxiety that Communists were secretly loyal to the Soviet Union grew into hysteria by the late 1940s. Anti-Communists whipped up America's fears and successfully conflated a miniscule domestic Communist threat with the real Soviet menace. The anti-Communist movement also broadened the exaggerated internal threat to include not only members of the Communist Party of the United States,[7] but also former Party members, socialists, anarchists, and those who had joined causes or allied organizations opposing war or fighting for civil rights or labor. The anti-Communist movement wildly succeeded in producing a massive overreaction that disrupted the lives of thousands of Americans and ruined careers and reputations. Thousands silently went missing from their former jobs at plants, schools, colleges, and government offices and would spend years trying to regain what they lost. Unknown thousands never realized that they had not been hired because an unseen process had labeled them subversive. A powerful anti-Communist movement instituted invasive and repressive legislation and a host of measures and exposures intended to ruin lives and careers. That oppression, generally known as McCarthyism, was the twentieth century's longest and most repressive red scare.[8]

The McCarthy anti-Communist era encompassed more than the four years (1950–54) its namesake, Senator McCarthy, dominated the movement. The House Un-American Activities Committee (HUAC) was established years earlier in 1938, and the movement remained active into the 1960s. The anti-Communist movement should perhaps more appropriately be named after J. Edgar Hoover, director of the Federal Bureau of Investigation, as he was its dominant personality and driving force. Having spent his lengthy career warning America of the Communist threat, Hoover was most responsible for the era's climate of repression.

When a group is feared, reviled, demonized, and dehumanized, society will sanction abuse, even crimes, against those so feared and hated. In the

1950s, the Soviet Union, posing a real threat to America, became feared and loathed. American Communist Party members took their ideological lead from the Soviet Party, but except for a tiny minority, they posed no security risk to the United States. Despite lacking evidence of illegal activity, the anti-Communist movement blacklisted individuals from working in their chosen careers; screened artists, writers, and teachers for loyalty; and hounded militant union organizers for years simply for their union work. Public opinion polls confirmed that an American super-majority would deny basic rights to Communists whose political conduct, in theory, was legal and constitutionally protected.

Despite the U.S. Constitution's promise of unrestricted right of belief, association, and expression, thousands of American Communists, socialists, and left-wingers were harassed and persecuted for their political beliefs and associations by the anti-Communist movement. Conduct as innocent as having one's name on a mailing list or signing a petition opposing seg- regation or war could cause loss of employment or placement on a dreaded subversive blacklist. In her classic anticommunism studies, historian Ellen Schrecker concluded that "although no single story can encompass every element of that repression, that of Clinton Jencks comes close."[9] In other words, the experiences of Clinton Jencks are emblematic of a time now seen as a national nightmare.

■

It was an impressive room. With cork floors and subdued, indirect lighting, the main courtroom of the New Deal-era, art deco U.S. Courthouse had an elegant formality and an imposing atmosphere.[10] Prosecutors and criminal defense lawyers practicing there routinely exchanged witness statements and reports once the witnesses had testified on direct examination, documents they called "Jencks Act material." Lawyers often cited cases and statutes such as the Jencks Act, but had little knowledge of their history.

Behind every criminal case there is a personal story, and the U.S. Supreme Court decision *Jencks v. United States* (along with the statute enacted to modify its holding, known as the Jencks Act) is no exception. For years, El Paso lawyers have routinely demanded and produced Jencks Act statements without realizing that Jencks, the defendant in the Supreme Court case and the statute's namesake, was tried and convicted in 1954 in that very El Paso courtroom for falsely denying that he was a Communist Party member.

This is the story behind that historic case, the story of how the nation's legal institutions, charged with upholding our basic law, acted instead to deny Clinton Jencks the Constitution's promises. His story is embedded within anticommunism's broader history, which includes McCarthyism, and the questionable strategies it developed to torment and disparage Communists and left-wing Americans.

Clinton Jencks lived to see the Supreme Court reverse his conviction, but in the minds of many Americans, his case was overturned on a legal technicality, and they were convinced that he remained a lying, guilty Communist. But it is only through new materials revealed here that we learn the surprising truth behind his conviction, and that is a story that has *not* been previously told.

The Federal Bureau of Investigation, Department of Justice lawyers and their high-ranking superiors, the Office of the Solicitor General of the United States, and John V. Lindsay, Special Assistant to the Attorney General and New York City's future mayor, pursued what they knew was an unjust prosecution against Jencks. All but one court willfully neglected to discharge their obligation to give Jencks a fair hearing, and in doing so, could not uncover the government's unethical and illegal conduct. Only by disregarding the intentional misrepresentations and arguments made to it by the solicitor general and Lindsay did the United States Supreme Court save the day for Jencks, an action that led many Americans to revile the court for freeing a Communist.

1

CLINTON EDWARD JENCKS

YOU COULD TELL from those attending his services that people were drawn to Clinton Jencks by something in his personality that grabbed individuals and pulled them into his story. It happened to many as they brushed with fragments of his incredible life.

EARLY YEARS

Clinton Edward Jencks was unusual even as a boy. When only ten years old, he showed the morals and ethics that would guide him throughout his life. Those values also drove his ideology, politics, and career choices. As a boy, Clinton was curious about miners and religious missionaries. He readily acknowledged that he was as deeply influenced by his family's faith, morals, and missionary history as he was by those who had toiled in the mining towns and camps around Colorado Springs, his birthplace and boyhood home. The inspiration he drew from missionaries and miners is evident in his life.

Jencks was born just over a century ago on March 1, 1918, to Horace Ebenezer Jencks and Ruth Shideler, both of whose families had roots in colonial America.[1] The immigrant Jencks progenitor was Joseph Jenks—as early generations spelled it—an English iron worker who in the 1640s helped establish an iron works on the Saugus River in Massachusetts. It is now a national historic site, and Jenks is prominently mentioned in its history.[2] His son, Joseph Jr., was among Rhode Island's first colonists, and Joseph Jenks III was its governor in 1727. A century later, descendant Leavens Jencks, a carpenter, migrated west to Killingly, Connecticut, where he and his wife Esther Kelley raised their six children in a devout Congregationalist home. Clinton's mother Ruth was a Shideler whose family had their roots in the Rhineland, and like the Jencks, they were also religious.[3]

A few months before the Civil War's end in 1865, Abraham Lincoln established the nation's first federal social service program, the United States Bureau of Refugees, Freedmen, and Abandoned Lands (commonly known as the Freedmen's Bureau), to assist newly emancipated slaves in the war-torn South. The South had prohibited educating slaves and, lacking a public-school system, neglected to educate many—if not most—whites as well. Congregationalists took on the mission of educating former slaves.

Leavens's son, Dewitt Clinton Jencks (our Clinton's grandfather and namesake), was passionate about his religion, his church's commitment to slavery's abolition, and the Congregationalist missions. He was among the first deployed to Georgia as a missionary teacher, an experience that undoubtedly left an impression on the young man. Accounts of white society's hostility toward Freedmen Bureau employees are legend, as the young missionaries enthusiastically engaged in upending the South's rigid caste and social order. Many white southerners considered Bureau employees traitors to their own race, and would refer to them as carpetbaggers or "nigger lovers."[4]

Young Horace Jencks, Dewitt Clinton's son, became a mail carrier, employment he would keep until his retirement in the 1940s. In 1912, nineteen-year-old Horace married seventeen-year-old Ruth Shideler in Colorado Springs's First Christian Church.[5] The couple would have four children, and their third child was Clinton Edward.[6] Faith played an outsize role in both Jencks and Shideler families, and Ruth was a devout Methodist Sunday school teacher at the First Christian Church. Horace Jencks seemed a distant and cold presence in the home, but Ruth made up for him. She instilled deep religious and moral values in her children. Although Ruth Jencks was a believer in social activism, hers was Bible-based and not political. Both Ruth and Horace were Republicans.[7]

As a boy, Clinton was drawn to the region's mining and labor history. He hiked to nearby towns and went into deserted mining camps, poking around looking at what the miners had left behind. He visited mining museums at Cripple Creek and Leadville. A friendly librarian noticed the boy's curiosity and supplied him with books, through which he became familiar with Ludlow and Cripple Creek histories as well as the Guggenheims and the Rockefellers, their mines and smelters, and their treatment of workers. An upset Jencks later wrote, "I felt sad and angered by the selfishness of some human beings against others, thrilled and full of admiration for those who sought to bring people together for their common welfare."[8]

Clinton was active in his church's Epworth League, became League president, and joined the church's Boy Scout troop. He described himself as "an agitator."[9] He often cited an incident that demonstrated the boyhood social activist in him. Each year, his Boy Scout troop distributed Thanksgiving and Christmas food baskets to the needy, a group that one year included striking miners. As he knocked on doors, Clinton noticed that the residences were cold and empty and had eviction notices tacked on the doors. These notices were signed by a Mr. Morris, a local bank vice president whom Jencks knew as his Sunday school superintendent. The next morning, instead of going to school, Clinton went to the bank and marched into Morris's office, put one of the eviction notices on the banker's desk, and demanded an explanation. When Morris explained that he was simply doing his job, Clinton responded, "Then you teach one thing in Sunday school and do something else during the week?" The boy's inability to reconcile lessons learned at Sunday school with life's realities led his worried mother to take him to see their pastor, who advised that Clinton should learn to separate business from religion: to render unto Caesar what was Caesar's and to the Lord what was His.

For young Clinton, who saw life as a battle between good and evil, the sides were clearly divided. He saw no option but to work for society's downtrodden—the only issue to resolve was *how*. In elementary and junior high school, his first inclination was to follow his family's path and become a missionary.[10] But the religious road continued to confuse him. He could not reconcile conflicts between religious teachings and life. How could they all be God's children, yet there was racial prejudice in churches with segregated congregations? After searching for consistently ethical faiths and finding none, he replaced his missionary ambitions with the desire to help workers. Young Clinton had an unusually deep sympathy and empathy for the poor, the discriminated against, the workers—miners especially—and society's underdogs, sentiments he would retain for life.

During his high school years, Clinton was an active student and worked summers at Pike's Peak, delivering newspapers and doing odd jobs. In his politics, he continued to drift left, always attracted to those who were committed and militant in the fight against greed and economic power. While he was still in high school, his reading progressed from labor and mining history to socialism and its leader, Eugene V. Debs.

BOULDER AND ST. LOUIS

Jencks was a good student. His Aunt Mabel and his minister encouraged him to go to college, but his father was unsupportive and lacked the resources to assist him. Clinton finished high school in 1935 and moved to Boulder, where he enrolled at the University of Colorado and worked several jobs to support himself. Soon after Jencks entered college, his father had "a nervous breakdown," and the family moved from Colorado Springs to Sheridan Lake, Colorado.[11] Despite his jobs and schoolwork, he was involved in university clubs and activities including the American Student Union, for which he later served as chapter president. He was a persistent peace advocate and pushed for racial and ethnic equality, successfully leading sit-ins at campus-area diners that refused to serve black students.[12]

Already a socialist, he attended campus meetings of the Student League for Industrial Democracy and the Young Communist League. He came to see the Socialists as a discussion society and the Communists as the group more dedicated to fighting for workers and against fascism and racial discrimination.[13] Impatient and uninterested in half measures, the Communist Party offered Jencks what no other organization did: a deep commitment to improving workers' conditions and to racial equality, and a militant membership relentless in pursuing those goals. In 1937, nineteen-year-old Jencks joined the Young Communist League.[14]

U.S. foreign policy was frustrating for such militant idealists, and they had no problem joining an organization that often took its marching orders from the Kremlin and was not yet the monster it would become to the American public a few years later. As Hitler's Germany, Mussolini's Italy, and Hirohito's Japan grew in strength, even pacifists such as Jencks pushed to fight fascists immediately. While Axis powers supported Francisco Franco's effort to overthrow the Spanish Republican regime, the Allies sat and watched. Only the USSR rose to the challenge. Poorly armed, equipped, and trained American Communists became cannon fodder in the conflict when they volunteered to fight in Spain with the Abraham Lincoln Brigade.[15] Jencks ached to go as well.

For a time, Clinton intended to pursue a career as a labor lawyer but abandoned those plans as too expensive and time-consuming. After graduation from the university, he went to Saint Louis, where in 1939 he married fellow Colorado Springs native Hermoine Heidbrink. He worked as an accountant at John Deere and later for a General Electric distributor. He joined the Harlem Place Methodist Church, a mixed-race congregation, served as a leader in its Epworth League, and headed the St. Louis Inter-Faith Youth Council, a religious ecumenical group. He became active in the American Youth Congress (AYC),[16] which he headed in St. Louis in 1939 and 1940. His service in the AYC won him an invitation to a White House meeting with President Roosevelt and First Lady Eleanor, a Youth Congress supporter.

Jencks and his wife had little in common, and Hermoine frequently complained about the time he spent on his civic and political activities. The marriage soon foundered, and the couple separated in 1940 and divorced in 1941.[17] Undoubtedly connected to his troubled marriage was the fact that in his work with the St. Louis Youth Council, Jencks had met and fallen in love with Virginia Derr, a St. Louis native who shared his political views. Derr had also been raised in a religious family. She was a year older than Clinton, and when they met she was married to Richard Halley and had a child, Linda. It was a troubled marriage, as Halley was mentally ill, and the couple separated and later divorced.[18]

Meanwhile, World War II burst onto the world. Hitler's Germany had annexed Austria in 1938 and Czechoslovakia in 1939 with the Allies unable or unwilling to resist. In August 1939, Stalin, trying to keep Hitler at bay, signed a nonaggression pact with Germany, a controversial act among American Communists and the socialist left. Jencks remained in the Party, perhaps seeing the pact as a desperate but necessary move by Stalin. A month later, Hitler invaded Poland, and Britain and France finally responded. In June 1941, Germany ripped up the Hitler-Stalin Pact and invaded Russia. The United States avoided war until Japan attacked Pearl Harbor in December 1941, and with that Jencks could finally fight fascists.

WORLD WAR II AND DENVER

In February 1942, Jencks volunteered for the U.S. Army Air Force. Accepted for service, he resigned from the Communist Party. The Army assigned him to navigation training in Texas, where in June 1942 he married Virginia Derr in a church ceremony. Once he graduated from training, the young second

Clinton and Virginia Jencks. *Courtesy Heather Wood.*

lieutenant went to Selma Field in Monroe, Louisiana, where for two years he was a navigation instructor. After Jencks was posted to the Pacific in early 1944, he moved Virginia and their children—Linda and the couple's son, Clinton Michael—to Long Beach, California.[19]

Once in the Pacific as lead navigator and a B-24 crew member, his unit received a perilous assignment. Their task was to plant Torpex mines in Japanese-held harbors from Guam to Okinawa. They were to do so by dropping the torpedoes at low altitude, 100 to 400 feet, making their B-24s vulnerable to ground and aircraft fire. Their commanding general had warned that they would not likely survive their mission. Navigation over the open, trackless Pacific was crucial to the missions, and several crews perished or had to be rescued because of navigation errors. The stars and sextants were their only guides. In April 1945, for his forty missions as lead navigator, Jencks was awarded the Distinguished Flying Cross and six air medals, the highest decoration short of a Congressional Medal of Honor.[20] Only one Flying Cross is awarded to an honoree, and each additional air medal is the equivalent of another Flying Cross. Jencks was reprimanded, however, for fraternizing as an officer with enlisted men—an act very much in character for him. After forty grueling missions, Jencks was sent stateside to finish his tour and was honorably discharged in December 1945.[21]

Once he was discharged, Clinton and Virginia settled in Denver, where he hoped to work as an airline navigator. With the return of thousands of GIs, the job market was poor, and all Jencks found was work handling baggage for Continental Airlines and later a job with flight control, work he soon lost when the job's GI subsidy expired. He had been unhappy at Continental, but was fortunate to soon find more enjoyable work in Denver as a laborer at American Smelting and Refining Company's Globe Smelter. He loved being alongside working people there and immediately joined the International Union of Mine, Mill, and Smelter Workers (Mine-Mill). He was quickly named a union steward, a job that fulfilled his boyhood dream.

Following an old pattern, when Jencks began his job at Globe Smelting, he also became involved in politics and civic activities. Always outgoing and gregarious, he organized the Denver chapter of the American Veterans Committee, whose goal was to reintegrate veterans into civilian life and promote programs Jencks held dear, such as "veterans' housing, adequate price control, fairness toward racial minorities, full employment, and a national health program." Jencks was soon elected national vice-chairman of the Veterans Committee over the Rocky Mountain Region. In 1946, within a year of his return, he was on the Democratic primary ballot running for state representative. He lost the September primary, but continued his work for the Veterans Committee.[22] Jencks loved leading an active and involved life. His optimistic, sunny disposition and sociable personality fit perfectly with his union and political activities. In 1946, he rejoined the Communist Party and became active in its eastside Denver chapter.

The Communist Party that Jencks rejoined had a complex history. Its close connection to the Kremlin might be the most difficult to understand. How could loyal Americans associate with their country's brutal Stalinist enemy? But it is important to note that Russia was not always the enemy, and Stalin's murderous purges, exterminations, and imprisonments were either unknown or not believed by many American Communists.[23] When

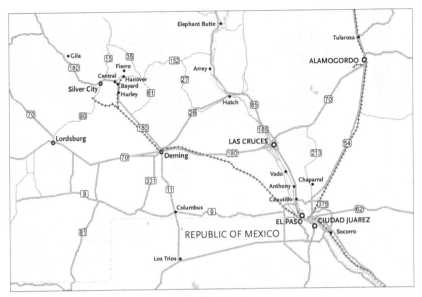

Southwest New Mexico. *Cartography by Olga Bosenko.*

biographer James Lorence asked him about his politics between 1945 and 1947, Jencks, although a Communist Party member in those years, described himself as a Christian Socialist in his youth and later a Democratic Socialist willing to work with liberals and Communist Party members on common policies. He joined the CP because he saw it as the way to achieve his goals, and he was attracted to those he saw as the "most committed" to fighting discrimination and improving workers' conditions.[24]

The Mine-Mill union that Jencks joined in 1946 began as the Western Federation of Miners in 1893, changing its name to the International Union of Mine, Mill, and Smelter Workers in 1916. In 1911, it had affiliated with the American Federation of Labor (AFL), and remained so until it was expelled with other industrial unions in 1937. Mine-Mill then joined other industrial unions in creating the Congress of Industrial Organizations (CIO). Mine-Mill experienced rapid growth during World War II, and by 1947 it had one hundred thousand members. Early in that year it experienced secession movements, raids, and jurisdictional fights with other unions. During that turmoil its president, Reid Robinson, was forced to resign, handing the presidency to Maurice Travis, a known Communist.[25]

Despite its internal problems, Mine-Mill's brass soon noticed the eager and engaged Jencks. In early 1947, Orville Larson, Mine-Mill regional vice president, asked Jencks if he would represent several locals in Grant County, New Mexico, home to large copper and lead mining operations.[26] The locals combined resources to support one paid organizer. Jencks discussed the job with Virginia, and they agreed to move.

The Grant County job and the Mine-Mill union were the perfect way for Jencks to fulfill his ambition of working for a militant labor union. Fellow Communists, moreover, were in Mine-Mill's top leadership. It is unlikely that Jencks recognized why his new assignment would be the perfect match for him, but in retrospect it is clear that his lifetime concern regarding racial and ethnic inequality allowed him to empathize with Grant County's Mexican miners and view southwest discriminatory traditions through their eyes. He too saw labor rights as civil rights and not merely as an economic struggle. Those shared views would allow Jencks and the Mexican miners to understand each other, communicate effectively, and make fighting discrimination their priority. When Jencks declared himself a Democratic Socialist—although he was a Party member—he was not alone in claiming an ideology alien to his Party membership. Mine-Mill's lawyer Nathan Witt described Mexican American Communists for whom, he said, "racial equality consistently superseded [Communist] ideology" and for whom it did not matter if they were "Red or not," as they knew that the Party fought for civil rights. As Anita Tórrez—wife of Grant County Mine-Mill leader Lorenzo Tórrez—said when Mine-Mill's leadership was attacked as Communist, "If this is what they're going to call Communist, fine; let's all be Communists then! Because we're fighting for our *rights*."[27] It was a happy coincidence for Jencks that he found a union with bottom-up, rank-and-file democratic rule in a working-class community where he could fight every day for civil rights alongside active leftists, including several fellow Communists. As a Mine-Mill labor organizer, Jencks could finally work with the miners he read about as a boy and be the missionary of his childhood dreams. But he also risked martyrdom, the fate of some unfortunate missionaries.

2

GRANT COUNTY, NEW MEXICO

SILVER AND COPPER had been mined in Grant County for a century and a half before Clinton Jencks arrived. Situated in the southern Mogollon Mountains at 6,000 feet, the area was the traditional home to Chiracahua Apaches, who lived there as hunter-gatherers and raiders.[1] Those mounted raiders had besieged and harassed the sparse settlements in northern New Spain since Spaniards arrived there in the late sixteenth century. Persistent Apache raids and poor transportation remained mining obstacles until after the 1880s, which brought Victorio's defeat and Geronimo's capture. In 1848 New Mexico became a U.S. territory, and a U.S. Army fort and rail solved remaining problems, allowing mining to flourish.

DISPARITY IN THE SOUTHWEST

After the U.S.-Mexican War the mines remained heavily dependent on Mexican labor, as did most mines in New Mexico and Arizona. Between 1850 and 1880, some 55,000 Mexicans immigrated to the region, many to work as miners.[2] Higher paying American jobs attracted Mexicans despite the fact that they received lower wages than Anglo-Americans for doing the same work.[3] The culture and mindset that Mexicans would work for lower wages than their Anglo

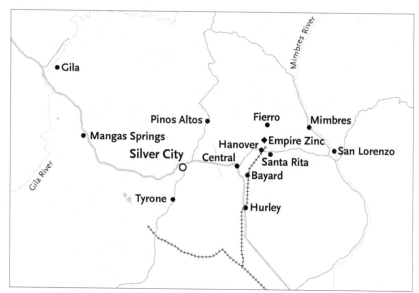

Grant County, New Mexico. *Cartography by Olga Bosenko.*

coworkers became the rule in the Southwest.[4] As the mines developed and larger corporations invested in new technology, the disparate wage structure persisted. Copper mining firms built their company towns, such as Grant County's Santa Rita, next to their operations. As in most Southwest company towns, everything was segregated, even the cemeteries at Santa Rita and Hanover.[5] The Anglo workers lived in their sector with better residences while the Mexicans lived in "Mexican Town," "Chihuahuita," Silver City's "Chihuahua Hill," or other similarly named districts. Residences in Santa Rita's Mexican Town usually had no plumbing, and often Mexicans would have to build their own homes on company-owned lots. Census enumerators inconsistently categorized the occasional Anglos who married Mexicans and lived in Mexican Town.[6]

Schools, theaters, and restaurants were also segregated. Workers had separate changing rooms, restrooms, and bathing facilities. There was not only a dual wage structure; there were separate pay windows for the two groups, and Mexicans drew the heavier and more dangerous work.[7] Anglo workers entered with higher wages and immediately stepped onto a promotional ladder; Mexicans started as laborers, and that was where many would remain.[8] The discrimination was against all those called "Mexicans."[9] Even after the dual wage was eliminated, the classification system remained to block Mexicans' promotion. In every way possible, Mexicans were openly discounted and disparaged. They deeply felt and resented this, and their aggrievement intensified when men returned from World War II to find that their service had not brought them equality.

The companies' discrimination against Mexicans was not simply to satisfy their Anglo employees; it was a deliberate strategy. For the companies, racial and ethnic discrimination was a substantial profit center.[10] First, it neatly divided the workforce, with Anglos typically more willing to side with the companies to preserve their economic and social advantage over blacks and Mexicans. Often, the company-friendly craft unions would not admit Mexicans, a strategy that pitted workers against each other rather than against the company. It was obvious that the companies reduced their labor expense in paying Mexicans lower wages, but companies also gained in how they paid their Anglo workers, who received lower wages than their counterparts elsewhere, such as in Utah or Nebraska. While the companies equated Mexicans with low wages, the predominantly Mexican Southwest mines also maintained lower geographical wages scales overall.[11] Southwest chambers of commerce like the one in Silver City routinely supported companies and their discriminatory wage structures even when the entire community was harmed. In other words, the business establishment supported companies that reduced communities' total income—and the chambers were not blind to this fact.[12]

LABOR IN GRANT COUNTY

Mexicans had their own Southwest labor history, one that included a radical element.[13] Mexicans played prominent roles in significant events throughout Colorado labor history, such as the 1903 to 1905 Cripple Creek strike or the 1914 Ludlow massacre. At Ludlow, several Mexican miners participated in that Western Federation strike,[14] and eight of Ludlow's eighteen fatalities were Mexican.[15]

Mexican anarchists had been active in nearby mining centers at Clifton-Morenci in 1903, 1915, and 1917, Bisbee in 1917, and other locations.[16] The largest strike in the area by Mexicans was in 1915 at Clifton-Morenci, where some five thousand Mexican miners organized under their mutual aid (mutualista) banner.[17] Mexican miners in Grant County also formed mutualista societies, including La Liga Protectora de Refugiados Políticos and the Alianza Hispano Americana.[18] Despite the strikes and labor unrest in Arizona, there is little documented union activity in Grant County mines before the 1930s. There was Western Federation organizing activity at Hanover, but it soon faded away. In 1912, Chino's open-pit shovel operators walked off the job and were fired the next day by the stridently antiunion Chino Copper Company.[19]

Franklin Delano Roosevelt's election dramatically changed the world for labor unions. Three months after he took office, FDR signed into law the National Industrial Recovery Act (NIRA), which protected a union's right to collective bargaining. The Act was part of the monumental legislative initiative to kick-start the depressed U.S. economy. Workers saw the Act as an invitation to join a union. In 1934, Santa Rita employees organized Mine-Mill Local 63, the first union in the area. By September, three hundred men had signed up with Mine-Mill.[20] Supervisors warned the men that if they voted for the union, the company would shut down.[21] The company kept its word. After Mine-Mill won its election at Santa Rita, the company closed the mine, laying off its employees, shutting down electric and telephone service, and closing the hospital. Santa Rita became a ghost town.[22]

In 1935, the Supreme Court declared NIRA unconstitutional, but Congress immediately passed the Wagner Act, which reestablished the right to organize and bargain collectively and created the new and independent National Labor Relations Board (NLRB). Santa Rita restarted operations in January 1937, but a blacklist prevented hiring Mine-Mill members. The union and those rejected employees filed charges claiming discrimination. The NLRB ruled against the mining company, finding that it discriminated against Mine-Mill members by denying their reemployment and improperly attempting to thwart union activities. The Board ordered the company, Nevada Consolidated, to reinstate the employees with back pay.[23] The case reached the U.S. Supreme Court, which in 1942 ruled in the union's favor.[24] It was a massive victory for Mine-Mill.

In the intervening five years between 1937 and 1942, metals production increased as the United States supplied Europe's wartime needs and then its own after Pearl Harbor. During the same period, many skilled Anglo workers left Locals 63 (Chino) and 69 (Hurley) to join company-friendly, segregated craft unions. What initially appeared to be a company victory in Anglo workers quitting Mine-Mill proved otherwise in the long term. The Anglo exodus left the Mine-Mill locals overwhelmingly Mexican.[25] The union's Supreme Court victory and the locals' Mexican composition left them free to advocate against discrimination, adding a civil rights component to the normal labor agenda. In July 1942, three months after the court victory, Mine-Mill had its first Kennecott contract. Kennecott had purchased Nevada Consolidated. Under Mine-Mill's constitution, its contracts contained a non-discrimination clause, so by entering into that contract, Kennecott agreed not to discriminate based on race, creed or national origin. Jobs, such as crane operator, never before open to Mexicans, now became available. Despite new contracts, federal wartime antidiscrimination directives in defense industries, and other advances, Kennecott continued some discriminatory practices.[26] Almost all of its employees in the "laborer" category remained Mexican,[27] and housing discrimination and segregation in public accommodations persisted.[28]

Confronting traditional racial and ethnic discrimination in the Southwest metals industry would test Mine-Mill's commitment to equality. Decades of excluding Mexicans and blacks from craft unions had already separated workers, as had the segregated company towns and facilities. Anglo workers would not easily give up the advantages they enjoyed over Mexicans. Anglo craft union members were reluctant to join Mine-Mill, seeing it as a Mexican union with forced equality should they join. Mexicans came to consider Mine-Mill as theirs and often saw the union's Communist leadership and the Communist Party as rare allies in their fight for equality.[29]

Fundamentally, there were two views of the labor fight. The Denver-based, predominantly Anglo Mine-Mill leadership saw their union work as the traditional economic struggle between labor and management. While Mexicans were also concerned with economic issues such as pay, benefits, and work hours, most were as interested in reversing discriminatory practices.[30] To Mexicans, the fight for labor rights became inseparable from the struggle for equal rights, and their union membership frequently accompanied their affiliation with civil rights organizations, such as the Asociación Nacional Mexicana Americana (ANMA). It was the returning GIs who gave voice and power to those demands. Veterans would not quietly accept the status quo when they returned home, and they would no longer accept discrimination. They would form groups and organizations that gave power to their demand for equality. Among those returning GIs were many Grant County miners, including their newly hired Mine-Mill organizer, Clinton E. Jencks.

To understand the events in Jencks's life between 1946 and his trial in the mid-1950s, one must comprehend anticommunism's fury in that decade.

That environment, which governed Clinton Jencks's world, would transform his life and work. The change was driven by a new "red scare," imprecisely called "McCarthyism": a cold war phenomenon that arose in postwar America when the Soviet Union became a world power challenging and threatening America's security. The scare also drove Americans to examine the Soviet-dominated American Communist Party.

3

RED SCARES AND ANTICOMMUNISM

THE DOMESTIC COMMUNIST THREAT to the United States during the 1940s and '50s was real, but it was exaggerated by anti-Communists and was never existential, as they claimed. Only a tiny fraction of American Communists was part of the postwar Soviet menace. Rather than being traitors, spies, or saboteurs, CP members were schoolteachers, miners, and workers going about their lives. Although any attempt to quantify CP members who were secret Soviet operatives is largely speculative and likely a low estimate, writers using the highest available figures put that number at three hundred out of fifty thousand members in 1944. Using that approximation, Soviet operatives were well below 1 percent of the membership, or only six out of every one thousand members.[1] An informed review of CP Soviet operatives reveals the nuanced levels of their cooperation as well as the specific international environment at the time some colluded, such as whether the Soviets were a U.S. ally or enemy. There were those who provided nuclear or vital military secrets to the Soviets and undermined American security in doing so. There were others who simply provided the Soviets information in the public domain at a time when the USSR was an ally. Others, such as John Abt and Lee Pressman, professed to be Party members who provided innocuous information about American agricultural programs. Often the information provided was not about the United States, but rather about events or conditions in Germany or Japan, then common enemies of the United States and the Soviet Union. So the percentage of Communist Party members who were Soviet operatives providing information harmful to American security was indeed tiny. While some reaction to the Soviet threat made sense given its menace, the anti-Communist hysteria produced a response grossly disproportionate to the risk.[2]

THE FIRST RED SCARE AND THE COMMUNIST PARTY

As noted, historian Ellen Schrecker wrote that the McCarthy era and its anti-Communist programs affected Clinton Jencks in more ways than anyone else, experiences instructive of anti-Communist methodology under J. Edgar Hoover,[3] Joseph McCarthy, and others. Anticommunism drove many Americans to disregard the Constitution in their attempt to ruin not only suspected Communists but also liberal and left-wing non-Communists, all but a small fraction of whom were law-abiding, loyal Americans.

In 1919, after Bolsheviks gained control in Russia, they took over international socialism's leadership. It was the Bolshevik model—violent, undemocratic, secretive, and conspiratorial—that Vladimir I. Lenin imposed on the movement, a result unforeseen by Karl Marx. Lenin organized the international Communist apparatus according to his model, the Communist or Third International, called the Comintern. Lenin's intent was to use Comintern to export Communist revolution worldwide to fight imperialism, what he considered capitalism's extreme form. In that same year, 1919, two American Communist parties organized under Comintern's umbrella.

Long before communism came to America in 1919, similar forces had already fought radicals and anarchists. Present even in those early times were elements that would become the antilabor, anti-Communist movement: private firms and business associations seeking to disparage and impede union activity; private detective agencies hired by the companies to infiltrate, surveil, and disrupt union operations and punish those who joined or worked to organize; and state and local law enforcement to oppose and monitor unions and radicals.

During World War I, the federal government expanded its role through its Bureau of Investigation, which would later become the FBI. The bureau brought its mission, which included national security and antiradical programs, to monitor and control "subversive" individuals and groups. It also introduced federal prosecution, immigration control, and military intelligence.

VANB

LOG

xxxxxxxx1392

3/16/2022

Item: ï¿½20010099357765 ((book)

In 1919, a large Soviet rally in the American capital raised the unrealistic fear that Bolsheviks might overthrow the United States, and in Seattle a general strike called by the Industrial Workers of the World paralyzed the city, with troops called in to restore order. In June, thirty mail bombs targeted prominent anti-Communists, and a device detonated at Attorney General A. Mitchell Palmer's home. A month later, Palmer named J. Edgar Hoover, a twenty-four-year-old Department of Justice lawyer, as his special assistant over the bureau's new antiradical General Intelligence Division.[4]

In September 1919, the two newly formed and competing American Communist parties, the Communist Party and the Communist Labor Party, advocated overthrowing the U.S. government.[5] In aligning and making American communism subservient to Lenin's Comintern, these two parties made a mistake that would dog American communism for decades. Three months after the American parties' formation, on December 22, 1919, Hoover issued orders to have 2,280 Communists and some five hundred anarchists and assorted radicals arrested around the nation. A week later, on January 2, 1920, the bureau carried out massive raids, the largest ever, in thirty-four cities in twenty-three states. Six to ten thousand individuals were arrested with 3,500 detained for deportation.[6] The raids, pinned on the attorney general, became known as the "Palmer Raids" and were controversial for ignoring due process and arresting thousands who had committed no crime. Palmer, stoking red fear, said that revolution was "licking at the altars of the churches, leaping into the belfry of the school bell, crawling into the sacred corners of American homes, seeking to replace marriage vows with libertine laws, and burning up the foundation of society."[7]

Congress held hearings to address the ruthless raids, which became a scandal and a "public relations disaster" for the bureau and the Department of Justice. Palmer, with Hoover sitting next to him, faced a congressional committee investigating the wholesale arrests. The committee asked Palmer about the raids, and the attorney general, shifting responsibility to Hoover, replied that the committee should address Hoover, "who was in charge of this matter." Hoover passed the hot potato along to his field offices, blaming them for having directed the raids.[8]

The Palmer Raids forced the American Communist Party underground, following Lenin's model that was ill-suited for America. Anticommunism often refused to distinguish between reformers and revolutionaries, unfairly labeling Socialists violent revolutionaries. In the red hysteria following the Palmer Raids, some lawfully elected Socialists were summarily denied access to their elected offices.[9]

It is a maxim in the United States: the First Amendment protects one's freedom to believe what one chooses, to express one's views, and to associate with whomever one wants. Antisedition laws would challenge those principles. In the Palmer raids, the government arrested and deported individuals not for what they did but for what they had joined. Many were arrested on suspicion of Communist Party membership or for simply being near someone who was an alleged Communist.

During World War I, some American Socialists who opposed the war, including Eugene V. Debs, were convicted of violating the Espionage Act by being antiwar. In 1919, the Supreme Court ruled that the First Amendment was not absolute and called for balancing individual and governmental interests with the "clear and present danger" test, holding that an antidraft speech given in peacetime was different than the same speech in wartime.[10] In *Abrams v. United States*, the Supreme Court upheld a conviction for printing two leaflets containing language that opposed sending U.S. troops to fight against the Bolsheviks.[11] With that, Americans could no longer proclaim that they had the freedom to say whatever they pleased.

President Warren G. Harding appointed Harry M. Daugherty as his attorney general and named Hoover as the bureau's assistant director under William J. Burns. Hoover continued the bureau's illegal "black bag jobs," which included break-ins and planting illegal listening devices, reading mail, and violating Americans' rights. One reporter described the bureau as "a private hole in the corner goon squad for the Attorney General. Its arts were the art of snooping, bribery, and blackmail."[12] After Harding's death, President Calvin Coolidge fired the unethical Daugherty and appointed straight shooter Harlan Fiske Stone to be attorney general. Stone named Hoover acting bureau director.[13] Stone understood, like few other attorneys general, the danger of investigative agencies acting as ideological police.[14] Taking policy direction from political appointees was alien to Hoover, who saw his political bosses as temporary annoyances he would manipulate, outlast, and often ignore.[15] Stone intimidated Hoover like no other attorney general. Hoover was now the man in charge, but he was forced to suspend the political red-hunting and illegal activities for as long as Stone was in office.[16] Over the decades, new anti-Communists would join and others would drop

FBI director J. Edgar Hoover. *Library of Congress.*

out, but the one constant shaping anticommunism between 1919 and 1970 was J. Edgar Hoover. Hoover would maintain his alarm over the red menace, and his anticommunism would be central to his work.

The Palmer Raids, the red scare, and other anti-Communist initiatives and legislation had their desired effect. Membership in the Communist Party—already small at ten to twelve thousand—declined, and by 1929 the secretive Party was reduced to a minor presence and low profile.[17] There were relatively few Communists remaining in the country, and 90 percent of those were foreigners. Then the 1930s Great Depression changed everything. Suddenly, the economy and the financial system collapsed. The number of unemployed mushroomed; desperation and economic insecurity absorbed the nation. Roosevelt was elected and immediately initiated the New Deal, his attempt to restart the economy and help those in need. He legalized unions and protected their right to organize and bargain for their membership. The Communist Party immediately saw its opportunity and made labor organizing its priority as the unions rapidly added members in the friendly New Deal environment. Communists would become among the most effective union organizers.[18]

Under FDR, it was a new day for the Communist Party. During his first year in office, FDR recognized the Soviet Union sixteen years and four presidencies after the Bolshevik takeover.[19] The left, including Communists, were delighted with the new emphasis on workers, the unemployed, and the poor. Many saw the Great Depression as capitalism's failure, exactly as Marx had predicted. Socialism and communism were now seen in a new light, and American-Soviet relations also improved.

By mid-1934, the violent anti-Communist and anti-Slavic Hitler quickly consolidated his power in Germany, and Stalin noted the new threat. Immediately, Stalin, after taking power and expelling Trotsky, had laid down a hard line in 1929 that prohibited the CP from working with other parties. Now he reversed and ordered a new, cooperative tone at Comintern. During FDR's first year or two, some American Communists complained that Roosevelt was no different than his Republican opposition. As the New Deal unfolded, their tune changed as Communists saw promise in the new administration's policies. These developments with fascism in Germany, Italy, and Japan brought a dramatic reversal at the Seventh Comintern Congress in August 1935, when it announced the Popular Front.

The Front was to be a broad coalition that would include Communists, Socialists, and liberals in a fight against fascism. To broaden the union, Comintern stopped calling for a worldwide socialist revolution. Communists became so open toward FDR that many members voted for him as they enthusiastically rolled up their sleeves, ardently supported the New Deal, and became the left wing in FDR's broad political coalition. Overthrowing the U.S. government was never a goal for most members and was no longer CP policy, a change that anti-Communists would consistently ignore.[20] As the CP softened its line, the nation became alarmed over the rise of fascism. The CP became a working and respected coalition partner, and as the threat of fascism increased, the Party attracted thousands of new members.

For many, including Clinton Jencks, the Spanish Civil War became the defining issue of the time. Antifascists appreciated that the Soviet Union was the only power to aid Spanish Republicans who were under assault by the fascist Francisco Franco. It was Franco and the Catholic Church, Germany, and Italy against the liberal and left Republicans, whose only ally was the Soviet Union. The Soviet Union sent supplies and troops to Spain and helped recruit 2,800 Americans, mostly Communists, who went to Spain in the Abraham Lincoln Brigade. The left saw the Party take a leadership role in

New Deal programs and unions, actions that endeared it to many. The Party adopted a pro-American image, with its Chair Earl Browder saying, "Communism is twentieth-century Americanism." Between 1936 and 1938 the party more than doubled in membership, from 40,000 to 82,000.[21] Following an old pattern, its membership was 40 percent New York City residents, many of them second generation Jews with Russian or Eastern European family roots, a group that would become its most conspicuous cohort. The New York CP could turn out thousands for its parades and rallies, and in 1938, the *Daily Worker*'s Sunday editions printed one hundred thousand copies. In addition, there were the tens of thousands who were small "c" communists who sympathized and believed but did not submit to party discipline.[22]

Among the new CP members signing on during the Popular Front period was nineteen-year-old Clinton Jencks, who joined in 1937 while at the University of Colorado. It was what many idealistic young people were doing, and overthrowing the United States government to install a Soviet regime or spying for the Soviets was not their agenda. All but a handful of them were loyal Americans who saw socialism as a preferred economic model for the nation. Jencks and many other new members consistently described Communist Party members as the hardest working and most committed to fighting fascism and racial discrimination and advocating for the oppressed and needy, characteristics that attracted them to the Party during the Popular Front period. Those who worked in unions were described as "unionists first, Communists second."[23] Communism manifested itself in union work mainly through resolutions passed at union conventions and locals' meetings and perhaps in choosing union officers, and it appealed to those who were uncompromising, militant, and impatient for the radical change they thought a depression-besieged America demanded.

Meanwhile in Europe, Hitler marched forward. In March 1938 Germany annexed Austria, and a year later, with German and Italian assistance, Franco's fascists took Spain all while the Allies stood by. In March 1939, Germany took over Czechoslovakia with the Allies again looking on. Stalin knew that Germany might invade Russia and that the Allies were not resisting Hitler but rather seemed to be encouraging him to move eastward. In an understandable but highly controversial move to keep Hitler from invading Russia, Stalin and Hitler signed a nonaggression agreement and carved up their eastern European interests. Immediately, the Communist Party USA shifted its stance from fighting fascism everywhere to advocating for peace and neutrality for the United

States. The abrupt change brought by the German-Soviet Pact ended good relations with the Communists, split the American Party, and caused many to resign.[24] Liberals split with Communists and quit many CP-dominated front groups. Party membership was almost halved in 1940,[25] and FDR went from being a friend one day to "a war monger" the next.[26] The range of those who stopped cooperating with the CP was wide, including former Communists, Socialists, and liberals.[27] As Party membership became a liability, resignation or not joining was not a bad option. Being a Party member was perilous and joining could easily cause one to lose employment and, in some extreme cases, one's citizenship.[28] Under threat, the Party opted for secrecy, but its reflexive alignment with the Soviet Union and its abrupt policy shifts were a "disaster."[29] After Party membership plunged in the 1940s, it would never recover.

ANTI-COMMUNIST STRATEGIES AND METHODS

Over the years, the anti-Communist movement developed strategies to confront, expose, and weaken the Communist Party and America's left wing, often sweeping up liberals who had joined allied organizations. The following are some anti-Communist practices, many of which Jencks was to experience: (1) Congressional investigations and public hearings, such as the House Un-American Activities Committee (HUAC) and the Senate Internal Security Subcommittee. (2) Use of the sixty-four-dollar question: "Are you now or have you ever been a member of the Communist Party?" This placed the sole focus on Party membership—a legal status—and not on whether an individual had acted illegally. The repression implicit in the inquiry was expanded to include membership or participation in "subversive organizations." (3) Employment or trade blacklists. Many on those lists were not Communists but had merely signed petitions or innocently joined leftist groups.[30] (4) Loyalty oaths and employment tests. (5) Smith Act prosecutions. (6) Deportation and denaturalization. (7) Using paid, professional anti-Communist witnesses. (8) Using informers, spies, and agents provocateurs. (9) Intimidating lawyers. (10) Using the press. (11) Under the Internal Security Act of 1950, using the security index for custodial detention. (12) Illegal surveillance and tactics, "black bag" jobs, and FBI blind copies.

HUAC, Hollywood, and the Blacklist

The famous Hollywood Ten case shows how the system came to work. For years, Hoover and the FBI had surveilled Hollywood leftists and became convinced that they were inserting Communist content into movies and brainwashing Americans. In 1942, Hoover instituted the Communist motion picture infiltration program (COMPIC) to keep files on Hollywood leftists. But because the filmmakers were not breaking any laws, Hoover grew frustrated at his inability to take action. Finding no Hollywood illegality, disloyalty, espionage, or sabotage, Hoover decided to provide the information to HUAC, the anti-Communist committee he had previously spurned.[31] When Republicans gained congressional control in 1947, HUAC's chair, J. Parnell Thomas, seized the opportunity to go after Hollywood's Communist community in high profile hearings. To prepare the committee's hearings, the FBI secretly assisted with black bag jobs, blind copy memos, phone taps, and leaking damaging information about Hollywood leftists and Communists, data lifted from the supposedly "sacrosanct" FBI files, including CP membership records the FBI had obtained in at least four burglaries of the Party's Los Angeles offices.[32]

The artistic community leaned left. Some were Communists, and this was true in Hollywood among writers, actors, and others in both the creative and technical jobs. By 1947, the FBI had identified as CP members ninety-two actors, one hundred twenty-seven writers, eight producers and fifteen directors. For its initial hearing in the U.S. Capitol, the committee subpoenaed nineteen prominent filmmakers the FBI had identified and whose CP membership cards they had seized.[33]

Those subpoenaed conferred with National Lawyers Guild counsel to devise a common approach to the hearings. The witnesses had three options: they could cooperate, answer the questions and go wherever that path took them, including admitting Party membership (if that was the case) and being forced to name others in the Party; they could assert the First Amendment and claim that their activities were constitutionally protected and the committee had no right to delve into their political views; or they could invoke their right under the Fifth Amendment's protection against self-incrimination. Much of the law in those areas was untested. Certainly, the Fifth Amendment option was unpalatable because the movie-going public would assume that anyone taking the Fifth was guilty and hiding information. The committee would condemn anyone invoking the Fifth as a "Fifth Amendment Communist," and it would also bolster the false notion that being a Communist was illegal. Moreover, because being a Communist was legal, it was not clear whether the witnesses could take the Fifth, as there was no incrimination risk. Despite everyone's ignorance about the First Amendment's untested consequences, the group chose that option. They planned to read their preliminary statements and then invoke the First. They also organized a prominent support group, Committee for the First Amendment, composed of Hollywood luminaries such as Humphrey Bogart.

Once the hearings began, Chairman Thomas did not permit some witnesses to read their prepared statements, and the testimony soon devolved into gavel-banging, shouting matches, accusations, and unanswered questions.[34] Neither the committee nor the witnesses emerged in good light; the committee appeared abusive and the witnesses evasive and furtive. The support of prominent producers and actors cratered after the first blast of publicity and the revelation that the Hollywood Ten were card-carrying Communists.[35] The producers distanced themselves from the witnesses; the initially supportive actors sought to assure the public that they were not CP members, and anti-Communist celebrities, such as Jack Warner and Robert Taylor, piled on. At a meeting in New York one month after the hearings, the producers issued their "Waldorf Statement" announcing that they did not support Communists and had fired the Hollywood Ten, who had appeared but refused to cooperate with HUAC. The Hollywood Ten were held in contempt of Congress and most were sentenced to serve one year in prison. The convictions were affirmed, and that was the end of the First Amendment option.[36] Not only were the Hollywood Ten sent to prison, but they were also blacklisted and banished from the movie industry. Despite having committed no crime, they could no longer work in films under their own names. They either left the country, worked under assumed names, or left the business altogether.[37]

Over the months, other Hollywood figures were called, suffered the same fate, and were blacklisted, except that they escaped prison because by then they had learned from the Ten's experience that the only refuge was in the Fifth Amendment. But even the Fifth had its perils: if witnesses answered one question too many, they could waive the privilege and lose it. Thus, caution dictated answering as little as possible, with some witnesses barely giving their names. Others, wanting to appear forthcoming, made the dreadful mistake and answered one question too many. To the famous sixty-four-dollar question, "Are you now or have you ever been a member of the Communist Party?" several answered that they had been Party members but had quit. Too bad. Anyone who admitted membership was then either obligated to name names, outing their friends, or be held in contempt for refusing to answer. It was a heartbreaking dilemma.

In a tale dripping with irony, one individual who did not continue to profit from his association with HUAC was its gavel-banging, law-and-order chair, J. Parnell Thomas. In 1948, Thomas, a former financier, was convicted and imprisoned for a sleazy fraud involving phantom congressional staffers whose salaries he pocketed. Being under federal criminal charges himself apparently gave Thomas a newly discovered appreciation for the Fifth Amendment he had previously excoriated others for invoking as he unhesitatingly "took the Fifth" in a futile attempt to avoid prison. To add to his discomfort, he found himself in prison with two of the Hollywood Ten he helped send there, including the screenwriter Ring Lardner Jr. Thomas's prison job was overseeing the institution's hen house, and passing by him one day, Lardner told Thomas, "I see you're still shoveling chicken shit."[38]

In those times, thousands of loyal Americans who had committed no crime lost their jobs. Any guess as to how many lost their employment is likely an underestimate. A detailed study published in 1958 put the number at ten thousand,[39] however the McCarthy era continued beyond 1958, racking up more cases to add to that total. The estimate does not account for the thousands who were simply terminated or laid off without explanation, or the other unaccounted-for thousands who were never hired and never knew why. In his later 1951 cooperative HUAC testimony, Hollywood Ten member Edward Dmytryk noted the confusion among Americans who were told that it was legal to be a Communist, only to find that exercising that constitutional right got one fired, blacklisted, or not hired.

Red hunting took a breather during World War II as everyone concentrated on the war effort. Despite cooperative Soviet relations during the War, the FBI obtained jurisdiction over all espionage and grew from 851 agents in 1939 to 4,600 by 1943, with illegal surveillance in the name of national security becoming a normal bureau activity. Hoover investigated even when the Justice Department refused permission, as in the National Lawyers Guild case. In an extreme example of the bureau's uncontrolled character under Hoover, it even investigated and collected derogatory information on his boss, Attorney General Tom C. Clark.[40]

For two years, from the time Hitler and Stalin signed their nonaggression pact until Germany invaded Russia in June 1941, American Communists were outcasts. Hoover began supervising counter espionage in 1939, and in December of that year he issued his "Internal Security" order: a list of individuals to be locked up in a national emergency, as in the Japanese internment. It was called the Custodial Detention Program. The list included some who would be immediately arrested and others who would be closely monitored.[41]

The Smith Act

Years before, Congress had already moved against Communists. Rules Committee powerhouse and Virginian Howard W. Smith sponsored the Alien Registration Act of 1940, thereafter known as the Smith Act, which required aliens to register and made it a crime to teach or advocate the government's overthrow. Once again, the Smith Act made certain speech criminal.[42]

There was "nothing intrinsically illegal about what Communists did."[43] Their conduct was constitutionally protected, and no prosecution was possible under the Smith Act because the Party no longer advocated the government's overthrow. To Communists, they were simply participating in the political process, running candidates, and advocating for change. Yet Hoover, whose FBI largely failed to make any espionage cases against CP members,[44] insisted instead on a Smith Act prosecution. For years, Hoover had pressed the Justice Department to prosecute Communists, but the department found nothing to prosecute. Other times, it was the bureau that put the brakes on a prosecution, sometimes because the evidence was from an illegal black bag job or the bureau did not want to burn an informant in court.[45] Among its black bag jobs, the bureau had a special interest in the National Lawyers Guild, and had burgled Guild offices a reported fourteen times. The Guild concluded that "on a strictly numerical basis, the FBI may commit more federal crimes that it detects."[46] The bureau later demurred on prosecutions because its witnesses were unreliable and problematic professional ex-Communists.[47]

Hoover began to accumulate records and files to build a Smith Act case, and Attorney General Clark told his lawyers to find a way to prosecute a case under the law. The department settled on a strategy in which, to ease its burden of proof and allow the admission of additional evidence, it would not charge a substantive violation but rather a conspiracy to violate the Smith Act. Finally in July 1948, eight years after its enactment, the department presented its first Smith Act conspiracy case to a New York grand jury that then indicted all but two national CP executive board members, including chair Eugene Dennis. The charge was that the defendants had conspired to "teach and advocate" the government's violent overthrow. The prosecution's problem was that board members had done no such thing. To overcome that hurdle, the government devised the strategy it would use over the next several years in prosecuting Communists.[48]

To sidestep the fact that these defendants had not advocated the government's overthrow, the Justice Department devised a "book" prosecution.

The prosecution found four publications by Lenin and other Communists that were sold in Communist bookstores or used as texts in Communist schools and claimed that by using such literature, the Party was teaching what Lenin, Stalin, Andrei Vishinsky, and other Communist thinkers wrote about advocating a government's overthrow—not the U.S. government, but any government. The same four books the prosecution relied on could be found in any large U.S. library, and their materials were taught in universities around the globe, including many in America.[49] As was already covered in the *Debs*, *Abrams*, and *Schenk* cases, what one read or advocated was generally protected by the First Amendment unless, as Justice Holmes wrote, it constituted "a clear and present danger"—that is, that what was being advocated posed an immediate peril. Selling or teaching from books that were decades old could hardly pose "a clear and present danger." After a nine-month trial, it was clear the evidence did not meet the "clear and present danger" test. In June 1951, the Supreme Court held that what was being regulated was conduct and not speech, and adopted a new test, upholding the conviction.[50] The Supreme Court did precisely what the anti-Communist movement had done, which was to exaggerate the danger to justify bending constitutional principles. As dissenting Justice Douglas observed, "only those held by fear and panic" could find a credible threat in *Dennis*. The case was a reminder of what the Supreme Court had done in times of hysteria and fear, as with Japanese internment.[51]

Supreme Court justice William O. Douglas was so concerned over the red scare that six months after his *Dennis* dissent, he wrote "The Black Silence of Fear," an article in which he analyzed the national hysteria and the practice of wantonly labeling individuals as subversive because they held unorthodox political views. "Fear has many manifestations," Douglas wrote.

The Communist threat inside the country has been magnified and exalted far beyond its realities. Irresponsible talk by irresponsible people has fanned the flames of fear. Accusations have been loosely made. Character assassinations have become common. Suspicion has taken the place of good-will. . . . Innocent acts become tell-tale marks of disloyalty. The coincidence that an idea parallels Soviet Russia's policy for a moment of time settles an aura of suspicion around a person. . . . Some who are opposed [to military solutions] are indeed "subversive." Therefore, the thundering edict commands that all who are opposed are "subversive." Fear is fanned to fury. Good and honest men are pilloried. Character is assassinated. Fear runs rampant.[52]

Paid Professional Anti-Communist Witnesses

The other strategy employed by the prosecution in *Dennis* and later cases was the use of professional anti-Communist witnesses. Those were former Communists or professed "experts" who claimed inside knowledge and expertise in Communist doctrine and tactics. The principal witness in the *Dennis* case was former *Daily Worker* editor Louis Budenz, whose job was to link the defendants and the Communist Party to the Lenin and Stalin texts. The *Dennis* decision broke the dam. It was soon followed by several major cases, including a second-tier New York case against Elizabeth Gurley Flynn and others in which both Budenz and Harvey Matusow were key witnesses. The Smith Act cases had their desired effect of ultimately breaking the Communist Party.[53] It would take several years before professional witnesses, such as Budenz, would be exposed for having "embellished" their testimony, but the bureau knew from the outset that they were not truthful. The bureau or the prosecutors would simply hint at the testimony they needed.[54] Budenz would be joined by Matt Cvetic and Harvey Matusow on the anti-Communist witness circuit, and Budenz and Matusow would follow McCarthy in claiming to have lists of Communists in government.[55]

Over the years, Hoover methodically and forcefully pushed his anti-Communist agenda. His views were those he grew up with in Washington, D.C., a city with southern values and culture. Hoover saw Communists as a threat against the social and religious values he cherished, a social order he felt was America's foundation. His anti-Communist agenda treated civil rights and economic activists with suspicion, and he frequently lumped them in with radicals and Communists. Although the South had the fewest Communists, it had more anti-Communist laws, which were in fact aimed at civil rights activists.[56] Hoover, moreover, had several unreconstructed southern segregationists as key congressional allies, such as in Mississippi's U.S. senator James O. Eastland and Virginia representative Howard W. Smith, among others. Their cries about Communist "outside agitators" stirring up blacks, or complaints, like Eastland's, that "integration was a Communist plot," rang true to Hoover. "Communist experts" such as J. B. Matthews believed that the NAACP was infiltrated with Communists.[57] The nation would pay a price later when civil rights activists understandably had a skeptical view of the FBI, their supposed ally and protector.

U.S. senator Joseph R. McCarthy (*standing*) and Roy
Cohn. *WHI-8004, Wisconsin Historical Society, Madison.*

Joseph R. McCarthy

In January 1950, Alger Hiss's perjury conviction started the year well for
anti-Communists, as it provided a connection between the Soviets, the
Party, and the State Department. Then in the same month, in preparation
for his 1952 reelection campaign, a little-known 41-year-old United States
senator from Wisconsin named Joseph R. McCarthy took a Catholic priest's
advice and made communism his campaign issue. The Republican Senate
Campaign Committee scheduled speeches for the senator, including one on
February 9, 1950 at a Lincoln Day event before the Ohio County Women's
Republican Club in Wheeling, West Virginia. McCarthy launched into a
speech critiquing the Truman administration for being soft on communism

and allowing Communists to work in the State Department. Looking at the assembled Republican women, McCarthy spoke in an ominous tone, "I have in my hand," he said, as if holding a nuclear secret, "a list of 205—a list of names that were made known to the Secretary of State as being members of the Communist Party and who, nevertheless, are still working and shaping policy in the State Department."[58] Days later, at speeches in Reno and Salt Lake City, he changed the number to fifty-seven,[59] and then to eighty-one.[60] McCarthy was elated—and surprised—that his unsubstantiated charges had created such a sensation. He was off to a good start in exaggerating the Communist threat with bogus but explosive lists, statistics, and allegations.

McCarthy hurled his wild charges in Senate speeches even after the 1952 elections, when Eisenhower won and Republicans gained control of the Senate. Under the Republicans, McCarthy became chair of the Subcommittee on Investigations of the Government Operations Committee. He named Roy Cohn the subcommittee's counsel, and he began his investigations. He continued pursuing the State Department, but as it was then under Eisenhower, McCarthy lost much of his Republican support. By 1954 McCarthy was investigating the Department of the Army, which was an overreach that caused him to self-destruct. By a 67 to 20 vote, he was censured by his fellow senators on December 2, 1954.[61]

Blind Memos

To note derogatory information in FBI files about an individual, the bureau anonymously leaked "blind memoranda" to HUAC, friendly journalists, and employers without the affected individual's knowledge. Another of the bureau's tactics was to send agents to an employer to ask if an individual worked there, making it clear that the FBI was interested in the employee. Harassment of those who had done nothing wrong could continue for years.[62]

Security Index and Custodial Detention

After Pearl Harbor, the bureau was ready with its detention program. Between 1941 and 1943, in addition to Japanese, the FBI arrested over 16,000 U.S. resident aliens as suspected subversives, though review boards released most as not being risks. The bureau simply added to its existing "Security Index" its Custodial Detention list—comprised of individuals to arrest and detain during a national emergency even though they had committed no crime. Attorney General Francis Biddle ordered Hoover to terminate the Index in 1943, but showing once again that he considered obeying his superiors optional, Hoover only changed its name to "Custodial Detention List."[63] By 1948, Hoover's FBI had two separate lists going: the Security Index and the Communist Index. The Security Index was the one that called for those individuals to be immediately and summarily arrested and detained in a national emergency. In mid-1949, the FBI had 10,744 individuals on the Security Index, a number that more than doubled by 1955. Almost all these individuals were active in the CP, the one characteristic that caused their classification as dangerous in a national emergency. Hoover then applied the same reasoning that was used to intern over one hundred thousand Japanese after Pearl Harbor: that those Communists would be disloyal to the United States and loyal to the Soviet Union, despite no evidence supporting this theory. The Communist Index listed all known current Party members, but also defined "Communists in the broad sense of the word," a group that included former Communists and those who "thru their activities and expressed sympathies strongly indicated affiliation or agreement with such ideologies." That last provision would brand many Americans as subversives because they were on friendly mailing lists, had signed petitions, or had joined organizations deemed to be Communist fronts.[64]

Jencks, those around him, and his union experienced most of the tactics outlined above. That background, in part, describes the environment in which Clinton Jencks operated in 1950.

4

CLINTON JENCKS AND LOCAL 890, 1947–1950

ONCE HE ACCEPTED his new job in New Mexico, Clinton and Virginia Jencks and their two children left Denver and headed for Silver City, where Jencks would work for Mine-Mill. Jencks loaded his family's goods onto a horse trailer and left Denver behind. During the trip the trailer broke down, but luckily they were able to complete the journey on Easter Sunday in April 1947 and settle into a roach-infested Silver City motel.[1]

The next morning, Jencks set out to survey the five locals, which had had little coordination before he arrived, including Santa Rita Local 63, Hurley Local 69, Local 530 at American Smelting and Refining's mine at Vanadium, Local 628 for the U.S. Smelting and Refining contract, and Local 604 at Hanover's Empire Zinc Mine. Each local had its own traditions, culture, rules, and grievance procedures. Often the membership knew little and was largely uninvolved in the locals' management.[2] The largest operation was the open pit at Santa Rita. In the early 1900s, with high grade copper ore long gone at Santa Rita, the company determined that processing low-grade material with expensive technology could result in a profitable mining venture. It would be done in an open pit rather than underground, and it would take huge shovels to dig and rail to haul the material to crushing mills and smelters. The mine was owned by Kennecott, as was the nearby smelter at Hurley.[3]

JENCKS 1947–1948

Jencks engaged his job with a passion. He purchased an old barracks to replace a small log cabin as the union's central office, meeting place, and community hall. He started a newspaper and a local Spanish-language radio program. He established uniform grievance procedures and ran classes for stewards in which they play-acted scenes to learn to process grievances. Jencks said that his ambition was to put himself out of a job by training Mexican leadership. His management philosophy was to run the union democratically by and for the rank-and-file membership. He said that "with the help of many active sisters and brothers, I was able to get folks to see that union strength flows from the bottom up, the power of 'one for all, all for one.'"[4]

The membership warmed up to the blond organizer whom they came to respect and treat as one of their own, calling him "Palomino" (a blond- or gold-colored horse), a nickname Jencks loved and kept.[5] With Jencks the locals got two for one, because Virginia also worked for the union, doing volunteer secretarial work and involving wives in the local's life, holding pot luck dinners, socials, Saturday night dances and movies, and forming a ladies' auxiliary.[6] Mine-Mill issued the auxiliary a charter, Local 209. By involving the women, the union became a family affair that strengthened the community as well as the local. In this work, Virginia was a key organizer.[7] Having husbands and wives work together was a model followed by several New Mexico Communists. Virginia often accompanied Clinton to Party meetings, as other wives did their husbands. According to Lorenzo Tórrez, besides himself and his wife, Anita, he knew of thirty-two Communists in Grant County in the early 1950s. Tórrez said Jencks was a Communist, but not openly so.[8]

At every opportunity, Jencks attacked anti-Mexican discrimination in the mines. He fought discrimination in hiring, promotions and seniority, housing, and work conditions, as well as geographic pay disparity by companies in the predominantly Mexican Southwest. He successfully recruited Mexican veterans who demanded equality and supported Mine-Mill organizer Alfredo C. Montoya, who formed the Asociación Nacional Mexicana Americana as a Mexican civil rights advocacy group.[9] Jencks also worked for bilingual communication to integrate the local's previously neglected Spanish speakers. To emphasize his own commitment, he took classes and in time communicated well in Spanish.[10] In joining Mexicans in their civil rights appeal and in voicing his union's militant labor demands, he quickly raised his profile in Grant County and was seen by the Anglo establishment and Silver City's newspaper as an Anglo troublemaker attempting to change the traditional social order. Jencks took on the same role Dewitt Clinton Jencks had after the Civil War: that of an unwanted outsider stirring up racial unrest and trouble for the establishment. Jencks recalled that the *Silver City Daily Press*, a pro-company publication, called him a "'tow-haired polecat,' a trouble-maker, a double-threat, a threat to the owners, a threat to the English-speaking community."

The environment for labor unions and their elected officers, especially the Communist Party members among them, changed dramatically during Jencks's first year in Grant County. In the November 1946 elections, Republicans took control of the House and Senate. It was an immense win for the business community and for anti-Communists, and it represented a turn to the right for the nation. Truman would call the new Republican Congress a "do nothing" Congress, but it was far from it, considering the impact of its legislation. Even Truman, who was criticized for being soft on Communists, saw the election's meaning. The ink was hardly dry on the election results when Truman signed Executive Order 9806 to study federal employee loyalty in anticipation of the coming Communist crackdown.[11] On March 12, 1947, Truman addressed a joint session of Congress and announced the Truman Doctrine, an American foreign policy whose purpose was containment, designed to resist communism in Greece, Turkey, and elsewhere. On March 25, further showing the nation that he was interested in eliminating Communists in government, Truman signed Executive Order 9835 establishing an elaborate mechanism to screen federal employees' loyalty, requiring clearance by a loyalty board and investigation by the FBI and the Civil Service Commission.[12] Executive Order 9835 led to the creation of the attorney general's list of subversive organizations. Finally on April 3, 1948, Truman signed the Marshall Plan to rebuild war-torn Europe, an initiative that the Soviets opposed as an American power grab. All of this happened just before Jencks arrived in Silver City, as did the introduction of the antilabor Taft-Hartley Bill.

To the unions, Taft-Hartley appeared designed to weaken legislation that labor held sacred, such as the Wagner and Norris-LaGuardia Acts. Taft-Hartley signaled just how politically weak unions had become in comparison to the business sector. Super majorities in the Senate and House passed Taft-Hartley, but the president vetoed the legislation with a passionate message. Days after Congress received Truman's veto, it overwhelmingly overrode it. On

June 23, 1947, Taft-Hartley became the law, and among its provisions was Section 9(h), a clause to eliminate Communists in unions by requiring that all elected union officials file an annual affidavit with the NLRB stating that they were neither members of nor affiliated with the Communist Party or any organization that advocated the government's violent overthrow. Section 9(h) immediately caused havoc in left-wing CIO unions that had CP members in their leadership and became an opportunity for some companies to refuse to deal with unions that did not comply, such as Mine-Mill.[13]

Although Taft-Hartley did not prevent companies from negotiating or dealing with noncompliant unions, some firms used the law as a pretext to weaken unions or put them at a disadvantage. The only penalty for noncompliance was a union's inability to invoke the Board's jurisdiction, including its supervision over elections and unfair labor practices. Companies chafed in dealing with leftist, industrial CIO unions with militant Communist Party leadership.[14] The CIO gave its unions the freedom to ignore the non-Communist affidavits, and at its February 1947 executive board meeting, that was what Mine-Mill decided to do. Mine-Mill's 1947 national convention fell just weeks after Taft-Hartley's effective date, and delegates voted to defy the law and refuse to file non-Communist affidavits, even if that meant boycotting the NLRB and its processes.[15] Perhaps Mine-Mill had little choice given that its then president, Maurice Travis, was a Communist, as were several in elected leadership positions.

The 1947 Mine-Mill convention was the first national meeting that Jencks attended, and he spoke twice there. The first time was to offer a resolution that the union vigorously combat discrimination of Mexicans and Spanish speakers. Jencks said, "We have in the Southwest second class citizens in the economic, political and social fields. The corporations . . . have brought in a system of segregation in housing, of differentials in wage rates and our union has been the greatest force for eliminating that." The resolution passed on a voice vote.[16] Presiding as convention chair that year was executive board member Kenneth Eckert—a name that comes up again later in Jencks's story. Normally, terms for the union's president were two years, but at the convention, Travis decided to demote himself to the lower profile secretary-treasurer position and pass the presidency to John Clark.[17]

When Jencks returned from the convention, he resolved that he would be even more militant if companies refused to negotiate new contracts. He would press stale grievances and insist that new ones be processed rather than postponed. He continued the daily consensus building that took hours. Instead of dictating what would be done—his predecessors' practice—he would involve the membership, which would decide the locals' course. The most important administrative change that Jencks made was to consolidate the five locals into one a few months after he arrived, creating Amalgamated Local 890—evidence that his consensus approach was working. Jencks was elected 890's president in January 1948, making it evident that he had gained the trust and confidence of the membership.[18] But by becoming an elected official, Jencks was then obligated to file a non-Communist affidavit if the union wished to invoke NLRB jurisdiction.

The presidential election year of 1948 was an especially complex and problematic time for labor. The incumbent, Democrat Harry S. Truman, had vetoed Taft-Hartley, an action that endeared him to labor. But Truman had confronted Soviet and Communist expansion and initiated several domestic anti-Communist measures. The old Democratic coalition fractured, and Truman was opposed on the right by the Dixiecrats, led by South Carolina's Strom Thurmond, and on the left by the new Progressive Party, led by Roosevelt's third-term vice president and former secretary of agriculture, Henry A. Wallace. The CIO usually gave its constituent unions freedom to support whomever they wished, but in 1948, with so much at stake, the CIO backed Truman and prohibited labor support for Wallace. To the CIO, Wallace was not a factor; it was a choice between Truman and Republican candidate Thomas E. Dewey, and for the left, Truman was the "lesser of two evils." The Communist Party, however, instructed its membership to back Wallace and the Progressive Party, which was what Mine-Mill and Local 890 did.[19]

It was then that two policies intersected to cause enormous problems for Mine-Mill. First, Mine-Mill supported Wallace against CIO policy, and then there was the non-Communist affidavit. Mine-Mill's affidavit and NLRB boycott policy allowed several companies in the die casting business to refuse dealing with Mine-Mill. Die casting was important to Mine-Mill and largely serviced the automobile industry. At a May 1948 union executive board meeting in Denver, die casting leader Kenneth Eckert proposed that the union allow signing the affidavits. Mine-Mill president John Clark urged the boycott's continuation, explaining that signing the affidavits would not solve any problems. In a June meeting held in Toledo, twenty-four of the district's thirty-seven die casting locals voted to secede from Mine-Mill, a huge blow to the struggling union, with the seceding locals migrating to United Auto

Workers. Mine-Mill vilified Eckert for his "treachery" and removed him from the board. Afterward Eckert said, "I found out that one cannot be a good union man and a Communist Party member, too, and I preferred to be a good union man."[20] Eckert's split from Mine-Mill was bitter.[21]

Meanwhile in 1948, U.S.-Soviet relations worsened, and the fledgling "cold war" intensified. In June the Soviets blockaded Berlin, forcing the Allies to supply the city in a massive airlift. Two months later, Whittaker Chambers appeared before HUAC and exposed a 1930s Washington, D.C. Communist group that included several individuals who later rose to prominence, such as Alger Hiss, Lee Pressman, and Mine-Mill's lawyer Nathan Witt.[22]

Not long after the die casting fiasco, Mine-Mill held its 1948 annual convention in San Francisco and readdressed the affidavit. With dissenters like Eckert out, the union found it easier to retain the affidavit boycott.[23] At his second Mine-Mill convention, Jencks was resolutions committee secretary, always a key committee for Communists. The committee resolved to repeal Taft-Hartley and to "persist in our refusal to subject ourselves to the Labor Board's procedures." Jencks argued for boycotting the affidavits, noting that "Taft-Hartley is but one of the steps along the road to fascism in this country. . . . Any attempt by us to submit to any part of Taft-Hartley will weaken the determination of our membership to fight the entire measure."[24] Jencks also presented a resolution condemning Eckert and other secessionists as "sell-outs," which broke the union's "solidarity to the glee and satisfaction of every employer, actively aided and encouraged company stool-pigeons in promoting secession." Jencks moved that Eckert be stripped "of every right and privilege" in the union and "that working men everywhere be warned against these traitors."[25] Finally, Jencks proposed a resolution to support the creation of a Southwest Regional office aimed at Mexican members, which included "Amigos de Wallace" and the "Committee to Organize the Mexican People."[26] Mine-Mill president Clark described Democrats darkly: "The Democratic Party under Truman is a party of witch-hunts and repression, speculation and inflation, brass-hat diplomacy, universal military training and war."[27] One could see that Jencks, in only his second convention, had a future in the union. He was a true believer and was dogged in pushing issues that were dear to him, such as fighting Taft-Hartley and Mexican discrimination, and he never let pass an opportunity to stand up for his Mexican membership.

Throughout 1948, Jencks and Local 890 campaigned for Wallace. As the largest Mine-Mill group in the state, Grant County controlled the New

Mexico Progressive Party. Communist Party member Craig Vincent led the Wallace effort in New Mexico.[28] Not only were Jencks and 890 early Wallace supporters, they ran Progressive Party candidates for almost every office. Jencks himself was candidate for U.S. Representative, B. G. Provencio for the U.S. Senate, Juan Chacón for state senate, and other Mine-Mill members filed for down-ballot offices.[29]

On Election Day, November 2, 1948, Truman pulled off the impossible and won. He and his running mate, Alben W. Barkley, took twenty-eight states; the Republican ticket of Thomas E. Dewey and Earl Warren won sixteen; Dixiecrats Strom Thurmond and Fielding L. Wright won four states; and the Progressive Party, with Wallace and Senator Glen H. Taylor, won none. Not only did Truman win a surprising victory, the "do nothing" Congress he had complained about was soundly defeated, with the Democrats regaining control of the Senate and House. In Grant County, all Mine-Mill candidates lost and received less than 10 percent of the vote.[30]

JENCKS 1949–1950

With Democrats in control, some in labor expected Taft-Hartley's prompt repeal. But party labels were deceiving: many southern Democrats were antilabor conservatives, as were several western Democrats. Elections have consequences, and certainly the 1948 election was a watershed. Labor split, and CIO unions that supported Truman did not forget what they saw as the left wing's and Mine-Mill's disloyalty. The election also caused estrangement between liberals and Communists, and ended whatever accommodation the two had. Going forward, liberals would be more willing to join the right in harassing Communists.

Rather than return to the Democratic Party after the election, New Mexico Communists formed the New or Third Party to replace the former Progressive Party. Leftist Mexicans, including Mine-Mill members, began to meet and organize a civil rights advocacy group called the Asociación Nacional Mexicana Americana (ANMA). Alfredo C. Montoya headed its organizing committee, and he was soon working for Mine-Mill. A chapter was organized among Local 890 members, and Jencks attended an early 1949 ANMA convention.

In May, a bar fight at the Fierro dance hall—just up the road from Hanover—involved several Mine-Mill members. The sheriff's office responded and used excessive force in dealing with what became known as the "Fierro Riot." ANMA adopted the altercation as a civil rights issue. With several Local

890 members in jail, Jencks and his lawyer attempted to visit the incarcerated. When he asked for the names of the arrested, the sheriff struck Jencks in the face with his fist while Jencks's lawyer was standing next to him.[31]

Mine-Mill's refusal to allow its members to sign affidavits continued to plague its negotiations. In May, Kennecott declined to negotiate a new contract with Mine-Mill so long as the union refused compliance. The Steelworkers' aggressive raiding pressured Mine-Mill to reexamine its policy. Mine-Mill's executive board met in Chicago in July 1949 and voted unanimously to reverse its affidavit policy, a decision ratified at the mid-September 1949 annual convention in Chicago, with cries that it was forced to do so by "the shameful betrayal of labor's fight for [Taft Hartley's] repeal." Before signing his affidavit, former Mine-Mill president Maurice Travis announced that he was resigning from the Communist Party.[32]

Local 890 members expressed bitterness over their "betrayal" by Truman and the Democrats in failing to repeal Taft-Hartley, and then they voted to permit its officers to sign the affidavit.[33] In October 1949, Jencks signed the affidavit form and mailed it to the NLRB regional office in El Paso. Jencks told his biographer that before signing the affidavit, "I sat down, wrote a letter resigning from the Communist Party. My affidavit was truthful and honest. Then I got on with my work as President of Local 890."[34] The existence of his October 1949 resignation from the CP is corroborated. His daughter Linda said that she saw the resignation in a book. Virginia Jencks, her mother, saw that she had it, took it from her, and said nothing further about it.[35]

In 1949, relations worsened between the CIO and Mine-Mill. The CIO and the left-wing unions were on a collision course reminiscent of the 1930s schism within the AFL that had given birth to the CIO. The main item on the agenda at the October CIO convention in Cleveland was the expulsion of "Communist-dominated unions." The CIO, determined to drive those unions from its ranks and Communists from their leadership, began the process by amending its constitution to empower its executive board to implement the ouster. The CIO board filed charges against ten left-wing unions, including Mine-Mill, for following policies dictated by the CP rather than those in the CIO constitution. A three-member committee was appointed to hear the charges, and the hearings began on January 18, 1950.[36]

During the expulsion hearing, committee witnesses, including former Mine-Mill executive board member Kenneth Eckert, detailed how Mine-Mill policies paralleled the Party's, especially regarding foreign affairs. Among those policies was Mine-Mill's opposition to the Marshall Plan and the Truman Doctrine, praise for the Communist coup in Czechoslovakia, and the mimicking of well-known twists and turns in Communist Party policies under Soviet Party orders. A Mine-Mill steering committee designed those common policies and coordinated in secret meetings with the CP. According to the committee, Mine-Mill refused to respond to the testimony. Mine-Mill leaders, the CIO reported, criticized the investigation as "biased," "phony," "red baiting," "witch-hunting," and a "sham." The committee unanimously recommended Mine-Mill's expulsion from the CIO, and on February 27, 1950, in a 34–6 vote, the CIO executive board did so.[37] To the expulsion, Jencks characteristically said, "We have been expecting this since last November's convention. Mine-Mill has been going for years, with and without CIO, and we feel that we can stand alone, if necessary."[38]

With Mine-Mill out of the CIO, it was now open season on its members and contracts. The defection of those who wanted no part of a "Communist union" intensified, as did raiding and poaching by rival unions. An economic recession reduced metals' demand and increased unemployment. Despite its problems in 1950, Local 890 was a different animal than the five weak locals Jencks found when he arrived in Grant County. His Local 890 was a well-oiled machine that processed its grievances, obtained wage and benefit increases, and showed no hesitation in calling strikes. It was no longer a union the companies could trifle with. Having gone through expensive battles, Mine-Mill's finances were poor, leaving the union ill prepared to face the harder times ahead. By mid-1950, with the union under siege, some companies sensed a vulnerability and an opening.

Mine-Mill's two-year contract with Empire Zinc (EZ) would expire in October 1950. EZ operated an underground mine and its associated mill in Hanover. It was a small operation compared to Santa Rita's open pit or other mines, but it would become a significant test for union and company, as it would for Hanover's men and women.

5

EMPIRE ZINC STRIKE

THE EARLY MONTHS OF 1950 were an ominous time for Clinton Jencks, as they were for Mine-Mill. By a lopsided vote, the CIO had voted to expel Mine-Mill, making the union vulnerable to member defections and raids by other unions. Red-hunters were on the attack against Communist Party union strongholds. The Cold War was reaching its greatest intensity, and the Communist Party, mostly through blunders and blind adhesion to Moscow's line, lost many allies and members. Congressional liberals and the CIO now joined conservatives in attacking Communists and their unions. In that setting, on April 28, 1950, after having quit the party the preceding October, Jencks filed his second non-Communist NLRB affidavit.

After a recession in which many Local 890 members were laid off, some Grant County mines began to rehire in 1950 when an increased demand for metals raised prices. In January, Local 890 signed its best ever Kennecott contract after a two-year negotiation. But 890 also experienced losses, with representation at Vanadium going to the company-backed union after the firm refused to rehire Mine-Mill members. Other companies sensed Mine-Mill vulnerability.[1] In May, American Smelting announced a wage cut, and Local 890 went on a thirty-six-day strike that brought the company to settle, giving its workers a five-cent increase.[2] Still, the strike was costly for Local 890 and depleted its meager strike fund, with later events further complicating Mine-Mill's environment.

On June 24, North Korea invaded the South, setting off the Korean Conflict with the United States and leading United Nations troops to defend the South. Three weeks after the Korean invasion, Julius and Ethel Rosenberg were arrested for providing the Soviets with American nuclear secrets. And then in late August, Lee Pressman testified in a HUAC hearing that Whittaker Chambers was correct to have named Pressman, Nathan Witt, John Abt, and Charles Kramer as members of the Communist Ware Group.[3] Witt was then Mine-Mill's general counsel. The nation now became open to the most repressive ideas.

On September 22, these explosive Communist exposures pushed Congress to pass over Truman's veto the most restrictive anti-Communist legislation to that time, the Internal Security Act of 1950, also known as the McCarran Act. Its purpose was to break the Communist Party by requiring registration for it and its members. It also established the Subversive Activities Control Board to name and monitor Communist and other organizations thought to be subversive. Article II of the Internal Security Act, known as the Emergency Detention Act, provided for the immediate arrest and detention of suspect individuals. The FBI kept a list of individuals to be arrested in a national emergency. With not a shred of evidence of disloyalty or illegality, the FBI put Clinton and Virginia Jencks on the list.

Despite the real threats to Mine-Mill, the resilient union hung on to most of its locals after some initial losses to the metals trade industry. It held its 1950 national convention in Denver in early September, and Jencks and Mine-Mill's leadership resolved to fight on. On its way to the Denver convention, the Jencks family stopped to vacation at the San Cristóbal Valley Ranch, a popular resort among Communists and leftists located about fifteen miles north of Taos and adjacent to the old D. H. Lawrence property. It was a fateful stop for Jencks: it was there that he met Harvey Matusow, who was there to see the ranch's owners, Craig Vincent and his folk singer wife, Jenny Wells. The conversations between Jencks and Matusow would later become controversial.

Jencks returned to Grant County just before the September expiration of Local 890's two-year contract with the Empire Zinc Company (EZ). EZ's operations at Hanover were among the Local's smallest, involving slightly more than 100 of its 1,400 members, but EZ would prove to be critical, and it became a famous Southwest labor dispute. Although EZ did not compare in size to Kennecott or ASARCO, it was no small firm. It was owned by the New Jersey Zinc Company, the nation's oldest and largest zinc producer, with the Hanover mine ranking fifteenth in the nation.[4] Zinc is a nonferrous metal essential to many industrial processes and defense-related products. It is used to make paint, rubber, pharmaceuticals, plastics, and ceramics. It is also used to galvanize steel and iron. Brass is 70 percent copper and 30 percent zinc. Of nonferrous metals, only aluminum and copper surpass its use.[5]

Among the companies with Local 890 contracts, EZ's labor record was one of intransigence and of working to break the union. Jencks believed that there was collusion between the companies to select a mine with smaller operations to test Local 890 and lower wages in the area.[6] Whether EZ was acting alone or was part of a larger plan, its refusal to bargain and negotiate with the local would challenge both sides as they approached the deadline. The company's negotiators seemed uninterested in a contract and refused to bargain in six of their eight meetings. In a secret meeting held on September 8, Local 890's EZ members overwhelmingly voted to authorize a strike should negotiations fail,[7] but Mine-Mill president John Clark wired Local 890 warning it not to go on strike unless it was "absolutely necessary."[8] On the contract's last day, EZ offered a five-cent wage increase, but insisted on also increasing the workweek from forty to forty-eight hours. The company negotiator left the area, and talks broke down. Local 890 waited three weeks before it voted to walk off the job. When the graveyard shift ended its workday at 6:30 A.M. on October 17, pickets stood to block the next shift. Local 890 member Lorenzo Tórrez said that in keeping with its democratic traditions of control by the rank-and-file, 890 members had voted to strike without consulting Mine-Mill's Denver headquarters.[9]

Local 890's demands were a fifteen cent per hour raise, "collar to collar" (meaning portal to portal) pay—that is, calculating time worked to include all time spent in the mine, including the meal break; six paid holidays; and meeting the terms achieved at other mines in the district.[10] EZ was not paying in full for the half-hour lunch period, choosing instead to pay ninety-six cents an hour or forty-eight cents for the daily lunch break. The principal economic point was calculating overtime pay, as the men were in the mine eight and a half hours rather than eight, meaning two and a half hours of weekly overtime that the company was not paying. To the mostly Mexican union men, collar to collar pay was also a civil rights issue. The muckers and miners—the underground workers—were mostly Mexican, but the shop and mill men were Anglo, so it was primarily the Mexicans who were at work the extra half hour without full pay, and it was the reason why the collar to collar point was so important to 890 members.[11]

It was typical for EZ to drive a hard bargain, and it was known for being hard-nosed.[12] EZ's goal was profit, and it did well by lowering its costs. The zinc produced at the Hanover mine was zinc ore, a material that was cheaper to process, giving the Hanover mine a competitive edge over other mines, as it could vary the zinc's quality from low to high grade through its smelting process.[13]

Before the EZ strike, Jencks and the 890 membership worked to strengthen the local, an activity in which Virginia Jencks and Virginia Chacón would play key roles. Women were invited to participate through the Ladies' Auxiliary.[14]

Unlike Santa Rita, Hanover was not completely a company town. There were company residences as well as some privately owned and rented homes near the EZ mine. The company homes were different for Anglos than those for Mexicans, which had no plumbing or running water.

Company and union conduct during a strike is an elaborate ritual governed by the federal labor code and regulations with a careful balancing of rights and interests. One goal of the labor laws was to encourage the parties to move toward amicable resolution by mandating negotiation with services such as mediation and conciliation. Picketing is the part of a strike the public gets to see. A striking union is entitled to inform the public of its grievance and that it no longer has a contract with the company. No threats or violence are permitted, and the pickets are not allowed to block other companies' employees or those making deliveries. Pickets are not permitted to block roads and entrances. Access to the Hanover mine was via a road that ran from the main highway north to Fierro. Local 890 established three picket lines on the road: one on the plant's south side, one to the north, and one at the plant entrance, with three shifts of six each manning the posts twenty-four hours a day. The locals' amalgamation in 1948 gave Local 890 a larger strike fund to sustain its members.[15] The local distributed strike rations consisting of food staples costing about $40.00 per month and a small $12.50 weekly allowance to pay bills.[16]

EZ's strike strategy was one of attrition in that it had the resources to outlast the stressed union and its needy strikers. In late October and mid-November 1950, the parties held five days of unsuccessful mediated negotiations. At the same time, EZ was foregoing a wartime economy—always a profit-making opportunity.[17] As fall ebbed into winter and the pickets braved Grant County's near alpine weather, confidence sagged. Strikers with large families could not live on the union's meager strike rations and asked for permission to find work elsewhere. Those allowed to leave were obligated to pay one quarter of their wages into the strike fund. This was later reduced to 15 percent, but even that remained a doubtful and painful proposition.

Folks at Mine-Mill's Denver headquarters regarded the EZ strike with the same practical economics of any labor dispute, balancing the costs versus possible benefits. In their eyes, the EZ strike looked like a loser that needed prompt resolution. Secretary-Treasurer Maurice Travis wrote Jencks in February 1951:

> I continue to be concerned about the Empire Zinc strike. Everyone tells me that the possibility of settlement is hopeless. I can't accept this point of view because I know that no strike can continue indefinitely without weakening and if we accept the idea that there is no possibility of settlement that is tantamount to accepting the idea that we abandon hope of retaining that section of our membership which is involved in the strike. At the coming Executive Board meeting on February 8th, I want to have a pretty down-to-earth discussion about the strike.[18]

After that ominous note, when Mine-Mill's executive committee met three days later, the Denver union voted to take control over the strike and act to resolve it.[19] Local 890 members had a different view. To his credit, Jencks understood what the international did not, that Mexicans had a different assessment of the dispute. To them, it was not just about economics; it was also about civil rights, fighting discrimination, and standing up for the Mexican community, values that defied economic analysis. To the Mexicans, the fight was existential. EZ was out to break *their* union, and they would not bend to the company's will—no matter the consequences.[20]

Later in February 1951, the international asked Jencks to work half time for Arizona locals and half time for Local 890, but the local refused to approve the arrangement while the EZ strike was pending.[21] In early March, the Federal Mediation and Conciliation Service brought the parties together for talks in El Paso, but the stalemate continued. The union increased its demands, and the company stuck to its old terms.[22] That failed effort was quickly followed by another in Hanover with the same result. Immediately after that session, the company mailed notices to all strikers that the mine would reopen and

Winter on the picket line of the Empire Zinc strike. *Michael Wilson Papers, Young Research Library, University of California at Los Angeles.*

they should return to work. With some dissenters, Local 890 rejected the offer. Anti-890 company attacks and those by the competing Steelworkers arose at other Grant County mines, making it imperative for the union not to lose at EZ. All sides intensified their public relations efforts.[23] In mid-April, Jencks's duties changed. He gave up 890's presidency to Cipriano Montoya and was to work half time organizing locals in Arizona.[24]

On June 7, 1951, a full-page ad appeared in the *Silver City Daily Press* announcing the EZ mine's reopening on Monday, June 11. The company claimed that "many" EZ employees were ready to return to work. The ad promised that EZ would pay the "highest mining rates in the district" and offered the fifteen-cent raise the union had been demanding but would not yield on the other points.[25]

The reopening raised the conflict to a different level. Whereas the pickets before had been informational, now they would take on a different role. Union members are expected to honor and not cross pickets. The company's move signified that it was prepared to start operating with non-union workers, strikebreakers, or "scabs." EZ executives obtained assurances from District Attorney Tom Foy and Grant County sheriff Leslie Goforth that the road to the mine would be open and accessible to EZ employees. To strengthen Goforth's efforts, EZ agreed to fund the hiring of twenty-four new deputies,

Strikebreakers taunting EZ strike pickets. *Mine-Mill Collection, Special Collections and Archives, University of Colorado Boulder Libraries.*

Grant County sheriff Leslie Goforth and strikebreakers. *Mine-Mill Collection, Special Collections and Archives, University of Colorado Boulder Libraries.*

with Goforth insisting that they would be under his and not the company's control. To union members, Goforth's promise rang hollow given his consistent company support, especially when Goforth hired strikebreakers and refused to hire union men as deputies.[26]

When the company opened the plant on June 11, strikebreaking employees were unable to enter, blocked by scores of strikers with pickets circling behind them. When a truck tried to pass through, the strikers picked it up and moved it away. Jencks told Sheriff Goforth that he and others could pass through, but the pickets remained in place. Goforth arrested Jencks and ten to twelve other pickets after they were ordered to stop blocking the road.[27] The district attorney and the sheriff claimed that the road was public and could not be blocked, but the union, noting signs on the road that warned, "Private Road, Pass At Your Own Risk," contended that it was private and company-owned. The union allowed EZ managers and office employees to pass, but told all others to use a back road to reach Fierro rather than the direct route that ran through EZ property. No strikebreakers passed that day.[28]

The next day, June 12, company lawyers filed their application for a temporary restraining order (TRO) against the international, Local 890, and the local's six-member negotiating team, which included Jencks. EZ asked the court to prohibit blockage and to allow returning employees passage. District Judge A. W. Marshall signed the TRO and set the matter for hearing on June 20.[29]

WOMEN PICKETS

On the evening that Judge Marshall signed the TRO against Local 890, the local held a meeting attended by a large crowd, which included Ladies' Auxiliary members. The TRO prohibited Local 890 members from blocking the road, which would leave the way open for strikebreakers. To people without resources, clinging to their jobs, saving their union, and keeping their strike alive, it was calamitous. After carefully reviewing their few options, Jencks and others, including many women auxiliary members, discussed having the strikers' wives take over the picket lines. Not being local members, the women were technically not covered by the TRO. But what would the men do when the women were doing men's work? Who would handle the home work and the child care? Many men opposed the move that endangered their wives and reversed domestic roles and duties, a change that "was as exhilarating for women as it was disturbing to men."[30] The crowd at the union hall argued for hours. Finally at 2:30 A.M., after several contentious votes, it was decided; the women would take over the picket line. Their vote was made possible by new union rules giving the auxiliary the vote. Although most men opposed the women pickets, Jencks wholeheartedly supported the idea. And so it happened, but what had seemed like a spontaneous decision had actually been planned earlier that afternoon by Virginia Jencks, Virginia Chacón, and Aurora Chávez.[31]

Within a few hours after the vote, the women organized their pickets and began their watch on June 13 while Jencks and eleven 890 members went on trial for blocking the road. Everyone was concerned about what could take place at the picket line given the tension and the armed, company-paid temporary deputies on duty. Goforth and the company appeared surprised by the development and took no action for two days.[32] Strikebreakers thought that they could go through but soon saw their error when they faced angry, determined women pickets. With the picket lines holding fast on June 15, Goforth went to District Attorney Foy and obtained arrest warrants for six women pickets, charging that they had grabbed at the strikebreakers or thrown rocks at their car. The next morning, Saturday June 16, Goforth went to arrest the women and open the road to traffic. Encouraged by the nearby men and others shouting *no los dejen* (don't let them), the women refused Goforth's order to clear out and pushed a deputy's car down the road. At 10:00 A.M., Goforth returned to the line and a deputy set off a tear gas canister, which temporarily scattered the pickets. But with a favorable wind direction, the pickets returned. Goforth then ordered the women's arrest. All told, they arrested some fifty-three women along with several children, including a newborn.[33] The arrested included Virginia Jencks and her daughter, Linda. The line still held, and individuals from the nearby group of three hundred women, many jeering at Goforth and his deputies, marched in to replace the arrested pickets. There was no end to the replacements. Two strikebreaker cars attempted to get through to the mine, but they were blocked and retreated. The line held. The entire time, the union men stood on a hillside nearby, gazing intently at the scene as their mothers and wives battled for the union's and their own survival. Jencks was not at the scene and claimed no involvement.[34]

Goforth was flummoxed, as his jail was jammed with women and small children. Late in the afternoon, with no solution in sight, he stopped arresting women. Goforth told the jailed women that they would be released if they promised not to return to the picket line, but the women would have none of it. They began singing and making noise to cause their jailors to regret the arrests. Goforth released some women with children, but others refused to leave the jail unless he released all, which he eventually did. At a hearing two days later, the women entered not guilty pleas to unlawful assembly charges and remained free on personal recognizance bonds. The courtroom was packed with the pickets and their supporters. As soon as they were freed, the women returned to the picket line, but rather than arresting them, Sheriff Goforth decided to wait before confronting the pickets again.[35]

After the June 16 events, the national media picked up the sensational story of women replacing their sons and husbands on a picket line and their return to the lines after being jailed. *Time* and *Life* magazines sent a crew, and larger newspapers, including the *New York Times*, as well as radio and television networks, followed the story.[36] On June 21, Judge Marshall held the scheduled hearing on whether the TRO should be converted to a permanent injunction against the union. At the hearing, Jencks and the others denied that they blocked the road and stated that they were instead on the road's shoulder. Jencks also testified that he did not advise union members or their wives or children to block the road or violate the judge's order.[37] To Jencks and Local 890, the women were not covered by the TRO or injunction and were acting lawfully. To Judge Marshall, the women were covered as union agents. In his view, the union men could not contract others to do that which they were prohibited from doing. The judge filed his findings on July 9 and issued a permanent injunction against the union and the individuals. Two days later, EZ moved to have the union defendants show cause why they should not be held in contempt of court.[38]

There was intense pressure on Jencks and Local 890 due to Denver's impatience, their meager resources, and the community's suffering. The strike committee and the local reached out to the Grant County business community and its residents, arguing that 890's demands were reasonable and agreed to by other district mines. EZ did not want a contract, the union alleged; it wanted nothing less than ending 890's representation. The strike committee's effort to gin up positive PR did some good. The Bayard City Council passed a resolution urging EZ to engage in good faith bargaining and to stop using strikebreakers and company-paid deputies. [39]

On July 21, the company filed a motion for the union and the individuals to show cause why they should not be found in contempt of court for having violated the June 12 temporary restraining order. After the hearing on July 23, Judge Marshall found Mine-Mill, Local 890, and the individuals guilty of contempt for having violated his June TRO. He fined the union and the local each four thousand dollars but offered to cut the fine in half if the union defendants stopped blocking EZ's access for one year. He found the six individual defendants, including Jencks, guilty of contempt and sentenced each to ninety days in jail, but he offered to suspend the sentences if the road to the plant remained open and unblocked for a year. The parties did not appeal the original suit but did appeal the contempt citations.[40]

As the strike wore on, racial tensions rose. Only twelve out of EZ's ninety-two union members were Anglo, and none took part in its strike activities; they had left to work elsewhere or became strikebreakers. Since Anglos were not underground workers, they were unaffected by the collar to collar pay dispute. Increasingly, it was a Mexican strike against Anglo forces. In Grant County, the strike mostly divided the community along racial lines.[41] To many in the Anglo community, the strikers were upsetting the peaceful social order they had always known, which was stirred up by Clinton Jencks, the Anglo

Communist and outside agitator. Adding communism to the mix quickly raised tensions in the area. The *Daily Press* contributed to the problem with its racially insensitive columns and openly pro-company stance.

With the case on appeal, the women continued picketing. Both the pickets and the deputies complained of violent incidents, but the judges only acted against the women pickets and in the deputies' favor. In some cases, the women's charges were not only disregarded but instead resulted in counter-charges against them.[42]

Union president Maurice Travis and Nathan Witt were in Grant County for the June hearings. Travis said that the injunction was "bought" by EZ, resulting in the Grant County Bar Association suing Travis for contempt of court.[43] The tension was such that EZ was calling for the governor to declare martial law.[44] On August 17, the NLRB ruled against EZ on a complaint filed months earlier by the union, stating that EZ's refusal to bargain constituted an unfair labor practice.[45]

The worst day of the EZ strike came one week later. August 22 was the day EZ decided to break the picket line. That evening, the company book-keeper sideswiped the union's strike coordinator with his car, and the pickets responded with a furious rock attack. Later, EZ employees met with the sheriff and planned the next day's definitive response. The local learned of the plan and called for picket line reinforcements the next morning. At 7:00 A.M., three to five strikebreaker cars approached the line of forty women and children. Goforth argued with the pickets for some time and finally told the strikebreakers that because it was a public road, they could drive through. When the vehicles advanced, the pickets attempted to push the cars back, and several pickets were injured in the incident. A strikebreaker shot at the pickets, hitting a striker. When word got out about the altercation, hundreds of union sympathizers walked off the job at other locations, and 600 to 1,400 supporters converged at Hanover. To the union, the attack was EZ's attempt to create a scene so the sheriff would demand that the governor call the militia. The state police arrived later and restored calm. Although twenty strikebreakers reached the mine earlier that day, they were unable to leave until after the state police arrived and escorted them out.[46]

The EZ strike incensed the Grant County business community. Angered by strike talk, Communists, and saboteurs during the Korean Conflict, the local radio station canceled Local 890's radio program, and the *Daily Press* warned of Kremlin influence and Communists in Mine-Mill. Antiwar talk by Communists in Mine-Mill's leadership helped convince the public that the union was attempting to thwart wartime production,[47] and they cited as examples speeches by Maurice Travis and Nathan Witt during their June visit.[48]

During the fall, District Attorney Foy, Sheriff Goforth, and EZ began harassing the pickets with peace bonds.[49] In September, Virginia and Linda Jencks were assaulted outside a grocery store that Virginia was picketing because it opposed the strike and refused credit to striking families. It was Virginia, however, who was charged and found guilty of unlawfully touching those who had attacked her.[50] In early October, Clinton Jencks went to get his mail and was engaged in conversation with the justice of the peace when he was attacked by Bayard druggist Earl Lett. The witness-judge fined Lett one dollar for the assault.[51]

In the altercation's aftermath, the antiunion "law and order committee" gave up on persuading the governor to declare martial law and focused instead on breaking Local 890 by encouraging its members to join the competing Steelworker organizing group that called itself the Grant County Organization for the Defeat of Communism. The Steelworkers did not understand the Mexicans' grievance over discriminatory treatment, did not emphasize the issue, and failed to recruit new members.[52] The Mexicans, men and women, came to believe that Local 890 was their union. Despite Steelworker raids and EZ's intransigence, Local 890 was doing well with the other firms. It obtained favorable agreements with Kennecott, Phelps Dodge, and American Smelting and Refining.[53] But EZ continued to stonewall bargaining talks, and the toll inflicted by the strike was bringing 890 to its knees. The litigation's cost, the many criminal charges, the peace bonds, and the picket lines' maintenance were devastating. By November, even Jencks was looking for an exit.[54]

STATE POLICE TAKEOVER

On December 10, Governor Mechem ordered the state police to take on security at the picket line and to open the road. The road was cleared without incident, and the pickets moved to the side. The strikers had more confidence in Mechem's evenhanded approach and felt reassured by the absence of company-paid deputies, some of whom were strikebreakers.[55] The possibility of state criminal charges also brought order, as did the reality that there were fewer pickets as time passed.[56] EZ's attrition strategy had not been foolish. EZ had the resources the strikers lacked, but the company was surprised by the local's

Clinton Jencks and bargaining committee in Grant County Jail. *Los Mineros Photographs, Chicano/a Research Collection, Arizona State University Library, Phoenix.*

Left to right: Nathan Witt, Maurice Travis, Clinton Jencks, Cipriano Montoya, and David Serna. *Mine-Mill Collection, Special Collections and Archives, University of Colorado Boulder Libraries.*

persistence and determination. By early January 1952, EZ claimed that it had resumed normal operations at its Hanover mill with non-union workers.[57]

Order held until mid-January when Judge Marshall called another hearing on a December 5 EZ motion to hold the union defendants (including Jencks), the negotiation committee members, and four union wives in contempt for violating the permanent injunction between July 10 and December 5. During the hearing, the sheriff and the company admitted that EZ paid for the temporary armed deputies at the mine. Goforth insisted, as did the company, that the sheriff was completely in control, but they were embarrassed by the revelation. Goforth admitted that it was his worst mistake.[58]

Jencks faced a dizzying number of attacks against him as well as other matters to handle. On January 18, 1952, during the EZ contempt hearings, the U.S. attorney served Jencks with a subpoena to appear before an Albuquerque grand jury. When told that Jencks was then in a hearing, the prosecutor agreed to postpone the appearance.[59]

EZ had filed another motion for contempt on December 18, 1951, for conduct it alleged occurred between December 5 and 18. That motion was not heard until February 1952. Sandwiched between the two contempt hearings, finally, were substantive negotiations that began on January 21 in El Paso. These negotiations came about when the company surprisingly accepted the invitation from the mediation and conciliation service as suggested by Mine-Mill.[60] First, the NLRB dismissed an attempt by EZ strikebreakers to decertify Local 890, because EZ had violated the NLRB's order to negotiate. Then on January 24, after three days of negotiation, the parties reached agreement in which the union gave up several demands.[61]

With thirty-two members in attendance, the local unanimously ratified the agreement, and some declared victory. Jencks said that it was not an economic victory. Local 890 members gathered during the weekend at the picket site and made the 11-mile pilgrimage to a church in San Lorenzo, a farming village to the east on the Mimbres, where three hundred attended a special Mass.[62]

In February 1952, Judge Marshall held a hearing on the third contempt case involving allegations that the union had violated the injunction between December 5 and 18, 1951. The judge found all defendants guilty and imposed additional fines.[63] Mine-Mill union and Local 890 were fined $38,000, and twenty members were also fined. Total fines neared $46,000. In addition, there were criminal contempt fines of nine hundred dollars and jail sentences totaling over one thousand days. Twenty-five criminal cases were resolved, but some ninety-one criminal charges remained pending against union members at settlement.[64]

It was unfortunate that the settlement did not expressly address the pending criminal and civil cases. Local 890 felt that EZ had implied in the settlement that the contempt and criminal cases would be dropped, but if that was the case, the company reneged and refused to relent on the pending cases, actions Jencks found "revengeful and vindictive." On March 10, 1952, Judge Marshall ruled against the union defendants in the two contempt cases.[65]

McCARRAN SALT LAKE CITY HEARING

With the EZ settlement in hand, Jencks finally began his new, divided duties, which had been postponed. He began to work half time for Local 890 and the balance for the international organizing in Arizona. Jencks no sooner began that schedule when, in April, the U.S. attorney in Albuquerque issued a new subpoena for him to appear before the grand jury. He advised the prosecutor that he would invoke his right under the Fifth Amendment, and he was excused and not questioned.[66]

In August, Judge Marshall began proceedings to have Jencks and others in Local 890 show cause why the one-year suspension of the ninety-day sentences pronounced the previous year should not be revoked. Marshall stated that he believed Jencks and the others had not complied with the suspension's conditions, and he set the matter for hearing on September 5.[67] At the hearing, Judge Marshall found that Jencks and his codefendants had violated the probation's terms and should serve their time.[68] Grant County's establishment had special scorn for Jencks, the outside Anglo agitator. The Anglo power structure claimed that Jencks was upsetting Mexicans who, they implied, had been previously content with their lot as second-class citizens. During his time in jail, Sheriff Goforth put Jencks into a solitary, tiny cell, isolating him from his fellow union inmates.[69] As ever, Jencks remained resolute and unapologetic and handled union duties while in custody. The union had a one-day sympathy strike to protest the sentences.[70]

While in the Grant County Jail, Jencks received a subpoena to appear in Salt Lake City before the Senate Subcommittee on Internal Security. The hearing's subject was the "Communist Domination of Union Officials in a Vital Defense Industry—International Union of Mine, Mill and Smelter Workers," and it was to be held October 6–9, 1952, with Senator Pat McCarran presiding. From jail before the hearing, Jencks wrote to 890 members, "This man McCarran is not by himself. This is no little scheme to 'embarrass' us. This Salt Lake hearing picks up where Taft-Hartley leaves off. T-H has not broken unions, only crippled them. Now liars, stool pigeons and company-minded men will give testimony that Mine-Mill . . . is a Communist union."[71] Seeking his release, writs were filed for Jencks with the New Mexico Supreme Court, which ordered him freed pending the case's resolution. On October 6, Jencks suspended for the time being his intense combat with roaches and bedbugs in his tiny cell.[72] Once released, Jencks had only a day or so to make the long drive to Salt Lake City and the hearing.

McCarran, a conservative Democrat, scheduled the hearing in Salt Lake City one month before the 1952 general election to help fellow subcommittee member and Utah Republican Senator Arthur V. Watkins, who was running for reelection.[73] By the time Jencks arrived at the hearing, other witnesses had already testified, including Maurice Travis and Nathan Witt. McCarran began the hearing with veteran, professional anti-Communist J. B. Matthews and former Mine-Mill executive board member Kenneth Eckert. Matthews described the broader environment and Eckert identified several Mine-Mill personalities as Communists, including Travis and, in so many words, Mine-Mill president Clark. As the committee questioned witnesses about their own politics and connection with the CP, Travis and Clark repeatedly refused to answer, invoking their right under the Fifth Amendment. Mine-Mill attorney Nathan Witt was called, and he too took the Fifth but seemed to enjoy sparring with and humiliating counsel for the committee. Jencks was a low-level Mine-Mill official among those called to testify, but the reason for his appearance would soon become evident.

At the subcommittee's evening session, the chair called Harvey Matusow, a rising personality on the anti-Communist witness circuit and professed CP expert. Committee counsel asked Matusow about his time at the San Cristóbal Valley Ranch. Matusow stated that in July 1950, he was on his way to California and stopped at the ranch, having previously met its owners in New York. He said that ranch owners, Craig and Jenny Vincent, were both "dues-paying" CP members. The ranch, Matusow alleged, catered mainly to Communists. Matusow quickly noted that one guest worked for the Czech United Nations delegation, and he intimated that the woman was involved in atomic espionage at the atomic laboratory in Los Alamos, New Mexico.[74] Continuing, Matusow noted that another guest he met during his one-month stay was Clinton Jencks, who was vacationing at the ranch and gave lectures there. Matusow testified that in their conversations, Jencks explained that Mine-Mill would strike to hinder metals production and hurt the Korean Conflict effort. They also discussed Jencks's CP status, with Jencks admitting that he was a Party member. According to Matusow, Jencks mentioned having contact with a Communist-dominated Mexican miners' union that cooperated in a cross-border courier operation. Matusow identified the National Mexican American Association (ANMA) as being a CP front organization.[75]

After McCarran and Watkins engaged in lengthy self- and cross-congratulatory statements, Matusow gave the committee a bonus revelation, a McCarthy-like nugget. He said that he was an American Newspaper Guild member and attended its New York City meetings in 1950. Matusow noted that "in New York City today there are approximately 500 dues-paying Communists working in the newspaper industry. The New York Times has well over 100 dues-paying members. Time, Inc., has 76 Communist Party members, working in editorial and research, and just a few months ago the Communist caucus regained control of that unit in the Newspaper Guild."[76] Having made that startling charge, Matusow was temporarily excused while Jencks was called to testify.

As Jencks took the witness chair, Nathan Witt entered his appearance for Jencks.[77] Counsel for the committee first elicited Jencks's work history and war record. As soon as he was asked any question about the CP, Jencks refused to answer, invoking the Fifth Amendment; the Chair insisted that he answer, and Jencks declined again. Jencks refused to answer whether he was elected to the Party's Colorado State Board, and when pressed further about why he refused to respond, Jencks replied that the Amendment was to protect "a witness against arbitrary and tyrannical procedures," adding that "it is my opinion that the intentions and procedures of this committee are arbitrary and tyrannical." Chair McCarran reminded Jencks that in the public's mind, by taking the Fifth Jencks was "inferentially declaring [himself] to be a Communist."[78]

In a moment staged for drama and maximum publicity—a stunt replicating Richard Nixon's staged Hiss-Chambers confrontation—while Jencks was still sitting in the witness chair, Matusow was recalled as a witness. In an unusual occurrence, committee counsel began to question both at the same time, the accused and his accuser in the witness chairs. The following occurred.

Counsel to Matusow: Will you identify this man, if you please?

Matusow: Clint Jencks.

Counsel: Mr. Matusow, did you have a conversation with this Mr. Jencks at the San Cristóbal Valley Ranch?

Matusow: I did.

Counsel to Jencks: Do you deny that conversation, Mr. Jencks?

Jencks: I decline to answer your question under the grounds of the Constitution and the fifth amendment to it that provides that right to decline to answer the question.[79]

The hearings went on for a few days, with Mine-Mill witnesses mainly taking the Fifth and the professional anti-Communists describing Mine-Mill as a CP-dominated labor organization. As designed, the hearings produced the expected publicity, and Senator Watkins was soon reelected. To the *Silver City Daily Press,* the EZ strike was the reason behind McCarran's Salt Lake City hearing.[80] Ranch owners Jenny and Craig Vincent denied Matusow's allegations, calling them "unfounded, undocumented and foolish."[81]

The consequences of the November 1952 election were profound. Eisenhower was elected the first Republican president since Herbert Hoover; Republicans kept a slim hold on the Senate and took the House. In Grant County, with strong opposition from Local 890, Sheriff Goforth was defeated. Despite all the challenges, Jencks and 890 did have some wins. Local 890 closed out 1952 signing a favorable contract with Kennecott for a hefty increase in pay and better benefits. But the dark clouds of Communist influence in Mine-Mill continued to gather over Jencks and his local. Matusow's explosive Salt Lake City testimony alleging a Czech espionage attempt on Los Alamos facilities made news again almost three months after the hearings. South Dakota Republican senator Karl E. Mundt called for a new investigation based on those allegations, with news accounts prominently mentioning Jencks and Mine-Mill.[82]

The EZ strike's consequences went far beyond the economic and local issues common to labor disputes. Much has been written about whether the EZ strike was a winner or a loser. In economic terms, the strike was a clear loser for the company and a perhaps a marginal loss for the union. The company had an opportunity loss in passing up fifteen months of maximum wartime production with high prices for its products had it met or even come close to what other mines in the district were paying their workers.[83]

EZ had a natural cost advantage given the zinc ore that it mined and could have paid its miners even more than other firms and remained competitive. The United States was only a few months into the Korean Conflict when EZ made that decision and stubbornly stuck with it. All in all, EZ's decision made little business sense. While EZ had the greater resources, it also had more to lose. Its competitors made money while EZ found itself mired in a self-inflicted labor dispute. But EZ was going for broke. It sensed a union weakness, wanted to break Local 890, and felt that it was the right time to do so. That strategy fit with EZ's harsh labor policy. If its goal was to destroy Local 890, EZ failed, and in doing so, made a significant miscalculation.

The union's choices were more limited. Local 890 made demands normal for unions seeking parity in the area.[84] When a union strikes a favorable deal with one company, it then pressures the rest to meet that standard. To a union, a favorable agreement made with one employer makes those terms per se reasonable. Those elements become the union's pattern contract demand to other companies.[85] In 1951, Local 890 confronted EZ, a company bent on destroying what members saw as their union. The local could have capitulated to EZ's offer, but it would not have been in keeping with a militant local like 890. Militant unions such as 890 under Jencks, and companies, such as EZ, intent on breaking unions, were more prone to strikes given their greater propensity to risk impasses. Mine-Mill's Denver-based executives saw the strike as a loser and essentially counseled dropping most demands, but to the 890 membership and to Jencks, it involved pride and self-respect. At various times, 890 told EZ that it would accept any contract 890 had with any other company, and EZ refused. That was an objective test proving that EZ wanted to pay less than any other firm. Those union men and their picketing spouses and mothers would die before giving in; they would not grovel. They saw no option but to fight. When Local 890 survived to sign a contract, even one with marginal gains after a costly, bitter, and painful battle, to them it was a win, an inspiring moral victory for a Chicano union against a determined and powerful foe.[86]

The EZ strike saga would be documented like few in the past.

6

SALT OF THE EARTH

THE NESTING-DOLL ASPECT of the Clinton Jencks story extended to the Empire Zinc strike, an event that was staged for cinema by blacklisted Hollywood filmmakers in *Salt of the Earth,* a film that was itself blacklisted, had its own story, and became a cult classic. In late 1952 and early 1953, blacklisted Hollywood filmmakers and Local 890 re-created the Empire Zinc strike for the moviegoing public, a course that would make the EZ strike famous. They made *Salt of the Earth* in an era when eight studios—five major and three smaller—ran Hollywood and there was nothing like today's independent film production.

In the 1940s and '50s, the studio oligopoly operated on an industrial scale with an iron-fisted control that many in the trade felt suffocated film's creativity. The studios had an authoritarian ethos with contracted stars treated like chattels. The studios owned or operated most theaters and were under pressure to produce a steady stream of movies.[1] They also controlled a film's content. For most films, the studios bought a story line and hired writers mechanically banged out scripts to fit. The frustrated artists and writers, treated more like hired clerks, longed for artistic freedom.[2] Although Hollywood had a large, vibrant, influential leftist and Communist community, in the main, its ideology did not find its way into the films they made, a point made by Ronald Reagan at the HUAC hearings. In that Hollywood, a Communist writer usually hammered out scripts for the likes of Hopalong Cassidy, and other than the rare *Grapes of Wrath, Casablanca,* or *Mission to Moscow,*[3] most never wrote about fascists, a worker's struggle, or corporate greed. Except for the good pay, in its lack of creativity Hollywood was less rewarding than writing pulp novels. The reality of the studios' control and their bland, nonideological product was the opposite of the Hollywood portrayed in anti-Communist allegations. To anti-Communists, Kremlin-controlled reds ran the film industry and surreptitiously propagandized Americans.[4] The anti-Communist movement had successfully purged Hollywood's Communist and left-wing filmmakers, hundreds of whom were blacklisted and banned from their moviemaking careers, including director Herbert Biberman.

THE HOLLYWOOD BLACKLIST AND THE INDEPENDENT PRODUCTION COMPANY

After serving six months in federal prison for contempt of Congress due to his refusal to answer HUAC's questions in the Hollywood Ten controversy, the blacklisted Herbert Biberman struggled over how he was going to make a living. Biberman's wife, the Oscar-winning actor Gale Sondergaard,[5] was also blacklisted after taking the Fifth during her 1951 HUAC appearance. Biberman recalled that back in 1942, left-wing theater impresario Simon M. Lazarus suggested that they form an independent film production company through which they could make quality films. Biberman had disregarded the idea before, but he recalled it when he found himself, along with hundreds of talented filmmakers, walking the streets with no hope of cinema work. Why not form a company that employed that blacklisted talent, so they could all make a living *and* make quality films? In the summer of 1951, Biberman went to Lazarus and suggested reviving the idea. But it was a different time and environment, with Biberman now a controversial and blacklisted figure. Lazarus had suffered some financial reversals in the meantime and could no longer finance the entire project. Biberman nevertheless convinced the somewhat reluctant Lazarus to serve as company president and to make a modest investment.[6]

Biberman learned that the blacklisted Paul Jarrico and fellow Hollywood Ten member Adrian Scott were working on a similar project, and he invited them to join him in forming the Independent Production Company (IPC). Despite Jarrico's reservations about Biberman, he and Scott agreed to join. While Jarrico found Biberman totally committed to his cause, he also regarded

Biberman as "rigid, abrasive, arrogant, and insensitive."[7] The normal studio film budget was five hundred thousand dollars, but Biberman thought that IPC could make films for one hundred thousand. They planned on three films to start their company, with a three-hundred-thousand-dollar budget, and quickly raised the first thirty-five thousand. Next, they looked for worthy projects to tell the untold stories of working-class blacks, Jews, and Mexicans in a genre called social realism.[8]

In 1950, Paul and Sylvia Jarrico vacationed at San Cristóbal, "the Communist dude ranch," or the red Chautauqua, where they met Clinton and Virginia Jencks.[9] Jarrico was a Hollywood screenwriter who was in the second group of Hollywood figures subpoenaed before HUAC in 1951, a cohort that included Biberman's wife Gale. By that time, the witnesses had abandoned the First Amendment and only invoked the Fifth, which Jarrico and Gale Sondergaard defiantly did. On the day he announced that he would be taking the Fifth, Jarrico was fired from the Howard Hughes-owned RKO Studios. He was an accomplished and successful writer with several film credits and an Academy Award nomination, but once blacklisted, he would find no work in Hollywood for twenty years.[10]

In 1951, the Jarricos returned to San Cristóbal for another two-week summer stay. The Jencks also went to the ranch, vacationing there during the intense events of the EZ strike. While there, Virginia Jencks told the Jarricos about the strike.[11] Paul Jarrico was immediately fascinated by the image of Mexican women and their children engaged in a class struggle with a national zinc corporation along with fighting scabs and armed, deputized company goons. If one wanted to see social realism in action, this was it. The Jencks invited the Jarricos to see it for themselves, which they did. The Jarricos not only visited Grant County to witness the picket line, but Sylvia and her eleven-year-old son also joined the pickets. For Jarrico, the EZ strike had all the elements IPC sought: a brutal, wealthy company intent on crushing a Chicano union; a dominant Anglo community determined to preserve its discriminatory dominance; an oppressed minority community fighting for equality and decent wages; in sum, a class struggle with the bonus of feminine empowerment and gender role reversal. Jencks was passionate in wanting the story told: "We in the Silver City area needed help in getting our story out of our little corner of the mountains." Jarrico needed no convincing.[12]

When Jarrico returned to Hollywood, he told Biberman that the EZ strike was the story they were seeking. Jarrico's eyes glowed, and his memory was "filled with the sounds and sights" of Grant County as he told Biberman about EZ and the women pickets. On hearing the story, Biberman agreed that it was the project to undertake.[13] Jarrico suggested that the only screenwriter who could do the story justice was his brother-in-law, blacklisted screenwriter and fellow Communist Michael Wilson. Jarrico and Wilson had married the Gussin sisters; Jarrico married Sylvia, and Wilson wed Zelma. Jarrico and Biberman described the project to Wilson. Although he was then at work on a novel, Wilson agreed to suspend his project and go to Grant County.

Jarrico and the Gussins had dramatically different backgrounds from Wilson's. The Gussins and Jarrico were generational Jewish leftists, and all three had joined the CP while at Berkeley. To Jarrico, socialists were too timid and lacked the militancy he wanted,[14] an experience and attitude he shared with Jencks. Wilson, on the other hand, came from a conservative Catholic Oklahoma family that had migrated to California where he, perhaps as a reaction against his father, became radicalized while at Berkeley.[15] Of the project's blacklisted participants, Wilson had the most impressive film credits, having won an Oscar for co-writing *A Place in the Sun* in 1951, the year he was blacklisted.[16] Later, he would receive a posthumous Academy Award for co-writing *The Bridge on the River Kwai* and a nomination after the fact for *Lawrence of Arabia*.

According to Biberman, Wilson said, "Fellows, we've got to give up trying to write stories of real people from our point of view. I think that's why the stories you have been doing are not coming off. If I do this story, I want to do a story from the point of view of the people of Local 890. And if I do this story, they are going to be the censors of it and the real producers of it . . . in point of view of its content. And I can't make any promises about how soon this script will be done. I've got a lot of reorientation to do." Then Wilson asked, "Terms satisfactory?" Biberman and Jarrico agreed.[17]

The EZ strike was still under way when Wilson went to see it for himself. Wilson spent a month in Grant County, hardly speaking, absorbing the strike and its personalities. Jencks called him "a sponge" for his intense study. Henrietta Williams, a picket, described Wilson: "When we saw Mr. Wilson up there on the little hill sitting down, we thought he was a scab. And we always kept an eye on him. We always were watching what he was doing, what time he came, what time he went. . . . We thought he was a company man. That he was writing down names to take us women to jail, like they used to do. He asked a lot of questions."[18] Wilson returned to Hollywood to work on a draft and then went back to Grant County in January 1952. He read the script to the strikers and the women. The community insisted on revisions, and Wilson made several significant changes to the script. One Mexican striker said that he objected to portraying Jencks as their Anglo savior. Wilson told Biberman and Jarrico that he found the story complex and multilayered. There were, he felt, battles for equality and against discrimination being fought on several levels; the men against the company, Mexicans in general against the community, and the women versus the men at home. To Wilson, the film's theme was the "indivisibility of equality."[19] Wilson then returned to the West Coast, where it took him six months to rework the script.[20]

While Wilson worked on the script, Biberman and Jarrico addressed the film's production side. The credits rolled out at a film's end show a project's complexity. From lawyers to plumbers, a project needs skilled craftsmen for cameras, lighting and sound, set designers and carpenters, wardrobe and makeup technicians. They must purchase or rent specialized film, lighting, and sound equipment as well as find and lease locations. Most skilled film workers belonged to craft unions, and IPC was adamant that its pro-labor film be made with union labor. In that, the company had a problem. The union representing most Hollywood technicians was the International Alliance of Theatrical Stage Employees (IATSE), a vehemently anti-Communist union led by the most vociferous Hollywood anti-Communist, Roy Brewer. IATSE grew to become a Hollywood monopoly. It became a vertically-integrated operation representing almost every craft associated with making, processing, and distributing a film, including cameramen, set builders and decorators, film processors, cutters and editors, film projectionists, and all the rest.

IATSE's unfortunate pedigree included the Chicago mob of Al Capone and Frank Nitti, complete with extortion and union goons. Under George E. Browne at the union's Chicago headquarters, extorting Hollywood studios had become a major revenue stream for IATSE, with its representative William "Willie" Morris Bioff handling its Hollywood operations. Between 1935 and 1941, rather than work for its membership, the union reduced its demands against the studios in return for huge under-the-table payoffs to Browne and Bioff. The studios carefully considered Bioff's thinly-veiled threats, as in an incident described by Warner Brothers Pictures' Harry Warner in which he paid Bioff $25,000 one Christmas after Bioff told him that "the boys in Chicago were expecting a Christmas present." After years of those operations, both Browne and Bioff were finally arrested and indicted for extortion, convicted, and sent to prison.[21] The evidence showed that Bioff would threaten a strike or violence to shut down filming or a film's screening, but call it off when the studios paid a bribe. It was a *modus operandi* common in Mafia-infested areas, where such bribes came to be a normal cost of doing business and the mob's main income source. For this reason, mobsters found unions attractive. Chicago thugs and extortion aside, the studios had one good reason for preferring the corrupt IATSE to a different, honest but militant union: money. Despite paying Bioff and Browne $1–2 million, a Hollywood executive testified at their trial that the studios had saved $15 million in labor costs by paying bribes to the pair.[22] That was the same reason companies did not like Jencks and the militant Mine-Mill. Jencks, some complained, was incorruptible.

In 1945, Roy Brewer was sent from Chicago's IATSE office to succeed Bioff in Hollywood. Brewer arrived there to handle a labor war within and against his union, a war between the mob-infested IATSE and the alleged Communist-influenced Conference of Studio Unions (CSU). The CSU offered to serve as a legitimate and militant union to replace the formerly corrupt IATSE. The NLRB ruled for CSU to represent several craft unions in films, but the producers refused to recognize CSU, preferring the lower-cost and "more compliant" IATSE. The refusal to bargain with the CSU set off a violent, months-long strike.[23] CSU's president, Herbert Sorrell, called the strike, and 750 pickets marched to block strikebreakers' entry into Warner Brothers Studios. The CSU strike lasted for months in 1945–46 and involved several violent episodes. With the studios in support, Brewer knew how to handle the uprising. IATSE goons and law enforcement clubbed and teargassed the CSU pickets, and the fire department hosed them down for good measure.[24] As the two unions competed for dominance in Hollywood, it did not take Brewer long to catch the scent of anticommunism in the nation's postwar tack to the right. On cue, Brewer devised a strategy to have the corrupt IATSE don the mantle of respectability and become Hollywood's protector against the Communist CSU threat. To defeat the CSU, Brewer exposed and purged every film industry Communist, CSU leftist, and liberal sympathizer that he could find, and in that manner rid IATSE of its CSU competition. Brewer was so successful in executing his anti-Communist strategy that, after fighting two years, CSU and Sorrell gave up, and IATSE regained its airtight monopoly.[25] Brewer was a magician. He had altered IATSE's image from that of a crime syndicate to the patriotic darling of the conservative Hollywood business establishment and the anti-Communist movement. It was quite a feat to go from FBI mob target to J. Edgar Hoover's handmaiden, and to have done so almost overnight.

No sooner had Brewer disposed of CSU in 1947 than HUAC, the studios' Waldorf Declaration, and the blacklists presented Brewer with new opportunities to lead Hollywood's Communist purge. Brewer's targets, which had formerly been stagehands, film technicians, projectionists, and back lot employees, now expanded to include high profile actors, writers, directors, and producers—that is, Hollywood's movers and shakers. When HUAC needed a friendly witness to set the table for the committee, Roy Brewer was its first choice. Brewer was the last friendly witness at the 1947 HUAC hearings before the committee undertook questioning the unfriendly Hollywood Ten. And no one relished IATSE's transformation more than Roy Brewer. Brewer, the man from the mob-infested union, joined Hollywood's conservative establishment and became its ant-Communist powerhouse. Hollywood producers gladly made Brewer their hatchet man carrying out blacklisting's dirty work. Moreover, given his background, Brewer was happy to display his ostentatious patriotism and do what studio moguls were too squeamish to do themselves.[26] When any upstart Communist wished to work anywhere in film, it was Brewer who stepped in. He would use his CSU-tested anti-Communist tactics and threats to destroy any Hollywood Communist, plus some leftists, liberals, and anyone else who might hire questionable individuals or get in his way.

With the studios' support, Brewer led various anti-Communist civic organizations and operations, including the Motion Picture Alliance for the Preservation of American Ideals, the AFL film council, the Motion Picture Industry Council, liaison to the American Legion, and blacklisting's rehabilitation apparatus.[27] Brewer's allies provided media outlet backing, including newspapers owned by Hearst and columnists like Hedda Hopper, to expose his targets; the FBI to exchange information; the FBI and Congress to investigate; and organizations, including the American Legion and the Catholic Church, to bludgeon.

This was the formidable anti-Communist machine facing IPC as the tiny, fledgling company attempted to produce its first film project, titled *Salt of the Earth*. IPC needed a film crew, and IATSE was the only game in town.

IPC's president, Simon Lazarus, volunteered to meet with Brewer, as he had a good past relationship with him and was early in recognizing the projectionists' union. For good measure, Lazarus took along a union man to vouch for him. At their meeting, the optimistic Lazarus told Brewer that IPC wanted to shoot a pro-labor movie and needed a union crew. But once Lazarus identified the blacklisted Biberman, Jarrico, Scott, and Wilson as IPC participants, it was essentially over. Brewer, playing a monarch dressing down an uppity subject, was brutally blunt with Lazarus, his responses constituting a resounding "No!" IPC's Communist players were, Brewer said, "a very disturbing influence." The movie, he threatened, would be made "over my dead body." Pounding the table, Brewer vowed that even if IPC made the film, it would "never be shown in the United States." This was no empty threat, as IATSE controlled the nation's projectionists.[28] Brewer "was able to say to Simon Lazarus, with all the authority of a sovereign, that if he proceeded with such persons [Biberman, et al.], he would be destroyed."[29] Brewer concluded, "I will see you in hell first." Lazarus, the highly successful and powerful theater owner, was shocked and shaken "by the ferocity of Brewer's attack."[30]

FILMING *SALT OF THE EARTH*

IPC was left to scramble in finding a crew. Jarrico recalled that there was an independent CIO documentary film union based in New York City that was not IATSE-controlled. When contacted, those at the documentary union expressed interest in the project but were apprehensive, as they were considering merging with IATSE. The CIO union agreed to "service" the film, but it would later renege on even that minor commitment. IPC struggled to hire a small crew from dissident individuals and some who simply were beyond threat. The team they finally assembled included some blacklisted individuals and three novice black cameramen available because AFL craft unions, such as IATSE, excluded blacks. The movie would remain "union made" because Mine-Mill would issue the crew temporary union cards.[31]

The executives on the project would be Jarrico as producer; Biberman's sister-in-law, Sonja Dahl Biberman, as associate producer; Biberman as director; and Wilson the screenwriter. They persuaded Mine-Mill to coproduce the film, which did not mean financial investment but rather union support and hopefully other unions' aid in the film's distribution. Film processing arrangements were made with Pathé Labs. The cast, they decided, would largely be the Local 890 members, the women pickets, and a few professional actors. After some discussion,[32] it was decided that Mexicans would play the lead roles of Esperanza and Ramón. Forty-two-year-old Mexico City actor

Rosaura Revueltas was cast as Esperanza, but filling the male lead remained a problem.[33] Mexican American actor Rodolfo Acosta initially agreed, but then his agent made him renege in fear that he would be blacklisted. Finally, just before the shooting began, Biberman handed the male lead to Local 890 president Juan Chacón. Clinton and Virginia Jencks would play themselves under the stage names Frank and Ruth Barnes. Among the hired professional blacklisted actors was Will Geer, who was contracted to play the villainous sheriff. Geer later achieved fame for portraying "Grandpa" in *The Waltons*.[34] Biberman struggled to persuade Local 890's Anglo members to play the roles of evil scabs and hired deputies.

Brewer's obstruction and threats caused vendors and providers to back out, and IPC struggled to organize the project. Routine moviemaking chores became formidable obstacles for the blacklisted group and drove up expenses. The crew they assembled was "motely" and inexperienced, the equipment was second rate, and they lacked a crucial script clerk, assistant director, and full-time wardrobe person.[35] They secured a shooting location by leasing a ranch from the eccentric Alford Roos—a self-proclaimed gun-toting Jeffersonian and Muslim convert—who insisted that his ranch be the location. They rented quarters for the crew at the Bear Mountain Lodge after its initially reluctant owner agreed.[36]

True to his commitment to involve the strikers and women pickets in writing the story, the script Wilson produced came from his consultation with many individuals. Whether the script was collaborative or written by committee, IPC marched toward filming with the script it had.[37] As Wilson conceived it, Esperanza, rather than her husband Ramón, became the film's focus. In doing this, Wilson confronted head-on "the woman question," the Communist term for feminism. Communists were not necessarily feminists, but they at least addressed and discussed the issue, mostly with good intentions. In looking at the EZ strike—DZ, or Delaware Zinc, in the film—through Esperanza's lens, Wilson examined the multifaceted discrimination faced by the wives of Grant County's Mexican miners and correctly decided that more could be seen through Esperanza's eyes than through Ramón's.

When the miners in the film, mostly Mexicans, go on strike over DZ's casual disregard for their safety in the underground mine, the women play their usual supporting role and the men handle the picket line. Months into the strike, DZ announces that it will reopen the mine with strikebreakers if necessary. After a picket line confrontation, the biased court sides with the company and enjoins the union pickets from blocking the mine entrance, with the sheriff and company-paid deputies there to enforce the court order. The union members face a dilemma. They have to block the strikebreakers to save their strike and jobs, but if they do so, they will be violating the court's order. After hours of heated argument at the union hall the night of the injunction, with most men in opposition, the women are permitted to vote and, with some men in support, swing the election to allow women to replace men on the picket line—in theory circumventing the court's order and resolving the dilemma. The women's insistence on becoming pickets threatens marital peace in many homes, as the women are overruling their husbands' opposition and challenging the domestic pecking order. While the men raise legitimate questions about the women's safety, they also resist the domestic role reversal implicit in the change, as women cannot be expected to handle the "men's" picket line *and* their housework *and* childcare while the men stand by doing nothing.

The film's women replace the men's mine safety issue with running water and sanitation. This was a lower-level priority for the men until, under the strike's domestic role reversal, the men are the ones hauling wood to heat water to wash, cook, and iron and carrying water to bathe, wash, and drink, laborious chores that consumed hours of the women's daily lives. Focusing on water and sanitation allowed for a broader examination of Mexican discrimination in the film, as Anglos living in DZ housing were, unlike the Mexicans, provided with running water, indoor plumbing, and better homes.

Flummoxed at first by the women pickets, the sheriff and DZ decide that the women will be easier to handle than the men. They are mistaken. The women pickets energetically and enthusiastically joust with the sheriff, the goons, and the scabs, obligating the sheriff to arrest them. When other women immediately replace those arrested, the sheriff finds his jailhouse packed with screaming and chanting women and children intent on making him miserable. The women succeed, and their detention, rather than deterring them, increases their determination.

In the film's most dramatic scene, sheriff's deputies execute a company order to evict one family from its tiny company shack. As their possessions are taken out the front door to the yard, neighbors and soon the entire Mexican community converge on the scene, menacing the evictors. Women then pick up the family's possessions from the yard and return them to the home, going through the back door as the deputies remove more items through the front.

Soon, the deputies recognize their task's futility and barely escape, leaving the community victorious. In the end, the women pickets hold fast, forcing DZ to negotiate and settle with the miners. The men recognize their spouses' value and equality and acknowledge that their courage and determination has saved the day. The women teach the men that they cannot gain respect and equality at work or in the larger community unless they first accord it at home. Coming long before the women's liberation movement of the late 1960s, the film's feminist message added to its controversial nature. Wilson, Biberman, and Jarrico did not forget from whence they came, and so the film's context remained the class struggle implicit in Esperanza's fight; the community's longtime discrimination against Mexicans; and the companies' mistreatment and exploitation of the miners.

With the story line settled, the crew went to the Roos Ranch and the Fierro bar to construct the sets. They built mock structures mimicking company housing at the ranch and interior sets at the bar. The cast was selected, and the actors began memorizing and rehearsing their lines. Finally everything was ready, and on January 20, 1953, IPC prepared to start shooting as a condensed five- to six-week project instead of the normal twelve.[38] For the first week or two, everything went as well as expected, and the Grant County community seemed supportive. Certainly, IPC's fifty thousand-dollar deposit to a local bank was evidence that the project was bringing money into the community.

Around February 8, the first ominous signs appeared. A Hurley school-teacher alerted Screen Actors Guild president Walter Pidgeon that Local 890 was making a film.[39] The *Hollywood Reporter* followed with a story that blacklisted Communists were filming a propaganda movie in Grant County. Claiming that the filming of *Salt of the Earth* was "a grave threat to national security," Pidgeon notified the FBI, HUAC, the State Department, Roy Brewer, the CIO, and labor columnist Victor Riesel. On February 9, Riesel escalated the threat, writing in his syndicated column that pro-Soviet Mine-Mill Communists were conspiring in an area near the nation's Los Alamos nuclear laboratory, absurdly implying that the very public film crew and striking miners were nuclear spies or saboteurs. Riesel obviously expected his terrified readers to be unaware that Grant County was as far a drive from Los Alamos as Richmond, Virginia, was from Manhattan. The film's propaganda involved, he claimed, the "so-called abuse of the foreign-born in the U.S.," inflaming the "anti-American racial issue."[40] The charge was that showing a labor dispute and discrimination against Mexicans helped the Soviets. After

Herbert Biberman *(on roof, seated, center)* with members of the *Salt of the Earth* film crew. *Wisconsin Historical Society, Madison.*

Riesel's column, Pathé Labs reneged on its agreement to process the film, leaving the crew unable to review film "rushes," a day's shooting.[41] After those initial jabs, the anti-Communist machinery then moved to a higher level, with the authorities converging to create mischief for the minor indie film.

On February 20, the *Silver City Daily Press* told the public, "It's time to choose sides." Pressures increased on IPC. Its Los Angeles accounting firm withdrew its services, and two insurance companies canceled the project's workers' compensation insurance.[42] On February 22, Immigration and Naturalization Service (INS) agents paid a threatening visit to Bear Mountain Lodge to interview Revueltas and review her immigration paperwork, which they took with them.[43] Two days later, California Congressman and HUAC member Donald Jackson took to the House floor. Jackson alleged that *Salt of the Earth* would be "a new weapon for Russia" and "is being made . . . not far from Los

Alamos by men and women who are part of the pro-Soviet secret apparatus in this country. . . . This picture is deliberately designed to inflame racial hatreds and to depict the United States of America as the enemy of all colored peoples." Repeating Roy Brewer's earlier threat, Jackson continued, "I shall do everything in my power to prevent the showing of this Communist-made film in the theaters of America."[44] Jackson asked several federal agencies to investigate the film project. In El Paso, the *Times* and *Herald-Post* repeated Jackson's allegations, as did local Grant County radio stations.

Two days after the Jackson speech, immigration agents arrested Revueltas. Revueltas had crossed into El Paso in an airport limousine, showed her papers at the border, and was waved through. INS claimed that her entry was illegal because her visa was not stamped. She was taken to El Paso and held in custody. INS assured Revueltas that the matter was not serious, and she could return to her work after posting a five-hundred-dollar bond. It did not turn out that way. After being questioned about her politics and the project, she was not released in El Paso nor was she allowed to post bond. Instead, INS moved to deport her. Days later, United States district judge R. E. Thomason agreed with INS and denied her relief. Defeated, she agreed to depart voluntarily.[45] The crew would scramble to complete the film with the female lead in Mexico.

What had been a peaceful filming changed after the Jackson speech turned the mood in Grant County's Anglo community from supportive or indifferent to hostile or violent.[46] On the morning of Monday, March 2, the local radio station rebroadcast the Jackson speech. That day, the crew had scheduled filming in Central, a community adjacent to Bayard where they had received permission to film from the mayor. The crew was approached by eight men—some of whom were armed—including Franey Foy, District Attorney Tom Foy's brother. They had formed a vigilante group called the Central Protective Committee, with the intention of harassing IPC. The group told the crew that if they did not leave, the Committee would smash their cameras. When the crew replied that they had the mayor's permission, the vigilantes said that the mayor did not run the place. To avoid a confrontation, the crew left.[47]

The following day, Tuesday, March 3, the crew set up to shoot a scene across from the Bayard union hall. As they finished filming the scene, an angry mob appeared. The mob was led by a local banker named Upton, who was Bayard's mayor, and druggist Earl Lett, with twenty or so others in tow. Lett said that they were not going to let Communists film, and for the second time he proceeded to grab Jencks by the coat and strike him in the face, blackening his eye. Lett proudly held up his fist for the press and photographers.[48] Union member Floyd Bostic was also injured, and the crew was threatened once again. The sheriff appeared but arrested no one. At 1:30 A.M. the next morning, four or five shots were fired into Jencks's automobile parked outside his home.[49]

The shooting was the final straw, and the state police were summoned. Within hours they showed up with seventy-five troopers in thirty-five squad cars. The tension and violence nevertheless continued to escalate. Encouraged by the anti-Communist movement and their own leadership, on March 4, Grant County's Anglo community made their biggest show yet. In a 250-car parade, the flag-waving Anglos rode around Silver City, Hanover, Bayard, Santa Rita, and past the Roos Ranch, where the crew was working. The "citizens' parade" was a demonstration, they said, to let everyone know that they did not approve of Communists. Later that day, seventy businessmen gave Jencks and the film crew an ultimatum: "Leave town in twelve hours or leave in black boxes."[50]

On March 4, State Patrol Chief Roach met with the new Sheriff Matthews, two local priests, Biberman, and Jencks. Roach suggested that with violence possible, it would be advisable for the crew to stop filming and leave. Father Francis Smercke disagreed, arguing that the crewmembers were innocent and that they should finish their work. That was the decision. After the meeting, Father Smercke met privately with Biberman and told him to tell the union and Jencks that Jencks "had outlived his usefulness in the area." The priest told Biberman that while Jencks had done much for the Mexicans there, because Jencks was an Anglo fighting for the Mexicans, he "had become the symbol of everything the rabid, racist elements in the area feared and hated."[51] Biberman did as asked and repeated the priest's comment to the union and Jencks. Jencks, as always, said it was up to the membership. After deliberating, the members unanimously voted that Jencks should stay so long as he wanted to and felt safe doing so. They said the vigilantes did not hate Jencks but rather what he stood for, "and what he stood for was decency in the community." Their fight was against "racism and vigilantism."[52] The racism the priest mentioned had always existed. It was Jencks, the Anglo, like the priest said, who drove his fellow Anglos wild with anger. Their perception was that Jencks was stirring up the natives, as though the Mexicans were blind to the racism and discrimination they lived with daily. In strikingly similar language, the *Daily Press,* the druggist Lett, and Bayard's mayor denied any racist feelings at all and blamed the problem on Mexicans from Mexico, to be distinguished from the better class Hispanics, the native-born Spanish Americans. To the *Daily Press,* Mine-Mill was mostly Mexican.[53]

Jencks was a hated man. Sometime late on the March 4, Jencks was fueling his car at a Bayard service station when the station owner, Richard Benjamin, punched Jencks in the head just because he felt like doing so. The proud Benjamin later "freely and cheerfully acknowledged to reporters that he had punched Jencks."[54] Lett, Benjamin, and others had learned that Jencks was nonviolent and would not strike back, and that law enforcement would let them go unpunished. Or it could have been as Alford Roos surmised: Jencks refused to be provoked into a fight so that they could not call him "a brawler, a rioter."[55]

The local radio station organized a demonstration to invite the crew to leave town by leaving their porch lights on. On March 5, the local businesses closed so residents could see the anti-Communist film *The Hoaxters.*[56]

Knowing that their time was limited and that they were unable to complete the Revueltas scenes, Biberman finished his work in two concentrated filming days. On March 7, the crew packed up and left Grant County.[57] The following day, Local 890's Bayard union hall was set on fire and damaged, and 890 member Floyd Bostick's home was torched and burned down.[58] It was no accident that Bostick's home was selected for arson. He was an Anglo, like Jencks, and especially reviled by the Anglo community for siding with Mexicans. That was what, under Jencks, made 890 more than a union. It "became a political and civil rights organization, too, attacking those institutions that favored rich over poor, Anglo over Mexican."[59]

Once Biberman and the others returned to Hollywood, they faced the daunting technical work of producing the film against a mountain of opposition. Congressman Donald L. Jackson, following up on his vow to bury *Salt of the Earth,* asked movie mogul Howard Hughes for advice. On March 18, the then merely eccentric Hughes outlined steps to stop the film. Hughes described what Biberman and IPC were up against. IPC, unlike the studios, lacked the skills and equipment to make the film, so if "the industry" denied them technicians and equipment, IPC could not complete it. Pathé Labs already refused the work, so IPC needed someone, somewhere to process the film. IPC needed film labs, film suppliers, musicians and recordings, technicians to do fades and dissolves, sound recording equipment and dubbing rooms, positive and negative editors and cutters, and labs to make the final prints. The industry had to detect dummy corporations and false names. All applicants for similar services and equipment needed to be investigated.[60] Over the next year and a half, IPC would battle to complete those tasks and work around the blacklist.

Salt of the Earth made news even while it was being filmed. *Time* and *Newsweek* gave the project prominent coverage in their film sections.[61] Making *Salt of the Earth* was challenging enough, but the film raised Clinton Jencks's profile in the community and made him a wanted man in Grant County and elsewhere.

7

UNITED STATES
V. CLINTON E. JENCKS

TEN DAYS AFTER Biberman and the IPC crew packed up and left Grant County, Congress held hearings on making Taft-Hartley even tougher on unions and controlling CP influence. On the hearings' second day, March 17, 1953, the committee heard from Richard B. Berresford, employee relations head at New Jersey and Empire Zinc. Berresford gave the friendly committee the company's version of the Empire Zinc strike and the film controversy. EZ, he testified, offered the union a raise before the strike and was always ready to negotiate. The strikers violated the court injunction and frightened Grant County citizens. He said that Jencks, Mine-Mill, and the filmmakers were inflaming race hatred where there had been none. At EZ, he swore, "we do not discriminate." The union posed as the Mexicans' champion against "the so-called white or anglo [*sic*]." Berresford described the scene as a violent union siege, and said the union had Communist goals and tactics. The "use of women and children on the picket line is a Communistic tactic," and a model, noted Berresford, whose name was "Vishinsky." Berresford denied that EZ was out to destroy the union. The company, he assured the committee, was only "trying to give it proper leadership."

The committee asked Berresford whether the anti-Communist affidavit was working. He answered that it was not; it needed to be strengthened. For example, he explained, if any union officer refuses to testify or invokes the Fifth Amendment, he should be barred from the union. Also, companies should be prohibited from dealing with Communist-influenced unions. Their contracts should be canceled. Jencks and other Mine-Mill officers, he reminded the committee, had taken the Fifth.[1]

Local 890's president, Juan Chacón, responded to Berresford's testimony, stating, "Neither the bosses nor the bosses' friends in government are going to tell us, the workers in the mines, mills and smelters, what union we can have or what unions we cannot have."[2] From Berresford's testimony, it appeared that EZ's executives were still intending to finish off militant, CP-influenced unions.

■

Late on Monday, April 20, 1953, Clinton Jencks was playing with his son, Michael, in the yard of his Bayard public housing residence. Suddenly, vehicles pulled up and men in suits got out. They were FBI agents, and, together with case agent J. Phillip Claridge, they arrested Jencks on an El Paso bench warrant. Jencks asked for permission to put on shoes and socks. The agents refused the request, put Jencks in the car, and took him for arraignment before U.S. commissioner George H. Keener in Silver City. Keener advised Jencks that he had been indicted that day in El Paso on two counts of making a false statement to a federal agency in violation of Section 1001 of the Federal Criminal Code. The crime charged was filing a false affidavit with the NLRB on April 28, 1950, in which Jencks attested that he was neither a member of nor affiliated with the Communist Party.[3] Each count was a felony and carried a maximum penalty of five years in prison. Judge Thomason in El Paso had set a five thousand-dollar bond, but Jencks was unable to make bond until the next day when Local 890 deposited the cash.[4] After another night in the Grant County Jail, Jencks was released. He blamed the mining firms and saw his indictment as "just another effort by the companies and their representatives to use the Taft-Hartley act to stop unions. I am guilty of nothing other than fighting for the rank and file of our local union, and I intend to keep right on doing that, Jencks said."[5]

The government had rushed to file the case a week before limitations— three years in 1953—would have barred prosecution. Jencks was among the first affidavit cases, but unlike the others, he was a low-level union officer.[6] In looking at cause and effect, it is tempting to see *Salt of the Earth* or the

Berresford testimony as the indictment's most recent precipitating events. Harvey Matusow was the only witness presented to the grand jury who testified that Jencks was a CP member after he filed the April 28, 1950 affidavit. Since Matusow was only contacted two or three days before the indictment, perhaps *Salt* was what moved the Department of Justice to indict. Historian Ellen Schrecker saw it that way.[7]

Matusow, who at that time was living in luxury after his marriage to a wealthy woman, was at his Washington, D.C. mansion when contacted by Justice Department attorney Joseph Alderman of the Internal Security Section. Alderman told Matusow that limitations was running the following week and that he was needed immediately in El Paso. Matusow left the next day for El Paso. Once there, he wrote, "I learned that it was my testimony that was needed to indict Jencks—mine, and only mine—I was in my glory. This was big league stuff, and I was the star. Without me there was no game." It placed him, he continued, on par with the other star anti-Communist witnesses of the day: Crouch, Budenz, Cvetic, "the stellar performers of the witness world." Matusow told the grand jurors that Jencks, the Communist, worked to undermine the U.S. effort in the Korean Conflict. He reminded the grand jurors that "the boys in Korea . . . were dying on that very day." Five minutes after Matusow testified, the grand jury indicted Jencks.[8]

Although Matusow habitually exaggerated, his statement that without him there was no case against Jencks was uncharacteristically on the mark. The government's problem in affidavit cases was that the statute required party membership or affiliation at the time an affidavit was executed, and Matusow was the only witness who testified that Jencks was a Party member after he signed the affidavit. Jencks expected that Matusow might be the main witness at his trial given their previous public confrontation in Salt Lake City and Matusow's testimony there. To Jencks and the union, it was "a frameup."[9]

The local and Mine-Mill quickly rose to support Jencks,[10] but for Jencks, it was a heavy blow that had landed on him and his family. Given his work in Grant County, he was always under pressure; first to learn the ropes and understand how to work with his Mexican membership; later to organize and run his amalgamated local, and finally to manage the EZ strike and complexities in making *Salt of the Earth*. It was clear that Jencks's continued tenure at Local 890 was problematic. First, there was his personal safety. He was struck three times with impunity for his assailants. His car was shot. The union hall and his fellow Anglo union member's home were torched. He was threatened. His wife and daughter were assaulted with no consequences for the attackers. Even the priest said that Jencks was so hated in Grant County that he had to go. Now he was under indictment and would have to prepare for the trial. Taking that into account, union headquarters decided to transfer Jencks to the Denver office in June.[11] The Jencks hated leaving Grant County. They felt at home there, where they made many friends and a life. Once in Denver, Jencks was to devote his time to raising money and support for his defense, and the union created the Jencks Defense Committee.[12]

In August, the court set the trial for October 6 but later changed the date to November 30, with pre-trial motions set for hearing on October 23.[13] Jencks and his lawyers, John T. McTernan, Nathan Witt, and El Pasoan E. B. Elfers, had little to go on to prepare the defense. Whose testimony or what documents did the government have regarding Jencks's Party membership on April 28, 1950? On membership, either he was or he was not a member. The second count, "affiliation," was more problematic for the defense. What did affiliation mean? How would the government prove that Jencks was affiliated with the CP when he filed the affidavit? Because this was among the first cases on the issue, there was little decided law to guide the lawyers. The defense moved for a bill of particulars to require the government to indicate what overt acts would show CP membership or affiliation. They asked for a witness list and the documentary evidence the prosecution would introduce. Given that the two counts punished identical conduct, the defense asked the judge to make the government elect one count. The judge overruled the motions but decided to postpone the trial again. The judge heeded pleas not to try the long case during the Thanksgiving to New Year's holidays and set the trial for January 11, 1954.[14]

Five days after Judge Thomason set the new January trial date, Texas attorney general John Ben Shepperd denounced Mine-Mill, the Fur Workers Union, and the Distributive, Processing and Office Workers of America (DPOWA) for being Moscow-controlled with a plan to take control over Texas industries. All three unions were, in Shepperd's words, "Deep Red and disloyal."[15] Shepperd, in office less than a year, picked up on the DPOWA strike in Port Arthur and the Jencks and Mine-Mill controversy in El Paso. Neither Shepperd nor Texas Governor Allan Shivers would miss such a political opportunity. Liberal Ralph Yarborough was opposing Shivers's reelection, and Shivers was painting Yarborough as an NAACP integrationist and a Communist labor union dupe. The DPOWA had targeted Port Arthur, Shivers's political home, to organize

Jencks family. *Clinton Jencks Papers, Special Collections and Archives, University of Colorado Boulder Libraries.*

with resulting labor strife. The McCarran Senate Subcommittee on Internal Security had investigated the DPOWA for being under Communist influence in early 1952, and now the same union was on strike at a Texas port. The announcement produced precisely the results Shepperd expected. The *El Paso Herald-Post* urged El Pasoans to "give their whole-hearted support to Attorney General Shepperd in his campaign to oust the Reds." The editorial noted that the alleged red takeover was "alarming news for Texas and especially El Paso where the Mine-Mill union has its greatest strength in this state."[16]

El Paso Mine-Mill union members were familiar with local red-baiting, but this was now coming from the Texas governor and attorney general, and it was making headlines a month before the Jencks trial. El Paso's Mine-Mill responded, "Mr. Shepperd's charges of 'Moscow gold' and 'Moscow plot' are a fantastic fabrication from start to finish. . . . It is unfortunate that his type of headline hunting has become such a surefire thing in the winning of political campaigns." Jencks realized that the flaming headlines made the chance of drawing a fair jury for his trial more remote. For the Jencks defense committee PR effort, Rod Holmgren drafted a letter that he sent to a selected El Paso mailing list. It said in part, "We don't expect the papers to observe ordinary journalistic rules of fair play in reporting the trial."[17]

"Governor Shivers Warns Reds to Stay Out of Texas," read the headline in the November 30, 1953, *El Paso Herald-Post* announcing that Governor Allan Shivers had asked the long-dormant and toothless Texas Industrial Commission to conduct "a sweeping investigation" of Communist-dominated unions. Attorney General Shepperd was to assist in the inquiry, and the "sweeping" investigation was to be conducted in several hours over one weekend.[18] Shepperd invited union officers to attend and announced the testimony of several professional anti-Communist witnesses, including Harvey Matusow as his first witness.[19]

Testifying against DPOWA was old hat for the twenty-eight-year-old Matusow, who had testified about the union before the McCarran subcommittee in 1952. Now Matusow would tailor his testimony for a Texas audience. Matusow assured the commission that the three unions conspired and that El Paso was a "way station in Communist courier operations." In front page headlined stories, Matusow and the other former Communist witnesses described Texas as a Communist and subversive hotbed, an allegation certain to add to the national hysteria over the domestic Communist threat.[20] The enterprising and skeptical Washington reporter Sarah McClendon, who represented several Texas newspapers in the capital, asked the Immigration and Naturalization officials about the border being a Communist hotspot and a courier way station. Several immigration officials told McClendon that "there is no such activity going on now or in the past in Texas that the Immigration Service knows about."[21] The Texas commission closed its Austin hearings on Sunday, December 6, harvesting the expected plethora of "commie" headlines.

With the trial scheduled to start in January, the timing could not have been worse for Jencks, an individual wearing the Communist label. The years 1950 to mid-1954 were the peak of McCarthy-era hysteria. The public was ready to punish Communists, and there seemed to be no limit to what it would allow done to them. Two months after the Jencks trial, in a final blow against Ralph Yarborough, his Democratic Primary foe, Texas governor Shivers proposed the death penalty for CP members. Already on the books since 1951, the Texas Communist Control Law required CP members to register or be charged.[22]

As everyone prepared to enter the holiday season before the trial, Craig and Jenny Vincent, who were subpoenaed to produce their guest records in November, announced that they were closing their San Cristóbal Valley Ranch and would operate the property in the future as a cattle ranch. The Vincents said the closing was a McCarthy hysteria casualty.[23]

As everyone prepared for the El Paso trial in January, Mine-Mill's *Union* newspaper carried a large Jencks family Christmas photograph. The caption had the family wondering, "Will we be together next Christmas?"[24] Everyone's attention would now be focused on the proceedings in El Paso.

8

THE JENCKS TRIAL PERSONALITIES

EVERY TRIAL IS A DRAMA. In contrast to most theater, a legal trial is put on by competing parties. As the prosecution stages its version, the defense attempts to enact a separate account. The warring parties often disrupt and contradict the other enactment as it is staged. The judge sometimes intervenes. The players in this legal theater are critical personalities in the ultimate outcome, as is the jury, about whom relatively little is known.

THE JUDGE

For half a century, U.S. district judge Robert Ewing Thomason, was a key public figure in El Paso.[1] Now seventy-four years old, he had been on the court since summer 1947, when President Harry S. Truman nominated the then-sixty-eight-year-old congressman to the bench. The people of El Paso were comfortable with Thomason, and he liked being the town's only federal judge, seeing the position as a cap to an impressive career. As he sat on the Jencks case, Thomason brought with him experiences that would shape his views of the defendant and the charges he faced.

Thomason was born in 1879 in Bedford County, Tennessee. His father was a Confederate veteran who later became a country doctor and moved his family to Cooke County, Texas. The family settled in Gainesville, its county

U.S. district judge R. Ewing Thomason.
Special Collections Department, University of
Texas at El Paso Library.

seat, located on the Oklahoma border 65 miles north of Fort Worth. Thomason
was expected to follow his father's medical career, but instead he chose the
law. He graduated from Southwestern University in Georgetown, Texas, and
received his law degree from the University of Texas in 1900. He practiced law
in Gainesville for a few years and served as Cooke County district attorney.
Malaria and a physician's advice to seek a high, dry climate took the young
lawyer to El Paso in 1911. Once there, he joined others to form the law offices
of Lea, McGrady, and Thomason, a firm of politically active trial lawyers. His
partner Tom Lea was elected El Paso's mayor in 1914, and Thomason won
a seat to the Texas House in 1916. Thomason was a wholehearted Woodrow
Wilson supporter and would remain a loyal, lifelong Democrat. If there was
one event in Thomason's life that indicated that he was a man who would
earn others' trust and respect, even those who disagreed with him, it was
his election as Speaker of the Texas House of Representatives in 1918. He
faced obstacles in that he had only served one previous term, and no one
west of the Pecos River had ever been elected speaker. Thomason supported
prohibition—although he was a moderate drinker himself—and backed
woman's suffrage, two contentious issues of the day. In his race for speaker,

Thomason was unopposed and was elected unanimously. He became the only El Pasoan to hold a similar position. Because Texas has a weak governor, the speaker and lieutenant governor posts are especially powerful. As speaker, Thomason became a public figure and gained statewide attention.[2] Under Thomason's speakership, Texas became the ninth state to ratify the Nineteenth Amendment giving women the vote. All other southern states failed to ratify the amendment until after its passage, one doing so as late as 1969.

In 1920, Thomason was persuaded to run for governor, but came in third. A friend teased that Thomason "was defeated by a large and enthusiastic majority."[3] Thomason returned to the full-time law practice that saw his firm prosper. They were the preeminent trial lawyers in the area. Thomason and his partner Lea continued their involvement in El Paso politics and joined the reform group, which in 1922 succeeded in deposing the powerhouse "Ring," the local political machine, and defeating a strong campaign by the Ku Klux Klan.[4] Following his law partner Tom Lea, Thomason returned to politics a few years later. He was elected El Paso's mayor in 1927 and reelected in 1929. Before he finished his second term, he was elected to represent El Paso and the sprawling Sixteenth District in the United States Congress. Thomason soon adapted to life as a congressman and was easily reelected time after time. He became a respected insider in the clubby House and was close to the powerful leaders in the Texas House delegation, such as John Nance Garner and Sam Rayburn, both House Speakers.[5]

Thomason served his first term under Herbert Hoover, and he was not inspired by the Iowan who sat in the presidency as the nation's economy plunged into the Great Depression. He won the primary for his second term in 1932 and, having no Republican opponent, was free to campaign for the Roosevelt and John Nance Garner ticket. On Roosevelt's election, Thomason joined many in Congress as enthusiastic New Deal supporters. In general, Thomason voted for the New Deal,[6] and he loved the charismatic and energetic FDR. Even late in life, Thomason spoke proudly of the Tennessee Valley Authority and emphasized the need to promote other navigation and hydroelectric projects. In the Depression years, he supported the Civilian Conservation Corps, the Works Progress Administration, and other programs that put people back to work. Thomason had a clear preference for helping working people. During his time in Congress, he rose on the seniority ladder to become ranking member on the House Military Affairs Committee, and as such came in touch with important wartime military and national figures.

His work on that committee and his focus on developing military facilities in his district would be his congressional career's centerpiece.

When it came to civil rights issues, the Texas delegation generally followed the South. Even then, Thomason was more liberal than the delegation. He opposed the poll tax as a restriction on one's right to vote, and he was adamant in supporting woman's suffrage. While Thomason was in Congress in the 1930s and '40s, the only "civil rights" bills were antilynching proposals. In his memoir, Thomason wrote that he opposed federal antilynching legislation and the Fair Employment Practice Commission as intrusions on states' rights. But he did support the weaker antilynching bill, applicable in cases where the victim was seized from federal custody.[7] In 1955, the year after the Jencks trial and *Brown v. Board of Education* and only weeks after *Brown v. Board of Education II*, Thomason issued his ruling declaring all Texas school segregation unconstitutional and ordered a black student's admission to Texas Western College. It was the first Texas desegregation decision after *Brown II*, and it put Thomason in the top rank among progressive judges.[8]

One writer who studied the Empire Zinc strike mistakenly described Thomason as "ultra-conservative."[9] The truth is, Thomason had a favorable voting record with organized labor,[10] except anti-Communist legislation or bills sponsored by his anti-Communist ally, Howard W. Smith.[11] Contrary to what Thomason and his editor wrote in his memoir, he voted against the Taft-Hartley Bill and voted to sustain Truman's unsuccessful veto. Thomason was only one of three Texas members and one of eighty-three in the House to vote to sustain Truman's veto. The other two Texans were Sam Rayburn and Albert Thomas, with fifteen Texas members voting to override, including Lyndon Johnson.[12] Among Thomason's papers is a letter from AFL's president thanking Thomason for his votes against Taft-Hartley.[13]

Although Thomason had a liberal voting record on social and economic legislation, he was and remained adamantly and rigidly an anti-Communist. In being so, he joined most Americans, including liberals and even left-wing labor organizations. Thomason could take pride in his moderate approach to most issues, but his strident anti-Communist views would challenge his ability to approach Jencks and the case with the detachment and objectivity he normally possessed. In his memoir, Thomason admitted that he was not a bookish lawyer or judge, but by reputation he possessed the more important qualities of good judgment, reasonable instincts, and common sense, attributes that would be tested by his personal distaste for Communists.

THE PROSECUTION

The lead prosecutor in the case was forty-year-old U.S. attorney Charles F. Herring. A Lyndon Johnson protégé, Herring went to Washington to work for Johnson. He was general counsel in the wartime Office of Price Administration and then an administrative assistant to Johnson before serving in the Navy during World War II. He returned to Austin, where he practiced law and served as state senator for seventeen years. In 1951 Truman appointed him the U.S. attorney for the Western District of Texas, and Herring was the last Democratic United States attorney still serving in the Eisenhower administration.

Sitting second chair for the prosecution was Holvey Williams. Williams had been an assistant U.S. attorney for some years and headed the El Paso office. He came closest to being considered a career assistant at a time when those positions were political patronage plums. Williams was first appointed under a Democratic administration, but continued serving under the Republicans. Francis C. "Skip" Broaddus Jr., also from El Paso, was the youngest prosecutor. He became a lawyer in 1948 and an assistant U.S. attorney in 1952. Joseph J. Alderman worked in the Internal Security Section of the Criminal Division at the Department of Justice in Washington, a section that was later converted into an entire division during the Cold War's anti-Communist era. Alderman was designated special assistant to the attorney general to work on Jencks and other Internal Security prosecutions.[14]

THE DEFENSE

The defense followed the common practice for visiting lawyers in hiring local counsel to help them navigate an unfamiliar community's peculiarities and personalities. They retained seventy-four-year-old E. B. "Bull" Elfers, an experienced El Paso lawyer. Elfers was a former assistant district attorney, former assistant U.S. attorney, and former El Paso Bar Association president.[15]

Unlike the prosecution, Jencks's defense lawyers had national notoriety. John T. McTernan of Los Angeles was the lead trial attorney, and Nathan Witt assisted. Both were proud, longtime members of and important figures in the National Lawyers Guild.[16] McTernan and his partner, Ben Margolis, were lawyers with national practices that represented leftists targeted in anti-Communist investigations and prosecutions. They were in the first rank and were prominent leaders in the Guild.

John Tripp McTernan was born in 1910 just outside New York City in Westchester County. He was educated at Amherst and Columbia Law and later worked at the federal Shipping Board and the Maritime Commission. In 1937 he went to the National Labor Relations Board as a trial attorney, and in 1942, he worked at the Office of Price Administration before joining Ben Margolis in his Los Angeles law office in 1944.[17]

Long before 1948, McTernan was documented by anti-Communist investigations for his activities.[18] For years, McTernan and his firm had stepped up when few others dared, taking on the defense in large, unpopular cases brought against Communists. In the late 1940s, Margolis and the firm represented some of the "Hollywood Ten." In 1950 and 1951, McTernan spent more than four months in trial in Pittsburgh representing accused Communist Steve Nelson. (This was an adopted name—Nelson, who was Croatian, was born Stjepan Mesarosh.)[19] While McTernan was in trial in Pittsburgh, Margolis was representing three of fourteen Communist defendants in the lengthy Yates case, a Los Angeles Smith Act prosecution.

In 1952 McTernan spent ten months in the Smith Act trial in New York City, taking the lead in defending four of fifteen Communist defendants. The lead defendant was Elizabeth Gurley Flynn, and Roy Cohn was a prosecutor. The case was considered the second most important Smith Act prosecution.[20] In that case, McTernan encountered personalities he would see again in the Jencks trial.

Moreover in January 1952, sandwiched between his Pittsburgh and New York trials, the House Un-American Activities Committee (HUAC), heard testimony from at least four lawyers who identified McTernan as a CP member who helped the Party recruit members and control the National Lawyers Guild. Interspersed among these and other trials and investigations, just between 1949 and 1952, McTernan briefed and argued three cases before the United States Supreme Court.[21]

One admirer described McTernan as "a tall, patrician-looking man who was always elegantly dressed. He spoke in a very measured way and sprinkled his conversations with Irish witticisms." It was said that Margolis and McTernan "displayed not only uncommon skill as lawyers but selfless courage in the face of personal and professional attacks of a ferocity that we can only imagine today."[22] One can sense the steel in McTernan from his appearance before HUAC, during which he refused to answer pointed questions,[23] or the grudging respect Senator Joseph McCarthy accorded the left-wing lawyer

John T. McTernan. *The New York Times/Redux.*

when he represented clients before McCarthy's committee.[24] Although an anti-Communist committee wrote that Margolis and McTernan were disruptive in court, Thomason would find this defense professional and respectful.[25]

The man who easily possessed the highest profile in that courtroom was Nathan Witt, who sat second chair for the defense. He would take no witnesses, make no summation, or say much during the trial. The FBI and the prosecutors might have known about McTernan, but Thomason, given his congressional experience, was certainly well acquainted with Witt's history, and many Americans would recall that they too knew the name. Witt's long Mine-Mill association brought the fifty-two-year-old lawyer to that El Paso courtroom.

Nathan Witt was born in New York with roots in the city's working-class Lower East Side. He was educated at New York University but drove a cab for several years before he saved enough for Harvard Law, from which he graduated in 1933. Jerome Frank was appointed general counsel at the Agricultural Adjustment Administration (AAA) where Frank, aided by Harvard Law Professor Felix Frankfurter, recruited several promising, idealistic law graduates, including Witt.

After only a year at AAA,[26] Witt moved to the old National Labor Relations Board (NLRB). In 1935, Congress enacted the National Labor Relations Act (Wagner Act) and created a new agency to administer it, the new NLRB, where

Witt became assistant general counsel. In November 1937, he was named NLRB secretary, the top administrative officer at the agency.[27]

As NLRB secretary, Witt was influential in labor circles during the first administration in which labor was important. Business interests always had an outsize voice in government, and now labor had a government that paid attention to its needs. Critics saw Witt as running the NLRB according to his own agenda, which they considered aligned with labor against management and with the CIO versus the AFL. There were also unconfirmed rumors and rumblings about his politics. In 1940, the House created a Special Committee to Investigate the NLRB and named powerful, arch-segregationist and anti-Communist Virginia congressman Howard W. Smith, a Thomason ally, its chair. From December 1939 until February 1940, the Committee probed Witt's handling of labor cases, strikes, and controversies.[28] Smith was intent on weakening the Labor Board, reducing its research capacity, and running off suspected Communists.[29] By the hearing's end, Witt was a weakened administrator under accusation that he "hewed" to the Communist Party line. Denying that influence, Witt wrote the Committee: "I do wish to go on the record that I am not now, nor have I ever been, a member of the Communist Party, a 'Communist sympathizer' or one who 'hews to the Communist Party line.'"[30] Unable to survive in that contentious environment, once FDR appointed a new Board chair, Witt left the Board in early 1941 and joined Harold I. Cammer in a New York law practice, Witt & Cammer.[31] They were soon hired by the CIO and other labor organizations—mainly left-wing unions, including Mine-Mill—as their general counsel. In Washington, the CIO and the Steelworkers hired Lee Pressman as in-house general counsel.[32]

Witt's firm was doing well until August 3, 1948, when HUAC subpoenaed and took testimony from senior *Time* magazine editor Whittaker Chambers. The hearing took place two months before the 1948 general election that saw Truman fighting his desperate campaign. Chambers entered and sat before a packed committee room that already anticipated his explosive revelations. In his opening statement, Chambers told the Committee that in the mid-1920s, disillusioned by the economy and by international events, he had joined the Communist Party. By the time Roosevelt won the presidency in 1932, Chambers was a paid Party functionary and active in an underground group known as the Ware Group, headed by Harold Ware. Chambers explained to HUAC that there were perhaps seventy-five Communist Party members in the larger, Washington Communist assembly and that the lead committee included Ware, Lee Pressman, Alger Hiss, John J. Abt, and Nathan Witt. The accusation against Alger Hiss was noteworthy because Hiss was a trusted, high-level government insider who went to Yalta with Roosevelt and served as a State Department official involved in the United Nations' formation. He was also at that moment the acting president of the prestigious Carnegie Endowment for Peace.[33] Chambers described the Ware Group's work and said that after Ware died in a car accident, the group faced naming his replacement. Chambers helped convince the group to have Witt be its new leader.[34]

The day after Chambers testified, front pages across the nation ran stories of the "Red Underground."[35] The names Alger Hiss and Whittaker Chambers would be joined for years in controversy, with conservatives supporting Chambers and the liberal establishment clinging to Hiss's innocence. The committee called on Hiss, who vehemently denied the Ware Group accusation and even denied having known Chambers. In light of Hiss's categorical denial, given his high rank, the committee delayed proceeding and resolved to find a solution. The decision was made to appoint Richard Nixon as chair of a select subcommittee which would determine who, between Hiss and Chambers, was truthful.

In the Chambers news accounts, Witt's name, as the former NLRB head, appeared just below Hiss's. At the end of August, the Committee called Hiss's former AAA colleagues Abt, Witt, and Pressman. Invoking the Fifth, each declined to confirm or deny whether they were in the Ware group or were Party members.[36] Having openly "taken the Fifth" themselves several times thereafter, Abt and Witt understood that the public saw that as tantamount to admitting guilt. Later, Abt wrote that taking the Fifth in those days was like "bringing the town madam to the Sunday school picnic."[37]

Witt and John Abt remained close friends, and years later Abt admitted having been in the Ware Group. But Abt agreed with Pressman that the underground group did not have espionage in mind. Working at AAA, he had no access to classified information, and he had only provided analyses of New Deal agricultural programs.[38] In 1952, the McCarran Senate Internal Security Subcommittee (SISS) called Witt and Jencks as witnesses,[39] and at a 1953 SISS hearing Abt and Witt again refused to answer questions.[40] Witt would continue representing left-wing unions, including Mine-Mill, and would testify at least six times before House and Senate investigatory committees, often invoking the Fifth Amendment and representing many witnesses who did the same, including Mine-Mill union organizer Clinton Jencks.

PRETRIAL

With the trial scheduled to start on Monday, January 11, 1954, pretrial motions were set for hearing the preceding Thursday and Friday. The Jencks team was desperate to learn about the prosecution's case. In criminal defense, it is critical to know the facts and the theory on which the government intends to prove guilt, the testimony, and the exhibits they intend to use. So far McTernan and his fellow defense lawyers were in the dark, as Thomason refused to order the prosecution to reveal its case. There was no way to find rebuttal testimony or documents. The only guess was that Matusow would testify, given the recent hearings in Austin. The defense issued a subpoena for all the government's evidence showing Jencks's affiliation with the Communist Party, and the government countered and demanded Local 890's records for the previous three years. Thomason quashed both subpoenas.

The judge then took up the government's subpoena for the San Cristóbal Valley Ranch guest register. Craig Vincent appeared and explained to the judge that Harvey Matusow had more than once accused the Vincents of being Communists and described their resort ranch as a Communist facility. Given the accusations, his lawyer said that he was advising Vincent to take the Fifth, which Vincent proceeded to do in response to more than a dozen questions. After the judge ordered him to answer, Vincent stood on his rights, and the judge found him in contempt of court. Thomason did not jail Vincent then, but said that he would deal with him later.[41]

The defense said that it had motions for change of venue and for continuance and would file them Monday morning as well as press other unspecified motions. Thomason set the matters for hearing on Monday morning with jury selection to follow. In its Sunday edition, the *Albuquerque Journal* ran a story on the coming trial, noting that "Jencks became a storm center last April when his Bayard union openly backed the Red-tinged movie, 'Salt of the Earth' filmed outside Hurley."[42]

On Monday morning, the judge denied the defense motion for a Bill of Particulars, leaving Jencks with no idea of how to defend himself from the accusation that he was affiliated with the Communist Party.

Next the defense filed a motion for a change of venue. This request was prompted by inordinate and prejudicial pretrial publicity brought about by the Austin hearings under Texas attorney general John Ben Shepperd and comments made by Governor Alan Shivers, both of which were prominently reported in the El Paso press. Not only was there explosive publicity against Mine-Mill; the union was unable to reach the public. Rodney Holmgren handled Mine-Mill public relations and stated that El Paso's four radio stations and both newspapers refused to accept the union's advertising scripts and ad copy.[43] The prosecutor called Holmgren to the stand and launched into what passed for cross-examination in those times, asking whether Holmgren was a Communist and then whether he "believed in the sincerity of an oath taken before God Almighty." The judge sustained defense objections to the questions.[44] McTernan told the judge, "The issues in this case have been publicly tried and pre-judged in the press." He urged the judge to move the trial to Los Angeles or, in the alternative, to delay the trial and allow the prejudicial publicity to "dissipate." The judge denied both motions.[45]

Finally, Jencks renewed his motion to quash the indictment and the jury panel because women were excluded, meaning it was not drawn from a representative sample. At that time, thirty-four years after women had received the right to vote, Texas continued to exclude women from jury service under state law, and the federal courts followed the Texas rule. Each federal court maintained its system for selecting potential jurors. In El Paso, the federal court employed a jury commissioner to assist the clerk in drawing names. The clerk kept 900 to 1,100 names in a jury box from which they would summon for both grand and trial juries. The defense called jury commissioner Laurence E. Stevens to explain how he supplied the names. Stevens, listed as a farmer in the city directory, explained that he had served as the court's jury commissioner for twenty-six years and that in that time no women were ever called to serve. Asked about how he supplied names, he insisted that there was no system—not even a random one, such as picking every tenth name in the phone book. Occasionally, the clerk's office would request more names, and Stevens would go to his regular sources to comply. He did not use voter registration rolls, but rather personally picked the names from the city directory, telephone directory, newspaper society pages, and from among his acquaintances—not surprisingly, quite a few of his fellow farmers made the list. When he needed jurors from other counties in the district, he called around to postmasters. He testified that the individuals who served on the grand jury that indicted Jencks and those fifty-four who were called to sit on the jury pool for the Jencks trial were representative of the hundreds of names in the jury box. The jurors called to serve on the Jencks case were characteristic of panels he had served up for twenty-six years.

John McTernan again objected to denying the defendant a fair cross section of the community for not only excluding women, but also for having an uncommonly large number of owners and managers in a working-class city with a union man on trial. After hearing the evidence, the judge again overruled the defendant's motion to quash the indictment and to reselect the jury panel.[46] Having ruled on all pretrial motions, the judge recessed until that afternoon at 2 P.M., at which time they would select the jury and commence the trial.

9

CLINTON JENCKS ON TRIAL

WHEN JENCKS AND HIS LAWYERS RETURNED for the afternoon session and reached the principal fourth-floor courtroom, union supporters were milling around, waiting for the trial to begin. In the courtroom, the bailiff accorded priority seating to the fifty-four men who had been summoned to serve. The press was at its special table while family, friends, and spectators vied for the remaining places. The courtroom clerk took his place and the lawyers sat at theirs, waiting for the judge. At 2:00 P.M., the bailiff rapped on the door, bringing the crowd to its feet. He cried out, "Hear ye, hear ye, hear ye! The court, the Honorable Ewing Thomason presiding, is now open pursuant to adjournment. All ye who have business before this honorable court draw nigh and ye shall be heard. God save the United States and this honorable court." Judge Thomason passed through the doorway and went up to the bench. He stood there momentarily, gazing at the assembled, and then took his seat.

The lawyers entered their appearances, and with the jury pool seated, the judge and the lawyers proceeded to question the first twenty-eight men on the panel, the minimum number needed for the government to exercise its six peremptory challenges and the defendant his ten. That would leave twelve for the jury. In this case, the court provided for two additional alternate jurors. As they began the voir dire, the prosecutor asked jurors whether they belonged to the Communist Party, were affiliated with the Party, or whether any were union men. They responded in the negative. The local defense attorney, E. B. Elfers, asked whether any juror knew the prosecutors or the main prosecution witnesses, and none did. One juror admitted that he had formed an opinion regarding the defendant's guilt, and he was excused.[1] The defense lawyers were correct to have complained about the panel's lack of diversity. Jencks was on trial not only for the non-Communist NLRB affidavit but also for the undercurrent of his militant unionism and his fight against discrimination and for Mexicans' equality and civil rights. Given those considerations, the defense had a greater need for a jury panel with fair Mexican representation and the inclusion of manual or industrial workers, groups El Paso possessed in abundance and that were an overwhelming majority in the population.

THE JURY

As Jencks and his lawyers studied the questionnaires submitted by the panel, the jury pool they faced hardly looked representative of El Paso, a working-class town in which over 60 percent of the population was Mexican. Of fifty-four on the panel, only six were Mexican,[2] and the working class was underrepresented as well. Of the panel members whose occupation could be found, business owners comprised the largest group (eighteen members), managers the next largest (twelve members). Seven members were in sales; six were professionals, such as accountants, chemists, and engineers; and two were bankers. Under the most generous interpretation, there were only four individuals on the panel who could be classified as laborers: a retired machinist, an elevator operator, a mechanic, and an individual in an unspecified civil service position. And yet over 77 percent of El Paso County residents worked for wages; only a reduced minority would be owners, managers, or farmers.

A jury panel that reflected the Mexican community would have had about twenty-six or more Mexicans—instead of the four or six present—and regardless of race or ethnicity, the number of workers would have been much higher than that day's panel and would have included Anglo laborers.[3] Included in that "representative" jury pool was the past president of the El Paso Chamber of Commerce, a current chamber vice president, the chamber's current manager, and the superintendent of the American Smelting and Refining Company's El Paso smelter, a company that had a long and contentious relationship with Mine-Mill.[4] While the Chamber of Commerce had three board members on the panel and undoubtedly other non-board members as well, not to be found in the jury pool was a union man, one of the thousands of El Paso smelter or railroad workers, or a sampling of the thousands of El Paso industrial laborers and service employees. There were at least 1,600 Mine-Mill members in El Paso, 8,000 if one included their families. A miner from Marfa was listed, but he never showed up.[5]

Nevertheless, in defending the jury panel's composition, the prosecutor pronounced "that there is nothing to prevent Jencks from getting a fair trial in El Paso." As he overruled the challenge to the panel and approved his commissioner's jury box selection, the judge added, "I think the defendant will be able to obtain a fair and impartial jury in this district and also obtain a fair and impartial trial."[6]

After the panel was questioned, the parties proceeded to exercise their peremptory challenges. The parties had their lists and would choose their challenges, or "strikes," by crossing through a name. They would concentrate their challenges on the first twenty-eight eligible names after the court excused several jurors. Given the skewed composition of that day's panel, even if the defense had been given twenty strikes, it would have struggled to get a fair jury. These first twenty-eight included only four Mexicans. In using its challenges, the prosecutors immediately struck all four Mexicans and still had two strikes to spare.[7] In selecting two alternate jurors, the prosecutors struck the retired machinist. This left the jury with no Mexicans and all managers, bankers, or owners except for one. That lone laborer was a seventy-five-year-old African American named Morie B. White, a retired railroad porter who was at the time employed as an elevator operator. In a strategic decision, the prosecution struck two Anglo jurors and left White to serve, perhaps thinking that White would support the African American Rev. J. W. Ford, one of the government's principal witnesses. The *El Paso Herald Post* noted in bold print that there was "a Negro on the jury," but neither the *El Paso Times* nor the *El Paso Herald-Post* mentioned the absence of Mexicans, an omission prominently reported in Mine-Mill's newspaper.[8]

Though it was a surprise was that there was a black man on the jury, it was no surprise that there were no Mexicans—that was a typical Texas jury in those days. It was normal for the judge and the prosecutors to have very few Mexicans on panels and to strike the few who might appear.

El Paso had occupied the remote, western tip of the Confederate States of America. Despite having only a few blacks—2.4 percent of the population—

El Paso in the year of *Brown v. Board of Education* carried southern baggage and retained the state's Jim Crow elements: racially segregated schools, public accommodations, restaurants, hotels, waiting rooms, restrooms, and water fountains at the Union Depot, and its city buses still had the obligatory order of "colored to the rear." As a black man on that federal jury, Morie White would be eating alone—most El Paso restaurants would not serve blacks—and using a separate restroom.[9]

As the judge looked out over the courtroom, he saw nothing abnormal in the fact that, with one exception, there were no Mexicans inside the bar as jurors or lawyers or clerks, bailiffs or marshals. The only Mexican inside the bar was court reporter-stenographer Ángel C. Valenzuela. It was as though more than half of the community were invisible. It was even worse than that with women missing, making more than three-quarters of the community invisible. This was a troubling sign for Jencks, a man who openly fought for Mexican civil rights and to upend the social order in Grant County. The jury he got, one excluding the few Mexicans called, was the Grant County environment Jencks had spent years fighting.[10]

The defense might have considered a broader challenge to the jury panel had they known of an argument taking place before the U.S. Supreme Court. The same day that the Jencks trial was getting underway, a Mexican American lawyer stood before the Supreme Court presenting his case in *Hernández v. Texas*.[11] The complaint was that Texas promoted jury selection practices that systematically excluded most Mexicans from jury pools and then allowed peremptory challenges to eliminate the balance. Court observers testified in *Hernández* that for years in some Texas counties, they had seen no Mexicans serve on juries. Four months later, at a time when it would do Clinton Jencks no good, a unanimous Supreme Court found that such a jury selection practice was unconstitutional and a denial of due process.[12] Although one had the right to a jury of one's peers, to a fair community cross section, serious complaints that Thomason stacked the deck against defendants and workers persisted.[13]

THE EVIDENCE

Once the Jencks jury was seated and sworn in, the indictment was read. It was impressive to hear a judge say, "The United States versus Clinton Jencks," pitting the entire nation against one lonely defendant. The prosecutor would lay claim to representing the people; jurors would know that they too were

Clinton Jencks at the federal
courthouse in El Paso. *Thirman
Studio, Courtesy Heather Wood.*

members of the prosecution. Given the proceedings, all defendants begin
at a disadvantage. After reading the indictment, Judge Thomason recessed
until the next morning when the first witness would be called.

On Tuesday morning, prosecutor Holvey Williams called his first witness,
but McTernan objected, insisting that Williams first give an opening statement providing a fair preview of the evidence.[14] That was no idle exercise on
McTernan's part. The defense had tried and failed to obtain witness lists, a
bill of particulars, or other indications of what they were supposed to defend
against. The second count—the Communist Party affiliation charge—was
clearly the more troublesome to the defense. Would the government attempt
to prove affiliation with the fact that Jencks was employed by a union widely
branded as Communist, or would it use as evidence his personal beliefs,
which were protected under the First Amendment? Did Jencks attend meetings or make statements, or would paid informers testify? The Communist
Party had many policies with which many, if not most, Americans agreed:

the right to unionize, fight racial and other forms of discrimination, and so on. The statute left the term "affiliation" undefined and open to almost any interpretation.

Prosecutor Williams gave a short opening stating that the government would prove that on April 28, 1950, Jencks was a Party member and that he had been associated with the Party since 1946, up to and including the affidavit filing date of April 28. Williams noted that the union chose not to file affidavits for 1947 or 1948, but that to invoke the NLRB's jurisdiction, Mine-Mill was obligated to change its policy and allow its officers to file affidavits starting in 1949. McTernan objected and complained that Williams was simply repeating the indictment and was not giving a fair preview of the evidence the government would be producing. The Supreme Court already held in a similar labor prosecution that the accused's mental state could only be proven with overt acts.[15] And that was precisely what McTernan was demanding to hear to properly defend his client. Thomason overruled the objection, stating, "The Court thinks counsel has made a substantial statement of what they expect to prove."[16] That ruling made any further comment unnecessary, and Williams called his first witness.

That morning's testimony established that Jencks filed the affidavit with the El Paso NLRB office, whose jurisdiction included Grant County in southern New Mexico. Two bankers testified that they recognized Jencks's signature on the affidavit. One banker, William James Upton, was the Bayard mayor present when druggist Lett assaulted Jencks and later led a mob that threatened the *Salt of the Earth* film crew. An FBI handwriting expert identified Jencks's signature on several documents, including the affidavit.[17] After a lunch break, the government moved into the substantive witnesses to show that Jencks had been a Party member.

First came James Edward Currie, a Denver printer who claimed to be a former Party member. He joined the Party in the late '30s and remained active until late 1946. Currie testified that he attended a closed Communist meeting with Jencks and others. He stated that Jencks was a Party member, although Jencks never said he was or identified himself as such, and it seemed to be a union meeting.[18] Currie had no contact with Jencks after 1946. McTernan objected so strenuously that he hardly let Williams question Currie. McTernan's complaint was that Currie's testimony was remote and therefore irrelevant.[19] Relevance works on a scale, balancing materiality versus the testimony's prejudicial quality. The more the evidence relates to the issue at hand—materiality—the more prejudicial it can be and still be relevant. If the evidence is high on the prejudice scale and low on materiality, then it is deemed irrelevant.

It was not difficult to prove that Jencks was a Party member before fall 1949. Jencks attended CP meetings but claimed that he resigned from the party before he filed an affidavit in autumn 1949, when it was still legal to be a Party member.[20] The testimony's danger was that the jury might assume Jencks continued being a Party member and remained one on April 28, 1950, even though the testimony did nothing to support this conclusion. The more remote the testimony was to April 28, the less probative it would be. Evidence that he was a Party member was highly prejudicial,[21] so great care had to be taken in admitting it.

In his arguments to the court, McTernan brought up the *Douds* Supreme Court decision,[22] a similar labor prosecution, reminding the judge that a union official could resign from the Party and be free to be a union officer.[23] He argued that to infer from 1946 membership that Jencks was still a member in 1950 would destroy the presumption of innocence and instead place the burden of proof on the defendant. When Thomason asked Williams for his view, Williams simply replied that this was just the start. They had "to start somewhere," and he promised the judge that it would all be connected without the need for inferences from earlier conduct.[24] McTernan asked for time to investigate, as Curie's testimony had been a surprise and the defense was unprepared to cross-examine. Thomason first denied the motion and insisted that McTernan proceed with cross-examination, but then relented and permitted the witness to be excused, subject to being recalled later. For the next several days, the prosecution would try to fill the gap in its case.

The next morning, the first witness was the Rev. J. W. Ford, a twenty-eight-year-old African American Methodist preacher from Los Angeles who previously belonged to the Communist Party in New Mexico and served on its state board. Washington-based Joseph J. Alderman questioned Ford. Ford testified that he met with Jencks and his wife, Virginia, at several New Mexico Party meetings around the state. Party state board members included Joseph DiSanti, Alfredo C. Montoya, Jencks, and Ford. What the group did not know was that for several years, Ford had been an FBI informant who reported Party activities in detailed oral and written dispatches. He was paid $150 per month ($1,572 in 2018, adjusted for inflation) when he was most active, and he reported to the FBI anywhere from four times a week to once a month.[25]

Ford testified that after an August 1949 meeting at a New Mexico ranch, he never saw Jencks again, although Ford continued to serve on the Party's board until he left the state more than a year later in September 1950. This meant that Ford did not see Jencks in the eight months before Jencks filed the April 1950 affidavit, which was the precise period when the union reversed its boycott policy regarding the affidavit and when Mine-Mill officer Maurice Travis publicly resigned from the Party so he could file his affidavit. Given his position on the state board, if Jencks was active in the Party, Ford would have known about it. In what would later prove to be critical testimony, Ford was asked, "To your knowledge, during the entire period of time, starting in 1949 and up to September in 1950, was Jencks ever replaced in his position on the State Board of the Communist Party?" Ford answered, "Not to my knowledge."[26] With that testimony, Ford and the prosecutor Alderman left the impression that Jencks had remained active in the Party and apparently remained on the board after August 1949 and until Ford left the state in September 1950. If Jencks was not replaced, logically he must have remained on the board.

When McTernan cross-examined Ford, despite Thomason giving the defense lawyer wide latitude in the examination, Ford's memory about the dates and events he had just recounted turned fuzzy.[27] Ford insisted that in preparing his testimony, the prosecutors had neither showed him his reports nor referred to them to refresh his memory. To hear Ford tell it, there was almost no preparation for his detailed testimony. After being on the stand the entire day, Ford was excused, but McTernan reserved the right to recall him to review the FBI payments he had received.

The next morning Williams called Clay Martin Brooks to the stand. Brooks, a mine driller and mechanic, was a Jencks neighbor in Hanover in early 1947. In an innocuous back porch conversation over a child sharing a Mother's Day card, Jencks remarked to Brooks that it was wonderful to see the child's loyalty to his mother. Another neighbor disagreed, stating that the child should have equal respect for the laws and the Creator. Jencks replied that such talk was nonsense, and Brooks responded that Jencks's comment "sounded to me like what I understood to be Communist beliefs." Jencks shot back that "he was a Communist and proud of it."[28] Even the court reporter in the transcript capitalized "Communist" to indicate a Party member rather than a general believer in communism. McTernan went to the bench and, out of the jury's hearing, moved for a mistrial. One issue was that the conversation took place more than three years before filing the affidavit. But more importantly, the comment attributed to Jencks was about his beliefs, not about Party membership or affiliation. The First Amendment protects beliefs—even communism—and it is inconceivable that it would ever outlaw a belief. What was prohibited was filing a false affidavit claiming that one was not a Party member or affiliated with the Party. Thomason overruled McTernan's objection and motion for mistrial.[29] Once again, McTernan asked for more time before questioning Brooks. Thomason agreed that those were "surprise witnesses" and allowed the defense to delay its cross-examination.[30]

The prosecution called George Knott, a former Mine-Mill representative then living in New Jersey who had helped the union hire Jencks and assign him to Grant County. Examined by prosecutor Broaddus, Knott stated that he was a Party member from 1937 until 1947. Knott was in New Mexico with Jencks only in 1947 and said that Jencks was a Party member. In meetings with Party members, they discussed strengthening the Party's hold on Mine-Mill locals in the area. McTernan repeated his request for more time to cross-examine Knott. The motion was denied.[31]

U.S. attorney Herring next called James E. Peterson to the stand. Peterson was a supervisor at Kennecott Copper Corporation. He admitted that he had been a Party member from 1942 until 1949 as well as a Utah Party central committee member. He identified Jencks, stating that he met him in 1947 at a Mine-Mill convention and knew him to be a Party member. He claimed to have attended three Party meetings with Jencks: one in mid-1947, another either in late 1947 or early 1948, and a final one in Denver in mid-1948.[32] Peterson was the fifth witness who could only testify about Jencks's Party membership months or years before the 1950 affidavit was filed, and before Jencks's October 1949 claim that he quit the party.

The day's last witness was Jesus Terrazas, a Bayard, Kennecott miner and former Mine-Mill member. Prosecutor Williams first tried to introduce discussion of ANMA, the National Mexican American Association, which some said was a Communist front organization. The judge stopped the prosecution from referring to ANMA. Williams then asked Terrazas, "Did you ever hear Clinton Jencks make any speeches concerning the Korean War and its connection with the United States?" McTernan objected, and the judge sustained the objection.[33] In a bench conference, McTernan reminded Thomason that this was the government's second reference to the Korean War, and the court had previously sustained the defense objection to that inquiry. A prosecution goal was to show Jencks's Party affiliation by noting policies the Party and Jencks supported in common, that is, their "parallel" views. Thomason noted that many people, presumably non-Communists as well, were against the Korean War, adding, "Simply because a man has fixed opinions about the Korean War, for or against, should not be held against him."

The prosecutors promised that their next witness would show that being against the Korean War as Wall Street aggression was CP policy, and they would persistently suggest that Jencks furthered Party policy by attempting to thwart critical war production. Continuing in that vein, Thomason said, "The Court . . . is not going to permit anything about the Korean War. Almost every person in the country at that time had some opinion about the Korean War, including the lawyers and the Court."[34] Just after the judge sustained the defense objection to the subject of the Korean War, Williams, acting as though he had not heard a word, asked Terrazas, "Did you ever hear Clinton Jencks say anything about the position the United States Government was taking in the Korean War?" A frustrated McTernan said, "That last question deals with precisely the same situation that Your Honor described as prejudicial. It was done in flagrant disregard of our ruling. I move for mistrial." The objection was again sustained; the motion for mistrial overruled, and there was yet another bench conference.

The prosecution was not to be denied. One way or another, that jury would know all about the Korean War and Jencks's attitude toward it. The prosecutors were apparently operating under a jury trial truism "that an ounce of prejudice was worth a pound of evidence." Make enough references, and all the judge's admonitions to disregard the testimony would be long forgotten, the old routine of throwing the skunk into the jury box. Terrazas was excused subject to being recalled later, and court was recessed for the day in anticipation of the trial's most controversial witness.

Every morning and afternoon during the trial, El Paso dailies treated their readers to sensational headlines and stories detailing the testimony, such as "'I Am a Communist—And Proud of It,' Witness Testifies Jencks Told Him"; "Witnesses Charge Jencks Plotted with Commies to Control Union"; and "Former Pastor Here Says Jencks A Top Communist In New Mexico." The El Paso Times added an editorial on Friday morning lauding the FBI and its investigatory prowess, entitled "FBI 'Delivers.'"[35] With a public relations machine second to none, it was only a few days later that the Times editor had in his hands another prized "thank you" letter from J. Edgar Hoover.[36]

On Friday morning before "another jam-packed courtroom,"[37] Williams called Harvey Marshall Matusow. Matusow, wearing a dark suit and sporting a bow tie, took his seat, and it did not take long to sense the twenty-seven-year-old's slightly cocky attitude. After stating that he was a New York actor and writer, Matusow laid out his Communist Party credentials. He said that he had joined the Party in 1947 when only twenty-one years old. He also joined as many as thirty Party-affiliated organizations. Matusow's occupation was that of a professional witness testifying about his time as an informer, outing suspected Communists, and becoming an expert on the anti-Communist circuit. Matusow started his career as a paid informer for the FBI and later became a Communist expert for congressional committees, including Senator Joseph McCarthy's.

Matusow recalled that in the summer of 1950, he decided to make his way to San Francisco and arrived in New Mexico with no plan in mind. He wandered into Taos and visited the San Cristóbal Valley Ranch, offering his services to Craig and Jenny Vincent, whom he had previously met in New York. Matusow identified almost everyone associated with the ranch as Communist, including the Vincents and their son-in-law, DiSanti. He repeatedly referred to Jencks as a Communist. He had met Jencks during his nine- or ten-day visit, and remembered engaging in several conversations with him regarding the Communist Party. While Jencks and a ranch guest helped Matusow unload books from his pickup, Matusow mentioned that he was considering transferring his own Party membership to New Mexico, to which Jencks responded, "'We can use you out here, we need more active Party members."[38] Matusow recalled that Jencks mentioned meeting with a Mexican miners' union and discussed a plan to coordinate their union contracts to have the same expiration date, the object being to thwart production of metals used in the Korean Conflict.[39] Matusow asked Jencks "what he and other Communists in New Mexico were doing in relation to the Stockholm Peace Appeal and the fight to put an end to the Korean War."[40] Matusow related that during his stay, Jencks lectured at the ranch library to vacationers and residents, describing unions' role in the peace effort and stating that the "United States was the aggressor nation" and had no business being in Korea.[41]

During his stay in Taos, Matusow, a prodigious joiner, enrolled in New Mexico's ANMA chapter, which he called a "proper Communist concentration work" of an organization important to and controlled by the Party.[42]

With Matusow's assertion that Jencks alluded to being a Party member in August 1950, some four months after the affidavit was filed, the government bridged a large gap in its proof. The prosecution already had ample proof of Jencks's Party membership before 1949, but with Matusow it could prove that Jencks was a Party member in August 1950. The inference that he was a member on April 28, 1950, was now a much shorter leap.

When McTernan stood to take on Matusow in cross-examination, it would not be their first encounter. Matusow had testified in the Flynn case, the New York Smith Act prosecution in which McTernan represented four defendants.[43] This was a witness McTernan knew well. As Matusow had testified perhaps twenty-five times in public, in court, and before investigative committees, there were volumes of his prior testimony that McTernan placed in a stack at the defense table. Under McTernan's cross-examination, Matusow said that he joined the Party out of conviction but was disillusioned by 1948. By early 1950 he was informing for the FBI, which he continued to do until he was expelled by the Party in January 1951. While he was an informer, he persuaded individuals to join the Party and then provided their names to the FBI. Regarding a report Matusow provided to the FBI, McTernan reminded the witness that in the New York case, the judge gave the defense those parts of the report related to the testimony. Williams immediately objected, trying to keep Thomason from doing the same.[44]

Despite having many pages of Matusow's testimony for impeachment, what McTernan wanted most were Matusow's FBI reports as they related to Jencks. The defense was convinced that Matusow was a professional fabulist whose reports differed from his testimony. Reports Matusow and Ford had made to their FBI handlers would become crucial in the Jencks case, and the defense insisted that without them, they could not properly cross-examine. Matusow testified that he tried to report weekly to the FBI in oral and written form, and that he had reported about the San Cristóbal Valley Ranch.[45] Matusow had testified in 1952 about the Valley Ranch episode before two congressional committees. McTernan questioned Matusow over his reports to the FBI and the fact that his testimony in the Jencks trial contained detail not previously mentioned. It was then that McTernan made a comprehensive demand and argument that the prosecution produce for the court's inspection Matusow's reports to the FBI. In the event those reports contained material that contradicted the witness's testimony, McTernan said, those portions of the reports pertinent to the testimony should be provided to the defense. He added, "We have pointed specifically to the reports we have in mind and we ask that they be produced, not for us to look at, because that would be improper before the statement's evidentiary value had been established, but we ask that they be produced for you to look at so you can determine whether or not they have evidentiary value."[46]

Williams asked the court to overrule the motion to produce for *in camera* inspection. Thomason denied production. Next McTernan asked Thomason to have the prosecution produce the reports, seal them, and make them part of the appellate record. Before Williams could object, the judge denied the motion.[47] It was a fateful decision on Thomason's part to refuse to examine the reports for himself or to make them part of the record.

Matusow resumed his testimony, stating that while he was in Santa Fe, using an alias, he wrote a plagiarized news article and placed it in the *Santa Fe New Mexican*. He was supposed to be paid for the article but never was. When shown a check with his assumed name, Matusow denied that he cashed the check or that the endorsement on the check was his signature.[48] Matusow insisted that he did not review his reports before testifying nor did he read summaries of their contents.[49] He recalled no mention by Jencks of any strike in Grant County at the time of their conversation. Matusow admitted that several of the points he made in the trial had not been mentioned in his previous testimony. McTernan brought out inconsistencies in Matusow's testimony, wrong addresses and pseudonyms, but without the reports, McTernan was unable shake Matusow's damaging testimony. Nathan Witt later conceded that as a witness, Matusow had been persuasive and able.[50]

McTernan then expanded his motion to produce FBI reports. He had already demanded Matusow's, and next he requested Ford's as well, covering all the meetings Ford reported on in New Mexico during 1948 and 1949. He asserted the same grounds as in the Matusow motion. Once again, Thomason denied the request for him to examine the reports.[51] Matusow's testimony ended the proceedings for the week.

News articles covering Matusow's testimony confirmed its impact and prejudicial power. Friday afternoon's *El Paso Herald-Post* had a banner headline, "Ex-Red Says Jencks Tried to Hamper Our War Effort," and this lede: "Union Leader Clinton E. Jencks plotted with Mexican and U.S. Reds to hamper the U.S. war effort in Korea by crippling metal production, a former Communist testified today." The *Herald-Post*'s reporter described Matusow as "an impressive witness who 'tangled repeatedly with Defense Attorney McTernan, who makes an impressive courtroom appearance.'"[52] Saturday morning's *El Paso Times* followed with the lede "Defendant as

Red in 1950. Clinton Jencks helped promote an international conspiracy to hamper production of critical materials for 'the imperialistic war in Korea,' a former Communist told a Federal Court jury here Friday."[53] The *Times* reporter wrote that Jencks was shown to be a Party member before and after the affidavit filing date. The reporter noted that he anticipated that the gap in the membership would be addressed the coming week. "With additional witnesses [the prosecution] presumably will try to show that Jencks was a Communist on the actual date of signing, or, by circumstantial evidence of his before and after activities, must have been a Red on that date." It remained to be seen whether the next week's witnesses would bridge the gap.

First thing Monday morning, prosecutor Charles Herring called Kenneth Eckert, a Grosse Point, Michigan, United Auto Workers (UAW) representative. Eckert was a Party member from 1931 to 1948, a Mine-Mill union man from 1942 until 1948, and on the union's CP steering committee. Eckert was the man Jencks had publicly denounced at a Mine-Mill convention for having moved die casting locals from Mine-Mill into the UAW, and he was also a key witness in the CIO hearings to expel Mine-Mill. Eckert met Jencks at an event in August 1947 through his work for Mine-Mill, and all in attendance were Mine-Mill Party members. He saw Jencks again in 1948 at a union executive board meeting. The prosecution called Eckert not only to place Jencks in the Party, but also to testify as a CP expert.[54] In that role, Eckert noted that Jencks and the Party shared policies, essentially repeating the testimony he had given at the CIO hearing to expel Mine-Mill. McTernan objected to common policies or parallel beliefs as not being relevant to anything. He noted that the undeniably conservative Senator Robert Taft was once called a Communist because he supported public housing, as did the Party. In his testimony, once again, Eckert could only place Jencks in the Party as late as 1948. This witness did not bridge the gap.

Following the model established by Louis Budenz in Dennis, the large Smith Act case, the prosecution tried its "book case" by using Eckert as its expert. Eckert noted the parallels between CP policy and Mine-Mill practices.[55] Eckert explained to the jury that the Party used unions as the means to "collect every drop of dissatisfaction that workers may have to channel it" into ever-growing streams to propel the revolution. The Party's position on wars depended on whether they were characterized as just or unjust, using terminology such as "imperialistic" or "reactionary." Once again the prosecution tried to inject the Korean War, but the judge continued to sustain McTernan's objection.[56] Thus far, only Matusow had put the Korean War into evidence, although the prosecution, violating the judge's ineffective admonitions, clearly succeeded in getting the point across to the jury. Claiming that he needed more time to cross-examine the surprise expert testimony, McTernan asked to postpone his cross-examination. Thomason granted the request, excused Eckert until Wednesday, and adjourned court until the next morning.

On Tuesday morning Williams recalled Jesus Terrazas, who testified that he was expelled from Local 890. Terrazas attended meetings at the local between 1950 and 1952, when Jencks encouraged union members to buy the *Daily People's World*, a newspaper Eckert said was controlled by the Party. The prosecutor again raised the Korean War, but once more the judge sustained McTernan's objection. Despite the ruling, the prosecutor asked what Jencks said at a union meeting about coordinating strikes with Mexican miners in 1950 or strikes to stop the Korean War, but Thomason struck the testimony, sustained the objection, and admonished the jury to disregard the testimony. Recognizing the futility in instructing the jury to disregard what they were continually hearing, McTernan moved for mistrial, but Thomason denied the motion. Immediately following that, the prosecutor asked Terrazas about Mine-Mill's cooperation with Mexican unions, and Terrazas twice repeated that the association related to the Korean War. Terrazas later explained that he was expelled from Local 890 because he fought communism on the job.[57] Terrazas did not address whether Jencks was a Party member, but noted that Jencks criticized the affidavit requirement.

Williams then called John P. Thompson, who was effectively the government's last witness. Thompson was a printer who published the *Union Worker*, Local 890's newspaper from 1948 until the first few months of 1950. Thompson identified an October 1949 article in the newspaper that related to efforts by the CIO to expel one-third of its member unions. It read, "now that our Union has signed the phony affidavits we can defend ourselves on a ballot in case of raids."[58] McTernan read the entire article, and the witness left the stand without providing any further explanation. With only half a day's testimony, the court adjourned until Wednesday morning, at which time Eckert's cross-examination was to continue.

When Eckert retook the stand, McTernan asked one inconsequential question and passed the witness. The government closed its case, and Jencks offered no evidence other than his military service record and honors, closing the evidence. The judge excused the jury until the next morning, when the lawyers would make their summations and the court would give his instructions to the jury.

SUMMATION AND VERDICT

On Thursday morning, the lawyers submitted their proposed jury instructions. McTernan's requests were standard for informer cases, such as asking that the court caution the jury about the danger of paid informer testimony, but for the most part, the defense remained focused on Party membership and affiliation. To be found guilty of Party membership, Jencks must have joined the Party and still been a member on April 28. The defense proposed that for affiliation, Jencks must have had a formal relationship with the Party; that it was more than a mere course of conduct, cooperation with an organization, or even repeated supportive acts. Moreover, Jencks himself must have known and intended to be affiliated with the Communist Party at the time he signed the affidavit. Thomason refused all the defendant's requested instructions.[59]

Once the jury was reseated, the court nodded to the prosecution to make the government's opening summation to the jury, a task handled by assistant U.S. attorney Francis C. Broaddus Jr. As the young prosecutor summarized the evidence, recalling testimony that placed Jencks in the Communist Party from 1946 until 1949, he focused on the Reverend Ford's testimony to bridge the case's weakest part: Jencks's Party membership at the time the affidavit was filed. At trial, when examined by Joseph Alderman, Ford testified that to his knowledge, Jencks had not been replaced on the Party's state board.[60] There is a critical difference between saying that one is not aware if someone was replaced to declaring that the individual was not removed or replaced. In the Broaddus summation, Ford's ignorance about Jencks's replacement was portrayed as a definite statement that Jencks had not been removed from the board. It was an explicit invitation to consider Jencks a Party and board member at the time the affidavit was filed. Not wishing to risk the jury missing the point, the prosecutor mentioned it at least six times, four instances in slightly more than one page of transcript and twice at the end of his summation.[61]

After Broaddus, defense attorney Elfers opened for the defense. Elfers went over the testimony witness by witness, pointing to inconsistencies and gaps. That took them to the noon break. In the afternoon, McTernan stood to make his summation. He covered the same ground as Elfers, spending time on

Matusow's troublesome testimony and credibility. There were inconsistencies, wrong dates and addresses, and the fact that he denied his own signature, admitted to submitting a plagiarized article, and confirmed informing on the same people he had persuaded to become Communists—and all of this for money. After McTernan questioned the credibility of the prosecution's thirteen witnesses, he devoted his argument's second part to what he called "the issue" in the case. McTernan asked, "Was he a member or affiliate of the Communist Party on April 28, 1950? . . . That is the ball. That is the issue."[62] The lawyer recounted the "before" evidence and noted that at best it ended with Ford in August 1949, nine months before the affidavit was filed. The only "after" evidence was Matusow's August 1950 San Cristóbal encounter with Jencks some four months after April 28. McTernan told the jury that they could make several inferences consistent with innocence, including resignation, withdrawal, or failure to comply with Party membership require- ments. All those interpretations mandated acquittal. "What reason is there to assume that he didn't drop out? Could he have resigned? What reason is there to assume that he didn't?" The fact that he was not disciplined did not mean that he did not resign or simply drop out.[63] Reduced to its core, that was the issue in the case.

When Holvey Williams went to close for the prosecution, he too would inevitably be drawn to the gap in his case. Williams was as explicit and insistent, although not as repetitive as Broaddus, in saying that it was the Reverend Ford's testimony that closed the gap for the government:

So, I say that he was still in the Party and we have direct evidence to that effect, when the witness, Mr. Ford, the minister. . . . And he was asked, "To your knowledge, during the entire period of time, starting in '49 up to September, 1950, way after this thing was signed, was Jencks ever replaced in the position on the State Board of the Communist Party?" And he said, "Not to my knowledge." Don't you think he would know it? Now why should you assume, as they ask you to, that maybe he withdrew?[64]

Williams continued, "McTernan says why would you not assume that he had withdrawn? I ask you, on what basis in the world could he ask you to assume that he did withdraw; and there is certainly no evidence of any withdrawal."[65] With all the resources it had, the government told the jury in every way that it could that according to the Reverend Ford, Clinton Jencks had not resigned or withdrawn from the Party and was a member on April 28, 1950. And on that thread hung Clinton Jencks's liberty.

Once prosecutor Williams sat down, the judge turned to face the jury and read his instructions on the case. The judge defined the term "affiliation" according to *Webster's*—to connect, ally, or associate oneself with an organization—and elaborated that "it means something less than membership but more than sympathy."[66] Thomason instructed the jury that they could find that Jencks was a CP member based on circumstantial evidence and by drawing reasonable inferences from all the facts. Finishing his charge at 4:32 P.M., the judge handed the jury over to the bailiff to start its deliberations.[67]

With the jury gone, the lawyers started gathering their papers, each ready to find some way to pass the time as they "sweated" the deliberations, which for many trial lawyers meant heading for the nearest bar. The jury had to elect a foreman, read the indictment, review the exhibits and discuss the testimony before they would vote one way or the other. At least that was what was supposed to happen. Everyone headed out, but no one could have gone far when the bailiff announced at 5:00 P.M. that the jury had reached a verdict after deliberating for only twenty minutes.[68] Everyone quickly reassembled, and the judge retook the bench. The courtroom that had been packed only minutes before was nearly empty, as few expected any further proceedings that afternoon. A few minutes later, the bailiff knocked on the door and ushered the jury into the box. Everyone sat while the judge asked the jurors if they had arrived at a verdict. The foreman, accountant Hubert Herndon Johnson, stood and said that they had. After the clerk handed him the form, the judge read it silently and handed it back. The clerk then read aloud that the jury had found Jencks guilty on both counts. The judge confirmed the verdict with the jury, thanked them for their service, and excused them.

As soon as they had left the room, Thomason told Jencks and his lawyers to stand before the bench, and he asked Jencks if he had anything to say. Jencks replied, "I have nothing to say." The judge then sentenced Jencks to the attorney general's custody for a term of five years on each count, with the sentences to run concurrently.[69] The marshal took Jencks by the arm, but his lawyers persuaded the judge to leave their client out on bond. Court was adjourned.

The reporter for the *Herald-Post*, El Paso's afternoon daily, quickly ran out to file his story. The daily added a few paragraphs to its final edition story and printed an Extra edition with a banner headline: "JURY FINDS JENCKS GUILTY."[70]

After court, a happy and relieved Holvey Williams said, "I was pleased with the quick response of the jury, especially in finding the defendant guilty on both counts. . . . The judge gave the defendant every right he could possibly claim. I see nothing in the record that could be used seriously in an appeal." The defense lawyers saw it another way. To them, it had not been a fair trial, with prejudicial pre-trial publicity and an all-male jury populated by owners and managers. Jencks had no comment when asked for his reaction, and Virginia said she was "glad it's over."[71]

The newspapers noted that the Jencks case held the El Paso record for the longest trial involving a single defendant. Despite a lengthy trial, the jury deliberated hardly long enough to have read the indictment and elect a foreman. Their choice of foreman might have had something to do with the quick verdict against an alleged Communist union man. According the jury questionnaire, foreman Hubert Herndon Johnson was an auditor and office manager at Darbyshire Steel. But what that record did not disclose is that for years before that Johnson had worked as an accountant for the Phelps Dodge Refinery in El Paso, another large copper company that had a long and contentious relationship with Mine-Mill.[72]

To Mine-Mill members the verdict was predictable, and the Jencks defense committee release noted, "The verdict was not surprising, in view of the whole situation in El Paso. It was a jury of businessmen and company managers, stacked from the beginning against any kind of union, much less a militant union such as ours. The fact that the jury was out only 22 minutes proves it was not interested in the facts, that its mind was made up long before the case was rested."[73]

A disappointed, worried, and saddened Jencks left the court that day, closing that chapter. With the unfortunate trial over, Clinton and Virginia Jencks returned to Denver and work at Mine-Mill. Jencks immediately resumed working on raising money and support for his defense. He wrote to several friends, telling them that the El Paso trial had been a "real lynching."[74]

New Mexico made noises indicating that it might prosecute Jencks under its new failure to register law, but did nothing.[75] Still pending before the New Mexico Supreme Court was the contempt case and a jail sentence against Jencks and Local 890's bargaining committee.[76] The Jencks lawyers began their work on the appeal in the El Paso case.

10

FALSE WITNESS: MATUSOW'S CONFESSIONAL

WITH THE TRIAL OVER, Clinton Jencks went his way, and Harvey Matusow returned to his anti-Communist work. If Jencks was victim to more of anticommunism's varied methods than almost anyone else, Matusow was his anti-Communist analogue, participating in more of those methods than anyone else. Fate would have it that their lives would intersect and be joined in controversy, much as with Hiss and Chambers.

Matusow was a member of the government's stable of paid informer-witnesses, a group numbering eighty-three, and he had become a star in a career that had begun only in 1952. When the Army discharged Matusow in 1946 after non-combat World War II service in Germany, he returned to New York City, where in 1947, he joined and worked for the Communist Party in several entry-level positions including switchboard operator, camp counselor, and bookstore clerk. Although the jobs were low-level, they exposed him to many CP members and activities. Working for the bookstore also placed him where he could purchase—or pilfer, according to the Party—hundreds of Communist and left-wing books, and he apparently read that literature.[1] The bookstore work also provided the platform for his later testimony in the New York Flynn case.

By 1950, Matusow had become disillusioned with the Party and decided to turn on it. He made a cold call to the FBI in February, and by July he was on the payroll as a low-level informer. His timing could not have been better. Matusow's anti-Communist career would coincide with McCarthyism's golden years. Within weeks, the peripatetic informer announced that he was off to a new life in California. In that summer of 1950, he stopped at the San Cristóbal Valley Ranch, a resort run by Craig and Jenny Vincent and patronized by Communists and left-wingers enjoying that season's mountain air. Matusow contacted the nearby FBI office and began reporting on ranch and Taos activities. He stayed in Taos for around five months and then returned to New York City, where the Party had filed charges and moved to expel him. The Party alleged that Matusow was dishonest, stole books, defrauded the Party in a *Daily Worker* subscription contest, and consorted with the enemy. Whatever defense Matusow raised was ineffectual, and he was thrown out. No longer useful to the FBI, his days as a paid informant ended the next month, and so did any official relation to the bureau.[2] The Air Force then granted Matusow's request to return to active duty. In early 1951, he was first assigned to Brooks Air Force Base and then transferred to Wright-Patterson Air Force Base in Dayton, Ohio. There Matusow suffered a mental breakdown and landed in the base psychiatric ward. After his discharge, the base chaplain connected Matusow to John and Martha Edmiston, former FBI undercover agents and later HUAC anti-Communist witnesses. They introduced Matusow to HUAC, where he renewed his anti-Communist activities. He later worked for HUAC's Ohio counterpart, the Ohio Un-American Activities Commission.

By November 1951, Matusow was testifying before HUAC in executive session. He was discharged from the Air Force and was free to pursue his new occupation. No longer undercover, he became a professional anti-Communist. For HUAC, he went through the individuals he identified for the Edmistons, a list that included Clinton Jencks and the San Cristobal Valley Ranch. Matusow mentioned Jencks only as a lecturer and did not specifically say Jencks was a Communist.[3]

A garrulous, boastful know-it-all, Matusow pleased HUAC members when he testified about communism and youth in the committee's February 1952 open sessions, in which he identified over two hundred CP members, including Clinton Jencks. Matusow said that Jencks was a Communist who was working with Mexican miners to reduce metal production needed for the Korean Conflict. Soon he became a three-hundred-dollar-per-month staffer at the Ohio Un-American Activities Commission, and in February 1952, New York Public Schools hired him as a consultant to ferret out Communist teachers. In addition to HUAC, he also testified for the Senate Internal Security Subcommittee.[4] In March 1952 he appeared again before the Senate Internal Security Subcommittee, this time opining on China expert Owen Lattimore. He accused Lattimore of being a Communist. The cocky Matusow quickly found his form and confidence in testifying about foreign affairs, unions, and the Party. Matusow told the committee about his Party work in New York City and said that he knew ten thousand New York Party members by sight.[5]

By December 1951, prosecutor Roy Cohn hired Matusow as an expert witness in the large, second-string New York Smith Act prosecution against Elizabeth Gurley Flynn and others. Matusow testified for HUAC and the Senate committee in the spring, and by June, he was back in New York City, where he spent six days on the witness stand in the Flynn case—a case that gave him a national profile. He testified that he had met the codefendant Alexander Trachtenberg at the Party's Jefferson School bookstore and that Trachtenberg had told Matusow to be sure to push the book *Law of the Soviet State* by Andrei Vishinsky. In the book's opening passages, Vishinsky advocates revolution by violently overthrowing governments.[6]

In the 1976 film *The Front*, Woody Allen portrays a false stand-in for blacklisted screenwriters. In the film, television and radio networks deny work to blacklisted writers and actors, and use an ad agency to screen and clear applicants. The Allen character presents others' work as his own to help banned writers evade the blacklist. The film echoes actual events that began in 1952, when Laurence A. Johnson, a supermarket owner in Syracuse, New York, launched a campaign to rid television and radio of those suspected of being Communists. Johnson persuaded an ad agency to hire Matusow to create a blacklist and clearance process for those under suspicion, or as others dubbed it, "smear and clear." As part of this effort, Matusow falsely accused producer-director Sidney Lumet and others of being subversives (but later withdrew the Lumet claim).[7] Years later, a famous libel case brought by blacklisted radio personality John Henry Faulk finally ended the Johnson's Super Market blacklist.[8]

With his nonstop 1952 activities, Matusow entered the professional anti-Communist pantheon, joining Louis Budenz, Elizabeth Bentley, Mathew Cvetic, and others. But he still hungered for more publicity. The highest-profile anti-Communist hearings then were Senator McCarthy's, but he was running

Harvey M. Matusow testifying. *George Tames/The New York Times/Redux.*

for reelection and recovering from surgery. In August 1952, Matusow walked into McCarthy's office, laid out his record, and offered to campaign for the senator in his Wisconsin primary election set for September. McCarthy agreed. They were successful, and McCarthy won. He retained Matusow to campaign in senatorial elections in Washington, Idaho, and Montana to help defeat Democratic candidates. In Utah, the objective was to reelect Senator McCarran's conservative Republican committee colleague. It was during that campaign that Matusow testified before the McCarran subcommittee in Salt Lake City, where he had his dramatic confrontation with Jencks, identified him as a Communist, and told the committee about their alleged San Cristóbal conversation.[9]

Not only had Matusow characterized several Democratic Senate candidates as soft on communism, but he also added controversial, gratuitous attacks against others. For example, in Idaho and Montana, he ripped a page from McCarthy's playbook and claimed that Communists had infiltrated all major churches, except the Church of Jesus Christ of Latter Day Saints. Speaking in

Great Falls, he said that the Methodist Church was under Communist influence, that there were five hundred Communist school teachers in New York City, that 126 Communists worked for the Sunday *New York Times,* and that the Farmers' Union was a CP front. Matusow alleged that there were seventy Communists working for *Time* magazine and that there were Communists on Montanan Mike Mansfield's staff.[10] In those western states, Matusow gave seventy-five speeches in a three-month period, many controversial. He implied that he was an undercover FBI agent rather than admitting the truth: that he had only completed a brief stint as a low-level paid informer in New York. Director Hoover received several inquiries from those surprised to learn that the FBI had hired someone so irresponsible. Hoover responded that Matusow was briefly an informer and emphatically denied that he was ever a bureau employee.

When the 1952 campaign ended, Matusow returned to the East Coast and was invited to an election night party hosted by the wealthy Arvilla Bentley. Matusow met and courted the divorced Mrs. Bentley, and they would marry the following March. So the impoverished Matusow became the squire of a large Washington manor complete with servants, and hobnobbed with anti-Communist luminaries of the day including Ayn Rand and George Sokolsky.[11] Matusow was barely a month in his new mansion when he was called to testify before the grand jury that indicted Jencks.[12]

MATUSOW'S CONFESSION

In May 1953, Matusow became a one-dollar-per-year McCarthy committee staffer. But he was under pressure. The FBI was pressing him to name the *New York Times* and *Time* magazine personnel he had said were Communists, a list Matusow had trouble producing.[13] By June 1953 Matusow's marriage was already on the ropes, and in July, Arvilla was in Nevada establishing residency for a divorce. Arvilla obtained a divorce on August 25, but a week later remarried Matusow in Santa Fe. Repenting over her second mistake, she divorced him again three weeks later.[14]

During that turbulent period, Matusow was depressed. He wrote to McCarthy intimating that he, Matusow, had been dishonest, but gave no specifics. In September, Matusow contacted the *New York Times* and retracted his claim about Communists on the Sunday edition staff. He said that he had extrapolated that number from the Newspaper Guild's membership. The *Times* immediately notified the FBI about Matusow's disavowal.[15] In another indication that Matusow was wavering, he told a New Mexico FBI agent that he did not want to testify in the upcoming Jencks trial. He said to others that he was working on a book about his time with McCarthy and apparently searched for a publisher. Yet as the end of 1953 approached, despite whatever doubts Matusow expressed, he responded when Texas attorney general John Ben Shepperd called him to testify before the Texas Industrial Commission hearing in Austin. And by January, Matusow was in El Paso appearing as the principal witness in the Jencks trial.[16]

In late March 1954, two months after the Jencks trial, Matusow continued to backtrack or deny outright his earlier accusations. Following his retraction to the *New York Times* the previous September, he provided two affidavits to *Time* magazine admitting that he had no evidence of Communist Party members on its staff. He said that McCarthy had encouraged him to make the claim.[17] His accusations regarding the *New York Times* and *Time* magazine were not simply allegations made in political speeches but rather in sworn testimony at the Salt Lake City Senate hearing. He was now admitting that he had committed perjury. It could be that Matusow sensed McCarthy's power waning, as indeed it was. The proceedings that brought McCarthy down—the Army-McCarthy hearings—had begun only a week before Matusow provided the *Time* affidavit. It was evident that Matusow's story was unraveling and that his days as a professional anti-Communist witness were numbered.

While shopping his McCarthy book proposal in the spring of 1954, Matusow told one lawyer that he was "an unreliable individual and a person who could not be trusted."[18] And on April 27 while in Washington, D.C., Matusow sought out Methodist bishop G. Bromley Oxnam, a man he had accused of being under Communist influence, prompting a HUAC grilling for the man. Matusow walked up to Oxnam after a broadcast and asked to meet with him. During their two-hour meeting, Matusow apologized for tarnishing Oxnam's reputation and causing him problems. Matusow explained that he had undergone a religious experience and was asking for forgiveness. On June 7, a week after their second meeting, the *Washington Evening Star* reported that Oxnam had revealed Matusow's confession at a Methodist conference. Matusow's private acts of contrition and retraction now made national news. On June 1, 3, and 7, Justice Department lawyers called him to testify for the government at a Subversive Activities Control Board hearing against the Abraham Lincoln Brigade and the National Council for American-Soviet Friendship. His appearance on June 7, the same day that

Oxnam's remarks became public, was to be Matusow's final appearance as a government witness.[19] It was Matusow's decision, not the government's, to end his career as a paid witness. Even at those last appearances, Matusow attempted to dissuade the lawyers from calling him, telling them that "my testimony in the past was not right in some cases." He advised that he was unstable and should not be a witness.[20]

After Oxnam's revelation, HUAC investigators immediately issued a subpoena to Matusow. Whatever his motivation, Matusow realized that he was in legal jeopardy for perjury and backtracked on the Oxnam confession. On July 12, Matusow appeared before HUAC and was asked if his prior testimony, including his Jencks grand jury and trial appearances, had been true. Matusow said, "Sir, I do not believe that I told any untruths at any time under oath." He was asked about Bishop Oxnam's statement that he had apologized to Oxnam for having lied about him. Matusow explained, "If he [the bishop] was correctly reported by the newspapers, the bishop is a dishonest man." Matusow concluded by assuring the committee that he was correct in his previous identifications of hundreds as Communists.[21]

After his appearances, the divorced Matusow was no longer the country squire. He moved to Dallas, where he worked selling theater programs and continued to look for a book publisher. In September the wandering and now-penniless Matusow hit the road again, this time on a bicycle trip. He roamed the Texas panhandle and headed toward Taos.

Meanwhile, Jencks and his lawyers continued to work his cases. On June 29, Judge Thomason denied Jencks's motion for new trial.[22] In late June, the New Mexico Supreme Court denied the defendants relief in the Grant County contempt case, meaning that Jencks and the others would have to complete the unserved thirty-some days of the ninety-day jail sentence.[23] The men's application for a pardon was denied, and by mid-July they were back in the Grant County Jail, from which they were released on September 8.[24]

Busy as Jencks's lawyers were with the various cases, Bishop Oxnam's public statement caught their attention in the summer of 1954. McTernan and Witt were always convinced that Matusow lied on the stand. They began preparing a motion for new trial based on newly discovered evidence—a recantation—but they were concerned about approaching Matusow, lest they be accused of tampering with a witness or spooking the skittish and unstable man. In September, McTernan suggested that Alfred Kahn offer to publish Matusow's planned book with the working title *Blacklisting is my Business.*

Kahn agreed to do so, but they had no idea where Matusow was. They left word with his parents, and in October, Matusow called Kahn's partner, Angus Cameron. Cameron and Kahn were just then starting a new publishing firm. Kahn, through Witt, obtained a commitment from Mine-Mill to purchase two thousand copies of Matusow's book and to draw a one-thousand-dollar advance from the Jencks defense fund. Matusow agreed to write the book. Kahn was professional in handling Matusow, though he had good reason not to be: Matusow had testified against Kahn in June's Subversive Activities Control Board hearings regarding Kahn's activity in the National Council for American-Soviet Friendship.[25]

Getting Matusow to write the book proved more difficult. Matusow rented a drab, cold-water flat in Greenwich Village during the process. Weeks went by with no production. Finally, Kahn suggested that he take Matusow's voluminous records and each day prepare questions for the following day, when Matusow would dictate his responses into a recorder. And that was how the book came to be written. As the writing began, Matusow continued to deny that he had committed perjury. He later said he denied lying because he did not yet trust Kahn. About four weeks later, he changed. At the December 14 session—two days after McCarthy was censured by the Senate—Matusow explained how it was that he knew that Jencks was a CP member. In Matusow's mind, Jencks may have legally quit the party, but he remained a member because he was still subject to party discipline. Matusow was concerned that Witt, who was given the recordings for safekeeping, might leak them to Jencks and Mine-Mill. Witt assured Matusow that the material would not be released without Matusow's permission.

With those assurances, Matusow came clean. He changed the book's title to *False Witness* and detailed how it was that he became a serial perjurer. He explained his work on the Jencks case and admitted that he was wrong to say that Jencks was a Party member when he might not have been as a legal matter. It was conjecture on his part. In the New York Flynn case, he detailed how prosecutor Roy Cohn developed his testimony with suggestions, indicating the testimony he needed to incriminate Alexander Trachtenberg and others.[26] Matusow also explained how it was that he emulated McCarthy and made wild accusations about hundreds. He was clearly unstable, an exhibitionist, and addicted to making a spectacle of himself.

Cameron and Kahn planned to release the book in May 1955, but their schedule was upset when they learned that in the Flynn case, the deadline for filing a motion for new trial based on newly discovered evidence was on February 3. Matusow was intent on making amends, and it made no sense for him to wait until May, when it would be too late to help the Flynn defendants. Matusow and the group resolved to draft affidavits for both Flynn and Jencks. Under the modified schedule, Matusow would provide the affidavits in late January and advance the book's release to March.[27] Matusow signed the affidavits on January 20, and on January 28, the Jencks team filed a motion for new trial in El Paso, attaching Matusow's explosive recantation. The Flynn defendants followed suit on January 31.[28] The environment for everyone had completely changed.

11

QUESTIONABLE WITNESSES AND THE MOTION FOR NEW TRIAL

IN SEEKING MAXIMUM PUBLICITY for Matusow's book, Albert Kahn selected columnist Stewart Alsop to receive an advance copy. Alsop had previously criticized the government's use of professional witnesses. After lawyer Harry Sacher filed the Flynn motion for new trial, Alsop's syndicated column, "Legal Lying," appeared in the *New York Herald Tribune* as well as more than a hundred other newspapers across the nation. Matusow's confession, Alsop wrote, "calmly explains how he made a business of bearing false witness; and how the American government made his business a profitable one, courtesy of the American tax-payer." Matusow explained the symbiosis between his false but libel-proof in-committee assertions and McCarthy's wild accusations. Matusow noted that in his McCarran Committee appearance, at McCarthy's suggestion, he had made his claim about CP members on *Time* and *New York Times* staffs. Then, Alsop wrote, "Once the 'facts' were in the record, McCarthy knew that he could accuse the *Times* and *Time Magazine* of being pro-Communist" and be safe from libel in doing so. To Alsop, the "cult of the ex-Communist . . . has grown like a cancer." He added that "Matusow's confession is likely to initiate a serious investigation of this new post-war profession of the informer, and this could have good results for the political health of the United States."[1] Matusow's recantation profoundly shook the anti-Communist world, especially within the FBI and Department of Justice.

The FBI and Justice correctly perceived the threat and promptly moved to create a counter-narrative that Matusow's recantation was a Communist conspiracy. Justice convened grand juries in New York and El Paso, and the FBI launched a huge, nationwide perjury investigation against Matusow and his left-wing publishers. Anti-Communist writers, journalists, and politicians rose to condemn Matusow and his retraction. For his part, Matusow was served with several subpoenas, and he would never be so occupied or preoccupied.

In El Paso on January 28, Jencks filed his motion for new trial. He issued his press statement that day explaining that Matusow's affidavit "proves what I always knew that this was a frame-up." Judge Thomason set a date of March 7 for the hearing on the Jencks motion.[2] Matusow's affidavit was not only important to anti-Communists, but also to the beleaguered Mine-Mill. To support the filing, Mine-Mill's leadership scheduled a large conference in El Paso the following day, at which the one hundred delegates in attendance attacked paid witnesses, racism, and segregation, controversial messages in El Paso with its Jim Crow elements and anti-Communist establishment.[3]

On Monday morning, January 31, barely three days before the deadline, lawyer Harry Sacher filed a motion for new trial for all defendants in the New York Flynn case. In the attached affidavit, Matusow claimed to have testified falsely several times in that trial and alleged that prosecutor Roy Cohn suborned his perjury. Cohn's star had fallen since the Ryan trial, as he was damaged by the scandalous allegations in the 1954 Army-McCarthy hearings. Cohn brushed off Matusow's charges, claiming that he had left for Europe by the time Matusow took the stand and adding that in any event, he would not "dignify any statement . . . in this Communist move."[4]

Kahn again advanced the book's release, this time to February 3, and scheduled a news conference at New York's Biltmore Hotel. The news conference broke into shouting matches, with Matusow unable to speak.[5] Amid the turmoil, FBI agents handed Kahn a subpoena to appear the next day before the grand jury—and they had one for Matusow as well.

The question raised was how anyone could believe a man who admitted to being a professional liar. Was he lying then, or was he lying now? Or was neither true? To the anti-Communist world, it was of course easier to believe that he was lying now and not back when he testified against Communists. That would support the anti-Communist narrative and the convictions based

1955 Herblock cartoon. © *The Herb Block Foundation.*

on Matusow's assertions. Across the nation, editorial and opinion pieces lined up for or against Matusow's recantation. They argued in favor of or against using professional anti-Communist witnesses; they accepted the recantation or rejected it as just another strategy to turn the nation over to the Soviets.[6] HUAC chair Francis E. Walter claimed that the Party had "planted" Matusow as a government informer. Matusow denied the charge and said that he had nothing to do with the Party since his expulsion in 1951.[7] Clearly underway was an epic battle for Americans' hearts and minds. Where would American public opinion land? Coupled with the Army-McCarthy hearings and McCarthy's censure, Matusow's recantation had the potential to tip the nation against McCarthyism. Matusow's confession was so powerful that on April 2, the author John Steinbeck wrote, "The Matusow testimony to anyone who will listen places a bouquet of forget-me-nots on the grave of McCarthy."[8]

But there were more immediate issues. Judge Dimock in New York ordered Matusow's grand jury appearance delayed until after he testified in his court on the motion for new trial. To show how serious the Justice Department was taking Matusow's affidavit, Manhattan's United States attorney J. Edward Lumbard personally took over the case. Kahn's subpoena ordered him to produce the Matusow book, papers, and recordings, but Kahn appeared empty-handed before the grand jury and was promptly taken before a judge, who found him in contempt and sentenced him to six months in jail. Kahn immediately reversed course and made public all the materials, and the sentence was vacated.[9]

The government was so anxious to put Matusow, Cameron, and Kahn in the dock that there was little they could do but go from grand jury to open court proceeding to Senate committee hearings, day after day. It was all happening almost simultaneously, with the events detailed daily in the press, placing all parties under unbearable pressure.

Matusow appeared before Judge Dimock on Thursday, February 10, on the New York motion for new trial. Matusow admitted that he lied, as prompted by Roy Cohn, and had gradually embroidered his testimony to implicate Alexander Trachtenberg. The following day, Matusow agreed that his recantation went far beyond his testimony in the Flynn case. He said that, encouraged by Senator McCarthy, he had also testified falsely to the Senate about Communists at the *New York Times* and *Time* magazine. He added that he also falsely accused television station owner Ted Lamb to convince the Federal Communications Commission to deny the man a broadcast license.[10] Matusow's testimony over the Lamb matter resonated when two other witnesses in that FCC hearing admitted that they, too, lied that Lamb had Communist ties.[11] Before Judge Dimock, Matusow detailed that as far back as 1953, long before he met Cameron and Kahn, he had admitted to others that he had testified falsely, including in affidavits to *Time* and the *New York Times*, in a letter to Senator McCarthy, and to Bishop Oxnam in two meetings.[12] During the court's weekend break, a *New York Times* editorial pondered philosophy in the Matusow conundrum and asked, "Can you believe a liar when he says he lied?"[13]

When Dimock's hearing resumed on Monday, the government pursued a new line: that Matusow was recanting his previous testimony for financial gain. It was an odd theory for the prosecutors to raise, given that Matusow had made a comfortable living for years as a paid government witness.[14] Matusow broadened his confessional to include his time running a blacklist for an advertising agency that screened radio and television personalities. He said that "many of the persons whom he had branded as 'Reds' were not known to him," including television producer-director Sidney Lumet. His work for the New York Public Schools was also baseless.[15] In his next-to-last day before Judge Dimock, Matusow stated that he lied in denying that he confessed to Bishop Oxnam. Matusow admitted that at that time, he was in fear and trusted no one. He now admitted that Oxnam had been truthful in his description of Matusow's confession, and that he was seeking to make amends for testifying falsely about the bishop and others.[16]

Under attack from Matusow's recantation as well Marie Natvig's, Attorney General Herbert Brownell promised a thorough investigation into the use of questionable testimony. He assured the public that government lawyers were "under instructions not to use witnesses whose credibility was suspect," adding that he "would be surprised if anyone used Matusow if there was any doubt as to his credibility."[17]

Matusow left Judge Dimock's court on Thursday, and on Monday afternoon in Washington, he faced Senator Eastland's Senate Internal Security Subcommittee, where he was about to undergo questioning for five days—between February 21 and March 2 and again on April 20. The large hearing room was packed, lit with floodlights, covered with banks of cameras and microphones, and overflowing with spectators and newsmen. Accustomed to the witness chair and loving the attention, Matusow readily admitted that he was "a perpetual and habitual liar." But he repeatedly insisted that on this occasion, he was telling the truth and had earlier lied in saying that Jencks was a Party member: "I did not know whether he was or was not a Communist." Matusow ascribed his career as a liar to "greed, need and fear." He then broadened his attack on the government's witnesses. Not only was *he* a liar; he said that Elizabeth Bentley had also lied and had admitted as much to him.[18] During his second day on the stand, he told the senators that other well-known, paid anti-Communist witnesses were liars, including Paul Crouch and Louis Budenz, the Communist "experts." As for Elizabeth Bentley and her untruthful testimony, Matusow repeated the professional witnesses' problem: if they wished to continue as witnesses, they continually had to find new items to expose. Because ex-Communists gave complete reports when first debriefed and no longer had access to their former Party associates, it was impossible to find new legitimate evidence, and so they were forced to embellish and fabricate. Matusow also detailed how McCarthy hired him for the 1952 campaign, paid him, and instructed him to lie about and smear Mike Mansfield, Henry Jackson, and others.[19]

McCarthy complained about the Democrats on the committee, claiming that they had encouraged Matusow's attack against him. "That," he said, "places them far below Matusow in my book."[20]

In the middle of the Senate hearing, Matusow had to travel to New York to testify before the New York grand jury investigating his possible perjury. After this brief departure it was back to Washington on Monday, February 28, when Matusow returned to the Senate witness chair. Matusow repeated that he had lied in calling Jencks a Communist. Finally, he returned to his fellow professional witnesses. He offered to take a lie-detector test and challenged Crouch, Budenz, and Bentley to do the same. The following day, he and the committee reviewed the 244 individuals Matusow had named as Communists for the committee. Matusow looked over the list, remarking that "some aspect of my testimony relating to every one of these people is false," although, he added, "there might be one or two names here I did not give false testimony about." Matusow was excused subject to recall.[21] The Senate subcommittee and its frustrated members had spent days beating a dead horse by calling Matusow a liar. Matusow, in the role of the repentant sinner expecting the lash, mostly agreed.[22] The senate committee recessed Matusow's testimony on Thursday, March 3, as the harried witness was due in Judge Thomason's court on Monday, March 7.[23]

EL PASO MOTION FOR NEW TRIAL HEARING

By the time he arrived in El Paso for the hearing on the Jencks motion for new trial, Matusow had already been in the witness chair eleven days, plus whatever time he spent before the New York grand jury. One could already feel the reaction from Matusow's recantation. Grand juries were convened in New York, El Paso, and Washington to investigate Matusow and other "turnaround" witnesses. The FBI and congressional committee staff were investigating every nook and cranny of Matusow's life. Government officials, including those in the White House and the cabinet, were discussing and working on the Matusow case, with the press deeply interested as well. On the day the El Paso hearings began, the Washington grand jury indicted recanting Federal Communications Commission witness Marie Natvig.[24]

As a further indication that the McCarthy era was on the wane, Democrats controlled Congress again and were working to reform McCarthy-era congressional excesses.[25] It appeared that a corner had been turned, and Matusow's recantation was central to the change.

Assistant Attorney General William F. Tompkins, heading the Internal Security Division, was in El Paso to prepare for the hearing but returned to Washington before the proceedings began. Staying for the hearing were Washington-based Justice Department lawyers David H. Harris and Brandon Alvey. They would join assistant U.S. attorney Holvey Williams and Russell Wine, the new U.S. attorney for the Western District of Texas. The defense replaced McTernan, who was unavailable at the time, with New Mexico attorneys A. T. Hannett, a former governor, and Harry L. Bigbee, a former state judge, who joined Nathan Witt and E. B. Elfers at the defense table.[26] Jencks was also present. He came in from Arizona, where he had been transferred by Mine-Mill in December 1954.[27]

As Jencks and his lawyers entered the El Paso federal court, they stood again in the lobby, waiting for an elevator to take them to the fourth-floor courtroom. The beautiful mural they saw gracing the lobby, titled *Pass of the North*, was a WPA-sponsored work by El Paso artist Tom Lea, the son of Judge Thomason's longtime law partner and fellow former mayor, Tom Lea Sr. What they might not have known was that Angus Cameron, the co-publisher of Matusow's book and his alleged Communist coconspirator, was the artist's close friend and, in his then-role as editor-in-chief at Little, Brown, had published Lea's bestselling *The Brave Bulls* in 1949. Little, Brown fired Cameron after he was named in *Counterattack,* the same anti-Communist blacklisting publication that once employed Matusow.[28]

Once in court, Judge Thomason opened the proceedings. Because it was a Jencks motion under consideration, lawyer Bigbee called Matusow as the first witness. Bigbee had Matusow review his witness appearances since his initial 1951 HUAC testimony. Matusow detailed how, before he testified in the Jencks trial, he made it known to a Santa Fe FBI agent that he no longer wished to testify on Communist matters. Matusow admitted that his testimony was false, especially the part about Jencks being a Communist.[29] He insisted that in his reports to the FBI, he had never said that Jencks was a Communist. The only conversations he had with Jencks were those at the San Cristóbal Valley Ranch. He testified, "My recollection is that at no time in my reports did I state Jencks was a Communist or make reference to the aspects of the conversation that I claimed he was a Communist."

Matusow testified about his attempts to retract his false testimony, to Senator McCarthy, Bishop Oxnam, commentator Elmer Davis, Drew Pearson, Senator Henry Jackson, *Time* magazine, and the *New York Times*. He said he did not tell government lawyers about his false testimony, as he was in fear for his life. While Matusow was on the stand that day, the grand jury, one of several that had been convened to investigate Matusow, Cameron, and Kahn, was sitting one floor below, hearing testimony in its Matusow investigation with everyone fully expecting his imminent indictment.[30] Bigbee took only part of the first day to end Matusow's direct examination.

Completing the direct, Bigbee repeated the same demands McTernan had made at trial: that the government produce all reports and oral and written material given by Matusow to Santa Fe agent Burttram to determine what Matusow said in 1950. Thomason denied the request, stating, "The Court holds that they are not required to do that. The Court holds that regardless of your request that they are not required in the decision and opinion of this Court to produce anything from the secret files of the FBI." Thomason again refused to review the files for himself in chambers.[31]

Department lawyer Harris then cross-examined Matusow for the next five days. Plus his time before the New York grand jury, that made approximately sixteen days that Matusow had been on the witness stand by the hearing's end—and all in one month. For one man to be subjected to hostile questioning for over sixteen days in one month, before four bodies in three cities two thousand miles apart had to be a record. Over several days, prosecutor Harris questioned Matusow in excruciating detail, with Matusow demonstrating patience, endurance, and a remarkable memory. While the defense and prosecution demonstrated his false testimony's incredible breadth, the prosecution was unable to shake Matusow's recantation. The prosecution's theory was that Cameron, Kahn, Witt, and Mine-Mill had bribed Matusow to recant, and that Kahn gave Matusow one thousand dollars to get him to travel to New York. Kahn stated that Matusow was given an advance for his book only after he arrived in New York.[32] Matusow had been so broke in Taos that he had traded his bicycle for a few days in a hotel and borrowed ten dollars from a friend. For days, the prosecutor probed and sought to create any discrepancy with Matusow's prior testimony. If prosecutor Harris could not pin major discrepancies on Matusow, perhaps he could find a conflict in the immaterial. As Harris dove into trivia, his examination had anesthetic potential. Perhaps Harris hoped that in a trance Matusow would suddenly confess to a Communist conspiracy. In 557 pages of transcript, Harris microscopically examined Matusow's bicycle trip from Dallas to Taos, down to having him list the contents of his knapsack and to state whether and when he had worn his beret or had put it in his knapsack. Harris dramatically ended his cross-examination, stating, "I put it to you, Mr. Matusow, that you are sitting in that witness chair paid by the Communist Party?" Matusow: "That is not a fact."[33] Matusow said that he "never had any knowledge of Clinton Jencks' membership in the Communist Party." He attributed his recantation decision to a desire to make amends; to hearing about the life sentence an American had received for collaborating with North Korea; to his conversion to the Church of Jesus Christ of Latter Day Saints; and to his work with sick children in Dallas.[34]

By agreement between the lawyers, Nathan Witt's transcribed testimony to the New York grand jury the previous month was read into evidence. In it, Witt detailed payments made to Matusow and their timing as well as the affidavit's drafting. Witt testified that after the defense team heard Oxnam's report that Matusow admitted lying, it was McTernan's idea to use the book publication to get Matusow to recant. Witt said that he obtained approval from Mine-Mill to spend up to one thousand dollars from the Jencks defense fund to help Matusow with his book, and he advanced $200 or $250. In sum, they paid Matusow $1,250 in four payments between October and December 1954. In January 1955, Mine-Mill agreed to pay an additional two thousand dollars and purchase more books.[35]

After Witt's testimony was read, with no warning, Thomason on his own called Witt to take the stand. The judge asked Witt about the affidavit's preparation and questioned Witt about why he had failed to bring the affidavit directly to his attention. Witt explained that the affidavit was signed on January 20 and was filed in Thomason's court eight days later. Witt said that he thought that he was acting properly in so handling the matter. Clearly not pleased, Thomason reminded Witt that he had an obligation to uphold the law. Thomason then asked Witt if he was a Party member. After objecting that it was not a proper inquiry, Witt took the Fifth.[36]

Done with Witt for the moment, Thomason turned his attention to Matusow, who was sitting in court. He told Matusow that he was holding him in contempt of court for his testimony, which constituted a conspiracy to obstruct justice. Matusow's lawyer, also present in the court, asked for a hearing, which Thomason granted and scheduled for the following week.[37] Finally, turning back to Witt, Thomason said, "The Court would like to announce, however, to all lawyers, not only in El Paso but anywhere else, that any lawyer in this Court who takes the witness stand and under oath invokes the Fifth Amendment on the ground that it might incriminate him will not be permitted to practice in this Court."[38] Based on this exchange, newspapers across the nation reported that Thomason had disbarred Witt.[39] The same day, Thomason entered his brief order denying the Jencks motion for new trial.[40] Seeing Thomason so forcefully and speedily reject the motion must have devastated Jencks and his family as they returned to Arizona, their hopes once again dashed.

THE MATUSOW IMBROGLIO

The sides were once again arrayed along McCarthy-era fault lines: those who favored McCarthy's methods in hunting reds and those who opposed political inquiries and the labeling of many as Communists or fellow travelers. The *Daily Worker* had a predictable response to Judge Thomason's ruling, criticizing the judge for being so certain that Matusow was lying now but had been truthful before.[41] Many lined up to cheer Thomason and his ruling. In El Paso, the *Herald-Post* wrote in its editorial, "The Liar Lies—In Jail. Federal Judge R. Ewing Thomason finished with the Communists and stooges of Mine-Mill Union yesterday when he sent the liar for hire, Harvey Matusow to jail for three years."[42] As for Judge Thomason, the same editor wrote the next day that "the Judge talked American to the Reds."[43] It certainly appeared that Thomason was the hero. In El Paso, his many admirers included a Mexican American civil rights activist who supported Thomason's rulings against Jencks and Witt.[44] In Washington, Senator James O. Eastland, Senate Internal Security Subcommittee chair, took to the Senate floor to praise, saying that "what Judge Thomason has done cannot help but add luster to the Federal bench and contribute to the confidence and respect which the people of America have for the judiciary."[45]

As Americans pondered the certainty in Thomason's opinion, doubts also arose. How could Thomason be so convinced that a liar such as Matusow was truthful at the trial when he left a trail of deception and confessed to lying months earlier? The answer was that it was difficult for anyone to determine which was the lie. And it was especially problematic for Thomason, who purposely remained ignorant of FBI reports and thus had no idea what Matusow had previously told the agents. The *New York Post* wrote, "We marvel at a judge who purports to be so confident that he can tell at what point in his life this implausible character [Matusow] told the truth. Would Solomon have dared to render judgment so swiftly, so categorically, and so self-righteously?"[46] There was also Thomason's summary contempt order against Matusow. Others thought the law dictated giving Matusow a jury trial on the matter, or perhaps referring the case to another judge.[47]

Soon what the government had known but withheld about Matusow was to be revealed in bits and pieces. The *Washington Post* reported that prosecutors had known since 1952 that Matusow "had a 'mild but acute' form of psychoneurosis while in the Army." Knowing of the diagnosis, the department went ahead and used Matusow as a witness, even after he himself had told government lawyers that he was not stable. The Immigration and Naturalization Service had earlier ceased using Matusow as a witness in its cases after being advised that Matusow had told his wife that he had committed perjury.[48]

Given the national controversy over paid informers, in a cabinet meeting on March 18, 1955, Attorney General Brownell decided to address the group even though the topic was not on the agenda. Brownell noted that Judge Thomason had found that Matusow's trial testimony was truthful, but he did not mention paid informants or their unreliability.[49] Brownell would find whatever comfort he had received from Thomason's ruling short-lived.

Perhaps what gave others pause over Thomason's March ruling was the contrast between his summary bench order denying the motion for new trial and Judge Dimock's compelling April 22 opinion in the New York Flynn case.[50] Lichtman and Cohen wrote that Thomason's comments and ruling involved no analysis and "bore little resemblance to the thoughtful and deliberate hearing conducted by Judge Dimock in the Smith Act case."[51] Whereas Thomason refused to review FBI records and refused their production, Dimock demanded to see records as well as trial, hearing, and interview transcripts, and intensely studied and analyzed them. The Jencks trial in Thomason's court was long—two weeks—but it could not compare with the ten-month Flynn trial, whose record contained thousands of pages featuring Matusow's six-day trial testimony and seven days on the motion for new trial hearing. The most important claim in Matusow's Flynn case affidavit was that in his interviews, prosecutor Roy Cohn had directed Matusow's testimony that ultimately incriminated Alexander Trachtenberg.

Besides studying the record, Dimock looked deeply into Matusow's character, finding in him an insatiable appetite for attention and publicity, a need to be "in the center of the stage," and an "inability to reconcile himself to the position of a man of no importance." Dimock found Matusow's falsity to have been caused by his "yearning for a place of importance. He had squeezed dry the orange of informing and was prepared to begin on the orange of recanting." Dimock found Matusow to be "a completely irresponsible witness." In a paragraph that should have damned Cohn, but did not, Dimock wrote:

"The Matusow who first brought his tales to the Government and who was being prepared to act as a witness by the Government lawyers and who was on the witness stand in the trial was a man without regard for the truth, with a passion for the limelight and with the need for a few dollars. The Matusow who retracted his testimony was the same man." Dimock went on to frame the issue: "Which was the lie, the original story or the retraction?"

Despite Dimock's and Thomason's differing approaches, in protecting its prosecutions, the government in Flynn, as in Jencks, contended that Matusow's retraction was the lie and his trial testimony the truth. At length, Dimock reached his reasoned and surprising conclusion. "The internal evidence," he wrote, "all points to the original story as the lie. The pattern of its development creates a probability of fabrication that becomes almost a certainty in light of Matusow's propensity to lie." This was also the opposite of Thomason's off-the-cuff conclusion. But Dimock was dealing with thirteen defendants. He carefully examined the testimony's impact against each defendant and granted new trials to only two, Alexander Trachtenberg and George Blake Charney.[52] Dimock's opinion let Cohn off the hook and found Matusow's subornation claim unsupported, yet he chided the prosecutors for being "credulous" in accepting Matusow's story.[53] Manhattan was not through with Matusow, however—not at all. On July 13, 1955, a grand jury indicted Matusow for falsely accusing Cohn of suborning perjury.[54]

During the summer of 1955, the Department of Justice continued its attack on Mine-Mill by filing a petition with the Subversive Activities Control Board seeking to find the union a Communist-infiltrated organization. Such a finding would cripple the union. Among those who signed the petition was Joseph Alderman, chief, Subversive Organizations Section of Justice's Internal Security Division.[55]

While the national debate raged, perhaps the best indication that the tide had turned against McCarthyism's excesses was the announcement by the attorney general on April 15, 1955, less than three months after Matusow's recantation, that Justice would no longer use paid witnesses.[56] As for Jencks, his case was now in the United States Court of Appeals for the Fifth Circuit, headquartered in New Orleans.

12

THE COURT OF APPEALS

WHILE THE JENCKS DEFENSE pursued the motion for new trial based on Matusow's recantation, the appeal in the main case proceeded in the U.S. Court of Appeals for the Fifth Circuit. McTernan filed his Jencks brief just six days after Thomason denied the motion for new trial, an order that Jencks also appealed. The appellate court set the trial case for argument in New Orleans on May 24, 1955. McTernan moved to consolidate the appeals, but the court refused and kept the May 24 argument date.[1] McTernan would argue for Jencks and Holvey Williams for the prosecution.

The lawyers likely did not learn which three judges would sit on their panel until they reached the court. Once inside the courtroom, the lawyers saw the judges enter and take their places. In the center seat, signifying his senior status on the panel, was Atlantan Elbert Parr Tuttle, who was appointed to the court the previous August and had only ten months' experience. But in comparison to the other two judges, Tuttle was an old hand. The next in seniority, sitting to Tuttle's right, was Benjamin Franklin Cameron of Meridian, Mississippi, who had been on the court less than two months. The junior man was Floridian Warren Leroy Jones, who was sworn in only a month before the argument. All three were Republican Eisenhower appointees. For Cameron and Jones, the cases on the docket that week were among their first assignments.

The Fifth Circuit would become the primary battleground during the civil rights era, then in its infancy. Tuttle would later serve as the court's chief judge in the era's peak years, 1960 to 1967. And all three judges would play consequential roles in those times. Tuttle would become one of the "Fifth Circuit Four," a reliably pro–civil rights cohort on the nine-member court. Cameron, on the other side, was a die-hard segregationist who, it was said, voted not once on the side of civil rights. He was so unyielding in his stance against integration that even though he was not on the assigned panel, he granted Mississippi a stay from the court's order admitting James H. Meredith as the University of Mississippi's first black student. Cameron's stay was overruled, but he disregarded court etiquette and rules and granted three more stays, all set aside when the Supreme Court issued the final order.[2] "The Four" on one side and Cameron on the other would be the bookends of the court, but Jones was a centrist. Although he often favored civil rights litigants, he did not reliably do so. He was proud of following precedent and claimed to abhor judicial activism.[3] The three judges, who at the time barely knew one another, would participate later in what passed for a scandal in those lofty and mostly private chambers, a controversy that would result in the bitter estrangement between Tuttle and Cameron.[4] But that would come later. On May 24, they were all just new colleagues on the court.

Except for one point, *Jencks* was not considered to be a civil rights case. Nor was it a typical criminal case. It was in all things a breed apart, a Communist case. In his exhaustive 124-page brief, McTernan raised twenty-eight points alleging errors, including evidentiary insufficiency, a faulty indictment, improperly admitting evidence, giving faulty jury instructions, and failing to produce the Matusow and Ford FBI reports.

Both McTernan and the government addressed the evidence concerning Jencks's party membership or affiliation at the time Jencks signed the affidavit. McTernan pointed to the lack of evidence that Jencks was a CP member on April 28, 1950. The government, he contended, relied on the presumption of continuing condition: that is, if Jencks was a member in August 1949, unless shown otherwise, he was presumed to be a member in April 1950. McTernan argued against using the presumption because the August 1949 membership was too remote, and the government did not exclude the reasonable proposition that Jencks could have resigned from the CP. Under the Supreme Court *Douds* case, the government could not punish Jencks for his past membership but only for his current association.[5] Several government witnesses were, after all, former Communists had who quit the Party, proof that one could resign.

The government relied once again on Ford's testimony, but continued its mischaracterization. As it had at trial, on appeal the prosecution changed Ford's professed lack of awareness to a categorical statement that there had been no resignation or replacement. The Government's brief asserted: "He [Jencks] ignores the evidence that he continued as a member of the State Board of the Communist Party through 1949 and to September 1950 without disciplinary action or replacement. And, aside from all this, he blithely ignores the other substantial evidence of his continued membership in and affiliation with the Communist Party after the crucial date of April 28, 1950. . . . The record is void of any evidence of resignation." The government's brief repeated its contention that there was no resignation, stating that in suggesting resignation as a possibility, Jencks was indulging in "frivolous speculation."[6]

Another point raised by Jencks was the trial court's refusal to produce the Matusow and Ford statements and to determine if there were any inconsistencies that could aid the defense in its cross-examination. The government continued to oppose production and said that the defense failed to demonstrate any inconsistency that would mandate the statement's production. Jencks also claimed that the trial court erred in refusing to grant the requested instructions defining Communist Party membership and affiliation. The instructions given to the jury, Jencks wrote, lacked guidance and may have punished innocent, protected conduct.

During the summer, while the court considered the main appeal, Jencks and the government submitted briefs in the appeal on the motion for new trial. There would be no oral argument on that appeal.

On October 26, 1955, the court issued its unanimous decisions in both cases in opinions written by Cameron.[7] Cameron ignored several points of error, including excluding women from sitting on grand or trial juries. He addressed evidentiary sufficiency on whether Jencks was a Communist when he signed the affidavit in April 1950, the central issue to McTernan. Cameron quite reasonably stated that proof of party membership before April 1950 was overwhelming, but he admitted that the evidence related to the critical hiatus between July 1949 and July 1950 was "not as satisfactory." Cameron ignored testimony that confidential informant Ford last saw Jencks in August 1949, and instead implied that there was continuous contact by noting that

Ford "was a security officer of the Communist Party during a great portion of the time from 1948 until September, 1950 in New Mexico, the place of appellant's residence and activities." The court upheld using the presumption of continuing condition in finding the evidence sufficient. Once a condition or state is proven, the law, he wrote, presumes that state continues until the contrary is proven.

As his final point, Cameron addressed the Ford and Matusow reports with a surprisingly misleading statement. He wrote, "Appellant argues at length that he should have been permitted to explore the Government's file with the hope of turning up inconsistent statements by government witnesses Ford and Matusow." The court repeated holdings in lower courts that to obtain statements a defendant must first show that they exist and second that they are inconsistent with the testimony. In the first place, once Ford and Matusow established the FBI reports' existence, the defense only requested that Thomason examine the statements for himself to determine if there was an inconsistency, which Thomason refused to do. At no time did the defense suggest that on its own it should be allowed to search and explore any FBI files. Thomason also refused to seal and attach the statements to the record. The court of appeals upheld Thomason's refusal to produce the reports. McTernan pointed out the nonsensical process suggested by the government, which Cameron had upheld. The defense had established the first step in proving the reports' existence. But how was the defense to show that the reports were inconsistent? Not only did the defense have no knowledge of their contents; neither Ford nor Matusow saw their own statements.

Courts sometimes disingenuously ignore and flush into oblivion troublesome, important points with comments such as "and the remaining points were found without merit." And it was in a similar fashion that Cameron summarily brushed off as "wholly unconvincing" the issue of faulty jury instructions on Party membership or affiliation. Cameron ended the opinion by praising Thomason and his conduct in the case.

In a separate unanimous opinion, also written by Cameron,[8] the court considered the motion for new trial. The court noted that the question for the court was whether Thomason had correctly determined that "the testimony given by Matusow at the trial was substantially true and that the testimony given on the hearing of the motion for new trial was corruptly false." Cameron wrote that it was a fact issue to be determined by the trial court, and it would not be disturbed unless it was unsupported by evidence and constituted an abuse of discretion. The court reviewed the record leading to Matusow's recantation as well as his previous statements that he was telling the truth under oath and had only recanted after he got into the hands of Witt, Cameron, and Kahn and was paid one thousand dollars. The court only mentioned the instances before Matusow's Jencks recantation when he said that he testified truthfully, ignoring his previous recantations to Oxnam, the lawyer Brown, the *New York Times, Time* magazine, and others. Cameron noted Judge Dimock's opinion in Flynn and found it both unpersuasive and inapplicable. Cameron wrote that Matusow did not have the same inducement to recant in Flynn as he did in Jencks.[9]

Matusow's recantation was a general confession, retracting his testimony not only for Jencks and Flynn but also in many other settings and cases. The money he received was to write a book about his activities that included both cases. Cameron found that Matusow's testimony in Flynn was uncorroborated but supported by other evidence in Jencks. When it came to Jencks's Communist Party membership or affiliation after August 1949, Matusow's testimony stood alone and was uncorroborated. Despite this, the court affirmed Thomason's new trial denial.

After his March 16, 1955 summary contempt conviction in El Paso, Matusow filed his own appeal to the Fifth Circuit. The case was argued, and on January 27, 1956, the same three judges—Tuttle, Cameron, and Jones—reversed the conviction.[10] In another opinion written by Cameron, the court found that Thomason should have given Matusow a jury trial and erred in acting on his own. They held that Thomason failed to certify the contempt process appropriately and that at most, only perjury was committed in his presence and more was required under the law. Those and other errors led to the reversal. But Matusow's troubles were far from over; in September 1956, he was convicted of perjury in New York.

Jencks worked in Arizona throughout the appeal, but it became apparent that he would not be able to retain his Mine-Mill job if the Court of Appeals ruled against him. Although Local 890 passed a unanimous resolution in his support, in January 1956, after his conviction was affirmed, the Mine-Mill executive board voted to ask both Maurice Travis and Jencks for their resignations. They did so to reduce pressure from competing unions and to ease an eventual merger with another union.[11] Jencks could have returned as Local 890 president, but he declined to do so because the funds were insufficient to pay both Jencks and Juan Chacón. He looked for work in Arizona but discovered that he was blacklisted. Thinking that the San Francisco area was his best hope, and perhaps to follow Travis and other friends, he and Virginia packed up the family and moved there.[12]

The next step in the Jencks appeal was to apply for a writ of certiorari to the United States Supreme Court, which he did, and on March 5, 1956, the Supreme Court granted its writ agreeing to hear the case.[13] This was the last chance Jencks would have to escape a prison sentence and clear his name.

13

THE SUPREME COURT

THUS FAR, local events and the national red scare had driven the Jencks prosecution. Anticommunism's rise, Taft-Hartley, the EZ strike, and the filming of *Salt of the Earth* occurred just before or at the McCarthy era's peak and the shift to the Republican Party and the right wing in post–World War II America. National currents would profoundly influence the Supreme Court, but not at all in the direction one would have predicted. Until the 1952 term's end in July 1953, the Supreme Court under Chief Justice Fred M. Vinson reliably supported government action against the CP. Of that term's nine cases, the court sustained the government in five, and the four the government lost were narrowly based decisions. Its last case was the controversial Rosenberg atom spy decision, handed down on June 19, 1953, which within hours sent the Rosenbergs to their execution. It was Chief Justice Vinson's final opinion. Vinson died in September, and President Eisenhower named Earl Warren as his successor.

THE WARREN COURT

Earl Warren brought strong law-and-order credentials to the court. He had been the district attorney in Alameda County (Oakland) as well as California attorney general. He was a popular and successful former governor and was

Tom Dewey's vice-presidential running mate in 1948. Warren had supported FDR's Japanese internment, but late in his life came to regret the decision.[1] But that background did not tell the whole story. As governor, Warren unsuccessfully pushed for health care, as had Truman, who commented that Warren was "a Democrat and doesn't know it." In fact, both Republicans and Democrats nominated Warren for governor when he ran for reelection in 1946.

In the term before Warren came onto the court, the Vinson court had been unable to decide *Brown v. Board of Education.* By the time the case was reargued and decided, the court was in its first term under Earl Warren. Instead of indecision, Warren brought a unanimous decision in *Brown,* and he wrote the opinion. In Warren's first four terms, new justices replaced those who usually supported the government in Communist cases, and in these cases, the court changed from the reliably pro-government Vinson court to one that was unpredictable, at times even trending against the government.

On Monday, October 8, 1956, most Americans were focused on that day's World Series game, when Yankee Don Larsen would pitch the only perfect game in Series history and break Dodger hearts. But that day in Washington, Earl Warren opened his fourth term as chief justice. The following Monday, Justice Sherman Minton retired from the court, and President Eisenhower immediately made a recess appointment. It was said that Eisenhower wanted a Catholic on the court, and with less than a month before the 1956 presidential election, he chose William J. Brennan Jr., who was from the New Jersey Supreme Court and a Democrat. Brennan took his seat on Tuesday October 16, the day before the *Jencks* argument.

The Supreme Court was the place where tough legal questions landed. The court's job each term was to settle and define the nation's laws and provide a comprehensive and coherent legal framework. Of the cases the court agreed to hear in the 1956 term, sixteen involved admitted or alleged Communists, including *Jencks.*[2]

Antipathy toward the Warren court had grown after its 1954 *Brown* decision and increased the following year with *Brown II,* the court's mandate that the nation desegregate its schools with all deliberate speed. "Impeach Earl Warren" billboards sprang up along the nation's highways. The court's rulings in Communist cases added to the anticourt sentiment. Segregationists called to reform the court or curb its power and jurisdiction. Virginia's Howard W. Smith filed such a bill, which proposed legislation to limit the Supreme

Court's state law preemption. In the court's 1955–56 term, several important cases heightened anticourt sentiment.

One case was that of Steve Nelson, *né* Stjepan Mesarosh, a prosecution under Pennsylvania's sedition law. Nelson, the top CP leader in the Pittsburgh area, was convicted for violating the Pennsylvania law. The Supreme Court reversed the conviction and invalidated the statute, holding that sedition was preempted by federal law. Several prominent legislators condemned the holding, including McCarthy, Howard W. Smith, and James O. Eastland. McCarthy stated that with the Warren court "there is just one pro-Communist decision after another." Eastland added, "What other explanation could there be except that a majority of that court is being influenced by some secret, but very powerful Communist or pro-Communist influence?" The Nelson case made many northern conservative Republicans allies of southern segregationists in Communist cases.[3] That term also saw Warren's alignment with the court's liberal Black-Douglas wing.

One 1955 term decision that would play an important role in *Jencks* was *Communist Party of the United States of America v. Subversive Activities Control Board* (SACB). The Internal Security Act of 1950 required the CP and other "subversive" organizations to register and disclose their members. The SACB, an administrative agency, found the CP to be subversive, and the CP sued to invalidate the law. The testimony relied upon by the board in making its finding against the CP included Harvey Matusow's. On March 8, 1956, during the court's second private Friday conference on the Communist Party case, Chief Justice Warren addressed Matusow's testimony. Warren and others on the court took their broad supervisory role over federal courts and agencies seriously; it was a duty they felt mandated an ethical and trustworthy process. Warren announced that he had decided to reverse the Communist Party case, and based his decision on Matusow's false testimony.[4] The government did not contest perjury accusations against anti-Communist witnesses Paul Crouch and Manning Johnson. Unlike the Supreme Court, the court of appeals had refused to consider CP claims alleging perjury by government witnesses. Warren assigned the opinion to Justice Felix Frankfurter, who noted that the administration of justice required a reversal even if other evidence had sustained the finding. The court found the process fatally tainted, and a majority rejected the government practice of using discredited witnesses and their testimony.[5]

Two days after Warren opened the 1956–57 term, the court took up *Mesa-rosh,* a Smith Act case. The court had reviewed Mesarosh's (a.k.a. Nelson) conviction on a state sedition prosecution the previous term. In *Mesarosh,* the government had relied heavily on professional anti-Communist Joseph D. Mazzei. At the oral argument before the court, discharging his duty of candor, the solicitor general advised the justices that Mazzei's testimony at other trials and before the SACB had been false. No longer able to rely on Mazzei's testimony, the solicitor requested that the case be stricken from the calendar and remanded to the trial court, where Mazzei's credibility could be examined. In an unusual occurrence at the oral argument on October 10, Warren called for a recess and the justices went into a private conference. When they emerged, Warren announced that they decided to reverse and remand the case, and he so ordered. Warren wrote, "The dignity of the United States Government will not permit the conviction of any person on tainted testimony. This conviction is tainted, and there can be no other just result than to accord petitioners a new trial. *** The government of a strong and free nation does not need convictions based upon such testimony. It cannot afford to abide with them."[6] In pre-Warren days, the court would more likely have overlooked the government's misconduct as "technicalities" and sustained actions against Communists.

JENCKS V. UNITED STATES

The 1956 term was a busy time for the Margolis and McTernan law firm. On October 8 and 9, Ben Margolis argued the term's first case, *Yates, et al. v. United States,* the significant second-tier Los Angeles Smith Act case involving fourteen defendants. On October 10 and 11, the court heard two more Communist cases, *Scales* and *Lightfoot. Jencks* was scheduled for the following week.

A month before the *Jencks* argument, Solicitor General J. Lee Rankin assigned the Jencks case to a lawyer working as a special assistant to Attorney General Brownell. That lawyer was thirty-six-year-old John V. Lindsay, who years later would become New York City's mayor.[7] *Jencks* would be one of the three cases Lindsay would argue to the court during his time at the Justice Department.

On Wednesday, October 17, McTernan and Lindsay entered the Supreme Court chamber to present their arguments. The day's first case was the continued argument that began the previous day, which had been Brennan's first day on the court. After that argument, Warren called the Jencks case, no. 23 on the calendar. As McTernan stood at the lectern and faced the court, he could almost touch Warren, who faced him. The nine justices, with Warren at the center, were seated by seniority, alternating first to Warren's right and then to his left. The justices were arrayed before McTernan from left to right as follows: Harlan, Burton, Frankfurter, Black, Warren, Reed, Douglas, Clark, Brennan

Of the points he raised in his brief, McTernan addressed only two in his argument: Judge Thomason's refusal to produce the Ford and Matusow witness statements and the jury instruction on Party membership. The court was already familiar with Matusow and his perjury from the previous term's Communist Party case. McTernan immediately seized on that principle and urged the justices to exercise their supervisory authority over the courts, as they had in *Mesarosh* the previous week. McTernan said, "We have here a problem which our courts face in seeing to it that the administration of justice is cleansed of the products of such people. And while this problem differed in details, we submit that it is the same in essence, as that which this Court disposed of last week in *Mesarosh*."[8]

McTernan continued and argued that the government could not bring a prosecution and then deny the defendant evidence relevant to his defense. By bringing the prosecution, the government had waived the privilege over relevant government documents. The issue was relevancy, not inconsistency, which the government argued the defense must show before the documents had to be produced. McTernan said that although inconsistency between a witness's testimony and a written statement was not necessary, it had been demonstrated in *Jencks*.[9] Matusow was the government's key witness and the only one to testify about post-affidavit matters, factors that made his cross-examination critical.[10] At the motion for new trial hearing, Matusow had testified that he did not tell the bureau Jencks was a Party member. He also said that he told an agent he did not want to testify at the Jencks trial and that his grand jury testimony had not been true. The agent had taken the stand at the hearing to deny both allegations, but Thomason refused to produce the statements Matusow had made to the agent, which might have settled the discrepancy. McTernan repeated that Thomason did not wait for the prosecution's objection before denying the statements' production, and refused to review the documents himself.

McTernan's second point was that Thomason's instructions permitted the jury to find membership where none might have existed. Under Thomason's broad definition, membership could be found for attending meetings with Communists or other innocent conduct. McTernan reminded the court that as decided in its *Douds* case,[11] the government must prove affirmative acts constituting membership. Furthermore, pre-affidavit conduct alone was insufficient proof. McTernan concluded on that point and reserved time for rebuttal.

Regarding witness statements and reports, Lindsay countered that the defense first had to establish that there was an inconsistency between the statements and the witness testimony. If there was an inconsistency, production was mandatory.[12] Lindsay asserted that to highlight an inconsistency, the defense could produce another witness; he then quickly corrected himself, acknowledging that it was impossible to produce such a witness if it was only a conversation between Jencks and Matusow.

Lindsay argued in favor of retaining the inconsistency rule, leaving disclosure to the trial court's discretion. Warren questioned how a court could fail to review a statement when a witness like Matusow claimed he told the agent one thing, and the agent contradicted him. Warren asked Lindsay, "Do you think, there, that the judge should have refrained from looking at it and—for the purpose of determining whether that was true after a man had confessed for being a perjurer?"[13] Lindsay then misstated what the agent said and was corrected by Black. Lindsay was losing his point in having to correct his misstatements. The frustrated Lindsay, rather than address the issue, next reached for the floodgates: "It seems to me that, in this case, in order to sustain the petitioner, you would have to be a very sweeping rule in this area, which, make convictions almost impossible."[14] Lindsay then doomed his argument by stating that because Matusow had not explicitly testified that Jencks was a Communist, accordingly there was no inconsistency between Matusow's statements and the report. Aghast, Frankfurter reminded him that Matusow was the key witness, and "the whole tenor of his testimony" was to describe Jencks as a Communist. Lindsay responded with a stammer: "Well, that—that's quite true. . . . I'll quickly concede that."[15] Warren and Black next separately sent Lindsay what must have been a depressing signal by asking him whether, if they found error in Thomason's refusal to produce, the court should reverse and grant Jencks a new trial or simply remand for a hearing to have the court examine the statements. Lindsay, not surprisingly, suggested a remand for a hearing rather than reversal and a new trial.

To extricate himself from the box he was in, Lindsay went on to state that Matusow's testimony regarding metals production for the Korean Conflict, even if it was an error, was harmless as cumulative and was corroborated. Warren forcefully reminded Lindsay that only Matusow had mentioned that fact, which Warren viewed as the most damaging evidence against Jencks. Later, Lindsay repeated that Matusow's testimony was harmless as it was corroborated, prompting Warren to ask Lindsay to show him where it was corroborated. All Lindsay could do was refer Warren in general to pre-affidavit testimony. Warren responded with a curt dismissal: "Never mind. . . . Finish your argument, Mr. Lindsay."[16] Once the argument was over, the case was in the court's hands.[17]

Two days after *Jencks* was argued, the court discussed the case in its regular private Friday conference. These conferences served several purposes. They allowed justices to attempt to persuade their colleagues, to determine whether the case would be affirmed or reversed, and to state the grounds on which they would base their decision. The main practical point was for the justices to give their initial votes on the case. The senior justice in any group determined who would write the opinion for the group.[18]

Thomason's most indefensible point was his refusal to review the statements and reports. He could not have exercised the discretion Lindsay and the government said he possessed. Warren opened the Friday conference discussion with this point: "The district court should have looked at the FBI reports to see if they [were] inconsistent with the testimony of Matusow." To Warren, a remand would normally follow such an error, but Warren found Thomason to have been biased in sentencing Matusow to three years. Warren apparently had no faith that Thomason would deal fairly with the statements should they remand the case. Warren also addressed and roundly criticized the jury instructions. The one regarding membership instructed the jury on "what circumstantial evidence it might consider, but not what it must consider." Warren concluded, "This paid informer [Matusow] is testifying to everything he can think of to incriminate a man over a period of years. He made written reports regularly. I reverse." Black quickly agreed with Warren to reverse. "You can't retain evidence and send a man to jail on it because it's too confidential. If the government wants to keep the evidence confidential, they should try the case without the evidence. Frankfurter felt that the reports should have been produced. He opposed private, in camera review by the trial court and favored an open process, stating, "There should be no *ex parte* rulings in a criminal case." Frankfurter advised that if they were going to reverse and grant a new trial, they should rule on the instructions "so that the same error will not be repeated." Next was Douglas, who was most succinct, saying only, "I reverse." Burton focused on the erroneous instructions and said he would reverse. On the reports, he noted that they should be given to the judge. Clark resisted giving FBI reports to the defense: "Ok to let the judge see them, but not the lawyers." He added, "We should not disturb the exercise of judicial discretion where two lower courts agree." Clark maintained that FBI reports were sacrosanct and would only go as far as allowing the court to see them. Harlan said he would reverse on both report production and the instructions.

Finally there was Brennan, who was only in his second day when the court heard *Jencks*. This was his first conference, and being the junior man on the court, he came last. He felt that the reports were not sacrosanct and resisted having the judge view them alone. Brennan was "bothered" by the instructions. At the court's Friday conference on November 2, Brennan articulated a new, simple, and radically different rule: "If a witness made a report, it should be produced." He saw "no possible basis for refusing production" when the witness made and signed reports as Matusow had done. His surprisingly broad proposal implied that the reports would be furnished directly to the defendant and not be filtered through a court.[19]

The final and most comprehensive Friday conference on *Jencks* was held on March 22, 1957. By that time, Justice Stanley Reed had retired and was replaced by Charles Whittaker. Whittaker took no part in the proceedings, leaving only eight justices on the case. A majority immediately indicated a willingness to reverse the case and remand for a new trial. Warren said again that he would not remand the case for a hearing, repeating his lack of confidence in Thomason, whom he found "prejudiced."[20] With the conferences over and the sides lined up, Warren assigned the majority's opinion to the junior justice, William J. Brennan.

Brennan went to work. He submitted his first draft opinion to his fellow justices on May 2, and his second draft May 6. In both the first and second drafts, Brennan organized the opinion in four sections: one addressing report production and three regarding jury instructions on membership, affiliation, and informer-witnesses. In his third May 13 draft, for reasons that are unclear, Brennan deleted the jury instructions, explaining in a footnote that "because of our disposition of this case, it is unnecessary to consider the alleged errors in these instructions."[21] It was still unclear why the court would reverse and remand for a new trial but risk repeating the erroneous jury instructions.

Associate Justice William J. Brennan Jr., 1972.
Library of Congress.

Brennan's majority suggested other changes in the opinion, and by the May 13 draft, Brennan had written assurances of support from Warren, Black, Frankfurter, Douglas, and Harlan. Burton stood for leaving the reports to the trial courts' discretion but found the jury instructions faulty. Clark was adamant for affirming and keeping FBI files secret. The decision was filed on Monday, June 3.

The court's decision contained three opinions: majority, concurring, and dissenting. In its factual recitation, the five-member majority adopted the government's erroneous characterization of Ford's testimony that Jencks had not resigned. The majority was clearly disturbed over Thomason's adamant refusal to examine the files and for ruling at the hearing even before the prosecutors objected. If there was a rule requiring defendants to lay an inconsistency foundation to obtain statements, that rule was changed.[22] Nor would the trial court first have to examine the reports and statements to see whether the defense should have them. As suggested by both Warren and

Frankfurter, Brennan noted that it was not just inconsistencies that made statements valuable to the defense; it was also omissions and "differences in emphasis." Brennan laid out a clear and simple rule: "We now hold that the petitioner was entitled to an order directing the Government to produce for inspection all Matusow and Ford reports, written and, when orally made, as recorded by the FBI, touching the events and activities as to which they testified at the trial. We hold further that the petitioner is entitled to inspect the reports to decide whether to use them in his defense." As for those, such as Burton and Harlan, who wanted the trial courts to make the determination, Brennan added, "The practice of producing government documents to the trial judge for his determination of relevancy and materiality, without hearing the accused, is disapproved. Relevancy and materiality for the purposes of production and inspection, with a view to use on cross-examination, are established when the reports are shown to relate to the testimony of the witness." Brennan made it simple; the defense was entitled to any statement made by a witness that related to the testimony given.

If the government refused to produce a witness statement, the case would be dismissed. In so ruling, the court held that the privilege the government had in keeping its records confidential gave way whenever it brought a prosecution. The government could no longer prosecute and then withhold evidence that was relevant and useful to the defense. In contrast to the court of appeals, which found no reversible error, seven of eight supreme court justices voted to reverse and grant a new trial, and five of the eight justices supported the sweeping new rule in the majority opinion that no longer considered FBI reports "sacrosanct."[23]

The two concurring justices, joined by Frankfurter, agreed with the reversal and remand for a new trial because they found the jury instructions on membership and affiliation faulty. [24] "This [membership] instruction failed to emphasize to the jury the essential element of membership in an organized group—the desire of an individual to belong to the organization and a recognition by the organization that it considers him as a member."[25]

In his dissent, Clark said that the majority changed federal law on statements. Clark read their previous *Gordon* decision as requiring a foundation before production, but he could not defend Thomason's refusal to examine the statements. "Perhaps here, with a recanting witness, the trial judge should have examined the specific documents called for, as the defense requested, and if he thought justice required their delivery to the defense, order such delivery to be made." Clark repeated Judge Cameron's misleading characterization of the defendant's demand. At trial, Jencks had only requested that the Ford and Matusow statements be produced for the trial court's review to see if they were impeachment material. At no time did Jencks ask that they be delivered to the defense, and Jencks in no way demanded direct access to FBI files. Mischaracterizing the decision in ways he knew would make headlines, Clark warned of catastrophe and invited congressional correction: "Unless the Congress changes the rule announced by the Court today, those intelligence agencies of our Government engaged in law enforcement may as well close up shop, for the Court has opened their files to the criminal and thus afforded him a Roman holiday for rummaging through confidential information as well as vital national secrets."[26] Clark's misleading language was variously described as "hysterical," "inflammatory," "extravagant," or "overwrought."[27]

Clark's irresponsible opinion proved useful to the court's enemies and those who were outraged by the decision, and his words landed in op-ed pages across the nation. Contrary to Clark's rhetoric, the *Jencks* decision limited discovery only to those statements made or adopted by a witness that were relevant to the testimony, period—no access to other files, no rummaging. Clark would continue to press his resistance, and remarked that his solo dissent in *Jencks* made him "'the highest-paid doorkeeper in the world' opposing demands for the release of Federal Bureau of Investigation files."[28]

Once the court announced its *Jencks* decision, the reaction was swift. Headlines in the *New York Times* ("Court Orders U.S. to Open F.B.I. Files or Drop Cases"), the *El Paso Herald-Post* ("Expect Dismissal of Jencks Case, U.S. Frowns on Giving Up Secret Data," "Internal Security System Threatened by Ruling"), and the *Washington News* ("FBI Ruling Spreads Confusion") mirrored Clark's inflammatory and near-hysterical mischaracterization.[29] The day after the decision, Pennsylvania congressman and HUAC chair Francis E. Walter introduced legislation to limit the holding in *Jencks* to protect FBI files.[30]

Three days after the decision, Thomason angrily spoke out—a questionable act, given that the case was still pending in his court. Echoing Tom Clark, the disappointed judge fumed:

> The case was fairly tried, and justice was done. If the present opinion is sustained and Congress does not act promptly to provide remedial legislation, the FBI might just as well close its doors. This decision has

probably given more comfort to guilty defendants and some criminal lawyers than any decision handed down in many years. The chances for conviction of Communists, narcotics peddlers, kidnapers [sic] and bank robbers will be lessened seriously if they are allowed to get into the private files and investigations of the FBI.[31]

Given all the hullabaloo, the public now imagined Communists and criminals freely rummaging through confidential FBI files and opening up the nation's secrets, all thanks to *Jencks*.

Storm clouds, already brewing before *Jencks,* darkened, but the tempest would not see its full fury unleashed until two weeks after *Jencks* was announced. In the 1956 term that was closing, the court issued eleven rulings in Communist cases—all against the government. The court issued four of those eleven decisions on Monday, June 17, a day that later came to be known as "Red Monday." As I. F. Stone wrote, "June 17, 1957 will go down in the history books as the day on which the Supreme Court irreparably crippled the witch hunt."[32] The decisions were shocking given the government's previous record, and that day's four cases raised a variety of issues.[33] The largest was *Yates v. United States*—the West Coast Smith Act conspiracy—a case argued by McTernan's partner, Ben Margolis, which became the decision that ended Smith Act prosecutions.[34]

THE JENCKS ACT

That term's decisions and the controversy over the eleven cases "transformed congressional criticism into militant opposition," and court analyst Robert M. Lichtman observed that *Jencks* was the decision "that most inflamed the Court's critics."[35] Congress was anxious to address the court's recent anti-government rulings, especially *Jencks*. On Monday, June 24, Senate judiciary committee members conferred with the Department of Justice. They drafted and introduced a bill to amend the federal criminal code relating to witness statements and reports. The bill's purpose was to correct what congress found wrong in the *Jencks* decision.[36] It was the same bill that Representative Kenneth Keating introduced on the House side. The legislation was put on the speediest of fast tracks. A hearing was scheduled four days later, and only government witnesses were called to testify.

The White House staff prepared for a June 28 cabinet meeting and put the Supreme Court decisions as the top item on the agenda, allotting it twenty of the meeting's forty-five minutes. The agenda item noted, "Top officials in all parts of the Administration [were] being faced with inquiries about the effect of [those] decisions both on the Executive Branch and on the Congress." Attorney General Brownell addressed the cabinet, acknowledged confusion over the Jencks case, and said that his department was preparing legislation to clarify the decision.[37] In later public statements, Brownell said that "the Jencks decision has resulted in a 'real crisis in law enforcement.'"[38]

When Judiciary Committee chair Senator Joseph C. O'Mahoney opened the hearing on the *Jencks* legislation, he spoke in a surprisingly measured tone in contrast to Clark's and Thomason's excited exaggerations. O'Mahoney said that he did not read the *Jencks* opinion as wantonly opening FBI files to defendants, adding that "a careful reading of the decision makes it clear that it was not the intention of the majority of the court. . . . There was a dissenting opinion written by Justice Clark which contained language that might be interpreted as saying that the FBI files would be released to any defendant." O'Mahoney explained that the bill intended to provide for an orderly procedure. The bill provided for report production related to the substance of the witness's testimony with discretion given to the trial court to excise unrelated parts. There was no requirement for showing conflict or inconsistency. The bill's intent was to clarify what the court in *Jencks* had left unclear. The subcommittee approved the bill immediately after the attorney general's testimony,[39] and both Senate and House judiciary committees filed their respective reports on the bills by July 5.[40]

As the Jencks legislation progressed, in August, finding the bill too harsh, three Senate liberals balked. A new compromise was fashioned.[41] Any delay was potentially fatal to legislation, as Congress in those days adjourned annually on August 31, and that year's calendar was already busy with the most contentious legislation possible. Moving simultaneously through Congress with the Jencks bill was the Civil Rights Bill, the first civil rights legislation since 1875, a legislative challenge that was to earn for Senate Majority Leader Lyndon B. Johnson the title "Master of the Senate." Court-curbing bills and anti–civil rights legislation often attracted the same legislators. In the Senate, legislation was in Johnson's hands.[42]

Behind the scenes, the FBI was pulling its levers to get the Jencks legislation through before Congress adjourned. The FBI wanted to limit disclosure to the witness's words and not an investigation's details. The bureau wished to avoid incidents such as the Coplon case, which revealed how the FBI had obtained evidence in a black bag job at the Soviet embassy. The bureau also wanted courts to excise raw and unedited data from the disclosure.[43] Hoover sent a letter to the acting attorney general urging him to limit the Jencks holding, noting that "the FBI certainly cannot continue to fulfill its responsibilities unless the security of its files can be assured. . . . Since the Jencks decision, however, we have faced one obstacle after another." Hoover added that "photostats of statements and documents taken from the files of the FBI and made available pursuant to the Jencks decision have actually fallen into the hands of the Communist Party."

The Department of Justice argued for the stronger House version rather than the Senate measure.[44] In the end, the House bill prevailed and the Jencks legislation passed, with the president signing it into law on September 2. Although session's end normally produced rushed legislation and excitement, the August 1957 tumult was unprecedented. The session closed on Friday, August 30. The Civil Rights Act of 1957 had passed the previous day, when South Carolina senator Strom Thurmond finally yielded the floor after a filibuster lasting a record twenty-two hours and twenty-six minutes. This allowed the Senate to hastily approve the conference report reconciling the House and Senate versions.[45] The Jencks Act passed on the session's last day.[46]

The legislation that came to be known as the Jencks Act settled the procedural questions related to witness statements.[47] Under the act, statements by a witness that were reduced to writing and that related to the witnesses' testimony would be produced after the defense made a demand. Any statements withheld by the government would be sealed and included in the record. If the government elected not to comply, the court could strike the witness's testimony or declare a mistrial if the "interests of justice" so required. The act made no allowance for dismissal as provided in the *Jencks* decision.

On the day the Jencks Act was signed into law, the current issue of *Newsweek* had J. Edgar Hoover on its cover. Its lead story asked if the *Jencks* decision had handcuffed the FBI, describing it as the FBI's worst defeat: "Yet on one day in early summer of this year, Hoover suffered perhaps the severest setback in FBI history. It came from an unexpected quarter—the U.S. Supreme Court. On June 3, the Court handed down a decision in the now-famous Jencks case that upset a long-standing Hoover order. FBI files must be secret and closed."

On September 19, a stern J. Edgar Hoover stood before the American Legion Convention in Atlantic City, New Jersey. Hoover had a lot on his mind given the threat that FBI files were no longer immune from discovery, although it was a limited exposure to be sure. Hoover, nevertheless, was used to winning, and the events following the *Jencks* decision were certainly not victories for him. McCarthy's fall in 1954 and the government's loss of all eleven Communist cases in the Supreme Court's 1956 term were worrisome signs that anticommunism had seen its best days. Hoover criticized those who were not helping to fight communism, stating, "There are those in this country who, through ignorance or design, confuse the basic issues of our constitutional freedom and muddy the waters of national unity." In a thinly veiled slap at the court, he warned, "There is a trend of softness toward wrongdoing which can cause irreparable harm. We are being stifled by technicalities and by throwing of roadblocks in the pathway of our traditional methods of justice." Despite the CP's huge membership loss, Hoover noted the continued Communist threat and deplored those who would hinder efforts to control communism. "The recent campaign to throw open the files of the FBI is a case in point. The bland refusal to recognize the right of the public welfare and the proper use of common sense result too often in a prostitution of the law in favor of evil." He attributed that weakness to the "cult of the pseudo-liberal," to "phony 'liberals,'" and to "fellow travelers and those of similar ilk." To Hoover, America risked committing national suicide if it stopped conflating the external Soviet threat with the internal Communist menace: "It would be the worst kind of folly to allow the spy and subversive immunity through technical rather than logical interpretation of the law, while they plot the destruction of our democratic form of government."[48]

With the *Jencks* ruling in the books, complete with legislation defining its scope, the Department of Justice was left to determine whether it was ready to try Clinton Jencks a second time. Obviously, it could no longer rely on Matusow, and so it lost its only post-affidavit evidence that Jencks was a Communist. In September, citing no sources, Scripps-Howard's Jack Steele reported that the department had decided to drop the Jencks case.[49] During the fall of 1957, the El Paso U.S. attorney's office expected to receive instructions on how to proceed. Jencks and his attorneys anxiously waited for a decision.

On December 31, 1957, assistant U.S. attorney Robert S. Pine appeared before Judge Thomason in a hearing to address the Jencks indictment. Jencks was not present, but as his El Paso lawyer E. B. Elfers looked on, Pine told Thomason, "On the available evidence the Government cannot successfully retry this defendant and, therefore, is reluctantly constrained to make this motion to dismiss the indictment against him." Thomason granted the motion, noting that "this court thought he was guilty then and thinks he is guilty now." The disappointed Thomason added that Jencks should be where Matusow was at the time—in prison. Looking at the lawyers, Thomason continued:

> Well, gentlemen, as you know and as courts and lawyers and the public generally through the country know, the Supreme Court has about disposed of this case. So when the District Attorney, speaking for the Attorney General and the Department of Justice, says in his motion that the Government cannot successfully retry this defendant *** this court has no alternative but to grant the motion to dismiss the case. *** In these dangerous days, men like Jencks and Matusow who have no respect for our law and courts and who will tear down and destroy our system of free Government should not be permitted to run at large if the evidence is sufficient for conviction.[50]

From California, John McTernan responded: "The dismissal of the prosecution against Clinton Jencks is an important step toward honest administration of criminal justice. We are slowly emerging from the age of the informer, and the *Jencks* case gives us an important assist."[51]

As for Clinton and Virginia Jencks, at last there was a break for the family. Perhaps, they hoped, their problems were finally behind them. Jencks, at the time living in Albany, California and employed as a machinist at an Oakland industrial plant, was working on his car when his daughter ran up to tell him she had heard on the radio that the charges had been dropped. Jencks later expressed his satisfaction, stating, "This decision was, of course, very gratifying to me. The whole thing is in keeping with the democratic traditions of the country. I am very happy."[52]

14

FBI FILES AND THE REVEREND J. W. FORD

WITH THE INDICTMENT against Clinton Jencks dismissed, the government could keep secret the facts behind his case, then safely entombed in FBI and Justice Department files. Once dismissed, in those days the case would be sealed and shrouded in a silence that not even the *Jencks* decision could have prevented or penetrated. Despite the dismissal, to Thomason, the FBI, and the public, Clinton Jencks was a liar and secret Communist on April 28, 1950, and would remain one until death. The only thing that saved Jencks from prison, they said, was a liberal Supreme Court, which had unfairly freed the man on a "technicality."[1] Given the harsh treatment accorded to former Communists who refused to implicate other Party members or fellow travelers, Jencks was rendered mute, unable to explain his version of events. Yet the FBI remained at liberty to stalk the man years after the dismissal and effectively hide its damaging harassment.

Noting the probable end to the Jencks case, I. F. Stone lamented that Matusow, the confessional, repentant perjurer, would pay the price for the government's misdeeds. Stone wrote, "It would be a great pity if the government in the wake of this decision, however, were to be allowed quietly to drop the Jencks case without the public ever coming to see the dirt swept under the rug, the ugly practices covered over, and the continued injustice done to Matusow. In a period when so many of the government's informers have been allowed to commit perjury unscathed, is there no way to get his just day in court for one informer who tried to go straight?"[2] Many joined Stone in condemning Thomason for having punished the repentant Matusow.

Fortunately, the case's dismissal did not end the story. A few years later, Congress passed, and Lyndon Johnson signed, the Freedom of Information Act (FOIA) legislation that gave the public access to the Jencks and other Communist files. Over the years, on demand and after suit, the government has released various Jencks and Matusow files. Initial releases were heavily redacted; later ones were more revealing. The files expose the reason the government fought disclosure and dismissed the charges: there was something in those files that it never wanted the public to see.[3]

JENCKS IN FBI FILES

Jencks, committed to left-wing labor and social reform from childhood, joined the Young Communist League when he was only nineteen years old. After college graduation, Jencks moved to St. Louis and continued to be active in the Communist Party and sympathetic groups.[4] It was in St. Louis in January 1941 that the FBI first opened a file on Jencks.[5] A lawyer-informant reported Jencks to the St. Louis Police Department on suspicion of being a Communist. Jencks was active in the Party and in left-wing organizations. He chaired the St. Louis American Youth Congress and was known to have supported Communist Earl Browder for the presidency. To investigate, an FBI agent illegally entered the Jencks' apartment along with the landlord, without either Jencks or his wife giving permission. The agent noted numerous Marxist books and publications and a card indicating that Jencks was a delegate to the Young Communist League's 1939 convention.[6] Jencks remained active in the Party, but in late 1941, the attack on Pearl Harbor finally brought the United States into World War II, and Jencks, anxious to fight fascism, quickly volunteered to serve. He enlisted in February 1942 and ceased being active in the Party. The FBI closed its file at that time.[7]

In 1946, after his discharge from the service, Clinton and Virginia resumed their Party memberships and activities in Denver. The FBI was soon back on their trail, reopened Virginia's file, and added Clinton to it. According to the file, the couple was active in the Party's eastside branch. Jencks joined the American Veterans Committee, a left-wing version of the American Legion, and led its Denver chapter. In 1946, he ran as a Democrat for the Colorado legislature and lost.[8] In the fall, the agent investigating Jencks submitted a detailed eight-page report listing Jencks's activities and recommending that a Security Index Card be issued for him, a process placing him under greater scrutiny and subjecting him to detention or search warrant in a national emergency.[9] When Jencks moved to Grant County in April 1947, the FBI transferred his file to its El Paso office. In its initial report, the El Paso office repeated the request that a Security Index Card be issued for Jencks. El Paso agents went to the Silver City area to interview local contacts regarding Jencks.[10]

Once he arrived in Grant County, Jencks was subjected to close FBI scrutiny that included non-security matters, such as union negotiations, contract provisions, demands for wage increases, and his efforts to fight racial and ethnic discrimination. Jencks had been on the Colorado Communist Party Board, and an FBI informant advised that Denver Communist leaders were on their way to New Mexico to meet with Jencks. The agent went to the local postmaster and put a thirty-day mail cover on Jencks to identify his correspondents. The El Paso agent again requested a Security Index Card on Jencks, and this time, headquarters agreed.

In 1949 the FBI, despite no indication in the files that Jencks participated in any criminal activity, untoward, or disloyal acts against the United States, included him in the DETCOM program for immediate arrest and detention in a national emergency and under the COMSAB program as a Communist sabotage suspect. DETCOM and COMSAB were used to indicate the danger posed by an individual.[11]

At the Jencks trial, the principal issue was whether Jencks was a Party member or affiliated with the Party when he signed the NLRB affidavit on April 28, 1950. The prosecution had ample proof that Jencks was a member as late as August 1949, some nine months before he signed the affidavit. There were only two witnesses who testified or implied that he was a member after August 1949, and both were paid bureau confidential informants. One was the Reverend Jerry W. Ford, a fellow New Mexico Party executive committee member.[12] The other evidentiary leg came from Harvey Matusow, who testified that Jencks was a Communist who had parroted the Party line on several issues when they met at the San Cristóbal Valley Ranch in August 1950, some four months after Jencks had signed the affidavit. If Jencks was a Party member in August 1949 and August 1950 and had not resigned or been replaced on the state committee, who would believe that he was not a member on April 28, 1950? In the government's eyes, the conclusion was logical: Jencks lied in the affidavit by saying he was not a member. In a nutshell, that was the government's case.

FORD'S TROUBLESOME TESTIMONY

The Reverend Jerry W. Ford was the FBI's principal and perhaps sole New Mexico Party informant in 1949 and 1950. Ford testified that Jencks was a member whom he saw throughout 1949 until a Party meeting at Tesuque near Santa Fe in August 1949, after which he never saw him again. It was critical for the government to address the gap between the meeting Ford described in August 1949 and April 28, 1950, when Jencks signed the affidavit. At the trial, the critical testimony was Ford's claim that he was unaware whether Jencks had resigned or was replaced on the state board.[13] The government changed Ford's lack of awareness into an assertion that Jencks had not resigned or been replaced to support the implication that he must have remained a board member and was thus a Party member on April 28, 1950.

Although he never testified at trial, Jencks always insisted that his affidavits were truthful. Over the years Jencks has consistently claimed that he was not a Party member after October 1949. He told his biographer, James Lorence, that once Mine-Mill changed its policy on the non-Communist affidavits, he wrote his resignation to the Party in October 1949 and ceased being a Party member.[14] Jencks notified New Mexico Party chair Joseph R. DiSanti of his resignation.[15] The government played a dangerous game in leading the jury, the judge, and the public to believe that Jencks had not resigned or been replaced on the state committee.

Ford had not been in the New Mexico Party long when he decided, in 1948, to become an FBI informant. It was fortuitous for the FBI when Ford contacted the El Paso Bureau office on July 6, 1948. In his role on the CP's state executive committee and as Party security head, Ford was strategically placed to give the FBI key, detailed information about the state Party. Over the next two years, there was little about New Mexico Communists that escaped the FBI. The FBI paid Ford a $75 to $150 monthly stipend which, adjusted for inflation, would amount to $786 to $1,572 in 2018. During 1949 Ford dutifully reported on Party meetings, noting that Clinton and Virginia Jencks were active and engaged members. Given its remote setting and small population, Grant County was the Party's New Mexico hotspot. On the executive committee, Jencks oversaw union activities and Virginia led the Party's political efforts, which in those days involved the New Party, a Progressive Party remnant. In 1949 the executive committee, including the Jencks, met on February 5, March 28, April 5, May 14 and 30, and August 1 and 16.[16] After August 16, neither Ford nor anyone else in the record would ever see Clinton Jencks at another Party meeting.

The next time Ford met with his FBI handler, Agent Claridge, was in December 1949, at which time Ford reported on a December 18 executive committee meeting held at San Lorenzo, New Mexico. Just as Jencks insisted that he had resigned in October 1949, the FBI report notes that Ford told Special Agent Claridge that Jencks had resigned from the Party and was replaced on the state executive committee. Claridge reported to the bureau:

> Confidential Informant AQ T-1 [Ford] has advised on numerous occa-
> sions since July, 1948, that JENCKS is a member of the Communist
> Party in the State of New Mexico and as such, has been a member of
> the State Executive Board since March of 1949 until he resigned from
> the Party in order that he could execute the non-Communist affidavit
> as required by the Taft-Hartley Act sometime during October, 1949.
>
> ■
>
> Confidential informant AQ T-1 [Ford] advised on December 22, 1949,
> that at a state meeting of Communist Party members held December 18,
> 1949, at San Lorenzo, New Mexico, the State Executive Committee was
> increased by three members in order that Mexican-Americans in the
> Silver City industrial area could be represented on the State Board. Infor-
> mant stated that vacancies were filled on the State Executive Committee
> which vacancies were created by the resignation of Clinton E. Jencks
> from the Communist Party and A.L. McMurry from the Communist
> Party. This informant further advised that the resignation of Jencks and
> McMurry from the Communist Party was occasioned by the fact that
> neither could enter into negotiations for their union or represent the
> union before the NLRB until they signed a non-Communist affidavit
> in compliance with the Taft-Hartley Act.[17]

Jencks's resignation and his state board replacement was not a minor matter hidden in a lengthy report. It was prominently noted in the FBI report's lead summary, and it was followed by several other reports repeating the same fact. Bureau headquarters quickly advised Agent Claridge that, considering the resignation, policy demanded an investigation to determine whether it was a true resignation from the Party.[18] The congressional intent in requiring the affidavit was to prosecute Communists for collateral crimes, such as perjury. Rather than make a case against Jencks, in the months following, it became evident that Jencks had resigned and was no longer involved in Party matters. FBI files include ten additional FBI reports, all documenting the Jencks resignation and replacement: December 2, 1949,[19] March 31,[20] April 5 and 17,[21] May 10,[22] June 5, 20,[23] and 22, 1950, and January 8 and 9, 1952.

On June 5, 1950, the Albuquerque case agent received orders to write a full prosecution memorandum, and he did so, including in it Ford's original December resignation and replacement report. The bureau forwarded the memo to the Department of Justice along with the agent's observation that few witnesses were willing to testify. The case agent repeated the same pre-October 1949 Party activities and, doing what the bureau advised, listed three of Jencks's post-affidavit "Communist activities": (1) He read the *People's World*, "a Communist dominated newspaper"; (2) He was listed as a subscriber to the *Daily People's World*; (3) He mailed postcards to Grant County government officials telling them to oppose the Mundt Bill pending in Congress. Those activities were clearly not evidence of membership, were open and available to nonmembers, and simply showed Jencks exercising his constitutional rights to read whatever he wanted and petition government officials. The agent turned up no incriminating Party activities in the eight months following Jencks's resignation.[24]

On June 22, 1950, informant Ford reported that at a Party meeting, Chair Joseph DiSanti stated that Jencks "is not to attend meetings of the Communist Party nor engage in any Communist Party activity at the present time." Apparently, contrary to a previous memo, Jencks was not supposed to do anything further for the Party, and there was no indication that he had engaged with the Party since his resignation or that he was a member. The bureau notified the Justice Department of the foregoing, and that being the definitive word, the Albuquerque agent closed the case on Clinton Jencks.[25] Or so he thought.

Two years later, FBI reports of January 8 and 9, 1952 noted that the Justice Department instructed the Albuquerque U.S. attorney to present the case on Jencks. The case agent told the attorney that they had no witnesses who could testify to Jencks's Party involvement after he resigned.[26] The record shows no Party activity by Jencks after mid-August 1949 to dispute the October 1949 resignation.

In 1950 at the end of the summer, the Reverend Ford left New Mexico for Los Angeles, where he attempted to become an informant again. Three years later, with Jencks under indictment, Justice lawyers wanted Ford to testify at the trial, but he resisted. He claimed that his bishop had criticized his informant work. Ford also said that coming out publicly would kill his career as a paid confidential informant. But government prosecutors were adamant that Ford was essential to their case against Jencks. Prosecutor Alderman promised to speak to the bishop, flew to Los Angeles to work on the reluctant Ford, and had to babysit the nervous twenty-eight-year-old preacher until the trial. At the January 1954 trial, instead of repeating the information he had repeatedly told agent Claridge regarding Jencks's resignation and replacement, Ford instead testified that he was not aware of Jencks's resignation or replacement. The prosecutors then went beyond Ford's misrepresentation and told the jury, the Court of Appeals, and the Supreme Court that Jencks had not resigned or been replaced and, contrary to what the prosecutors and the FBI clearly knew, that Jencks remained an active state board and Communist Party member on April 28, 1950. Despite the defense's vigorous attempts to examine Ford's conflicting FBI statements, knowing what the reports would reveal, the government succeeded in preventing their disclosure.

The prosecution also got past another dangerous point during the March 1955 hearing on the motion for new trial when Matusow recanted. Thomason again refused to provide Ford's or Matusow's statements to the defense and once more refused to review them for himself in chambers or to seal them and make them part of the appellate record.

Of the original prosecutors, only Holvey Williams and Joseph Alderman remained on the case and handled the appeal, which the Court of Appeals for the Fifth Circuit affirmed in late 1955. In the spring of 1956, the Supreme Court granted review of the case, causing the environment for the case to change dramatically.

Once the Supreme Court agrees to hear a federal criminal case, the government's file is turned over to the office of the solicitor general of the United States, a special office. It is prestigious, highly professional, and recruits only from the top legal rank. It also maintains a special relationship with the Supreme Court, so much so that the solicitor is nicknamed the "tenth justice." Tradition has it that the office of the solicitor has "special credence," that is, its word and opinions are especially valued by the court, because the solicitor is expected to be brutally honest. The office is proud of its absolute "duty of candor." If the government has erred, the solicitor is expected to confess error. The office is not a normal advocate; it is more of a fiduciary. Lawyers are not supposed to lie to a court, but the solicitor has the affirmative duty to reveal the truth to the court even when it damages the government's case, and it is expected to play a nonpartisan role. The Jencks case would test the solicitor's traditional obligation.[27]

The solicitor's office had already failed in being candid in its brief to the Supreme Court. The brief, most likely prepared by Justice legal divisions, opposed the Jencks petition by contradicting the truth about his resignation and replacement. Furthermore, following the trial prosecutors, the government changed Ford's professed lack of awareness to a positive assertion that the Party had not replaced Jencks and he had not resigned. It was possible—although unlikely—that in that early stage, unlike the FBI and Justice Department lawyers, the solicitor might not have known about Ford's numerous resignation and replacement reports and relied on the trial court record. But in the government's brief, the solicitor misrepresented Ford's statements, writing, "To [Ford's] knowledge, during the period from 1949 through September 1950, no disciplinary action was ever taken by the Communist Party against [Jencks] and [Jencks] had not been replaced as a member of the State Board of the Communist Party."[28]

In autumn 1956, as the solicitor's office prepared for argument, Solicitor General J. Lee Rankin and the lawyer he assigned to argue the case, John V. Lindsay, began to review the file. They knew that the principal issue involved the Ford and Matusow witness statements. Normally, the solicitor's office went by the court record, but given the notoriety of Matusow's recantation and the problem they were experiencing in *Mesarosh*, discretion in this case advised that they review witness statements that were not produced or inspected at trial and that Thomason had refused to examine for himself.

The solicitor instructed the Department of Justice to produce Ford's statements forthwith, and the department in turn instructed the FBI to immediately deliver all the Ford and Matusow statements. The top Justice and the FBI officials furiously exchanged memos over the reports. The bureau turned over most of the memos. It took only a few days for the lawyers at Justice and the solicitor to narrow their focus to Ford in the Claridge memos of December 1949, January 1950, and later reports documenting Jencks's resignation and replacement. The department asked the bureau whether Informant T-1 mentioned in the reports was witness Ford who had testified

John V. Lindsay. *Library of Congress, Prints and Photographs Division, Washington, D.C., LC-USZ62-1334-1.*

at trial. The bureau answered that he was. Once the lawyers read Ford's trial testimony and the numerous misleading, flat-footed statements by the prosecutors at the trial and on appeal—and by the solicitor himself in his opening brief—and compared them to the very clear reports by Ford noting Jencks's resignation and replacement, the problem was obvious. Whether one characterized Ford's trial testimony as a misstatement, misleading, or perjury, it was clearly not the truth. Solicitor Rankin was facing a moment feared by that office. Was it time for him to reveal the false record? How would he address the problem?

The Jencks case was important to the department, and it was a major case for Hoover and the FBI. It was a high stakes game that put everyone under enormous pressure, as the nation would be watching. With the files on resignation and replacement now open for discussion within the government, the FBI argued that the discrepancy in the reports was not fatal. The bureau wrote that Jencks could still be guilty if he had resigned but agreed to continue his affiliation with the Party. In so arguing, the FBI invited Justice to ignore the clear, documented resignation and replacement. Given his position as head of the state Party's security, Ford would have known and reported any activity by Jencks until Ford left New Mexico in September 1950, and there was none after August 1949.

Justice Department lawyers argued that the resignation was a mere "technicality," and that Ford's false testimony made it appear that Jencks had not resigned or been replaced. The FBI added that it would be unfair to demean Ford's testimony without first giving the informant the opportunity to explain what he had meant in saying that he did not know about the resignation and replacement.[29] But as Justice Department lawyers were well aware, what Ford *meant* was irrelevant; what was important was what he had said at trial, what was heard by the jurors, and what was repeated and expanded upon insistently by the prosecutors. Internally, Justice lawyers admitted that Ford knew about the resignation and that his testimony that he was unaware of it was "inaccurate."[30]

Solicitor Rankin surely brought dread to the FBI and Justice when in early October, just days before the argument, he advised them that he was "debating whether or not he must advise the Supreme Court of this," the "this" being Ford's resignation and replacement reports. Assistant Attorney General J. Walter Yeagley of Justice's Internal Security Division "stated that [Solicitor General] Rankin feels that Ford's answer to this one question casts a doubt on his credibility as FBI reports reflect that Ford knew that Jencks was replaced on the CP state executive committee and Rankin is debating whether or not he must advise the Supreme Court of this."[31]

Justice attorneys opposed advising the Supreme Court, but the call belonged to the solicitor. Having already misled the court in the government's opening brief, it remained to be seen whether Rankin and John Lindsay would continue the deception and again rely on Ford's misstatement in their argument. Would the solicitor do in *Jencks* what he had done the previous week in *Mesarosh* and admit that the informant's testimony was false?

On the day the lawyers argued the Jencks case before the Supreme Court, John Lindsay, representing the United States, stood at the lectern and in his opening sentences addressed the troublesome resignation/replacement issue that McTernan had raised in his argument. Lindsay, having just spent days reviewing Ford's FBI statements detailing Jencks's unequivocal resignation and replacement, looked at the justices and said, "He [Ford] also testified that, as an officer of the Communist Party, as a member of the New Mexico State

Board of the party, and also as the security officer of the party for all of that period, nothing had come to his attention up to the time of his severance from the Communist Party [September 1950] to indicate that the petitioner [Jencks] had withdrawn from the Communist Party."[32]

Lindsay's statement—an intentional misrepresentation made with Rankin's obvious approval—swept away the Ford problem with the hope that Ford's numerous statements, all to the contrary, would remain hidden. The deception worked, as the Supreme Court in its opinion accepted as fact the solicitor's false assertion that Jencks had not resigned from the Communist Party and had not been replaced on the state board.[33]

15

FBI FILES AND
HARVEY MARSHALL MATUSOW

WITH MATUSOW'S RECANTATION AFFIDAVIT, the FBI faced a dilemma. On the one hand, it had long warned the Justice Department about Matusow's mental state and unreliability as well as the perjury he committed regarding allegations against the *New York Times* and *Time* magazine in his sworn Salt Lake City testimony. On the other hand, the bureau wanted to be on the anti-Communist side and save the Flynn and Jencks prosecutions. The course it chose was to hide from the public what it knew about Matusow and join the Department of Justice in its claim that the recantation was false and a Communist plot. Matusow was critical to the Jencks case, as he offered the government's only direct post-affidavit evidence that Jencks was a Party member. Released FBI files now reveal that Matusow's testimony and his FBI statements would prove even more problematic for the government than Ford's.

Matusow confessed in public, in his book, and in court affidavits that he falsely and systematically branded scores as Communists when he had no evidence that they were. His scandalous recantation produced headlines across the nation, sent shockwaves through the bureau and the department, and put anti-Communists on the defensive. FBI records show that immediately after the recantation, supervision over the Jencks and Flynn cases shifted to

Hoover and the top men at the FBI and to Attorney General Brownell at the Justice Department. FBI and Justice reports and memos demonstrate that the government knew it had played a dangerous hand in using Matusow as a witness. They also show how Hoover, above all, protected his image and the Bureau's reputation. The FBI's own reports tell the story.

Soon after he became an FBI informant, New York agents evaluated Matusow. They quickly sized up the fast talker as "vain, egotistical, self-centered and inclined to 'blow up' his CP background in order to make an impression." They checked his military file, where they found documentation in his VA records that he suffered from "headaches and dizziness which was diagnosed as psychoneurosis of a mild yet acute form." The diagnosis and the agents' observations disclosed that Matusow's personality was home to a collection of psychiatric maladies.[1]

While Matusow was at the Taos ranch in 1950, he contacted the Santa Fe FBI agent Julian H. Burttram, who interviewed him on August 10 and 11 about his visit. According to Burttram, Matusow told him Jencks had said, in so many words, that he was a Communist. Matusow said that Jencks also told him his union was attempting to work with Mexican miners to have their contracts expire simultaneously and bring about a work stoppage to hinder U.S. war production during the Korean Conflict. Burttram relayed the information to the Albuquerque case agent, who prepared a report.[2]

In October 1950, two months after Matusow's reports, the Albuquerque case agent apparently did not consider the reports significant, as he wrote that "no present Communist Party activity has been developed on the part of [Jencks]," and placed the case in a pending but inactive status.[3] After Matusow was expelled from the Party, FBI headquarters instructed its field offices to have no further contact with Matusow or obtain information from him.[4]

Following Matusow's initial 1951 HUAC testimony, Cincinnati FBI agents arrived in Dayton to interview him. They met with him on December 7 and 29, 1951, at which time the agents thoroughly debriefed him. Matusow signed a three-page sworn statement at the interview on the 29th. The statement mainly related to his meeting with Jencks at San Cristóbal. According to Matusow, Jencks had mentioned that his local union established relations with Mexican miners—which was true—and that Jencks was against the war in Korea—which was also true. Matusow made no mention of the explosive allegation that the two unions were working together to hinder metals production during the Korean Conflict.[5] Matusow's statement continued:

I wish to state that I have never attended a meeting of the Communist Party in New Mexico, and have never been present at a Communist Party meeting where Jencks was in attendance. I have never been told by Jencks that he is a member of the Communist Party, and have never seen any direct evidence to prove that he is a member of the Communist Party. However, there is no question in my mind but that Jencks is a member of the Communist Party.[6]

What Matusow described was that Jencks passed the "duck test." Jencks spoke like a Communist, had Communist friends, and held several views in common with Party members. As Matusow acknowledged, none of this offered "direct evidence" that Jencks was a Party member or affiliate, a fact corroborated by the reality that most CP members over the years had quit but might have retained their old political views and friends.

During the 1952 campaign, Matusow made seventy-five speeches while on McCarthy's payroll, mostly in western states. He made many outrageous statements, eliciting numerous complaints, and implied that he was an FBI agent. In December 1952, the FBI brought Matusow into the New York office to lecture him about his representations. The agents "forcefully impressed upon Matusow that he had given a false impression concerning his statements and the fact the information was available to the Bureau." Matusow had written an exposé for the *New York Journal-American*, and he "frequently made irresponsible public statements . . . usually being publicized as a former undercover agent for the FBI."[7] Bureau headquarters and field offices repeatedly warned, long before the Jencks trial, that Matusow was a problem witness.[8] After the *New York Times* advised the FBI that Matusow had disavowed his allegations against the newspaper, Hoover suggested to the Justice Department that Matusow be prosecuted for perjury. This was one month before the Jencks trial.[9]

Matusow always considered himself a stage actor, and he was glib, fast-talking, agile minded, intelligent—and convincing. But anyone who spent much time with Matusow eventually saw a different side, as was the case with the Edmistons. After escorting Matusow to Washington, they changed their minds as well. To them, Matusow started as an unassuming airman but became an "overbearing individual" full of self-importance. After his appearance before HUAC, Matusow bragged that he had become a national figure and deserved to be treated as such, and that a film should be made about his life. Matusow confessed to Martha Edmiston that he had been depressed, suffered crying spells, and experienced a mental breakdown at Wright-Patterson, where he was hospitalized. During 1952, the Dayton-based Matusow worked for the Ohio Un-American Activities Commission, investigating and accusing various Ohio institutions and individuals of being Communist. John Edmiston recalled that on one occasion, Matusow asked a newspaper reporter friend for his file on Antioch College. The reporter told Matusow that there was nothing useful in his file. Matusow responded, "Never mind, if the files don't show anything, I'll make a case out of them anyhow." With that, the Edmistons had enough of Matusow.[10]

In April 1953, the bureau noted that it had been issuing warnings about Matusow since 1951, writing that the FBI had "washed [its] hands of Matusow and that he was a free agent" as far as they were concerned.[11] Despite those FBI warnings, the department proceeded to schedule Matusow as a major witness before the Subversive Activities Control Board on November 3, 1953.[12]

Although FBI headquarters, several field offices, the Edmistons, and others had noted that Matusow was a liar, untrustworthy, and problematic, the Department of Justice found the man suitable for its purposes. The challenges for Justice would be hiding Matusow's messy FBI file from the Jencks defense team and keeping Matusow in line. A Jencks prosecutor recalled in 2016 that he found Matusow repugnant, and "there was a lot of worry about him because he just had an aura of falsity and deceit." He added that "Matusow was trouble from the beginning, that there [were] a lot of questions about maybe he'd given conflicting statements to the FBI even."[13] Despite that history and those warnings, Justice lawyers and U.S. attorney Herring called on Matusow to present their case for indictment against Jencks and made him the principal witness in the January 1954 trial. Matusow testified for the department until summer 1954, almost a year after Hoover himself had advised the department that Matusow was a fabricator and perjurer.

The Jencks trial was months before the Ford and Matusow FBI statements would surface, and so it was a different time and environment. After the Jencks jury deliberated only a few minutes and returned a guilty verdict on both counts, Thomason and the prosecution became renowned. Awash in congratulatory headlines, editorials, and news reports, the prosecution, the FBI, and Thomason, all now in the national limelight, were pleased, some even ecstatic over the conviction. FBI files document their delight. In those days, Hoover was a god, or as close as you could get to one in the United States. He had expertly crafted and burnished an enviable image.[14] In the mid-1950s, the bulldog-faced director's public persona was that of a no-nonsense tough guy, a man of the law, and an unparalleled defender of truth, justice, and the American way. Decades would pass before Hoover was exposed to be otherwise. Nothing was more prized than praise from the beloved director, and thousands of scrapbooks held the valued Hoover congratulatory letters. The special agent in charge of El Paso's office, Charles W. Brown, wasted no time cranking up the FBI PR machine. The day after the Jencks verdict, he sent a personal note to Hoover extolling the trial's heroes, U.S. attorney Herring, his two assistants, and Alderman from the department, mentioning each by name and suggesting that the director send letters.[15] A few days after the trial, while the case was still pending in his court, Thomason marched into the FBI offices and told the agent in charge that the FBI "did an outstanding job and he desired that [Hoover] be so advised."[16] Thomason wrote to agent Brown that day expressing the same thoughts: "Now that the trial of Clinton E. Jencks (Communist) has been concluded in my court and he has been found guilty, I want to congratulate you." He signed the letter "with all good wishes to you and your organization, and hoping you will remember me to my old friend, Mr. Hoover."[17] U.S. attorney Herring wrote to Hoover commending the FBI office and agent Brown specifically for their excellent work "in successfully prosecuting this Communist"; Hoover in return sent his thanks to Herring, and Alderman thanked Hoover for the letter he received from the director.[18] Even Harvey Matusow received his commendation from U.S. attorney Herring, who expressed the prosecution's gratitude for his testimony, telling Matusow, "Your testimony was absolutely essential to a successful prosecution, and you presented it in a fine, intelligent manner."[19] Jencks, on the other hand, was a dispirited and worried man, knowing only that he faced a terrible future.

FBI FILES ON MATUSOW POSTTRIAL

In the months after the trial ended, Matusow went from erratic to eventually producing a book and affidavits recanting just about everything he ever said about anyone being a Communist. On January 25, 1955, three days before Jencks filed his motion for new trial based on Matusow's affidavit, Assistant FBI Director Alan H. Belmont alerted FBI offices that Matusow was retracting his testimony and had given the defense an affidavit. Though the FBI had previously claimed partial credit for the Jencks trial success, the bureau now shifted its position, preparing to separate itself from the Justice Department and from Matusow.

Sensing that Matusow and the Jencks case had the potential to greatly embarrass the FBI, the bureau prepared to blame the Matusow fiasco on the department. Belmont knew that Matusow's retraction would "shake public confidence" and harm the bureau. Belmont wrote that two years before Matusow testified in the Jencks case, the FBI had furnished the Cincinnati memo containing Matusow's affidavit, "which indicated that Matusow did not have information concerning Communist Party affiliations of Jencks which would make his testimony valuable in [that] case." Matusow's testimony in the Flynn case came long before the Jencks case, and in Flynn, he was already known to be less than accurate. Given Matusow's troublesome background, Belmont emphasized that "on its own initiative, the Department interviewed Matusow and based on the results of that interview decided to use him as a witness in the Jencks case." Fully informed about Matusow's problems and about the Jencks case specifically, "the Department went ahead and used Matusow as a witness despite the information furnished by the Bureau indicating that he did not have knowledge of some of the facts to which he testified." The memo's routing indicated the FBI's concern, as almost every top bureau executive's name was checked.[20]

When Jencks's lawyers filed the motion for new trial and attached Matusow's affidavit, the filing made national headlines and editorials, and Matusow was summoned to hastily called congressional hearings. Alarm bells rang loudly at the FBI and the Department of Justice, which immediately swung into action not only to destroy Matusow but also to save the Jencks and Flynn prosecutions—and themselves from embarrassment.

On the day the Matusow affidavit was filed, Assistant Attorney General Foley called the FBI, spoke with Inspector Victor P. Keay,[21] and requested a conference that day so he could brief the attorney general about the Matusow crisis. Attending the meeting with Foley was trial prosecutor Alderman. Foley acknowledged the department's problem in that "Matusow in his testimony in the Jencks case had gone far beyond the signed statement which he had turned over to the Department."[22] Sitting there with Foley, prosecutor Alderman understood that Matusow had extravagantly embellished and extended his previous Jencks allegations, all with Alderman's knowledge. The men recognized that they were looking at a public relations disaster and months of work to defend against Matusow's recantation. Prosecutor Holvey Williams told the FBI that Matusow was the "only witness who placed Jencks in the Party after filing the affidavit, thus the Jencks case failed if Matusow's testimony went down."[23]

Preparing for the intramural fight, Hoover asked Assistant FBI Director Leland V. Boardman to brief him as to when and how the bureau had called Matusow's unreliability to the Justice Department's attention. Boardman listed for Hoover several instances when the department was so advised, including the January 1952 Cincinnati memo. Boardman reminded Hoover that "despite Matusow's statement that he had no direct evidence to prove that Jencks was a member of the Communist Party, he was used as a witness in this case."[24] Boardman also advised the director that in Matusow's 1952 testimony in the Flynn case, he acknowledged submitting a plagiarized article to the *Santa Fe New Mexican* but stated that he was not paid, even after examining a canceled check bearing his signature. Wrote Boardman, "This indication of possible perjury on the part of Matusow was, of course, known to the Department of Justice attorneys handling the second Smith Act [Flynn] trial."[25] The Flynn trial was almost two years before the Jencks trial, and Alderman was deeply involved in both. Hoover had already suggested that Matusow be prosecuted for perjury regarding his Senate subcommittee hearing testimony about *Time* and the *New York Times*. The FBI was correct in alleging that by the time of the Jencks trial, the Justice Department was familiar with the fantasies springing from Matusow's fevered imagination.[26]

The bureau had established practices for dealing with crises that threatened its reputation. It was perhaps the best connected and most respected institution in the capital and had many journalist supporters ready to do its bidding. The highest FBI ranks considered the Matusow recantation a crisis, and one way to deal with it was leaking to friendly sources and suggesting supportive columns and editorials.[27]

Thomason set the hearing on the motion for new trial for March 7, 1955, and soon the top lawyers from Justice's Internal Security Division packed up and headed for El Paso and their confrontation with Matusow.[28] In preparation for the hearing, the Department of Justice demanded all FBI Matusow statements, especially the Burttram August 1950 reports documenting Matusow's conversation with Jencks at San Cristóbal. But the bureau refused to hand them over because they contained a major inconsistency. In the

August 11 report, Burttram noted that Matusow had described Jencks as a Communist Party member from Silver City, but in the August 28 memo Matusow described him as a "former Communist from Las Cruces." With all the effort the FBI and the prosecution had already invested in ignoring the Jencks resignation and replacement, any mention in a report that Jencks was a *former* Communist was bound to create a problem. The Albuquerque FBI office strenuously objected to furnishing the August 28 "former Communist" memo.[29]

The knotty issue was handled by Belmont, the FBI director of domestic intelligence, who recommended that while the decision on whether to use the memos would be the Department's, the bureau cautioned that using the Burttram letters would lead others to dig deeper into the files and might necessitate calling Burttram as a witness, something the FBI wanted to avoid. Burttram was no longer with the bureau and was unable to help untangle the discrepancy. In the New York Flynn case, Justice lawyers had persuaded the judge to block the disclosure of FBI memos. To avoid leaving a paper trail, Belmont suggested that the bureau "orally" advise the department that Burttram had previously monitored "technical or microphone surveillance," that is, that the agent had worked with bugs or phone taps—illegal "black bag jobs" that were potentially embarrassing to the bureau and the department.[30] This was obviously done with the intention of scaring Justice away from the memos.

On March 1, Hoover reported to his top staff that he had conferred with the attorney general that day and was advised that President Eisenhower, concerned about unreliable witnesses like Matusow, requested that the attorney general report about the issue to the cabinet the following week. The administration wanted to know specifically what action the FBI was undertaking to assure its informants' reliability. Hoover ordered the staff to prepare a memo for the attorney general.[31] There was no doubt that the Eisenhower Administration, the Department of Justice, and the FBI were aware that with Matusow's recantation, the use of paid, unreliable informants had finally metastasized into a huge crisis and scandal.

The nation's newspapers raged with editorials, columns, and letters on the issue. "Who Established Matusow's Credibility?" asked a *Denver Post* editorial, continuing, "Harvey Matusow, self-confessed liar for hire, has put the department of justice and the FBI in a nasty spot. He has raised questions and doubts that may seriously impair the usefulness of any and all professed ex-Communists in the future as informants for the FBI and government witnesses in the trials of Communists in federal courts."[32] On February 21, 1955, the attorney general issued his internal "Brief on Ex-Communists as Witnesses" in which the bureau insisted that it had already taken all the necessary corrective actions and alleged that Matusow's recantation was "a Communist plot against the Department of Justice" and an attempt to "smear" the FBI. And a month later, though the department knew Matusow to be a liar before the Jencks trial, the attorney general repeated the assertion that Matusow's recantation was a Communist conspiracy to "wreck the informant system of the FBI."[33]

At the March hearing on the motion for new trial, the prosecution executed its plan to show that Matusow's retraction was a Communist conspiracy. Contrary to what it knew, the Justice Department alleged that Matusow was lying in his retraction but was truthful at the Jencks and Flynn trials. The FBI and the prosecution once again avoided disaster when Thomason followed the prosecution line and continued to refuse to provide any FBI statements to the Jencks team, examine them himself in chambers, or seal the reports and include them in the appellate record.

The week after Thomason denied the motion for new trial, he held Matusow in contempt, sentenced him to serve three years in prison, and then excluded Nathan Witt from practicing in that court for having invoked the Fifth. The proceedings and Witt's exclusion made headlines, national news, and the editorial pages, with many congratulating the El Paso jurist, including Hoover.[34] Prominent in Thomason's scrapbook is the letter he received from Hoover noting that with the Matusow case, Thomason had established himself as "one of the most outstanding Federal Judges in our country, ranking along with Judge Medina as a stalwart American dedicated to the ideals of our Constitution."[35] Days after the Supreme Court reversed the Court of Appeals, Judge Cameron wrote to Hoover and to the bureau protesting that his overturned decision had been correct and that defendants should not have access to witness statements absent a showing of inconsistency. Hoover thanked Cameron for his support.[36]

Despite the behind-the-scenes battle over Matusow's known false statements, in public, the government—the department and the bureau—consistently asserted that Matusow had testified truthfully at the Jencks and Flynn trials and insisted that he began fabricating with his January 1955 recantation affidavit. The government would not admit that it had knowingly put a liar on the witness stand to support its prosecutions and actions against the CP.

During his presentation to the Supreme Court, John Lindsay, representing the solicitor general and that office's "unflinching duty of candor," continued painting the false picture and told the court, "At the [Jencks] trial—the trial itself, there was no question about Matusow's reliability as a witness. It [Matusow's reliability] came up after Matusow recanted."[37] Much later, FBI files would expose the government's grave deception.

16

CLINTON JENCKS AFTER THE TRIAL

IT TOOK ABOUT A YEAR TO PROCESS *Salt of the Earth* for distribution and showing. IPC resorted to pseudonyms and other evasive measures to avoid Roy Brewer's long reach. Brewer's threats were credible given that the studios controlled 85 percent of theaters and that projectionists belonged to Brewer's union. The American Legion visited the remaining independent theaters, threatening pickets and other demonstrations should they attempt to show *Salt*.[1] Under union and public pressure, IPC had limited showings in March 1954 in New York, where it ran for weeks at the third-rate Grand Theater on East 86th Street. But IPC could not obtain a projectionist at another theater or a showing in the union meccas of Chicago and Detroit. In Denver, Mine-Mill's home city, only one theater in suburban Arvada ran the film for a mere four days, and even then, IPC could not get a firm commitment until ninety minutes before the first private showing. IPC did have limited success in the Bay Area and Los Angeles, where the film ran for eleven weeks.

Salt of the Earth opened in Silver City in May. Threatened, local theaters refused to show it. Catholic Bishop Sidney M. Metzger warned his flock not to see the Communist movie,[2] opposition Virginia Chacón understood well. "We were Communists," she said, "How were they going to support us?" The Sky Vue Drive In Theater owner was the last man standing. He disregarded threats and pressure and agreed to show *Salt*. The theater's playbill advertised, "Salt of the Earth, A Picture 90 Per Cent of the People of Grant County Want to See." In a town of fifteen thousand, five thousand lined up in their cars for five days to see the film. To Virginia Jencks's disappointment, no Hollywood personalities attended. There were also no showings in the mining states of Utah, Montana, or Idaho, where theater owners succumbed to the threat, "If you play that film, you'll never get another."[3]

All told, *Salt* ran in only thirteen theaters nationally. IPC claimed that one hundred thousand saw the film in the United States. Finally, all they had left was the international market, but even it, though laudatory, produced negligible revenue. The film had a ten-month run in France, was an award-winning hit in Czechoslovakia, and ran in China for fifteen years but produced no revenue for IPC. What remained for IPC was litigation, but it too proved a failure. In all, IPC lost its $250,000 investment. Sixteen-millimeter prints played to college and university audiences for years, and the film became a cult attraction. In 1992, the Library of Congress added *Salt* to the National Film Registry to conserve and protect it as part of the nation's heritage. Although the film's thirty-five-millimeter version was an economic loss, in time its other versions would be an artistic success and an inspiration to many.[4]

THE JENCKSES

After the trial, Clinton and Virginia moved to the California Bay Area where they did not expect to be so controversial and could find work in a more liberal atmosphere.[5] Once in the Bay Area, Jencks applied for a job with Stauffer Chemical, passed its employment tests, and showed up for work with his machinist tools. When he reported, the foreman told Jencks that the manager wanted to see him. The manager told Jencks that executives had vetoed his employment.[6] Later, he found work as a millwright at CertainTeed, a roofing material manufacturer. After successfully working there, the shop steward stopped by and told him, "Jencks, I don't know what you have done to get the boss so stirred up, but he is demanding that I get you out of here immediately!" Jencks described his controversial background, and the steward insisted on talking to the manager, saying that he could not be fired for what he had done. The steward returned and explained to Jencks that the "manager claims two guys came into the office saying that you are a Communist known for stirring up stuff on the job." The manager promised a good recommendation if Jencks voluntarily quit. He was terminated. A review of years of FBI surveillance explains the two CertainTeed visitors dressed in suits.[7] After the Denver FBI office removed Jencks from the key figure list, the bureau questioned the decision. Jencks's conviction may have been vacated and his case dismissed, but this did not mean that he was no longer subject to FBI scrutiny. Far from it. The FBI and anti-Communist personalities were determined to see Jencks ruined.

Jencks's employment difficulties continued. He found work as a machinist for General Foods, but after several months he was terminated, told to leave the plant the next day, and given no explanation. Next came machinist work at Litton Industries where, after being there for some time, he was given some forms to fill out. In time, he was terminated without explanation. He was unemployed for some time before finding his next job, as a millwright-machinist at American Can Company in Oakland. He was happy in his job there until an engineer pointed to an article about the Supreme Court and Jencks in *Time* magazine. Jencks explained his predicament, and this time, his boss said that he could keep his job until management said otherwise. Although Jencks was happy about his Supreme Court victory, he was determined to move on from his employment problems and find a new career.[8]

In October 1958, Jencks's daughter Linda showed him an ad in a student newspaper advertising Woodrow Wilson Fellowships for graduate study at the University of California at Berkeley. Jencks, wanting to escape the blacklist, applied for the fellowship and for admission to the economics PhD program. He succeeded in both. In March, the foundation announced the recipients of the prestigious fellowships.[9] Soon thereafter, HUAC chair Francis E. Walter announced that the committee would hold hearings to investigate California teachers and the Wilson fellowships, including the one Jencks received. Anti-Communists were outraged that a Communist had received a grant to become a teacher. Just as Jencks prepared to enter the 1959 school year in a challenging program, he was subpoenaed to appear before HUAC that summer in Washington.[10]

On July 22, 1959, HUAC questioned Jencks in an executive session in Washington, D.C. The obvious purpose in calling Jencks was to embarrass the Woodrow Wilson Foundation and the university and end Jencks's academic career. Risking the trap of answering enough questions to waive his constitutional rights, Jencks walked a fine line that bordered on belligerence. He questioned the pertinence of the interrogation and the hearings' legislative purpose. He did his best to avoid stating that he was refusing to answer on grounds of self-incrimination, and when forced to do so used different terminology. HUAC wanted to know who had supported his fellowship and pressed him on whether he told the foundation about his CP background or his conviction. Did he tell the fellowship committee whether he had signed a false non-Communist affidavit? Clearly the committee, at a minimum, wanted Jencks to leave the hearing room "a fifth amendment Communist." Jencks denied that he was then a Communist. "I am not now a member of the Communist Party nor was I at the time I was nominated for a fellowship by the Woodrow Wilson National Fellowship Foundation. However, as to questions covering any prior period, I must object."[11] The committee then went through the back door and asked if Jencks was against the CP. Jencks avoided the question, but noted, "Certainly I have many differences with the Communist Party, many, many differences." Jencks was asked if he ever resigned from the CP but remained under its discipline. He denied that he had ever done so.[12] The committee resented but was powerless to prevent Jencks's statement that he had been vindicated by the Supreme Court. Of course, Jencks was correct in saying so, and it was the committee that demonstrated its ignorance of the presumption of innocence.[13] A conviction removes the presumption and replaces it with a guilty finding; a conviction's reversal reinstitutes the presumption of innocence as though there had been no trial. HUAC resorted to practices that had ruined witnesses in the past.[14] Normally, the FBI and the committees exposed suspected subversives, and private industry and institutions completed the damage by ending employment or tarnishing a reputation. The committee fully expected that Jencks would not be a Woodrow Wilson Fellow. Even though Jencks had resigned from the CP in 1949 and did not again engage in Party activities, the FBI continued to monitor the man and keep his name on the Security Index with a DETCOM tab, meaning that Jencks would be immediately arrested in a national emergency.[15]

Once Jencks completed his testimony, the worried Wilson Foundation director called him and asked to meet at the organization's Princeton headquarters. Jencks arrived at Princeton to find the director concerned, because agents had asked to review foundation files. Jencks was told that the foundation would notify him of its decision in a month or two. Two months later, the foundation confirmed that he would be a fellow, and the university admitted him to its fall semester.[16] The anti-Communist tide seemed to be in decline.

For the next several years, Jencks would be grinding out the difficult life of a married graduate student. He served as a teaching assistant during his second and third years, but still worked at odd jobs to support the family. By 1962, the Jencks children were grown and had left home. Jencks later explained that at this time, long-standing marital differences with Virginia surfaced, causing the couple's separation and eventual divorce. He admitted that his "own shortcomings were sufficient to prevent [him] from being able to create solutions for our marital problems." Virginia, for her part, may have precipitated the couple's separation when she went on a tour around the world sponsored by a friend.

For his fourth year, Jencks was nominated for a Fulbright Fellowship to finance a stay in Great Britain to conduct research for his doctoral dissertation. The program was federally funded and administered under the State Department. Though he was initially approved, the application was later declined by what Jencks called "the political screening process." The university made up for the slight by awarding Jencks a Newton Booth Traveling Fellowship in Economics.[17] In March 1962, Jencks left Berkeley to spend eight months studying British coal miners, the subject of his dissertation. After his British research stay, he returned to Berkeley to write his dissertation. By December 1963, he was ready to look for an academic position. He expected his past to be an issue, so he was open about his union activities and the Supreme Court case. Around this time he remarried, to Florence "Chickie" Bird, but that marriage soon ended in divorce.[18]

In June 1964, he graduated from the prestigious University of California at Berkeley and became Clinton E. Jencks, Doctor of Philosophy. He received several job offers, and accepted one from San Diego State University, which allowed him to be near his father and family in Long Beach. He reported for work in August 1964.[19]

One week after he began teaching, Jencks was given a bulletin called "Evolve" published by the Young Americans for Freedom, a conservative campus political organization. The publication carried a cartoon connecting Jencks to overreaching by the Supreme Court, calling it "Government by Gavel." A month later, a reporter from the *Daily Aztec,* the campus newspaper, called Jencks and told him that a John Birch Society member had provided material on Jencks. The *Daily Aztec* interviewed Jencks and published a straightforward story about his background and his Supreme Court case. The economics department chair was not troubled by the commotion, saying that Jencks was qualified to teach economics and would be retained. Four days later, the *San Diego Union* followed up with a story titled, "SDS Hires Ex-Labor

Aide," noting Jencks's Communist past. After speaking with the university's president, Jencks met with the faculty senate. Its members noted that the university had been hurt "during the earlier witch-hunts of the McCarthy period" and urged Jencks to stay calm and keep a low profile.

Jencks went on to serve the university with distinction. He received a grant to spend a year at Boulder, Colorado, assembling and organizing the Mine-Mill Union and Western Federation of Miners archives as well as his own papers.[20] Jencks moved up the academic ranks, becoming full professor in the economics department and director of the Institute for Labor Economics. He remained a committed leftist, supporting various causes, but he also joined others in showing independence from the Party long after he quit.[21] In 1971, he married Muriel Sobelman-Brodshatzer, became devoted to her family, and converted to Judaism. He had open-heart surgery in 1985 and retired from teaching in June 1988. Jencks died in San Diego at age eighty-seven on December 15, 2005.[22]

After her 1962 divorce from Clinton, Virginia Jencks met and married Thomas Chambers, another UC Berkeley graduate student. Eventually, the couple moved to Grand Rapids, Michigan, where Chambers taught, and Virginia continued being an activist. She died on February 22, 1990, at age seventy-two. She requested that her ashes be spread at Local 890's Bayard union hall.[23] Their daughter, Linda Halley Rageh, remained in the East Bay area, where she died in 2017. Son Clinton Michael had a troubled life and died in Grand Rapids in 1996.

THE REVEREND JERRY W. FORD
AND HARVEY MARSHALL MATUSOW

After the Jencks trial, the Reverend Jerry W. Ford continued with his ministry in the African Methodist Episcopal Church. In 1980, he was considered for the position of bishop for his church's general conference. He was an active speaker at churches in his region. He was pastor at churches in Phoenix, Los Angeles, and finally in San Francisco, where he died in 1979 at the age of 53.[24]

And, of course, there was Harvey Marshall Matusow, without whom there would have been no trial, Supreme Court case, or Jencks Act. Matusow's New York perjury conviction was affirmed, and he served forty-four months in federal prison. He was released in 1960 and returned to New York City, where he was active publishing art books and a counterculture Village newspaper. He married briefly and had one child, a daughter. In 1966, he went to London, where he became involved in underground entertainment and performance. He married again in 1967, and in 1973 returned to the United States, where he separated from his wife. He lived for a period in a Massachusetts commune and married a minister, Emily Babbitt. The marriage was to be his longest and ended with her death in 1989. Matusow then moved to Tucson, reconnected with the Church of Jesus Christ of Latter Day Saints, and worked in children's theater. Late in his life he became involved in public access television in Utah and finally in New Hampshire, where in 2002 he died at age seventy-five from injuries he sustained in a traffic accident. After his time in prison, Matusow appears to have led a well-intentioned, productive life devoted to charitable endeavors. In its obituary on the man, the *New York Times* estimated that Matusow had married around a dozen times. No one would dispute Matusow's claim that his life had been "a lifelong three ring circus."[25]

17

SOME OBSERVATIONS

AMONG THE RESEARCH MATERIALS for this book are thousands of pages of FBI reports and memos detailing how government agents monitored and surveilled Clinton Jencks, his union brethren, and fellow Communist Party members. Because the FBI's work is to investigate criminal activity and that which imperils the nation's security and domestic order, its reports have an implicit conspiratorial undertone suggesting sinister and illegal activity on the part of those being monitored. Yet after reading those Jencks and Mine-Mill reports, one is left to conclude that there was nothing illegal or sinister going on at all in those files; it was like reading volume after volume of Elks Lodge minutes. What the FBI reported were the regular membership activities of legal and legally protected institutions, including the Communist Party, labor union locals, left-wing associations, and clubs. The evil is not found in Jencks's or his associates' conduct; rather it was in the skewed perspective of the government and the FBI, which viewed the surveilled as dangerous and disloyal individuals who belonged to suspect organizations. The national hysteria over communism drove this view, which was fanned by Hoover's FBI and followed a tradition of left-wing repression going back to the 1886 Hay Market Affair.

What exactly *was* illegal about what Jencks did at those meetings or in life? There is no evidence, not even a hint, indicating that Jencks and his union brothers were disloyal, spies, traitors, or saboteurs. They were union men and women legally working in their manner for what they believed was a better life, and whatever political views they had were protected by the Constitution. Anti-Communists persuaded Americans to fear communism and believe that Party members' activities were illegal. It was akin to the thinking that led to the internment of Japanese Americans during World War II, so flimsy in its logic that the pervasive anxiety resembled a mass sociogenic illness.

In logic, the thinking behind FDR's Japanese internment was based on what is known as a syllogism. As applied to Fred Korematsu, one of the interned Japanese who took his case to the Supreme Court, it goes like this: the major premise was that all Japanese were loyal to the Empire, would collude with the Empire, and constituted a threat to U.S. security. The minor premise was that Korematsu was Japanese. The inescapable conclusion was that because Korematsu was Japanese, he would collude with the Empire and constituted a security threat. The Ringle report exposed the major premise's fallacy that all Japanese would collude with the Empire. And did we really need a Ringle report to know that U.S. Japanese were not disloyal?[1] The fact we as a nation arrived at the opposite conclusion demonstrates the power of unreasoning fear.

The McCarthy era's premise was that Party members were loyal to the USSR and would collude with the Kremlin; Jencks and others were Party members; therefore, they would be Soviet operatives and a threat to U.S. security. Using that logic, all it took was CP membership to conclude that a person would be disloyal and a national security threat—ignoring the fact that membership was a legal status.[2] And so membership became the heart—and usually the end—of any inquiry. Any crimes associated with membership would almost always be collateral, such as perjury, contempt, a false statement, etc., rather than substantive violations such as treason, espionage, sabotage, or an attempt to overthrow the government. Fear over revealing CP membership often induced those collateral crimes despite that membership's legal and protected status.

McCarthyism's major premise was not only far off the mark; it was almost the truth's opposite. Hoover's FBI knew that it employed a false syllogism. It knew then what we know today—now that we too have access to FBI files—that Jencks and almost all CP members were neither disloyal nor a threat to the United States. While some in the Communist Party's leadership worked to recruit Soviet spies during World War II, an estimated 49,700 out of its 50,000 members were "uninvolved in espionage, even taking the highest estimate of communist participation in the KGB's network."[3] The FBI made few cases supporting the theory that CP members were Soviet operatives, and later projects, such as the Venona cables, revealed that less than one percent of CP members colluded in any respect. The Soviets had a large American espionage operation, but the FBI never objectively assessed the actual risk posed by Party members, especially the rank and file.

Between 1945 and 1953, the Soviet Union's intelligence assets in the United States dried up, and the Soviets realized that recruiting from Communist Party ranks had been an error.[4] The FBI caught only a handful of spies, and the bureau recognized that McCarthy was ineffectual in finding them as well. Thomas Powers wrote, "As a spy hunter McCarthy was a complete failure. His elastic numbers, never the same two days running, were much derided at the time; he never found even a single genuine Communist in the government; none of those he named recklessly during his hour on the stage was ever proved to have been a spy; and none of them appear in the Venona traffic or the documents published by [Allen] Weinstein and others."[5]

Why would the FBI and high government officials sell a premise that they knew was wrong? Because the fear and the anxiety their exaggerations generated empowered them and weakened their political opposition. It also weakened the CP and its political programs. Anticommunism's excesses decimated the Party and certainly blunted the left wing—the progressive edge of what had been a broad political coalition—while it strengthened the opposite end of the political spectrum. The shrinkage and weakening of the progressive left wing continued until anticommunism's excesses convinced Americans that enough was enough.

Communists and the left wing threatened the social and economic fabric that included segregation and discrimination, which spread far beyond the South. In some ways, CP members resembled the post–Civil War Freedmen's Bureau. Communists were decades ahead in pushing for stronger unions, civil rights, and equality for women, blacks, Mexicans, and others, while many important anti-Communist figures did the opposite and were on the front lines in promoting antilabor and Jim Crow laws and forcefully resisted the civil rights movement. Southern arch-segregationists played prominent roles on HUAC and the Senate Internal Security Subcommittee.[6] Although

Communists were hated and feared by the right for their alleged—although minimal—Soviet connections, they were reviled more for their work to upset the domestic social and economic order. Communist-dominated labor unions such as Mine-Mill led much of that work. The same hatred would later come down on Martin Luther King, who had no pro-Soviet agenda but rather one that threatened the South's social order.

More than the Soviet menace, many anti-Communists resisted the fearsome foreign hordes, blacks and browns threatening white America. It was no accident that anti-Communists successfully pushed repressive immigration legislation to accompany southern Jim Crow laws, including the Alien Registration Act of 1940 (Smith Act), the immigration provisions in the Internal Security Act of 1950, and the Immigration and Nationality Act of 1952. The "others" they sought to repress, deport, and control were a convenient bundle of anti-Communist targets not considered American enough: people of color, those who spoke with an accent or in a foreign language, and immigrants, especially those from Russia and Eastern Europe, many of whom were Jews. It gave anticommunism a distinct racist, xenophobic, and anti-Semitic cast. To novelist Philip Roth, anti-Communists "could transform a personal prejudice into a political weapon by confirming for Gentile America that, in New York as in Hollywood, in radio as in movies, the Communist under every rock was, nine times out of ten, a Jew to boot."[7]

The closest Jencks and his fellow union men and women came to illegal activity would be in actions surrounding the EZ strike, during which both sides engaged in violent acts, rock throwing, blocking cars, and the like—activities commonly associated with picket line altercations. Only the antiunion side, engaged in shootings and arson. Certainly, Jencks was himself the victim of several assaults and was never the attacker.

The significant criminal and unethical acts to emerge from the anti-Communist era—and they are numerous—were in fact committed by the FBI and the Justice Department. There are references to illegal and unethical FBI black bag jobs, illegal entry and search of Jencks's apartment, subornation of perjury, wanton civil rights violations, and certainly threats without cause against the civil liberties of those they were duty bound to protect.[8] The Department of Justice staff repeatedly misled the courts, either suborned perjury or knowingly permitted it to occur in their presence, and tried to hound a man they knew was innocent into federal prison rather than leave him and his family alone. And that was just the government.

There was also the conduct of the FBI's anti-Communist allies, such as Roy Brewer and others, who received federal protection and assistance despite violating the commercial and civil rights of those who simply wanted to make a union film. The violence and threats against Local 890 and the film crew by Anglo vigilantes and the Grant County establishment were also criminal and were ignored by law enforcement, making them complicit in the illegal behavior.

What are we to make of the main actors in the Jencks case?

JUDGE THOMASON

Thomason was a rigid, committed anti-Communist and a fervent admirer of J. Edgar Hoover. Justice Department lawyers and the FBI misled the judge, but Thomason willingly played into their hands by refusing to examine reports when he should have done so. The judge was unwilling to follow routine procedures, which might have prevented his mistakes or allowed appellate courts to correct his errors. Two years after the trial, Thomason wrote a column for the *El Paso Times* and mentioned *Jencks* as one of his significant cases. Thomason was clearly proud of the way he had handled the case. He went to his grave ignorant that he had been misled by the Department of Justice and the FBI, had committed grave errors, and nearly sent an innocent man to prison.[9] The appellate court judges were equally negligent in that they saw and then overlooked Thomason's errors. Not even Tom Clark, his fellow Texan and lone defender on the Supreme Court, could explain Thomason's failure and adamant refusal to review the Ford and Matusow reports, because his action was indefensibly erroneous.

Thomason had another side that cannot be ignored: he was intelligent and knew his community. How, then, could he have allowed his jury commissioner, year after year, to serve up panels that were so unrepresentative of the community? As a former trial lawyer himself, Thomason could not have been blind to that, especially since it was brought to his attention. This problem cannot be written off as an omission. The method used to select names for the jury box was known and intentional. One can only speculate as to how many in addition to Jencks were deprived of a fair trial as a result.

Thomason leaves a confused and paradoxical record. On the one hand, his history reveals a man of moderation, decency, good instincts, fairness, progressive traits, and liberal views on race, despite having a Confederate veteran father. But when it came to Communists, Thomason exhibited none of those qualities. Lawyer Nathan Witt was a keen observer who saw Thomason's interactions with immigrant defendants. To Witt, the judge seemed a "very humane, very kind, and very patient man," but with Communists, "we had a tough judge to deal with, who was a wild man on the red issue."[10] While judges may not like the defendants who enter their courtrooms, they are obligated to set aside their personal distaste and accord the accused a fair trial. That Thomason failed to do for Jencks. He was no longer a judge; he became part of the prosecution, unreasonable and biased toward Communists. It was not just Witt who observed that bias: Earl Warren made mention of it at least twice in the court's Friday conferences, and it is also evident in the trial record. Thomason was not a detached arbiter in the case, and he allowed his views to steer him into committing grievous judicial error.

THE GOVERNMENT

FBI reports and the government's conduct in the Jencks case raise serious questions over how the FBI and Justice Department planned the Jencks prosecution and handled the controversy following Matusow's retraction. Given the Rev. Ford's numerous reports that Jencks had resigned and the government's realization that Matusow was untrustworthy, it is difficult to escape the conclusion that the government could not build a case unless it distorted the record, possibly suborned perjury, and certainly relied on known untrustworthy witnesses. Bureau executives expressed incredulity regarding the department's use of Matusow, yet the FBI remained complicit in his use as a witness and in covering up his file. Recently released government records prove that the FBI knew by December 1949, and the Department of Justice knew by 1952, that Jencks had resigned, was never again active in the Party, and was not a Party member or affiliate when the 1950 affidavit was filed. They knew that they were prosecuting an innocent man.

In its attempt to convict Jencks and prove that he was a Party member or affiliate on April 28, 1950, the prosecution called the Rev. J. W. Ford as a witness. How could prosecutor Alderman put Ford on the stand knowing he would testify that Jencks had resigned from the Party and had been replaced on the New Mexico executive committee? They had Ford's statements, which confirmed over and again that Jencks had resigned. Ford testified that the prosecutors chose not to show him his own statements to refresh his memory.[11] Even so, it was improbable that Ford had forgotten about the Jencks resignation, considering that he had reported it so many times. This begs the question: who encouraged Ford to say that he had no knowledge of the resignation? The prosecution would certainly have known how Ford would testify on the trial's key issue before putting him on the witness stand, so they must have known that he would falsely deny knowledge of the Jencks resignation. Keeping Ford's reports secret was crucial to their strategy, and in that, Thomason was a cooperative, if unwitting, player. Had the resignation reports surfaced, they would have ended the case.

Then there is Matusow's testimony. Instead of admitting that Matusow was a liar who frequently fabricated testimony and confessing error, the government twisted itself into a pretzel arguing that though Matusow was a habitual liar who had lied in his retraction, he had been uncharacteristically candid at the Jencks and Flynn trials. Publicly, Hoover vouched for Matusow's 1954 Jencks trial testimony, but FBI records now reveal that in 1953, the director himself had urged the Justice Department to prosecute Matusow for perjury. Led by Hoover and Attorney General Brownell, the government compounded its unethical misbehavior and alleged that Matusow's retraction was a Communist plot to damage the anti-Communist effort, making yet another false accusation.

It is impossible at this date to piece together what prosecutors in El Paso knew. The prosecutors observed at the time of the Jencks trial that Matusow had an air of "falsity."[12] It is possible that apart from U.S. attorney Herring, who handled Matusow as a witness, the local prosecutors might not have read all of the Ford or Matusow statements, as they were relatively far removed from the case's ultimate handlers. One of the local prosecutors denied knowing that Jencks had resigned from the Party. But Alderman and the Washington lawyers, who handled Ford and had an extensive history with Matusow, certainly read the critical memos.[13] The FBI, as author of the reports, absolutely had all the facts, and as the FBI contended, the Justice Department in Washington had the memos. Washington-based department lawyers were all fully knowledgeable about Ford and Matusow at the hearing on the motion for new trial. There were countless opportunities, including at the Supreme Court argument and afterward, for the government to act honorably, correct the record, and give Jencks the justice he deserved. While Judge Thomason's error was a grave omission, Hoover's FBI and the Department of Justice acted knowingly.

During the McCarthy era, the government recklessly used unreliable anti-Communist informants and witnesses and willingly permitted illegality and perjury. These practices, coupled with the red scare's ginned-up hysteria, likely resulted in the unethical prosecution or mistreatment of many others. At this date, we can only speculate as to how many.

THE JENCKSES

It was legal to be a Communist Party member and to run as a Communist candidate for public office. Unfortunately, in the early years, except for a few individuals, the Party chose secrecy for its members even when they could have been open. Later, when Party membership—although still legal— became a liability, ended many careers, and exposed members to criminal prosecution and economic ruin, secrecy became a necessity. This secrecy and conspiratorial nature made Communists appear guilty and suspicious, and by adopting it, Communists themselves helped stoke the fires that engulfed them in the 1940s and '50s.

As the U.S. Party followed the abrupt reversals in Soviet policy and remained silent as a murderous Stalin exterminated or imprisoned millions, many Party members failed to speak out. Most American Communists either engaged in studied ignorance of Stalin's crimes or managed the cognitive dissonance of maintaining idealism on the one hand while supporting Stalin's policies on the other. Perhaps they refused to admit that the idealistic group they joined in the '30s and '40s had turned murderous under Stalin. To Paul Jarrico, a former Communist and friend of Jencks, it had been "stupid" to accept "Stalin as the fount of all wisdom" but, he added, "stupidity is not treason."[14] Isserman and Schrecker wrote that "American Communist Party recruits in the 1930s believed that they were signing onto a worldwide class and antifascist struggle, not enlisting on one side in a superpower conflict. . . . Communists remained deeply, willfully, and, yes, tragically, blind to the true nature of Stalin's regime."[15]

American Communists like Jencks were, after all, individuals who had paid a high price for their beliefs and associations in a nation that claimed to prize and protect the right to believe, express, and associate with the most despicable and odious ideas, groups, and individuals. The 1940s and 1950s was a time when the unthinkable became not only acceptable but also legal, including the mass arrest, internment, and dispossession of innocent West Coast Japanese of all ages or the wholesale attempt to destroy many Americans for their left-wing beliefs or associations despite no proof of criminal conduct or any credible threat to the nation's security. It was in such an environment that Clinton and Virginia Jencks lived.

Given the Party's secrecy, the little we know about Clinton Jencks, the Communist, we know from limited sources. Government files reveal his actions and associations, but we have few reports regarding his membership, whether he believed in the Party's policy choices, and what he thought of Stalin and his measures. We are ignorant of his stripe or type of communism, on what issues he might have disagreed with the Party, or whether he opposed its policies. It was apparently only with trusted fellow members that he might have been open and revealing, but they have not been forthcoming about his views, an understandable discretion and reluctance with such a sensitive and precarious subject.

Jencks granted numerous interviews, including several to his biographer James J. Lorence, but in them he was reticent and unrevealing for the most part about his Communist past, guarded as he should have been given his tribulations. Even to Lorence, with whom he developed a trusting friendship and longtime correspondence, Jencks did not reveal his former Party membership until some twelve years into their relationship, and that confession seemed to be a spontaneous outburst and afterthought.[16] Jencks wrote to Lorence and said that he believed that "all human beings are created equal, that we are endowed by our Creator with certain inalienable rights." He stated that he never believed in a dictatorship in whatever form and always believed "in economic and social forms that seek to empower and mutually benefit all."[17] Certainly his life supported that contention. In 1977, Jencks described his ideology as Christian socialism; at other times, he referred to it as democratic socialism.

What was it about Clinton Jencks that would take him down this path, one that would wreck part of his life, endanger his family, and cause him grief over the years? For his views and career, he and his family suffered abuse and harm. But it did not have to be that way. He had a college degree at a time when few were so qualified. He was intelligent and engaging. He could have been successful in any career he chose. What was it about communism and its real peril that attracted him? Clearly, Jencks was fulfilling a childhood ambition. He became both a missionary to and a fighter for the weak and oppressed. He was attracted to the Party because he found that its members were the most committed and militant in fighting for workers, the poor, and the marginalized. Every cell in his body was dedicated to that task, even when it hurt his wife, children, and the family's economic well-being.

Although Virginia and Clinton Jencks were committed to their union work and were steadfast left-wing activists, their children certainly paid a price for their parents' dedication. Jencks appeared altruistic, that is, one who is generous to a fault. But that generosity might also have fit into a personality that hungered for recognition, even when the publicity he sought might hurt him and his family. Nathan Witt described Clinton and Virginia in that manner. Jencks, Witt said, "was one of the more, without using the term 'invidious' invidiously, one of the best known, most notorious of the Mine, Mill personnel. He liked publicity—very active, very combative. . . . Scarcely a day went by during the [EZ] strike where there wasn't some episode, either an altercation on the picket line or a big argument" in Grant County. While the Jencks were secret Communists, they were notorious left-wingers. Several individuals described Virginia as being equally aggressive and political.[18]

What Witt described as the Jencks' attraction to publicity is consistent with the couple's desire for Jarrico make a film. There was reported tension between the Jencks and the filmmakers as well as between the Jencks and the Mexicans about the roles Clinton and Virginia would play. It was said that Jencks was going to give himself the lead, an Anglo arriving to fight for the Mexicans. Apparently, two Los Angeles African American Communists pressured Michael Wilson to change the film's focus to the Mexican strikers and their wives and have the Jencks assume subsidiary roles. It was not only Jencks who made others envious; Juan Chacón was roundly criticized for receiving too much attention as the male lead. There was no question that Jencks's high profile and the film's publicity raised tensions within Local 890.[19]

The film aside, Jencks was completely devoted to his union work and the membership. Many leftists were both union organizers and Communists. For Communists in Local 890, including Jencks, their union work seemed more important and appeared to be their focus. His daily work with the union appeared to have little to do with his Party membership. It seemed that membership added little except grief to his life. Virginia summed up her life after the prosecution, "My marriage ended. My children have been badly burned. *** Personally, I feel that our lives as a family was a defeat and not a victory."[20]

Years later, daughter Linda still had difficulty discussing what the family had experienced. Granddaughter Heather Wood felt the same. Even they, at such a remote time and place from the Grant County events, lost employment over Jencks's Party affiliation.[21] To Heather Wood, her grandparents' Party membership remains a delicate subject. While it seems that Clinton Jencks did leave the Party in his past, Virginia might have remained longer in the fight, although not as a Party member. Heather Wood wrote that Clinton Jencks was scarred by his experience and retreated from his prior activism, whereas Virginia did not.[22]

His activism in the past, Jencks settled into his fourth and final marriage and his life as an economics professor. He was a doting and warm grandparent. Despite some evidence that he earlier had a roving eye and had neglected his alimony payments,[23] Clinton Jencks was in most ways a deeply moral and ethical man. Early in his life, he developed an ethical framework based on his family's religious views. His mother's teachings seemed to have had a profound effect. He attacked greed, poverty, and racial inequality throughout his life. Aside from his impressive war record, which was inspired by his hatred of fascism and his need to fight what was to him a great evil, he appeared to be a pacifist. There is no mention of Jencks defending himself or striking back, even when his wife and daughter were attacked. In that sense, he turned the other cheek and perhaps invited more assaults for having done so.[24]

Anyone looking at his photographs soon notes a common feature: Jencks smiling, no matter the situation. He could be in negotiations or at the union hall, in jail or walking to and from his criminal trial. His was not a toothless grin but rather an open-mouthed, ear-to-ear, joyous smile. That smile went along with his sunny and optimistic personality. He clearly wanted to be loved and appreciated by the local's members, and that seems to have been the case. In remaining positive despite what must have been enormous stress, Jencks apparently internalized his fears and the unbearable pressure he must have experienced. While overcoming his trials, Jencks never turned his back on Local 890 or his Mexican friends there. He returned and participated in several reunions and commemorations. His tombstone bears the name the Mexican miners bestowed, "Palomino."

As for his and Virginia's legacy in Grant County, it may have been ephemeral. There is no union local today in Grant County. The underground mines are closed, and the union was decertified at the large Santa Rita Chino open pit mine. Santa Rita, the company town, was itself swallowed up by the pit, and today its relocated housing is scattered around Grant County. And what of the local women, who played such a crucial role in the EZ strike? According to some observers, they returned to their old ways; Jencks said that the women "slid back into the old way but not all the way back."[25] What does remain are the memories and record left by Local 890; the EZ strike; its leaders, such as Jencks and Chacón; the trailblazing women like Virginia Jencks, Virginia Chacón, and Anita Tórrez. *Salt of the Earth* has survived. It remains an inspiration to thousands of college students and others who have seen and studied it, and it remains a staple in Chicano studies.[26]

What has not been ephemeral is the impact and legacy of *Jencks v. United States* and the Jencks Act. For decades, it has been mandatory for criminal defense lawyers to demand *Jencks* statements and exculpatory *Brady* materials.[27] The *Jencks* decision made more effective the right to confront a witness and partially opened the hitherto closed, "sacrosanct" FBI files. It is difficult to overstate the importance of *Jencks v. United States.* Had its benefits existed for Clinton Jencks, it is doubtful that the government would have brought his prosecution in the first place.

The power of their personal story is in the idealism Clinton and Virginia Jencks clung to even in the face of enormous abuse. Their lives leave no doubt that they each had an overwhelming drive to fight for economic, social, and racial justice. Clinton Jencks arrived in Grant County already holding the same civil rights views as Grant County's Mexicans, views at odds with his union's Denver leadership. In advocating for the Mexican membership's views, Jencks never wavered for one minute, and for that Local 890 Mexicans looked on him as a brother.

■

It was unreasoned and unjustified fear, about which Franklin Roosevelt warned us, which drove this nation to deny Jencks the right to pursue happiness, his political beliefs, and his chosen career. The government improperly filed criminal charges against him and denied him several constitutional rights in handling his case. It would have denied him even more civil liberties had there been a national emergency, which would have immediately brought about his unwarranted arrest and internment under the various FBI security programs. The overblown domestic Communist threat produced the unreasoned fear that wrecked a part of Clinton Jencks's life. Even those who later admitted the threat's overstatement went along with the era's repressive measures, yielding to political pressures generated by that national hysteria. Many Americans chose to join rather than be crushed by the anti-Communist stampede. Given more than a decade's hindsight, even former attorney general, Justice Tom C. Clark, whose "overwrought" *Jencks* dissent was part of the hysteria, later confessed that indeed, "the Communist scare was highly exaggerated."[28]

NOTES

INTRODUCTION

1. "Text of the Inaugural Address; President for Vigorous Action," *New York Times*, March 5, 1933. Roosevelt apparently paraphrased Henry David Thoreau, who wrote, "Nothing is so much to be feared as fear." Emerson, *Henry Thoreau*, 72.

2. Executive Order 9066, F.R. [Federal Register] 1407, February 19, 1942; Executive Order 9102, F.R. 2165, March 20, 1942, and related military proclamations.

3. *Korematsu v. United States*, 323 U.S. 214 (1944); see also, *Hirabayashi v. United States*, 320 U.S. 81 (1943). Recently, in upholding a presidential order restricting entry by those from certain named countries, and seventy-six years after *Korematsu* was decided, the Supreme Court finally set aside its 1944 holding. "*Korematsu* was gravely wrong the day it was decided, has been overruled in the court of history, and—to be clear—'has no place in law under the Constitution.' 323 U.S., at 248 (Jackson, J., dissenting)." *Trump v. Hawaii*, 585 U.S. ____ (2018).

4. *Hohri v. United States*, 782 F.2d 227, 234 (D.C. Cir. 1986); rehearing denied in 793 F.2d 304; vacated and remanded by the Supreme Court in 482 U.S. 64 (1987). See also *Final Report, Japanese Evacuation from the West Coast 1942*; Peter Irons, *Justice at War*.

5. Edward Ennis, director of the Alien and Enemy Control Unit in the Justice Department, came across the report of Lt. Comm. Kenneth D. Ringle of Naval Intelligence and advised the solicitor general that "we should consider very carefully whether we do not have a duty to advise the Court of the existence of the Ringle

memorandum and that this represents the view of the Office of Naval Intelligence. It occurs to me that any other course of conduct might approximate the suppression of evidence." *Hohri v. United States*, 782 F.2d 227 at 234.

6. Katyal, "The Solicitor General," 3037.

7. The Communist Party of the United States will be referred to as "CP" or "Party."

8. Schrecker, *Many Are the Crimes*, x; Schrecker, *Age of McCarthyism*, 2.

9. Schrecker, *Many Are the Crimes*, x, 309–10.

10. The building, no longer the federal court but still a federal building, was named after United States district judge R. E. Thomason in 2017.

CHAPTER 1

1. The Jencks personal and family history is found in *Genealogy of the Jenks Family of America*, the handwritten family history Dewitt C. Jencks deposited with the Colorado Springs Century Chest Collection; Bicknell, *The History of the State of Rhode Island and Providence Plantations*; Browne, *Jenks Family in America*; Cleary, *Jenks Genealogy with Allied Families*; and Chapin, *Chapin Genealogy*. Most of what is written about Clinton Jencks's boyhood and early years comes from "Palomino," his unpublished memoir, Box 1, Folder 1, Jencks Papers, University of Colorado; International Union of Mine, Mill and Smelter Workers (hereafter IUMMSW), "Portrait of a Labor Organizer," c.1956, Box 1, Folder 5, Jencks Papers, University of Colorado; a short, biographical note in his personal papers (Jencks, Biographical note); Jencks's autobiographic note in Fariello, *Red Scare;* Jencks to James J. Lorence, letter, June 17, 1999, Jencks-Lorence Correspondence Folder, Jencks Papers, University of Colorado; Lorence, *Palomino;* undated memoranda from Clinton and Virginia Jencks to Michael Wilson, found in Folder 7, Box 45, Michael Wilson Papers, UCLA; an undated (possibly 1950s), typewritten note by his mother, Ruth Jencks, to an unknown individual who was writing an article about Jencks, found in Box 1, Folder 23, Lorence Papers; Jencks interview by Patricia Burch Vaughn, c. March 1987, Vaughn Papers; Jencks interviews with James J. Lorence, June 19, 1996 and October 3, 1997, Lorence Papers; letters from Linda Rageh to James Lorence, Box 1, Folder 22, Lorence Papers; and an interview of Jencks by Albert Kahn, July 26, 1977, Box 1, Kahn Papers.

2. A description of the Saugus Iron Works by the American Society of Mechanical Engineers credits Jencks with inventing the scythe and building America's first fire engine. "Saugus Iron Works," National Park Service, June 15, 1975. In a work by the University of Notre Dame Library, Jenks is also assumed to have cut the dies for the first coins minted in Boston. "Joseph Jenks," https://coins.nd.edu/ColCoin/ColCoinIntros/MASilver.Jencks.intro.html.

3. The name Shideler is also found as Scheidler, Scheydler, Scheideler, Scheitler, etc.

4. Only scalawags, southern whites who sided with carpetbaggers, were more hated. See the numerous references to Freedmen's Bureau employees in Margaret Mitchell's *Gone with the Wind*.

5. "Horace Jencks and Miss Shideler Married," *Colorado Springs Gazette*, October 25 and 27, 1912.

6. The other three children were Arthur, Mervyn, and Rosemary. Lorence, *Palomino*, 3–5.

7. Horace and Ruth Jencks never agreed with Clinton's politics. Later, after he joined the CP, his mother wrote, "We all love Clinton very dearly and it has caused us a great deal of heartache because of all the trouble he has had. We do not agree with him politically." Ruth Jencks, undated note, Box 23, File 23, Lorence Papers.

8. Jencks, "Palomino," 2, Box 1, Folder 1, Jencks Papers, University of Colorado; Jencks to Lorence, June 17, 1999, 2, Jencks-Lorence Correspondence Folder, Jencks Papers, University of Colorado.

9. Some of the biographical material comes from an undated five-page memo from Jencks to Michael Wilson, Box 45, Folder 7, Wilson Papers.

10. "About that time I got religion. My mother was active in the Methodist-Episcopal Church, and through her I came to believe that the church was the one hope of eliminating injustice and bigotry. And if this was true, it seemed to me that a missionary was the highest calling of all, for it meant bringing brotherhood to the oppressed peoples of the world. Dreaming about what I would do for a poor benighted heathen, I must have figured brotherhood would be realized in Colorado Springs long before I grew up." IUMMSW, "Portrait of a Labor Organizer," 3, c.1956, Box 1, Folder 5, Jencks Papers, University of Colorado.

11. Undated note by his mother Ruth Jencks, Box 1, Folder 23, Lorence Papers.

12. There was a Jim Crow-like atmosphere at Boulder before 1938, and the ASU led by Jencks worked to eliminate the discrimination. David Hays, memorandum on minorities at CU, Box 2, Folder 3, Lorence Papers. Jencks's early commitment to civil rights is documented in the transcript of a 1938 Jencks radio interview. Transcript, KFKA Greely, Box 2, Folder 3, Lorence Papers.

13. This is a common description of the reasons many chose to become Communists. Whittaker Chambers said that socialists and fellow travelers were in the main "sitting and talking." Chambers, *Witness*, 159. Young New York City schoolteacher David Friedman described how in his union, the Communists were "the most active and most dedicated" and the hardest working individuals. He knew that they were the ones he wanted to join in the work, and that was how he joined the Party. Schrecker, *The Age of McCarthyism*, 101.

14. Jencks to Lorence, June 17, 1999, 9a, Lorence Papers. The League was listed as a Communist organization by the attorney general. Schrecker, *The Age of McCarthyism*, 171.

15. The Brigade was listed as Communist by the attorney general. Schrecker, *The Age of McCarthyism*, 168.

16. Like other organizations, it split over the 1939 Hitler-Stalin Pact and lost the support of Eleanor Roosevelt. Despite its one-time White House support, broad base, and many prominent members, the congress made it on to the Attorney General's list as a Communist organization. Schrecker, *The Age of McCarthyism*, 169; Lorence, *Palomino*, 26–28.

17. Jencks, "Palomino," 7, Box 1, Folder 1, Jencks Papers, University of Colorado.

18. Linda Rageh to James Lorence, February 23, 2010, Box 1, Folder 22, Lorence Papers.

19. Jencks, "Palomino," 9, Box 1, Folder 1, Jencks Papers, University of Colorado; Lorence, *Palomino*, 30–31.

20. One of the citations read, "To First Lt. Clinton E. Jencks. Distinguished Flying Cross. For flight to Bonin Islands where they dropped medium altitude mines around the harbor to retard construction work. Had to fly very low with intense antiaircraft fire and possible air interceptors. "Extraordinary heroism" and "cool courage in the face of great danger." IUMMSW, "Portrait of a Labor Organizer," c.1956, Box 1, Folder 5, Jencks Papers, University of Colorado.

21. Ibid., 6, 7.

22. Lorence, *Palomino*, 39.

23. To the once-Communist Paul Jarrico, "The answer is that we did not want to know. We either refused to read works critical of the Soviet leadership or refused to believe what we read." Ceplair, *The Marxist*, 39–168.

24. Jencks interview by Albert Kahn, July 26, 1977, Box 1, Kahn Papers; Jencks to Lorence, June 17, 1999, part 4a, p.9a, Lorence Papers.

25. Guide to the Western Federation of Miners and International Union of Mine, Mill, and Smelter Workers Collection,

26. According to one writer, the Anglo Mine-Mill organizer at the ASARCO mill in Grant County had threatened to secede, and Jencks was detailed there to combine the locals and solve the problem. Hudson, "Mine-Mill," 68.

27. Lorence, *Palomino*, 50–51. Anita and Lorenzo were among those in Local 890 who became Communists. Arturo Flores said, "If Clint is a Communist, the Communists must be very good people." Flores did not believe that Jencks was Communist and stated that if he was, it would have made no difference to him. Interview of Arthur Flores by James Lorence, Box 2, Folder 10, Lorence Papers.

CHAPTER 2

1. Huggard, *Santa Rita*, 11; Lundwall, *Copper Mining*, 15, 16.

2. Acuña, *Corridors*, 48–49.

3. Ibid., 128.

4. Baker, *On Strike*, 17.

5. Huggard, *Santa Rita*, 110.

6. Census enumerators made marginal notes on the forms indicating residential districts. Perhaps living in Mexican Town was a state of mind. Census enumerator Lloyd A. Nelson, a Santa Rita mining engineer, surveyed the community for the 1920 census. As he mentally processed complex societal factors, he became the town's sociologist, deciding for posterity who resided in Mexican Town—and who did not. On the 1920 census form for Mexican Town, Nelson noted that Edward Moulton, a Texas-born Anglo with Irish parents, was a Mexican Town resident as he was married to Juliana, a Mexican. But in the brackets he drew to indicate Mexican town residents,

Nelson excluded Moulton's next-door neighbor, the popular Anglo deputy sheriff James Blair, from living in Mexican Town. Blair was also married to a Mexican; his wife Inez and their children lived in the same residence as Blair. The brackets included them as Mexican Town residents, but excluded Blair. 1930 U.S. Census, Santa Rita, Grant County, New Mexico, Precinct 13, Dist. 9-15, Sheet 22B; 1920 U.S. Census, Santa Rita, Grant County, New Mexico, Precinct 13, Dist. 49, Sheet 20B.

7. Baker, *On Strike*, 23.

8. Of the 484 Mexican workers in 1930 at the Santa Rita Chino mine, 420 were laborers, whereas only five Anglos were in that category. Of the 152 Mexicans at the Hanover mine, 113 were laborers in comparison to only eight who were Anglo. Baker, *On Strike*, 32.

9. "Mexicans" included U.S. citizens and native-born generational New Mexicans known as Spanish Americans, other U.S. citizen Mexican Americans, permanent U.S. resident Mexicans, temporary Mexican workers, and undocumented Mexicans.

10. Large U.S. firms pursued the profitable dual wage until the Civil Rights Act of 1964 finally outlawed the practice. In what is perhaps the most important U.S. employment case, Duke Power Company fought to retain the dual wage into the 1970s when it resorted to contrived testing to classify its black workers as "laborers" or janitors and continue to pay them a lower wage than whites, even after the Civil Rights Act. *Griggs v. Duke Power Co.*, 401 U.S. 424 (1971).

11. Jencks estimated that pay discrimination was costing Local 890 $440,000 annually and could have been twice that if one considered the cost of barriers to promotion. Jencks provided the example of a local in Laredo, Texas. Nationally, between 1947 and 1951 industry workers had received raises of fifty-four cents per hour, but in Laredo they received only twenty-three cents. Jencks, "Palomino," 53–54, Box 1, Folder 1, Jencks Papers, University of Colorado. Kennecott paid its workforce in Nevada more than 2 percent more than miners in New Mexico. Hodges, "Making and Unmaking," 49–50.

12. Paying lower wages to Mexicans and to residents of predominantly Mexican areas remained common in the Southwest and Texas. The state of Texas had for years used its border areas as a cash cow to fund statewide operations. Texas used block grants to redistribute federal funds, intended for low-income border residents, to wealthier areas of the state. Also, Texas had traditionally invested little in border areas, utilizing a skewed spending system that allowed other areas of the state to enjoy enhanced state funding at the border's expense. Border educational institutions were few, and those were inadequately funded. A 1987 LULAC lawsuit determined that the entire border region had few doctoral programs, a finding that prompted reform. Al Kauffman, "Lawsuit leads to improvements in border area higher education," *The Monitor* (McAllen), May 29, 2016, www.themonitor.com/opinion/columnists /commentary-lawsuit-leads-to-improvements-in-texas-border-higher-education /article_cc92bd68-2469-11e6-8543-371e9abe9135.html. The State of Texas also used the dual wage system in paying its border-area employees, Anglo and Mexican, less than those elsewhere. Unfortunately, some border business communities helped

perpetuate their addiction to a low wage structure by advertising that fact to attract bottom-feeding companies seeking low wages and unskilled labor. Later, NAFTA and a worldwide labor market revealed this to be a disastrous economic strategy from which those communities have yet to recover. It was the equivalent of giving a community's talented youth a one-way ticket out of town, as was revealed by the 2000 census and other censuses, which showed high rates of out migration by their educated. Shapleigh, *Texas on the Brink*.

13. To Jencks, the Mexicans in Grant County "had inherited a long and proud history of radicalism that had already welded them to the militant unionism represented by the WFM-IUMMSW [Mine-Mill] tradition." Their activities there became class-based to combat "racial discrimination and economic injustice." Lorence, *Palomino*, 43, 46–47.

14. *Regeneración*, December 23, 1911.

15. *Regeneración*, May 2, 1914. *Regeneración* noted that the Ludlow massacre was the deadliest strike in U.S. history.

16. At the Morenci strike, Mexicans did not strike as members of the WFM, which had discouraged Mexican membership, but rather as members of a *mutualista* society. The WFM took notice and no longer ignored the potential of Mexican membership. Mellinger, *Men Have Become*, 328, 332–33. Organized in a mutual-aid (*mutualista*) society, Mexican miners in Clifton-Morenci, one hundred miles from Silver City, went on strike in 1903. In 1906, Práxedis Guerrero started a Partido Liberal Mexicano (PLM) affiliate in Morenci and was joined by Manuel Sarabia. Together they started Obreros Libres (Free Workers). Albro, *To Die*, 30, 52. Guerrero requested that PLM recognize his group as party members. Guerrero arrived in Morenci by October 1905 and remained there until June 1907. Martínez Núñez, *La Vida Heróica*, 78. *Regeneración*, the radical Magonista newspaper, noted that in November 1911, several named Mexicans in Morenci formed the Grupo Obrero Comunista (Communist Labor Group), which sought affiliation with the PLM. *Regeneración* also reported that on April 18, 1912, a group of Mexicans employed at Hurley—a Grant County smelter—were expelled from the town because they were attempting to strike. The newspaper wrote that they were preparing to celebrate the May 5 holiday. *Regeneración*, May 11, 1912. *Regeneración* listed several Grant County residents as subscribers and contributors. *Regeneración*, August 5, 1911, February 3 and 10, March 23, May 4, 1912. Most of the subscribers were in Santa Rita with some in Mogollon. *Regeneración* also carried articles about labor incidents at Santa Rita. *Regeneración*, March 30, 1912.

17. Mellinger, *Men Have Become*, 323–24, 347.

18. Acuña, *Corridors*, 172; Huggard, *Santa Rita*, 94–95.

19. Cargill, *Empire and Opposition*, 9; Acuña, *Corridors*, 112; Huggard, *Santa Rita*, 93.

20. Lorenzo Tórrez attributes this early Mine-Mill organizing to Arturo Mata who, like Tórrez, was a member of the Communist Party. Tórrez also said that Kennecott forced workers to sign "yellow dog" cards, that is, agreements that the employees

would not join a union. Lorenzo Tórrez interview by Cargill, December 8, 1977, Box 1, Folders 6 and 19, Cargill Papers.

21. *Nevada Consolidated Copper*, NLRB Decisions, 26:1182, 1191; Baker, *On Strike*, 49.

22. *Nevada Consolidated Copper*, NLRB Decisions, 26:1182, 1189, 1192.

23. *Nevada Consolidated Copper*, NLRB Decisions, 26:1182, 1193–1200, August 24, 1940.

24. *National Labor Relations Board v. Nevada Consolidated Copper Corporation*, 316 U.S. 105 (1942), reversing *Nevada Consolidated Copper Corporation v. National Labor Relations Board*, 122 F.2d 587 (10th Cir. 1941).

25. Huggard, *Santa Rita*, 99.

26. Executive Order No. 8802; Dinwoodie, *Rise of Mine-Mill*, 50, 53–54. The advances included the Fair Employment Practices Commission that held hearings in the Southwest in 1943 and the Non-Ferrous Metals Commission under the wartime NLRB, the National War Labor Board, that mandated an end to the dual wage system. Case No. 111-718-D Non-Ferrous Metals Commission Files. 14 War Labor Reports 146, and 18 War Labor Reports 591.

27. Baker, *On Strike*, 60, 62–63.

28. Dinwoodie, *Rise of Mine-Mill*, 46.

29. James Robinson complained that the Mexican organizers sent to help him in Grant County were making his life difficult. "The average Anglo in this district considers the Spanish worker about three degrees below a dog," he wrote, "and our Spanish organizers continue to aggravate this condition by continually harping on equality." James Robinson to Allan D. McNeil, December 21, 1941, Box 35, Western Federation of Miners and International Union of Mine, Mill, and Smelter Workers archives, University of Colorado (hereafter cited as Mine-Mill archives). It was an understandable bitterness on the part of Arturo Mata, the organizer Robinson complained about, who was a child when his entire family was deported from Bisbee for his father's labor activities and did not return to the U.S. for some time. Dinwoodie, *The Rise*, 51. Spanish speaking Anglo organizer Harry Hafner had the same problem, and said that "Anglos were against him because he 'stressed the race discrimination issue entirely too much.'" James Robinson to Howard Goddard, October 27, 1941, Box 35, Mine-Mill archives.

30. Lorenzo Tórrez, for one, stated that the Communist Party successfully added those social concerns to the historic economic issues that interested unions. Lorenzo Tórrez interview by Cargill, December 8, 1977, Box 1, Folders 6 and 19, Cargill Papers.

CHAPTER 3

1. Isserman and Schrecker, "Dangerous Tendency," 159; Maurice Isserman, "They Led Two Lives," *New York Times*, May 9, 1999. Isserman wrote, "The average Communist in 1944 was far more likely to be a fur worker or a public school teacher than a policy maker in the Treasury Department, and thus an unlikely candidate

for Elizabeth Bentley to approach for workplace gossip. Of the approximately 50,000 party members in those years, 49,700 were not involved in spying, even taking the highest estimate of Communist participation in the spy network."

2. Athan Theoharis wrote that most of the information given to the Soviets "did not compromise U.S. security interests, including 'analyses and commentary,' reports on the plans of foreign (non-U.S.) officials, simple political intelligence, and the monitoring of Trotskyites and Russian emigrés." Theoharis, "Venona," 209; Schrecker, *McCarthyism*, 3.

3. Schrecker, *Many Are the Crimes*, x, 309–10.

4. Powers, *Secrecy and Power*, 86.

5. Morgan, *Reds*, 56–57, 58, 63, 65, 74–76.

6. Weiner, *Enemies*, 34; A reported seven hundred were arrested in New York City alone, two hundred in Philadelphia, and four hundred in Detroit. "Reds Raided in Scores of Cities; 2,600 Arrests, 700 in New York; Deportation Hearings Begin Today," *New York Times*, January 3, 1920, 1. The numbers increased in later reports. By the next day, raids had been reported in fifty-one cities. "5,483 Arrests Reported," *New York Times*, January 4, 1920, 2.

7. Morgan, *Reds*, 81–82.

8. Montana Senator Thomas J. Walsh asked Palmer how many search warrants were issued. Palmer replied, "I can not tell you, Senator, personally. If you would like to ask Mr. Hoover, who was in charge of this matter, he can tell you." Hoover: "The search warrants were entirely a matter which the agents in charge of local offices handled." *Charges of Illegal Practices of the Department of Justice: Hearings*, 19; Morgan, *Reds*, 85. Not only were the raids a PR liability, the Immigration Act of 1917 was held unconstitutional. Palmer ran for the presidency in 1920, and the raids proved to be his undoing. Hoover learned a valuable lesson about leaving his fingerprints on controversial orders, a lesson that would return to haunt him fifty years later.

9. Five Socialists were barred from the New York Assembly when the sergeant at arms marched them out of the chamber after passage of a resolution expelling them. "Albany Assembly Bars Out Five Socialist Members," *New York Times*, January 8, 1920, 1. Not everyone approved of the expulsion. Then Senator Warren G. Harding said, "We should dangerously abridge American liberty to deny a place in any State Assembly or in Congress to any man eligible to the office and honestly elected thereto." "Would Not Bar Socialists," *New York Times*, January 9, 1920, 4.

10. The Supreme Court upheld Debs's ten-year sentence for the crime of telling a gathering, "You need to know that you are fit for something better than slavery and cannon fodder." *Debs v. United States*, 249 U.S. 211 (1919); Lichtman, *Supreme Court*, 8; *Schenck v. United States*, 249 U.S. 47 (1919).

11. *Abrams v. United States*, 250 U.S. 616 (1919). All told, the Supreme Court sustained all eight sedition and espionage cases it considered at the time. Thirty-five states enacted repressive antiradical laws. Lichtman, *Supreme Court*, 8; Schrecker, *Many Are the Crimes*, 58, 60.

12. Morgan, *Reds*, 109–10.

13. The Church Committee, 2:24, fn. 7 noted: "Although Hoover had served as head of the General Intelligence Division of the Justice Department at the time of the 'Palmer Raids' and became an Assistant Director of the Bureau in 1921, he persuaded Attorney General Stone and Roger Baldwin of the American Civil Liberties Union that he had played an 'unwilling part' in the excesses of the past, and he agreed to disband the Bureau's 'radical division.'"

14. Stone announced his thoughts: "There is always the possibility that a secret police may become a menace to free government and free institutions, because it carries with it the possibility of abuses of power which are not always quickly apprehended or understood. . . . It is important that its activities be strictly limited to the performance of those functions for which it was created and that its agents themselves be not above the law or beyond its reach. . . . The Bureau of Investigation is not concerned with political or other opinions of individuals. It is concerned only with their conduct and then only with such conduct as is forbidden by the laws of the United States. When a police system passes beyond these limits, it is dangerous to the proper administration of justice and to human liberty, which it should be our first concern to cherish." *Final Report of the Select Committee (Church Committee)*, 2:23.

15. *Final Report of the Select Committee (Church Committee)*, 2:23–24.

16. Morgan, *Reds*, 113–14.

17. Schrecker, *Many Are the Crimes*, 11–12.

18. Ibid., 13–14, 66.

19. "United States Recognizes Soviet, Exacting Pledge on Propaganda," *New York Times*, November 18, 1933.

20. Morgan, *Reds*, 168, 173; Schrecker, *Many Are the Crimes*, 14–15.

21. Schrecker, *Many Are the Crimes*, 13–15. In the 1930s the party's membership grew from 7,500 to 55,000. Schrecker, *McCarthyism*, 5.

22. Schrecker, *Many Are the Crimes*, 15; Schrecker, *McCarthyism*, 5.

23. Schrecker, *McCarthyism*, 6.

24. Schrecker, *Many Are the Crimes*, 15–16. Stalin's show trials, purges, and executions in 1936 and 1937 also demoralized many American Communists.

25. Although Party membership figures are inconsistent, the trend line was clear. The Communist Party was hemorrhaging members after the Stalin-Hitler pact. Lichtman notes 1940 CP membership at one hundred thousand its peak year. Lichtman, *Supreme Court*, 14.

26. Morgan, *Reds*, 203–4.

27. Fights broke out in several leftist organizations to smoke out and expel Communists, including at the ACLU, the National Lawyers Guild, the CIO, and others. One tactic was to propose "Communazi" resolutions condemning totalitarian governments of the right and left, proposals many Communists would not favor as they offered explicit criticism of the USSR. Schrecker, *Many Are the Crimes*, 82–85.

28. Only thirteen cases of denaturalization succeeded between the years 1945 and 1956. Caute, *Great Fear*, 226–28.

29. Schrecker, *McCarthyism*, 7.

30. Schrecker, *Many Are the Crimes* 329–30.

31. Theoharis, "Lawless Agency," 418–19. HUAC had an earlier run at Hollywood Communists in August 1940, but it was then under Martin Dies and soon abandoned the effort.

32. Theoharis, *Chasing Spies*, 144–45, 151–56; Ceplair, "Film Industry's Battle," 406; Theoharis, "Lawless Agency," 418; Ceplair, *The Marxist*, 96.

33. Theoharis, "Lawless Agency," 418; Ceplair, *The Marxist*, 96; Schrecker, *Many Are the Crimes*, 320–22. Forty-three individuals were summoned, of which nineteen were considered "unfriendly." Only eleven of them (noted below in italics) were called, and of those eleven, ten invoked the First Amendment, refused to answer questions, and became the "Hollywood Ten." The eleventh, Bertolt Brecht, said he had never been a Communist and answered the questions. The numbers in parentheses note the pages in HUAC's record where each individual's testimony appears. The nineteen were: *Alvah Bessie* (383), *Herbert Joseph Biberman* (412), *Bertolt Brecht* (491), *Lester Cole* (486), Richard Collins, *Edward Dmytryk* (459), Gordon Kahn, Howard Koch, *Ring Lardner Jr.* (479), *John Howard Lawson* (290), *Albert Maltz* (363), Lewis Milestone, *Samuel Ornitz* (402), Larry Parks, Irvin Pichel, Robert Rossen, Waldo Salt, *Adrian Scott* (466) and *Dalton Trumbo* (329). *Hearings Regarding the Communist Infiltration of the Motion Picture Industry.*

34. Biberman testified on October 29, 1947. *Hearings, Committee on Un-American Activities*, 412.

35. Humphrey Bogart was among those who went to Washington in support of the Hollywood Ten and later regretted the trip, although Bogart remained critical of HUAC's anti-Communist hysteria and was unfairly called a Communist. He insisted that the group was not in Washington to defend the subpoenaed Hollywood Ten but to defend freedom of speech and the Bill of Rights. Humphrey Bogart, "I'm No Communist," *Photoplay*, May 1948, 53.

36. One judge sentenced two of the ten, Biberman and Dmytryk, to serve six months, and another judge sentenced the other eight to a year. Biberman, *Salt of the Earth*, 7. The Ten were out of luck. They were counting on a reversal by the Supreme Court, but two justices likely favorable to them died while the case was pending. Justice Robert Jackson, who had once agreed hear the case, changed his vote, and certiorari was denied. *Trumbo v. United States*, 176 F.2d 49 (D.C. Cir. 1949), cert. denied; *Lawson v. United States*, 339 U.S. 934 (1950).

37. Schrecker, *Many Are the Crimes*, 321–28.

38. J. Parnell Thomas, HUAC Chair in 1947 and 1948, came under investigation a month after Whittaker Chambers testified and exposed Alger Hiss at the August 1948 HUAC hearings. The day after Chambers's testimony, columnist Drew Pearson exposed Thomas's fake employee-kickback fraud. Thomas had his secretary, a Ms. Campbell, put several of her friends and family members on his House payroll. The fake employees kept a small part of their federal pay—for which they did no work—and endorsed their checks over to Ms. Campbell, who immediately issued checks to

Thomas, keeping none of the proceeds for herself. The scheme lasted several years. A Washington grand jury took up the case, and Thomas proudly announced that he would not take the Fifth. Addressing Attorney General Tom Clark and standing tall the week before the November 2 election day, Thomas said, "Not only do I choose to appear before the grand jury but I insist upon that right not only for myself but for the members of my family who have been subjects of your political harassment." "Thomas, Accepting Clark Bid, Asks Grand Jury Hearing After Nov. 2," *New York Times*, October 25, 1948. On November 2, even as the Democrats took control of Congress, Republican Thomas was reelected. Immediately after reelection and facing the grand jury appearance, Thomas lost his bravado and refused to testify, invoking his right against self-incrimination under the Fifth Amendment. The grand jury indicted him on multiple counts of defrauding the government. "J. Parnell Thomas Indicted for Fraud in Office Payroll," *New York Times*, November 9, 1948. Despite the strong documentary evidence against him, Thomas, playing the insulted upstanding citizen, insisted that he was innocent and that the charges were political. Three days into his trial, in which he and Ms. Campbell were in the dock, he changed his plea to no contest, and was found guilty by the judge and sentenced to prison. He served nine months at the Danbury Federal Prison, where he found as fellow inmates two of the Hollywood Ten, Ring Lardner Jr. and Lester Cole. In an interview, Lardner said that Thomas was already in Danbury when he and Cole arrived. Lardner interview in Fariello, *Red Scare*, 263; Richard Severo, "Ring Lardner Jr, Wry Screenwriter and Last of the Hollywood 10, Dies at 85," *New York Times*, November 2, 2000; Lily Rothman, "The Real Story Behind the Movie *Trumbo*," *Time*, November 6, 2015. See also, "J. Parnell Thomas, Anti-Red Crusader is Dead," *New York Times*, November 20, 1970, 44.

39. Brown, *Loyalty and Security*, 182.

40. Clark learned that Hoover was collecting derogatory information about him while he was attorney general. Clark found out when William Rogers, investigating voter fraud for a committee, got access to the file and showed it to Clark. Clark asked Hoover about it, and when confronted, Hoover said he knew nothing about it, blaming it on a deceased assistant director. Clark interview by Hess, October 17, 1972, 112–16.

41. Weiner, *Enemies*, 83–86.

42. Schrecker, Many Are the Crimes, 98;

43. Schrecker, *McCarthyism*, 41–42.

44. Theoharis, *Chasing Spies*, 32, 34.

45. The Judith Coplon case is instructive. Hoover told the Justice Department to drop the case because the documents involved contained references to the bureau's black bag jobs. The department persisted in the prosecution. They got the conviction, but it was reversed on appeal, and the FBI's illegality was revealed. Hoover vowed never to allow a recurrence. Schrecker, *Many Are the Crimes*, 223.

46. NLG's New York City offices were "burgled more than a fur company in the Bronx." Schrecker, *Many Are the Crimes*, 223–25.

47. Schrecker, *McCarthyism*, 23.

48. Ibid., 41–43.

49. The four books relied on were Stalin's the *Foundations of Leninism*, Marx and Engel's *The Communist Manifesto*, Lenin's *State and Revolution* and the *History of the Communist Party of the Soviet Union*. Lichtman, *Supreme Court*, 44–47.

50. *Dennis v. United States*, 341 U.S. 494, 510 (1951).

51. *Korematsu v. United States*, 323 U.S. 214 (1944).

52. Douglas, "The Black Silence of Fear," *New York Times Magazine*, January 13, 1952, 7 at 37.

53. Morgan, *Reds*, 319.

54. Schrecker, *Many Are the Crimes*, 230–31.

55. Lichtman, "Louis Budenz."

56. This would be true in the case of the NAACP and CORE, and later with Martin Luther King.

57. Schrecker, *Many Are the Crimes*, 73–75.

58. Rovere, *Senator Joe McCarthy*, 123–25. The best guess is that a friend had provided McCarthy a copy of a 1946 letter from Secretary of State James F. Byrnes, noting that three thousand employees had been screened for loyalty. Of those, 284 received a negative committee recommendation and of those, seventy-nine had been terminated. McCarthy's deduction was that 205 remained and were Communists. McCarthy later said that what he held in his hand was a copy of the Byrnes letter. No one knows the source of the other numbers McCarthy used.

59. On February 11, two days after the Wheeling speech, McCarthy made public a letter he wrote to Truman alleging that fifty-seven Communists were still working at State. "McCarthy Insists Truman Oust Reds," *New York Times*, February 12, 1950, L5.

60. Harold B. Hinton, "M'Carthy Charges Spy for Russia Has a High State Department Post," *New York Times*, February 21, 1950, 13.

61. William S. White, "M'Carthy Censure Wins, 67 to 20, in Tentative Vote on 2 Counts, Knowland Widens Split in G.O.P.," *New York Times*, December 2, 1954, 1.

62. Schrecker, *Many Are the Crimes*, 211–12.

63. Ibid., 106. In October 1948, a month before the election, Hoover made another run at his prohibited Index. He explained the details of the list to Attorney General Tom Clark as though it were a recent project, rather than a program in existence for several years. He raised the subject because there were elements he needed for his plan that required presidential approval, such as the suspension of the writ of habeas corpus and the potential approval of a sweeping presidential arrest warrant. In the emergency, the president would sign a "master warrant" with the Security Index attached. Hoover revealed that the index at that time numbered twelve thousand individuals, of whom 97 percent were citizens. Each detainee would be afforded a hearing, but there would be no rules of evidence. The plan contemplated the construction of six detention camps. Although Congress financed the secret construction of the camps, no president until George W. Bush seriously considered Hoover's plan for mass incarceration of suspect subversives. Weiner, *Enemies*, 160–61. In a June 19, 1948, memorandum, the unknown author wrote that "practice of maintaining custodial detention cards"

had been instituted some years before. Part 1 of 29, Custodial Detention Security Index, FBI File No. 100-358086.

64. SAC Letter No. 97, October 19, 1949; X to X, June 17, 1955, Section 35; both in FBI File No 100-358086. FBI memos describe the program in detail: "Our Security Index was originally established in order that all individuals determined through security investigations to be dangerous to the internal security of the nation in time of emergency might be catalogued for immediate apprehension and detention. In the past, it has been our policy to include in the Index only the names of those individuals who have been the subject of complete security investigations. As you know, because of personnel limitations we have never attempted to investigate all members of the Communist Party which today has approximately 59,000 members. Our security investigations have been selective and we have investigated only the more active members of the Communist Party and have included in the Security Index out of the number investigated only the names of those individuals who it would appear would constitute an actual threat to the country in time of an emergency. We have today 10,744 subjects catalogued for apprehension and detention." X to X, July 1, 1949, FBI File No. 100-358086.

CHAPTER 4

1. Virginia Jencks undated note in Box 45, Wilson Papers, UCLA.

2. Jencks, "Palomino," 11–12, Box 1, Folder 1, Jencks Papers, University of Colorado; Lorence, *Palomino*, 48.

3. Baker, *On Strike*, 26–28.

4. Jencks, "Palomino," 12, 34, Box 1, Folder 1, Jencks Papers, University of Colorado.

5. Jencks's grave marker lists his name as "Palomino."

6. Jencks, "Palomino," 13–14, Box 1, Folder 1, Jencks Papers, University of Colorado; Lorence, *Palomino*, 55–57, 71.

7. Jencks wrote of Virginia's work, "Virginia was an inspiring organizer, friend and partner in all his work. Her help was vital. She was held in high regard by the women and most men in Local 890." Incorporating women into the life of the union set the stage for their takeover of the picket lines in EZ strike. Jencks to Lorence, June 17, 1999, 14, Jencks-Lorence Correspondence Folder, Jencks Papers, University of Colorado; Jencks, "Palomino," 14–15, Box 1, Folder 1, Jencks Papers, University of Colorado.

8. Lorenzo Tórrez interview by Cargill, December 8, 1977, Box 1, Folders 6 and 19, Cargill Papers.

9. Lorence, *Palomino*, 58, 80.

10. Jencks, "Palomino," 13, Box 1, Folder 1, Jencks Papers, University of Colorado.

11. Executive Order no. 9806, 11 F.R. 13863, November 25, 1946.

12. Executive Order no. 9835, 12 F.R. 1935, March 25, 1947.

13. Section 9(h) of the Act provided: "No investigation shall be made by the Board of any question affecting commerce concerning the representation of employees, raised by a labor organization under subsection (c) of this section, no petition under section 9 (e) (1) shall be entertained, and no complaint shall be issued pursuant to a charge

made by a labor organization under subsection (b) of section 10, unless there is on file with the Board an affidavit executed contemporaneously or within the preceding twelve-month period by each officer of such labor organization and the officers of any national or international labor organization of which it is an affiliate or constituent unit that he is not a member of the Communist Party or affiliated with such party, and that he does not believe in or teaches, the overthrow of the United States Government by force or by any illegal or unconstitutional methods. The provisions of section 35A of the Criminal Code shall be applicable in respect to such affidavits."

14. Wrote Jencks, "In New Mexico, the mining, smelting and refining companies used the affidavit issue as part of their effort to get more compliant union leadership, sow division and confusion, encourage more conservative unions to split workers, used the Red issue to weaken community support, to get cheaper contracts or no contracts at all." Jencks, "Palomino," 18, Box 1, Folder 1, Jencks Papers, University of Colorado.

15. *Proceedings of the 43rd Convention of the IUMMSW*, 1947, 197–98, Box 36, Folder 3, Mine-Mill archives; Jensen, *Nonferrous Metals*, 210–11.

16. Santa Rita Local 63 delegate Albert Muñoz supported the Jencks resolution and said that corporations used discrimination as a tool to maintain lower wage rates and a lower standard of living. Muñoz did not blame the corporations, who did it for profit, but asked labor to end the practice for its own welfare. *Proceedings of the 43rd Convention of the IUMMSW*, 1947, 266–67, 268–69, Box 36, Folder 3, Mine-Mill archives. A month after the convention, Jencks was urging Mine-Mill to support COMP (Comité para la Organización del Pueblo Mexicano). Jencks to Maurice Travis, September 29, 1947, Box 94, Folder 1, WFM, Mine-Mill archives.

17. Jensen, *Nonferrous Metals*, 204–5.

18. Local 890 member Arturo Flores recalled, "Clint right away floated the idea that we could amalgamate into one strong effective Local. (I said floated because Clint never pushed anything on us.). The old timers opposed it, but us youngsters who wanted to fight for our rights were all for it. . . . Clint taught us '*Unidos Venceremos*' (United we Shall Overcome)." Arturo Flores, December 27, 2005, Box 1, Folder 37, Lorence Papers; Lorence, *Palomino*, 49, 53, 71.

19. "N.M. Union Endorses Wallace for President," *El Paso Herald-Post*, March 5, 1948; Hudson, "Mine-Mill," 135.

20. Jensen, *Nonferrous Metals*, 221. Jencks was at that meeting and criticized Eckert for creating disunity in the union. Jencks, p. 3 of nine-page chronology found in Box 2, Folder 2, Lorence Papers. See also, "Non-Red Oath Is Issue in Bargaining Election," *New York World Telegram*, May 4, 1948; "CIO Group Bolts in Red Oath Spat," *New York World Telegram*, June 30, 1948.

21. "Union Sues Ex-Officer," *The Advocate* (Newark, Ohio), July 28, 1948.

22. C. P. Trussell, "Red 'Underground' in Federal Posts Alleged by Editor," *New York Times*, Aug. 4, 1948. The CIO fired Pressman for supporting Wallace. What is called the McCarthy era actually began before the Wisconsin senator rose to prominence and continued after his death.

23. *Proceedings of the 44th Convention of the IUMMSW*, 1948, 115, Box 36, Folder 4, Mine-Mill archives; Jensen, *Nonferrous Metals*.

24. *Proceedings of the 44th Convention of the IUMMSW*, 1948, 114.

25. *Proceedings of the 44th Convention of the IUMMSW*, 1948, 114–15, 158.

26. *Proceedings of the 44th Convention of the IUMMSW*, 1948, 159, 161, 173.

27. "Mine-Mill Convention All-Out for Wallace," *The Score*, September 20, 1948.

28. Vincent to C. B. Baldwin, June 5, 1947, Box 2, Folder 13, Lorence Papers.

29. Progressive Party 1948 Campaign matters, Box 2, Folders 11, 13, 15, Lorence Papers. Jencks was out for Wallace in writing by September 1947: "We need a figure of the stature of Henry Wallace. Wallace himself if possible." Jencks to recipients, undated but stamped September 29, 1947, Box 94, Folder 1, Mine-Mill archives. A New Mexico political action committee for Wallace was set up on January 31, 1948, and Jencks was named chairman. "New Mexico CIO Unions Step Up Political Action Campaign," Press Release, January 31, 1948, Box 102, Folder 11, Jencks Papers, University of Colorado.

30. Lorence, *Palomino*, 76–77.

31. Jencks, "Palomino," 28, Box 1, Folder 1, Jencks Papers, University of Colorado.

32. *Proceedings of the 45th Convention of the IUMMSW*, 1949, Box 37, Folder 1, WFM Collection, University of Colorado; Jensen, *Nonferrous Metals*, 248–49. On a positive note, Jencks obtained a resolution of support for ANMA from the convention. 1948 Convention *Proceedings*, 259–60.

33. Jencks, "Palomino," 29–30, Box 1, Folder 1, Jencks Papers, University of Colorado. Local 890 resolved: "The Truman Administration and the Democratic Party have completely sold out on their promises to repeal Taft-Hartley. The corporations, the FBI and other agencies will try to scare your officers, and may even try to persecute them in court. They will steal our union from us unless we stay awake, unless we continue to battle for it. We have been forced to make a retreat that is part of the increasing loss of freedoms for the common people of America. We can go from this retreat to win back our freedoms, to win new and better wages and working conditions for all."

34. Jencks to Lorence, June 17, 1999, 9a, Lorence Papers. In the draft of his memoir, "Palomino," Jencks scratched out the sentence, "I sat down and wrote a letter resigning from the Communist Party and ending any and all affiliation with that Party." Jencks, "Palomino," 30, Box 1, Folder 1, Jencks Papers, University of Colorado.

35. Linda Halley Regeh email to Lorence, May 17, 2010, Box 1, Folder 22, Lorence Papers.

36. Jensen, *Nonferrous Metals*, 251–68.

37. "Report on the Committee to Investigate Charges Against the International Union of Mine, Mill and Smelter Workers," Box 2, Folder 18, Lorence Papers; Jensen, *Nonferrous Metals*, 266–67.

38. Lucien A. File, "History of Labor in Nonferrous Metal Mining Industry in New Mexico," Box 2, Folder 18, Lorence Papers.

CHAPTER 5

1. Cargill, "Empire and Opposition," 57–58, 63. A January strike at a Carlsbad potash mine represented a loss to the union, and no doubt there were other firms hoping to repeat the union's humiliation there. The Carlsbad strike was a disaster

for Mine-Mill. Three hundred union members lost their jobs, and many lost their seniority. While other zinc mines closed when prices dropped in 1949, Empire Zinc, as a low-cost operator, remained open.

2. Jencks, "Palomino," 31–32, Box 1, Folder 1, Jencks Papers, University of Colorado.

3. C. P. Trussell, "Pressman Names Three in New Deal as Reds with Him," *New York Times*, August 29, 1950.

4. Cargill, "Empire and Opposition," 62.

5. Yates, "Samuel Wetherill," 469.

6. Lorence, *Palomino*, 92. Lorence, Hodges, and Cargill found no evidence to support Jencks's collusion theory, and Cargill believed that EZ was simply following its practices in maximizing profits and attempting to control its labor environment. Hodges, "Making and Unmaking," 61; Cargill, "Empire and Opposition," 63.

7. "Empire Zinc Workers Vote Strike," *Union Worker*, September 1950.

8. Cargill, "Empire and Opposition," 67.

9. "Miners Walk Out As Talks Collapse," *Silver City Daily Press*, October 17, 1950; Lorenzo Tórrez interview by Ellen Baker, October 4, 1995, Box 2, Folder 14, p. 15, Tórrez Papers.

10. The other demands were a fifteen-cent-per-hour raise in wages; foremen to supervise and do no productive work; the elimination of three pay rates for one job class; the filling of vacancies on basis of seniority; and for safety reasons, no solitary work. "Miners Walk Out As Talks Collapse," *Silver City Daily Press*, October 17, 1950; Jencks, "Palomino," 33, Box 1, Folder 1, Jencks Papers, University of Colorado.

11. Cargill, "Empire and Opposition," 84.

12. Ibid., 60–62.

13. Low grade ore was mostly used for galvanizing iron and steel, and high grade was used in making brass and for casting. Cargill, "Empire and Opposition," 62–63.

14. Ibid., 64–65.

15. Ibid., 66. Cost of the strike was paid by the international (13 percent), other locals (24 percent), and 890 (63 percent).

16. Baker, *On Strike*, 83; Lorenzo Tórrez interview by Ellen Baker, October 4, 1995, Box 2, Folder 14, p. 6, Tórrez Papers.

17. "Empire Talks End; Strike Continues Here," *Silver City Daily Press*, October 27, 1950; "Empire, Union Break Off New Negotiations," *Silver City Daily Press*, November 18, 1950. The wartime government was expected to buy $1.4 billion of strategic metals. "Predict 'Rebirth' of Lead, Copper, Zinc Mines," *Silver City Daily Press*, November 6, 1950.

18. Travis to Jencks, February 5, 1951, Box 1, Folder 6, Cargill Collection.

19. Cargill, "Empire and Opposition," 67.

20. Local 890-member Ernest Velásquez said, "The issue in the Empire Zinc strike was equality. We were trying to end discrimination at Empire Zinc, to bring wages and working conditions up there into line with contracts our union had already won from other big companies. The company wouldn't negotiate. It soon became clear they were determined to break the union—to starve us into submission, to force us

back to work on our knees." IUMMSW, "Portrait of a Labor Organizer," 27, c.1956, Box 1, Folder 5, Jencks Papers, University of Colorado. Although Maurice Travis of the international thought the strike was lost, Lorenzo Tórrez saw it as a winner. Lorenzo Tórrez interview by Kent Hudson, January 16, 1978, Box 2, Folder 64, Lorence Papers.

21. Jencks to Larson, February 27, 1951, Box 1, Folder 6, Cargill Collection. With the election of Cipriano Montoya as 890's president in April 1951, he became the first Mexican to be a full-time union representative, achieving one of Jencks's goals of moving Mexicans into leadership positions. Jencks, "Palomino," 34, Box 1, Folder 1, Jencks Papers, University of Colorado.

22. "New Attempt to Settle Strike Fails," *Silver City Daily Press*, March 8, 1951; "Union Claims It's Ready to Talk to Empire," *Silver City Daily Press*, March 9, 1951.

23. "Empire, Union Resume Talks to End Strike," *Silver City Daily Press*, March 13, 1951; "Empire Parley Breaks Off As Strike Continues," *Silver City Daily Press*, March 14, 1951; The company's ad read, "Empire Zinc Offers 'Back to Work' Wage Increase," *Silver City Daily Press*, March 26, 1951; Cargill, "Empire and Opposition," 70.

24. "Montoya to Head Union; Jencks Moving," *Silver City Daily Press*, April 18, 1951.

25. Empire Zinc had been signaling as far back as April, in a newspaper ad, that EZ employees were demanding an end to the strike so they could return to work. "Many Empire Zinc Employees Want to Return to Work," *Silver City Daily Press*, April 2, 1951; "To Empire Zinc Employees and to Men Seeking Employment, Empire Zinc Resumes Work," *Silver City Daily Press*, June 7, 1951;. A news article claimed that "some 40 workers signed a petition asking that Empire offer them jobs," *Silver City Daily Press*, June 7, 1951.

26. "Union Protests Hiring of Special Deputies for Monday," *Silver City Daily Press*, June 8, 1951; "Goforth Says Extra Men to Enforce Law on Both Sides," *Silver City Daily Press*, June 9, 1951; Cargill, "Empire and Opposition," 74.

27. Arrested along with Jencks were David M. García, Wallace M. García, Claudio Padilla, Mariano Zamora, Tomás Gomes, Julián Perea, Daniel Salas, Salvador Vásquez, Ray Marrufo, Vera Molano and Max Dónez. "Jencks Held After Sheriff Orders Empire Road Cleared," *Silver City Daily Press*, June 11, 1951; Jencks, "Palomino," 38, Box 1, Folder 1, Jencks Papers, University of Colorado.

28. A company ad asked, "Who Owns the Highway? The Union or the Public?" *Silver City Daily Press*, June 9, 1951; Jencks, "Palomino," 37, Box 1, Folder 1, Jencks Papers, University of Colorado; Cargill, "Empire and Opposition," 71–73.

29. *New Jersey Zinc v. Mine-Mill International, Local 890, Clinton Jencks, Cipriano Montoya, Ernest Velásquez, Vicente Becerra, Pablo Montoya and Fred Barreras*, No. 12812, 6th Judicial District Court for Grant County, New Mexico; "Company Says 'Some Employes' [sic] Have returned to Jobs," *Silver City Daily Press*, June 13, 1951. In a newspaper ad, EZ wrote, "As a public service, the company is determined to establish that no Mine Mill dictatorship will be imposed on the citizens of this county. Every public spirited citizen should do his part to preserve the law in Grant County." *Silver City Daily Press*, June 13, 1951.

30. Baker, *On Strike*, 88.

31. Ibid., 85–87; Cargill, "Empire and Opposition," 73–75.

32. The *Daily Press* did not on this first day seem to realize the significance of women replacing men as pickets. It noted, "At Hanover this morning, the picket line scene was quiet. Women and a few children made up the line and traffic was being allowed, for the most part, to pass unhampered." "Empire Begins Operations," *Silver City Daily Press*, June 14, 1951.

33. Those named were Mrs. Lorenzo Tórrez, Mrs. Vicente Becerra, and Mrs. Daria Chávez. "Warrants issued for Six Pickets," *Silver City Daily Press*, June 15, 1951; Bert Steele, "Pickets Defy Officers," *Silver City Daily Press*, June 16, 1951. The weekly *Silver City Enterprise* had the number arrested at sixty-two women and seventeen children. "Strike Stalemated as Law Attempts New Action Against Local 890; Use of Women on Line Noted by Nation," *Silver City Enterprise*, June 21, 1951. Jencks wrote that in addition to the fifty-three, fifty others were arrested and lodged in hotels. Jencks, "Palomino," 39, Box 1, Folder 1, Jencks Papers, University of Colorado.

34. Jencks said, "I'm an outsider. These women have taken over and they tell me to go peddle my papers. They won't tell me a thing. But I know that there will be more and more women to take the places of those who are arrested." "Pickets Defy Officers," *Silver City Daily Press*, June 16, 1951; Cargill, "Empire and Opposition," 77.

35. "Fear New Violence," *Silver City Daily Press*, June 16, 1951. At court, the women pleaded not guilty to charges of unlawful assembly. They showed little concern over their predicament while they exhibited a steely determination. "It's like a picnic," said one, "We're having fun and we're going to stay on the picket line, too." Among the names of the defendants were Virginia Jencks, Virginia Chacón, and Amelia Montoya. "Deny Charges of Unlawful Assembly in Hanover Trouble," *Silver City Daily Press*, June 18, 1951.

36. "Strike Stalemated as Law Attempts New Action Against Local 890; Use of Women on Line Noted by Nation," *Silver City Enterprise*, June 21, 1951; "Women Again Picket Mine," *New York Times*, June 18, 1951. With the increased national interest, Mine-Mill officers, including Maurice Travis and Nathan Witt, were on the scene. "Union Officials Due Here," *Silver City Daily Press*, June 20, 1951.

37. Trial transcript, 195–223, New Mexico Supreme Court, No. 5579 (hereafter cited as trial transcript).

38. "Judge to Grant Injunction Against Pickets at Empire," *Silver City Daily Press*, June 30, 1951; "Judge Signs Strike Injunction," *Silver City Daily Press*, July 10, 1951.

39. See, for example, the June 25, 1951 letter from Ernest Velásquez to local merchants and the June 28 City resolution. A group of Bayard merchants and individuals circulated an opposing leaflet critical of the union. Box 2, Folder 3, Cargill Collection.

40. The six defendants were Clinton Jencks, Cipriano Montoya, Ernest Velásquez, Vicente Becerra, Pablo Montoya, and Fred Barreras. *New Jersey Zinc Co. v. Local 890 of International Union of Mine, Mill & Smelter Workers et al.* No. 12812, Sixth Judicial District Court for the State of New Mexico, record pp. 5–15 in New Mexico Supreme Court No. 5579; "Union, Six Officials Found Guilty," *Silver City Daily Press*, July 23, 1951.

41. Cargill, "Empire and Opposition," 85–86.

42. Baker, *On Strike*, 129–33.

43. These charges related to the comments Travis made at the Fierro nightclub. "Travis Faces Charge," *Silver City Daily Press*, July 24, 1951; "Union Officials Face Charges of Attacking Integrity of Judge," *Silver City Daily Press*, August 4, 1951.

44. "Lawyers, Judge Ask Mechem to Act in Tense Strike Dispute," *Silver City Daily Press*, July 23, 1951.

45. "Labor Board Rules Against Empire," *Silver City Daily Press*, August 17, 1951.

46. "Four Sent to Hospital After Fracas at Line," *Silver City Daily Press*, August 23, 1951; "Roach Probes Blockade" (with photographs of the injured pickets), *Silver City Daily Press*, August 24, 1951; "4 Hurt in Mine Riot," *New York Times*, August 24, 1951, 9; Jencks, "Palomino," 41, Box 1, Folder 1, Jencks Papers, University of Colorado; Lorence, *Palomino*, 100–101; Baker, *On Strike*, 130–31; Cargill, "Empire and Opposition," 99–101.

47. Jencks and Mine-Mill were rumored to be Communist or under Communist influence. Jencks was not public about his Party membership, and even close union friends said that Jencks did not speak of communism to the membership. Flores written interview by author, 7. Flores: "I never heard Clint openly discuss communism with anybody."

48. Cargill, "Empire and Opposition," 87, 105; Baker, *On Strike*, 141–42.

49. They would claim assaults, threats, and threatening behavior and ask the courts to impose peace bonds to ensure the law was followed. Once jailed, the accused were obligated to post bonds of $250 to $500 to be released. Union and personal resources were taxed by the strategy. Finally, after Judge Marshall was disqualified, the union appealed to a judge in Socorro, who released them and condemned the wholesale use of the practice. Violence at the picket line was poised to spread into the larger community.

50. "Mrs. Jencks Pleads Not Guilty To Charge," *Silver City Daily Press*, September 14, 1951; "Mrs. Jencks Found Guilty, Others Freed," *Silver City Daily Press*, September 27, 1951; Local 890 Press Release, September 29, 1951, Box 1, Folder 10, Burch Vaughn Papers.

51. "Talk Over New Union Prelude to Bayard Fight," *Silver City Daily Press*, October 3, 1951; IUMMSW, "Portrait of a Labor Organizer," 30–31, c.1956, Box 1, Folder 5, Jencks Papers, University of Colorado; Jencks, "Palomino," 44–45, Box 1, Folder 1, Jencks Papers, University of Colorado.

52. Baker, *On Strike*, 145; Cargill, "Empire and Opposition," 107–8.

53. "Mine-Mill Reveals 20½ Cents Pay Hike in Agreement," *Silver City Daily Press*, October 20, 1951; "ASR, US Sign Contracts With Unions," *Silver City Daily Press*, November 8, 1951.

54. Cargill, "Empire and Opposition," 109.

55. "Pickets Cleared from Empire Road," *Silver City Daily Press*, December 10, 1951; "Quiet Reigns After State Police Order Pickets to Clear Highway," *Silver City Daily Press*, December 11, 1951; Richard W. Everett, "Grant County Strike Nearly a Civil War," *New Mexican*, January 20, 1952.

56. The union and EZ both agreed that there was attrition. The strike involved around 120 in the EZ bargaining unit. According to EZ, forty of the men had asked EZ to reopen in the summer of 1951 and of those, twenty-eight had been willing to sign a petition. EZ hired about twenty men after August 1951 and increased that to forty or fifty after November 1951. Most of the Anglos at EZ wanted to return to work, but a number of Mexicans joined them. Testimony of Richard B. Berresford, Hearings, March 19, 1953, 1199–1200.

57. "Empire Zinc Mill Resumes Normal Operations," *Silver City Daily Press*, January 8, 1952; Baker, *On Strike*, 147–48; Cargill, "Empire and Opposition," 109–10.

58. "'Co. Gunmen' Charge Hurts Empire Zinc," *New Mexican*, January 20, 1952.

59. "Jencks Called to Testify in Labor Hearing," *Silver City Daily Press*," January 18, 1952; Jencks, "Palomino," 52, Box 1, Folder 1, Jencks Papers, University of Colorado.

60. "Empire, Union Continue El Paso Peace Talks," *Silver City Daily Press*, January 22, 1952.

61. "Company Gives More Pay, Union Concedes On Collar-to-Collar," *Silver City Daily Press*, January 24, 1952; "Notify Workers Jobs Waiting for Them," *Silver City Daily Press*, January 25, 1952. The terms were as follows:

Wage increases of 19.5 to 39.5 cents per hour.

Payment in lieu of collar to collar pay increased from 6 to 11.5 cents per hour. Keeping the 8.5-hour day was hard for the union to swallow, but the union did receive an increase in such pay from 48 to 92 cents for the half hour.

Payment in lieu of holiday pay increased from 3 to 3.5 cents per hour.

Three weeks' vacation after twenty-five years.

Pension plan of eighty dollars monthly after twenty years and one hundred dollars monthly after twenty-five years after age sixty-five.

Health and welfare benefits of twenty-six dollars per week for twenty-six weeks, and $2,500 in life insurance.

Reinstatement with seniority rights. The strikebreakers kept their jobs.

Assurances that EZ would provide running water at Mexican housing and "cooperation" in settling pending court cases.

62. Jencks, "Palomino," 48–49, Box 1, Folder 1, Jencks Papers, University of Colorado; Cargill, "Empire and Opposition," 114–15.

63. "Judge Ponders Decision in Contempt Case," *Silver City Daily Press*, February 3, 1952; Jencks, "Palomino," 49, Box 1, Folder 1, Jencks Papers, University of Colorado.

64. Local 890's summary of the fines and jail sentences resulting from the EZ strike. Box 1, Folder 4, Cargill Collection. Later, on September 18, 1952, Judge Marshall took up the criminal cases pending against sixty-four defendants. After the defendants entered guilty pleas, the judge fined them a total of $750 and dismissed the cases with his admonishment that they observe the law. Eighteen other defendants with more serious charges also entered pleas and were fined twenty-five dollars in court costs. "Judge Clears Docket of Hanover Strike Cases," *El Paso Herald-Post*, September 18, 1952. The following is a recap of the litigation and the criminal cases.

First contempt. Violation of the temporary restraining order between June 12 and July 9, 1951.

Mine-Mill and Local 890 each fined four thousand dollars, for total of eight thousand dollars.

Jencks and five other members of the negotiating committee sentenced to serve ninety days in jail.

Second contempt. Violation of the permanent injunction between July 10 and December 5, 1951.

Mine-Mill and Local 890 each fined $12,450, for a total of $24,900.

Jencks was fined one thousand dollars and the members of the negotiation committee, plus four women pickets, were fined varying amounts from $1,150 to $70, for a total for all of $6,970.

Third contempt. Violation of the permanent injunction between December 6 and 18, 1951.

Mine-Mill and Local 890 each fined $1,350, for a total of $2,700.

Clinton Jencks and seventeen others, including several women, fined varying amounts totaling $3,050.

Criminal contempt. These were charges brought alleging that the court was insulted when it was said that the injunction could be bought by EZ. The local bar association brought the case. Maurice Travis was fined seven hundred dollars and was sentenced to serve 180 days in jail, but the sentence was suspended. Jencks was fined one hundred dollars and sentenced to serve sixty days, but the sentence was suspended.

65. At least in its public statements, EZ was clear that the criminal and contempt cases would go on. EZ spokesperson S. S. Huyett said that the items had been discussed but no agreement was reached. "We did not feel that legal actions were negotiable." *Silver City Daily Press*, January 24, 1952; Jencks, "Palomino," 49–50, Box 1, Folder 1, Jencks Papers, University of Colorado; "Pickets and Unions Get Heavy Fines," *Albuquerque Journal*, March 11, 1952. The union had more than EZ to contend with. Conn Brown, the Grant County Clerk, sued the union, Jencks, and others for libel, claiming that he was defamed when he appeared in a photograph in the union newspaper seemingly as a striker. A jury awarded Brown ten thousand dollars in actual damages and five thousand dollars in punitive damages. The court reduced the total award to $12,500. Both sides appealed. *Conn Brown v. Local 890, Cipriano Montoya, Clinton Jencks and Ernesto Velásquez*, Civil No. 12988, 6th Judicial District Court, Grant County, New Mexico. "Claims pending in District Court, Grant County, or on appeal from that court," undated, unsigned memorandum most likely from Nathan Witt to the union, Box 1, Folder 4, Cargill Collection. See "Libel Suit Opens Against Union in Silver City," *Albuquerque Journal*, April 8, 1952; "Photo 'Hurt' Him, Grant County Clerk Testifies," *Albuquerque Journal*, April 9, 1952.

66. Jencks, "Palomino," 52, Box 1, Folder 1, Jencks Papers, University of Colorado.

67. "Seek Jail Terms for Mine Union Representatives," *El Paso Herald-Post*, August 22, 1952; "Mine, Mill Union Men May Face New Legal Action," *Albuquerque Journal*,

August 22, 1952; "N.M. Judge Sets Contempt Hearing for Union Leaders," *El Paso Herald-Post*, August 23, 1952.

68. "Six Union Men Begin Jail Terms for Contempt," *Albuquerque Journal*, September 6, 1952: "Union Men Blast Court Ruling at Silver City," *El Paso Herald-Post*, September 8, 1952.

69. Jencks later explained the judge's thinking in ordering his isolation. "Their theory, of course, was the usual racist kind of theory that all this trouble was an outside agitator, and after all these Mexican-American people were just children anyway. And, they wouldn't have gotten involved in this if I hadn't—so if I looked silly the leader of the whole thing would fall apart." Jencks interview by Albert Kahn, July 26, 1977, Box 1, Folder 13, Lorence Papers.

70. Lorence, *Palomino*, 105; "Strike Threatened Over Jailed Union Leaders," *El Paso Herald-Post*, September 6, 1952.

71. Jencks to 890 members, October 5, 1952, Box 1, Folder 25, Lorence Papers.

72. Lorence, *Palomino*, 106; "Kennecott to Shut Two Lead-Zinc Mines in Grant," *Albuquerque Journal*, October 3, 1952.

73. Matusow, *False Witness*, 152.

74. *Communist Domination*, Hearings, 150–52.

75. Ibid., 153–55.

76. Ibid., 162–63. In his memoir, Matusow wrote that he had planned his *New York Times* bombshell and had discussed it with Senator McCarthy. He inserted the surprise testimony when he saw an opening to do so. Matusow had no facts to support his allegation, but he knew that it could not be disproven, which was the method behind many of McCarthy's baseless charges. Matusow, *False Witness*, 155–56.

77. *Communist Domination*, Hearings, 163.

78. Ibid., 167–75.

79. Ibid., 175.

80. "Mine Union Leader Defies Red Probers," *El Paso Herald-Post*, October 8, 1952; "Empire Strike Was Focal Point of McCarran Tie-In," and "Ex-Spy Hints Jencks Had Knowledge of Red Activities," *Silver City Daily Press*, October 9, 1952.

81. "Union Says Solons' Charges Unfounded," *El Paso Herald-Post*, December 29, 1952; "Union Leader Denies Spy Ring Operated in N.M.," *El Paso Herald-Post*, December 30, 1952. In the report, Jencks claimed that he had never seen or met Matusow before the Salt Lake City hearing.

82. "Solon Asks Probe of Alleged Spying on 'Hill,' Sandia," *Albuquerque Journal*, December 30, 1952; "Solons Urge Union to Oust Commies," *El Paso Herald-Post*, December 29, 1952.

83. As evidence of a large loss, company-wide, New Jersey Zinc's profits doubled from prewar to Korean War production levels. Lorence, *Suppression*, 14.

84. Local 890's Ernest Velásquez: "The issue in the Empire Zinc strike was equality. We were trying to end discrimination at Empire Zinc, to bring wages and working conditions up there into line with contracts our union already won from other big companies. Jencks didn't 'stir up' that strike. The issues were there, and would

have been there even if El Palomino had never been born. . . . The company wouldn't negotiate. It soon became clear they were determined to break the union—to starve us into submission, to force us back to work on our knees." IUMMSW, "Portrait of a Labor Organizer," 26–27, c.1956, Box 1, Folder 5, Jencks Papers, University of Colorado.

85. Jencks explained that the strike began with "just a simple straightforward refusal of the company to follow the wage and working condition pattern . . . already established at the other mines in the district." Wilson and Rosenfelt, *Salt of the Earth*, 117.

86. To Lorenzo Torres, the strike was a success. Local 890 gained members, and EZ never took on the union again. EZ also installed plumbing in the homes. The positive influence lasted until Phelps Dodge broke the union in 1980. Lorenzo Torres interview by Baker, October 4, 1995, Box 2, Folder 64, p. 15, Lorence Papers. Jencks was ambivalent in his assessment, but decades later wrote that the settlement scored "important gains for the workers." Jencks, "Jencks vs. U.S.: Part of the Cold War Attack on Labor," 1, Wood Collection. Hodges also saw the strike as a success. It helped solidify the union's power base and challenged racism and the Anglo power structure. The strike shed light on gender and ethnic discrimination. Hodges, "Making and Unmaking," 43–45. To Virginia Jencks, "Company won when it came to pure and simple economic issues." To her, the court cases broke the union's resolve. Virginia Jencks to Michael Wilson, February 24, 1952, Box 6a, Folder 86, Jarrico Papers.

CHAPTER 6

1. Far from inserting revolutionary ideas into film, according to Paul Jarrico, "We were unable to get anything more than the most moderate kinds of reform messages into our films. If we thought we got some women treated as human beings rather than as sex objects, we thought it was a great victory." Ceplair, *The Marxist*, 41.

2. Baker, *On Strike*, 183–84.

3. Reagan testified, "I do not believe the Communists have ever at any time been able to use the motion-picture screen as a sounding board for their philosophy or ideology." *Communist Infiltration of the Motion Picture Industry*, HUAC Hearings, 1947, 217. The blacklisted Howard E. Koch wrote the script for *Mission to Moscow* and shared the screenwriting Oscar for *Casablanca*.

4. Edward Dmytryk, one of the Hollywood Ten who later cooperated with HUAC, testified, and named names, found absurd the idea of a Communist propaganda conspiracy. At the second HUAC hearing, when asked if he had seen Communists insert propaganda into films, he said, "It is absolutely impossible, unless we had Communists running the studio." Dmytryk interview in Fariello, *Red Scare*, 301.

5. Sondergaard won an Academy Award in 1936 for best supporting actress in *Anthony Adverse*. Biberman, *Salt of the Earth*, 23–26. Sondergaard was the first to receive an Oscar in that category.

6. Biberman, *Salt of the Earth*, 31; Lorence, *Suppression*, 54; Hodges, "Making and Unmaking," 85–86.

7. Ceplair, *The Marxist*, 137–38.

8. Biberman, *Salt of the Earth*, 35; Hodges, "Making and Unmaking," 88–92. Paul Jarrico, UCLA interview, March 13, 1990; Virginia Jencks to Jarrico, August 18 and 28 and December 14, 1950, Box 6a, Folder 86, Jarrico Papers. Biberman and IPC had difficulty finding worthy, shootable screenplays and unsuccessfully tried to persuade experienced screenwriters, such as Dalton Trumbo, to participate. Cook, *Trumbo*, 227–28.

9. Lorence, *Suppression*, 52–53.

10. His Oscar nomination for *Tom, Dick and Harry* lost out to Orson Welles for *Citizen Kane*; Jencks, "Palomino," 56–57, Box 1, Folder 1, Jencks Papers, University of Colorado; Ceplair, *The Marxist*, 122, 139, 140; Biberman, *Salt of the Earth*, 37–38; Lorence, *Suppression*, 58. RKO also denied Jarrico credit for his screenwriting, action that was upheld in court. Ceplair, *The Marxist*, 126–27.

11. Weeks after Virginia Jencks's death, Jarrico wrote that she was "the mother" of the film, and he added, "Without discounting Clint's contribution, the idea of the film was born out of the pleasure and excitement Virginia communicated when she talked about the women involved in the strike—the growth of their self-esteem, the way their men were reacting. *** Virginia's compassion for the disadvantaged, her ability to help people to help themselves, to lead without patronizing, to enter into individual lives and leave those lives enriched—these qualities found expression not only in a film that has now become a classic, but in every field she touched." "A message from Paul Jarrico," March 10, 1990, Box 69, Folder 86, Jarrico Papers.

12. Ceplair, *The Marxist*, 140; Biberman, *Salt of the Earth*, 37–38.

13. Biberman, *Salt of the Earth*, 37–38.

14. Ceplair, *The Marxist*, 13; Hodges, "Making and Unmaking," 17–18.

15. Baker, *On Strike*, 182; Hodges, "Making and Unmaking," 21–22, 25–26.

16. When blacklisted, Wilson could either decline to claim credit, use a pseudonym, or be denied credit. Among others, he worked on the following films: *5 Fingers, Lawrence of Arabia, The Court-Martial of Billy Mitchell, The Bridge on the River Kwai, Friendly Persuasion, Planet of the Apes, Che!,* and *The Sand Piper.*

17. Biberman, *Salt of the Earth*, 38–39.

18. Ceplair, *The Marxist*, 140.

19. Biberman, *Salt of the Earth*, 39.

20. Baker, *On Strike*, 192–93, 194, 196; Biberman, *Salt of the Earth*, 39–40.

21. Reported studio payoffs to Bioff and Browne range from $550,000 to $2.5 million, huge sums for those days. Bioff was suspected of many crimes, including murder, but was only convicted for pandering and the IATSE extortion scheme. Browne was sentenced to serve eight years and Bioff to ten, but both turned on their former mob associates and were released after two years. Bioff provided evidence against Frank Nitto, aka Nitti, and other members of the old Capone gang. Nitto committed suicide within hours after the indictment. The government gave Bioff a new life in Arizona complete with a new identity, and he may have been the first individual provided with anonymity in what later became the witness protection program. But the Chicago mob had a long memory. In 1955, twelve years after he

"turned state's evidence," Bioff was killed by a bomb attached to his truck. "Gang Guns May Blast Veil of Anonymity from Bioff," *Oakland Tribune* (CA), August 24, 1954; "Blast in Truck Kills Willie Bioff, Once Hollywood Racket Leader," *New York Times*, November 5, 1955; "Bioff, Browne Guilty; Facing 30-year Terms," *New York Times*, November 7, 1941; "8 Capone's Aides Indicted in Fraud; One Kills Himself," *New York Times*, March 20, 1943; Gang Leader Nitti Kills Himself in Chicago After Indictment Here," *New York Times*, March 20, 1943; "Bioff Describes Gang Rule of Union," *New York Times*, October 7, 1943.

22. Fariello, *Red Scare*, 256 n2.

23. Ibid., 256.

24. "Hollywood Riot Flares in Strike," *New York Times*, October 6, 1945; "78 Persons Hurt in New Film Fight," *New York Times*, October 9, 1945; "50 Hurt, 13 Seized in Film Strike Tilt," *New York Times*, October 24, 1945. See IATSE Local 728's history of the strike in "The War for Warner Brothers," www.iatse728.org/about-us /history/the-war-for-warner-brothers.

25. Fariello, *Red Scare*, 256.

26. Biberman, *Salt of the Earth*, 42.

27. Brewer was also involved with the Motion Picture Industry Council. Lorence, "*Salt of the Earth* and Free Expression," 416; Biberman, *Salt of the Earth*, 41–42. When Hollywood Ten member Edward Dmytryk decided to submit to rehabilitation, he had to be interviewed by the FBI and HUAC investigators, appear voluntarily before HUAC, name names, and have his recantation published in a magazine. Ceplair, *The Marxist*, 118.

28. Biberman, *Salt of the Earth*, 441; Lorence, *Suppression*, 62–63.

29. Biberman, *Salt of the Earth*, 42.

30. Jarrico, *Marxist*, 144.

31. Lorence, *Suppression*, 68–70.

32. The lead roles were initially intended for blacklisted Anglo actors. Wilson had written the role of Esperanza for Biberman's wife, Gale Sondergaard. Others complained and persuaded Biberman that Mexicans should be cast. Biberman, *Salt of the Earth*, 43–44; Rosenfelt, *Commentary*, in Wilson and Rosenfelt, *Salt of the Earth*, 131. Also, originally, the film's focus was to be the Jencks character, but Frances William, a black CP personality, convinced them to make it about the Mexicans. Frank Barnes and his wife, the film's stage names for the Jencks characters, would become part of the union crowd playing supporting roles rather than having the lead as first contemplated. Jencks approved of the changes. Lorence, *Suppression*, 59. Biberman later admitted his mistake, writing, "We had planned to use Mexican-Americans in all the small parts. But we couldn't entrust Mexican-Americans with the *important* Mexican-American roles. The Hollywood tradition. And we were the carriers." Biberman, *Salt of the Earth*, 43–44.

33. Rosaura Revueltas Sánchez, an actor, dancer, and writer, was member of a famous and talented Mexican family of artists, composers, and writers. It is rare to find such an accomplished family whose celebrated members occupied places in the

234 Notes to Chapter 6

top rank of several Mexican arts and in politics. Her brother José was a prominent, gifted writer and controversial political figure for more than a generation, and her brother Fermín was an important painter and muralist. Her third brother, Silvestre, was a well-known musician and composer. All were Communists.

34. The production company, cast, and film crew included the following members who were blacklisted, called as unfriendly witnesses before HUAC, or both: Herbert Biberman, Gale Sondergaard, Simon M. Lazarus, Michael Wilson, Will Geer, Herbert Waldman (aka David Wolfe), David Sarvis, and Mervin Williams. They took on the investigating committees in unapologetic, aggressive testimony while declining to name names.

35. Lorence, *Suppression*, 69–70, 75; Biberman, *Salt of the Earth*, 76; Hodges, "Making and Unmaking," 133.

36. Roos told them, "You come here and shoot the whole damn thing here. I'll stand at the top of the hill with a gun in my hands and say, 'Yes, I've got the whole gang here. What're you going to do about it? This is a thousand acres of Jeffersonian America and don't any reactionary, un-American hoodlum put his foot on it!'" Biberman, *Salt of the Earth*, 51, 58–59.

37. Jarrico estimated that four hundred individuals read or heard the script by the time it was filmed. Jarrico and Biberman, "Breaking Ground," 60; Wilson, *Salt of the Earth*; Lorence, for one, examined the script's criticisms. Lorence, *Suppression*, 60.

38. January 20 happened to be the day that Dwight David Eisenhower took the presidential oath.

39. The schoolteacher was June Kuhlman, but James Lorence's review of SAG files turned up four other informants. Three were from the *Silver City Enterprise*, including its publisher, Paul Wright, and the fourth was Kennecott's public relations person, Ward Balmer. Lorence to Jencks, December 3, 1997, Lorence Papers.

40. Lorence, *Suppression*, 77–78; Elizabeth Kerby, "Violence in Silver City, Who Caused the Trouble," *Frontier*, May 1953, 5–11.

41. Biberman, *Salt of the Earth*, 87; Rosenfelt, *Commentary*, 131.

42. Hodges, "Making and Unmaking," 165, 168.

43. Revueltas, "Reflections on a Journey," 174–75.

44. *Congressional Record*, 83rd Cong., 1st Sess., February 24, 1953, vol. 99, pt. 1, 1371–72; "Jackson Attacks Film," *New York Times*, February 25, 1953; Weinberg, "Salt of the Earth," 42; Jencks, "Palomino," 60–61, Box 1, Folder 1, Jencks Papers, University of Colorado; Baker, *On Strike*, 221, 224–25.

45. Revueltas, "Reflections on a Journey," 175–77; "Actress in Film Under Fire Is Seized as Illegal Alien," *New York Times*, February 27, 1953; "Star of Union Movie Being Held Without Bond," *Silver City Daily Press*, February 27, 1953; "Moves to Free Actress," *New York Times*, February 28, 1953.

46. Hodges, "Making and Unmaking," 167.

47. Biberman, *Salt of the Earth*, 91; Baker, *On Strike*, 227; Hodges, "Making and Unmaking," 173; Elizabeth Kerby, "Violence in Silver City. Who Caused the

Trouble," *Frontier* (May 1953), 5–11, 8; "Community Near Silver City Bars Movie Crew," *Albuquerque Journal*, March 3, 1953; Lorence, *Suppression*, 34.

48. The *Albuquerque Journal* photograph showed Lett smiling and holding up his right fist for the camera, with the caption: "Eye-Blackening Fist: Earl Lett, Bayard druggist, cheerfully displays right fist with which he blackened mine union leader Clinton Jencks' eye Tuesday. The fracas in which townspeople, here offering silver dollars for any fine Lett might have to pay, stopped filming of a controversial union movie scenes." The same issue carried a photograph of Jencks next to his bullet-damaged vehicle with his eye clearly injured. *Albuquerque Journal*, March 6, 1953.

49. "Street Fight Halts New Mexico Filming," *New York Times*, March 4, 1953; Hodges, "Making and Unmaking," 173. Later that day, Jencks filed charges against Lett and requested that Lett be put under a peace bond, Baker, *On Strike*, 227, 228.

50. "Citizens Parade in Film Protest," *Albuquerque Journal*, March 5, 1953; "Violence is Avoided in Protest on Film," *New York Times*, March 5, 1953; Hodges, "Making and Unmaking," 175; Jarrico and Biberman, "Breaking Ground," 61.

51. Jencks was in danger. A Mimbres farmer noted, "I think Jencks will get killed if he doesn't leave town." But to Joe "Fat Joe" Morales, "It wouldn't make any difference if Jencks did leave. The problem is racial, and it will still be here after he leaves." Both in Elizabeth Betty Kerby to Michael Wilson, June 2, 1954, Box 45, Folder 7, Wilson Papers.

52. Biberman, *Salt of the Earth*, 113; Hodges, "Making and Unmaking," 176, 177.

53. Lett: "Some of my best friends are Spanish Americans." Bayard Mayor Bill Upton: "We have Spanish-American families here who are just as fine a people as you ever saw. But on the other hand the laboring class is not the same class of people. . . . We're just sitting on dynamite here until something is done about these Communists." The *Daily Press*: "Most of Mine-Mill's devoted following are Mexican background—as distinguished from New Mexico's own native people, who are Spanish-Americans and proud of it." Baker, *On Strike*, 230. Another writer recorded more extensive remarks by Mayor Upton. "The good Spanish American here can and does command social prestige—the *gente decente*, well-descended people. They are just as fine a people as you ever saw. But on the other hand, the laboring class are not the same class of people." Elizabeth Betty Kerby to Michael Wilson, June 2, 1954, Box 45, Folder 7, Wilson Papers.

54. "Mining Film Near Finish, Backers Say," *Los Angeles Times*, March 6, 1953, 10.

55. Alford Roos in IUMMSW, "Portrait of a Labor Organizer," 31, c.1956, Box 1, Folder 5, Jencks Papers, University of Colorado.

56. Baker, *On Strike*, 228; Hodges, "Making and Unmaking," 178.

57. "Union Finishes Move Today, Crew Leaving Area Saturday," *Albuquerque Journal*, March 6, 1953; Jules Schwerin, "On Location," in Wilson, *Salt of the Earth*, 179; "Mobbed Film Crew Quits New Mexico," *New York Times*, March 8, 1953.

58. "Mine-Mill Gets Arson Expert to Probe 3 Fires," *Albuquerque Journal*, March 18, 1953; Baker, *On Strike*, 232.

59. IUMMSW, "Portrait of a Labor Organizer," 33, c.1956, Box 1, Folder 5, Jencks Papers, University of Colorado; Baker, *On Strike*, 99, 146–47.

60. Howard Hughes to Jackson, March 18, 1953, in Wilson, *Salt of the Earth*, 181–82.

61. "Reds in the Desert," *Newsweek*, March 2, 1953; "Salt of the Earth," *Time*, March 16, 1953; "Salt & Pepper," *Time*, March 29, 1954; "'Salt'—One Brand," *Newsweek*, March 29, 1954.

CHAPTER 7

1. Testimony of Richard B. Berresford, *Matters Relating to Labor-Management Act of 1947: Hearings*, March 17, 1953, 1199, 1202, 1204; "Firm Urges Ban on Negotiations with Red Unions," *El Paso Herald-Post*, March 18, 1953.

2. "Men Will Fight for Our Own Union, Chacon Asserts," *Albuquerque Journal*, March 19, 1953; "Mine-Mill Head Fights Red Hunt," *Arizona Republic*, March 19, 1953, 3.

3. The indictment charged in Count 1. "That on or about the 28th day of April, 1950, in the Western District of Texas, Clinton E. Jencks, the defendant herein, in a matter within the jurisdiction of the National Labor Relations Board, an agency of the United States, did unlawfully and willfully make, use and cause to be made and used and file and cause to be filed with the National Labor Relations Board a false writing and document namely an 'Affidavit of Non-Communist Union Officer' (Form NLRB-1081) knowing the same to contain a false fictitious and fraudulent statement and representation to wit: that he was not a member of the Communist Party, whereas the said Clinton E. Jencks then and there well knew he was a member of the Communist Party. In violation of Section 1001, Title 18, United States Code." Count 2 was the same except for the representation that he was not affiliated with the Communist Party. Original Trial Transcript, 1–2.

4. Jencks, "Palomino," 69, Box 1, Folder 1, Jencks Papers, University of Colorado; "Clinton Jencks, Mine-Mill Leader, Indicted, Held," *Albuquerque Journal*, April 21, 1953; "Jencks Makes Bond," *El Paso Herald-Post*, April 21, 1953.

5. "Mining Concerns Scored," *New York Times*, April 22, 1953; "Jailed Mine, Mill Union Official Blames Companies," *Albuquerque Journal*, April 22, 1953. Jencks also wrote that the Jencks case was "part of a more general attack on Mine-Mill, the labor movement, and all sections of the population who work or hope for more economic, social and political democracy." Jencks, "Jencks vs. U.S.," 3, Wood Collection.

6. Another early case was the one against Hugh Bryson, the national president of the National Union of Marine Cooks and Stewards. *Bryson v. United States*, 238 F.2d 657 (9th Cir. 1956), cert. denied, 355 U.S. 817.

7. Matusow, *False Witness*, 190. Schrecker, "Since Jencks was a relatively minor functionary, it was clear that the furor about *Salt of the Earth* had prompted his arraignment." *Many are the Crimes*, 336. Union president Juan Chacón said that the "indictment was the outcome of 'violence and hysteria caused by Congressman Jackson'" who attacked *Salt of the Earth* as "a new weapon for Russia." "Jencks Foresees 'Paid Witnesses' at Perjury Trial," *Albuquerque Journal*, April 24, 1953.

8. Matusow, *False Witness*, 190–92.

9. "Jencks Foresees 'Paid Witnesses' at Perjury Trial," *Albuquerque Journal*, April 24, 1953.

10. "Mine, Mill Union Official Urges Aid for Jencks," *Albuquerque Journal*, April 28, 1953.

11. "Mine-Mill Transfers Jencks to Denver," *Silver City Enterprise*, June 4, 1953; "Clinton Jencks Shifted to Denver," *Albuquerque Journal*, June 2, 1953.

12. "Board Launches Campaign Against Jencks Frame-up," *The Union*, July 13, 1953.

13. "Union Leader's Trial Scheduled," *El Paso Herald-Post*, August 17, 1953; "Jencks Hearing Scheduled for Oct. 23," *Albuquerque Journal*, October 15, 1953.

14. "Labor Board Ruling Hits Jencks Union," *Santa Fe New Mexican*, October 25, 1953; "Jencks' Motion Ruling Said Due in Several Days," *El Paso Times*, October 25, 1953; "Judge Overrules Plea to Dismiss Jencks Indictment," *Albuquerque Journal*, November 5, 1953; "New Date Set for Jencks Trial," *Albuquerque Journal*, November 20, 1953.

15. "E.P. Union Linked with Commie Plot by Atty. General," *El Paso Herald-Post*, November 25, 1953.

16. *Subversive Control of Distributive, Processing, and Office Workers of America: Hearings*; "Oust the Commies," *El Paso Herald-Post*, November 26, 1953.

17. "Clinton Jencks Group Warns of Prejudice," *El Paso Times*, November 28, 1953. One of the letter's recipients was Art Leibson, the *Times* reporter who was to cover the trial, who promptly turned the letter over to the FBI.

18. "Governor Shivers Warns Reds to Stay Out of Texas," *El Paso Herald-Post*, November 30, 1953.

19. Shivers Invites Union Officers to Red Hearings," *El Paso Herald-Post*, December 1, 1953; "Probers Hunt Reds in Texas," *El Paso Herald-Post*, December 4, 1953; "Shepperd Links Three Groups with Commies," *El Paso Herald-Post*, December 4, 1953.

20. "EP Red 'Way Station,' Ex-Communist Reveals," *El Paso Times*, December 5, 1953: "Ex-Red Says Texas Main Concentration Point for Commies, *El Paso Herald-Post*, December 5, 1953.

21. Sarah McClendon, "Immigration Service Unaware of Texas Reds," *El Paso Times*, December 10, 1953.

22. Texas Communist Control Law, Art. 6889-3, Texas Revised Civil Statutes. The Texas Attorney General announced in December 1953 that unregistered union organizers would not be allowed to operate in the state. Holmgren to Nathan Witt, December 30, 1953, Box 302, Folder 62, Jencks Papers, University of Colorado. In February 1954, Governor Shivers proposed legislation mandating the death penalty for Communist Party members, and the next month a member of the Texas legislature introduced death penalty legislation. "Texas Governor Urges Death Penalty for Reds," *New York Times*, February 12, 1954, 8; "Death Asked for Reds," *New York Times*, March 17, 1954. In 1954, Texas passed its version of sedition and Communist control legislation. Chapter 557, Texas Government Code. In August 1954, Congress passed the Communist Control Act of 1954, Title 50, United States Code, Sections 781 and 841, et seq.

23. "San Cristóbal Valley Ranch Closed by McCarthyism," *Albuquerque Journal*, December 12, 1953; "Ranch Described as Communist Indoctrination Center Closed," *Lubbock Avalanche-Journal*, December 13, 1953.

24. *The Union*, December 1953.

CHAPTER 8

1. His biographer noted, "No one rises to challenge in any substantial measure his local preeminence. His towering prestige . . . held him firmly in place as El Paso's number one citizen." Thomason, *Thomason*, 57.

2. Ibid., 1–19.

3. Ibid., 23–24.

4. Thomason and Lea backed Richard Dudley, El Paso's anti-Klan mayoral candidate. Lea had joined the Klan earlier but apparently quit by 1922, when he was the Dudley campaign point person against Klan candidate P. E. Gardner. Lay, *War, Revolution*, 144. Lea could not have been in the Klan long, because it was only organized in El Paso in July 1921, and Lea campaigned against its candidate in 1922. Alexander, *Ku Klux Klan*, 39, 127; Lay, "Imperial Outpost," 73; Sonnichsen, *Pass of the North II*, 11, 12. The Klan quickly lost its appeal in El Paso, where it never took hold, and Thomason would later find himself allied with former Klan personalities who agreed with him on issues like prohibition and controlling the perceived illegal Mexican vote. Alexander, *Ku Klux Klan*, 156. In 1922, the Democrats nominated Earle B. Mayfield, a Klan sympathizer and the Klan's candidate, for the U.S. Senate. Thomason, a "yellow dog Democrat," saw no alternative but to support Mayfield, a position that obligated Thomason to deny any Klan ties of his own. In a letter to the editor, Thomason wrote, "I am for Mayfield for Senator. To borrow the language of a friend, 'There is nothing else a Democrat can do.' I do not belong to the Ku Klux Klan, and never have." "Mr. Thomason to Support Mayfield for Senator," *Bartlett Tribune and News*, August 4, 1922, 2.

5. A fellow member in the powerful Texas delegation later noted what others have said: "Thomason of El Paso, was a marvelous member. There were so many able men from Texas, as well as elsewhere. . . . The Congress of the United States has many able men." Judge Marvin Jones, oral history, 85.

6. Thomason voted for the National Industrial Recovery Act of 1933, the Civilian Conservation Corps of 1933, the Agricultural Adjustment Act of 1933, the Tennessee Valley Authority in 1933, the Works Progress Administration of 1935, the Social Security Act of 1935, the National Labor Relations Act of 1935, the National Housing Act of 1937, and the Fair Labor Standards Act of 1938.

7. Thomason's vote against the Fair Employment Practices Commission (FEPC) could have been a product of following the lead of Howard W. Smith, an unremitting segregationist and anti-Communist. The FEPC had a short life, 1941–44. Smith and other segregationists brought about its termination. Smith, *Race, Labor, and Civil Rights*, 17–18. A review of congressional votes shows that while Thomason opposed the stronger 1937 antilynching bill backed by the NAACP, so did every member of

the Texas delegation except for the aptly named Maury Maverick, who was the only southern member to do so. But Thomason supported the weaker antilynching bill that only applied to federal prisoners. In doing so, Thomason was one of four in the twenty-member Texas delegation to support the bill, joining Sam Rayburn, Hatton Sumners, and Maury Maverick.

8. "Thomason Enters Order Outlawing Segregation," *El Paso Herald-Post*, July 27, 1955; "All Segregation in Texas Schools Declared Illegal," *Albuquerque Journal*, July 28, 1955; "E.P. Federal Judge Rules Segregation is Illegal in Texas," *El Paso Herald-Post*, July 18, 1955; "Judge Thomason Refuses to Dismiss Suit, Issues Declaratory Judgment in White Case," *El Paso Times*, July 19, 1955; Thomason Papers.

9. Cargill, "Empire and Opposition," 131.

10. Despite having relatively few union constituents, Thomason had a positive record in the eyes of organized labor, a political stance from his days in the Texas House. In the Texas legislature, he opposed the use of the National Guard to break strikes, and as a congressman, he gained labor's praise, such as in 1932 when he received 100 percent pro-labor marks. Thomason, *Thomason*, 21, 56–57. In 1932, he received a perfect labor rating for his votes in four important labor votes, including the Norris-LaGuardia Act.

11. In 1942, Thomason called the AFL and asked for his record on votes important to the AFL. The AFL sent a list of 23 labor votes cast in the years Thomason served, 1932 to 1941, noting that Thomason voted favorably to labor in 15 of the votes, voted unfavorably in only 5, and did not vote on three occasions. Thomason cast no votes against labor from 1932 to 1939. His first unfavorable vote was in support of Virginia's Howard W. Smith to establish a committee to investigate the NLRB. Responding to pleas from the business community, Smith sought to curb what he saw as a pro-CIO bias at the NLRB and to investigate possible Communist influence at the agency then administered by Nathan Witt. Thomason, like Smith, supported the AFL's side in its contention that the NLRB was favoring the CIO industrial unions over the AFL's craft unions. Most of Thomason's unfavorable labor votes related to amendments or legislation sponsored by Smith, the author of the famous anti-Communist Smith Act and no friend of organized labor. It was likely that Thomason was a Smith ally and fellow anti-Communist. Although his vote in 1943 for the Connally-Smith Act (War Labor Disputes Act) earned Thomason a place on labor's enemies list, the vote was predictable given his strong support for the military, his opposition to any disruption of wartime production, and his record of supporting Smith. The voting record confirmed that Thomason was friendly to labor, except when questions of Communist influence were involved. Hushing to Thomason, July 14, 1942, Box 5, Folder 5, Thomason Papers. Thomason was one of 238 House members, along with all but two of the Texas delegation, to vote for the Connally-Smith Act, which Congress passed over FDR's veto. "The Roll-Call of Labor's Enemies," *American Federation of Labor*, June 8, 1943.

12. The signature federal labor legislation was the Wagner Act, also known as the National Labor Relations Act, the law that established the National Labor Relations

Board and the principal law supported by organized labor. The postwar climate and the Republicans' taking control of Congress in the 1946 election brought about a reversal in pro-labor legislation, and the primary law to do so was without a doubt the Taft-Hartley Act. To organized labor, there was one standard by which to judge a legislator: "How did he vote on Taft-Hartley?" Overwhelming congressional majorities passed the Taft-Hartley Bill, but Truman vetoed the legislation. Congress overrode the President's veto by a wider margin than it had in passing the bill. In his memoir, both Thomason and his editor noted that Thomason voted for Taft-Hartley and for overriding the President's veto. To the contrary, the Congressional Record is clear about Thomason's vote *against* Taft-Hartley and in support of labor's and Truman's opposition to the bill. Sitting in the House chamber and voting on Taft-Hartley at that time were three presidents-to-be, John F. Kennedy, Richard M. Nixon, and Lyndon B. Johnson. The Congressional Record notes three critical House votes on Taft-Hartley. The first vote was to return the legislation, H.R. 3020, to committee. The vote was taken on April 17, 1947, and it failed 122 to 291. Thomason, Sam Rayburn, and Kennedy voted to return the legislation to committee, and Nixon and Johnson voted against the resolution. That effort failed, the bill itself was immediately brought up, and Taft-Hartley passed by a vote of 308 to 107. In the minority voting against Taft-Hartley were Thomason, Sam Rayburn, and John Kennedy. Johnson and Nixon voted for the law. After the Senate passed the same legislation and Truman vetoed it, the House again took up the bill on June 20, 1947, where House members voted 331–83 to override the president's veto. It represented a crushing defeat for Truman, who lost more votes between the passage and the override. Voting to sustain the veto were Thomason, John Kennedy, and Rayburn, with Nixon and Johnson voting to override. *Legislative History of Taft Hartley Act*, 1:861–62, 915; *93 Cong. Record*, 80th Cong. 1st Sess., April 17 and June 20, 1947, 3746, 3747, 7504.

13. William Green to Thomason, June 24, 1947, Box 22, Thomason Papers.

14. Alderman became chief of the Subversive Organization Section in the Internal Security Division, the section that compiled the attorney general's growing list of subversive organizations.

15. The prosecution also hired Mine-Mill member Isadore Salkind to help with the El Paso research.

16. *Report on the National Lawyers Guild.*

17. *Investigation of Communist Activities in the Los Angeles, Calif., Area*, 4061–62. In 1989, Margolis wrote a biographical note about his then former law partner McTernan, which is found in Box 59, Folder 6, Jencks Papers, University of Colorado.

18. California Legislature, *Sixth Report of the Senate Fact-Finding Committee on Un-American Activities*, 1951, 260.

19. Steve Nelson, *The 13th Juror*, 8. After Nelson was unable to find any lawyer in the Pittsburgh area to take his case, McTernan agreed to represent him. He was charged with violating Pennsylvania's version of the Smith Act. Schrecker, *Many Are the Crimes*, 303. McTernan spent more than four months in that trial before his client was severed out of the case as the result of an automobile accident. Nelson

was convicted after a second trial, but the Supreme Court reversed the conviction. *Pennsylvania v. Nelson*, 350 U.S. 497 (1956). Nelson was well-known to the Bureau long before his Pittsburgh indictment. The bureau had Communist Steve Nelson, aka Mesarosh, under surveillance since 1942. His phone had been tapped and his home bugged. He had been recorded having a conversation in Berkeley with a physics student about the Los Alamos project, information he relayed to a Soviet agent. Until then, the bureau did not know about the Manhattan Project and had little knowledge of the Soviet espionage apparatus. That one meeting gave Hoover the link he needed to allege that CP members were involved in spy rings. Weiner, *Enemies*, 119–20; "Steve Nelson, Ex-Communist Tied to Ruling on Sedition, Dies at 90," *New York Times*, December 14, 1993.

20. McTernan was described as the "chief defense counsel." Russell Porter, "All 13 convicted in Red Trial Here by Jury Out 7 Days," *New York Times*, Jan 22, 1953, 1. Elizabeth Gurley Flynn and her codefendants in the New York case were turned down by more than two hundred lawyers before finding representation. Schrecker, *Many Are the Crimes*, 303.

21. *Investigation of Communist Activities in the Los Angeles, Calif., Area*, 4061–62.

22. *Los Angeles Times*, April 4, 2005.

23. *Investigation of Communist Activities in the Los Angeles, Calif., Area*.

24. *Security—Government Printing Office: Hearings*, 114.

25. California Legislature, *Sixth Report of the Senate Fact-Finding Committee on Un-American Activities*, 1951, 260. El Paso Times editor agreed that Jencks's defense was respectful. "During the trial, the defense attorneys conducted themselves with utmost decorum. As a matter of fact, their court room manners brought considerable praise from El Paso judges and lawyers." "Abuse of Freedom?" *El Paso Times*, January 23, 1954.

26. Today, it is odd to think of the Department of Agriculture as attractive to left-wing radicals. In general, the sober agency was run by and for the benefit of large food processors and millions of four-hundred-plus-acre farmers. Generally ignored were the millions of tenant farmers and sharecroppers and the much larger number of farm workers. Roosevelt appointed Henry A. Wallace to run the department, and Wallace brought new ideas and people. In addition to Witt, Frank recruited future Supreme Court Justice Abe Fortas, governor and presidential nominee Adlai Stevenson, future Nuremberg prosecutor Telford Taylor, John J. Abt, Lee Pressman, and Alger Hiss. Weinstein, *Perjury*, 132.

27. *Special Committee to Investigate National Labor Relations Board, House of Representatives*, 76-3, HR 258, 1:895 (Washington, D.C.: GPO, 1940).

28. Ibid., vols. 1–30.

29. Hiba Hafiz, "The Red-Scare Relic That Holds Back Smart Labor Policy," *New York Times*, May 1, 2018. Smith not only got rid of Witt, but he also ran off its chief economist and eliminated the Board's Division of Economic Research. "David Saposs, 82, Labor Economist," *New York Times*, November 16, 1968.

30. Witt to Committee, October 16, 1940, *Special Committee to Investigate National Labor Relations Board, House of Representatives*, 76-3, HR 258, 25:7487–88 (Washington, D.C.: GPO, 1940). McTernan had made a similar disclaimer in his application for his NLRB job. *Investigation of Communist Activities in the Los Angeles, Calif., Area* 4063, 4065.

31. Cammer later represented Ben Gold, who had been charged with filing a false Taft-Hartley non-Communist affidavit. The Supreme Court reversed Cammer's contempt conviction for having communicated with the grand jury. *Cammer v. United States*, 350 U.S. 399 (1956).

32. Zarnow, "Braving Jim Crow," 1013.

33. *Interim Report on Hearings Regarding Communist Espionage in the United States Government*, 6–9.

34. Chambers, *Witness*, 287, 322.

35. C. P. Trussell, "Red 'Underground' in Federal Posts Alleged by Editor," *New York Times*, August 4, 1948.

36. It did not take long for the Chambers testimony to affect former Ware Group members. By mid-1949, Hiss resigned his Carnegie position, and Nixon was on his way to higher office, but not before Nixon had another run at Abt, Witt, and Pressman. Pressman had recently separated from the Witt, Cammer, and Pressman law partnership and publicly resigned from the American Labor Party for its stand against the Korean Conflict. In August 1950, HUAC and Nixon again subpoenaed Pressman, Abt, and Witt. Just before the hearing, Abt and Witt learned that Pressman had decided to cooperate with the committee. On August 28, 1950, Pressman appeared. He seemed anguished as he stated that he had decided to split with his former Communist friends over the Korean Conflict. He was now for the United States in that conflict, and they were opposed. He mentioned Hiss and the Ware Group and his membership, but at first, Pressman declined to identify Ware Group members. Finally, pressured by Nixon, Pressman identified Abt, Witt, and others as members. Pressman did not wholly impress his new anti-Communist friends, and he lost a host of old ones, including Abt and Witt. Although Pressman admitted that the Ware Group was Communist, he was vehement that its object was not espionage or disloyalty. *Hearings Regarding Communism in the United States Government, Part 2*, 2844, 2847, 2852–55. Years later, in memoirs published posthumously, Abt, still angry as a result of Pressman's betrayal, confirmed the existence of the Ware Group and the membership of Hiss, Witt, Abt, and others. Abt with Myerson, *Advocate and Activist*, 39–42.

37. Abt with Myerson, *Advocate and Activist*, 153.

38. Ibid., 42.

39. *Communist Domination*, Hearings.

40. *Interlocking subversion in Government Departments*, Hearing, 621–40, 640–55.

41. Craig Vincent testimony, Pretrial Transcript; *El Paso Times*, January 6, 8, and 9, 1954; *El Paso Herald-Post*, January 8, 9, 1954

42. "Jencks Plans Final Fight to Prevent Trial in Texas," *Albuquerque Journal*, January 10, 1954.

43. *Mine-Mill Bulletin*, January 11, 1954; Holmgren to McTernan, December 30, 1953, Holmgren correspondence, Box 62, Folder 302, Jencks Papers, University of Colorado; Holmgren to Miller Robertson, January 7, 1954, Box 62, Folder 2, Jencks Papers, University of Colorado.

44. "Jury for Jencks Trial Chosen in 90 Minutes," *Albuquerque Journal*, January 12, 1954.

45. The union charged that it was a "Trial by Headline." *Mine-Mill Bulletin*, January 11, 1954. See the defendant's motion for continuance and change of venue and the affidavit of Rod Holmgren, who handled the union's public relations. District Court record for January 11, 1954.

46. Mine-Mill wrote that it was a "Stacked Jury Panel." *Mine-Mill Bulletin*, January 11, 1954; Motion to dismiss indictment and against the jury array. NARA District Court record for January 11, 1954.

CHAPTER 9

1. "Start to Select Jencks Case Jury," *El Paso Herald Post*, January 11, 1954.

2. Two of the Mexicans did not have Spanish surnames. The six Mexican panel members were Manuel Y. Baisa, Felipe Hernández, George F. LeBreton, Guillermo Villarreal, Leo A. Collins, and Roberto Alberto García.

3. At the time of the trial, El Paso's population was over 194,000, 100,000 of whom were men. Of the forty thousand males over twenty-one years of age, thirty thousand, or 75 percent, were native born citizens, and of the balance, three thousand were naturalized. That would leave about 82 percent as eligible to vote, or about 33,200. The Mexican population in El Paso in 1954 would have been over 60 percent, and with 82 percent of those eligible to vote, that would have made about 49 percent of the male population Hispanic and eligible to vote. In "Stacked Jury Panel," the *Mine-Mill Bulletin* noted that "of the 63 panel members, there are only 3 Mexican-Americans, in contrast to a Mexican-American percentage of 60 to 65 percent in the County." *Mine-Mill Bulletin*, January 11, 1954.

4. Jury information list, Box 59, Folder 5, Jencks Papers, University of Colorado.

5. As *Mine-Mill Bulletin* reported, McTernan pointed out that 62 percent of those on the panel were managers, officials, or business owners when only 10 percent of El Paso males were so employed. The panel was only 9 percent manual workers, whereas 60.5 percent were so. *Mine-Mill Bulletin*, January 11, 1954.

6. "Start to Select Jencks Case Jury," *El Paso Herald Post*, January 11, 1954.

7. The government struck all four Mexicans among the first twenty-eight names, Manuel Y. Baisa, Felipe Hernández, Guillermo Villarreal, and Roberto Alberto García.

8. "NOT ONE . . . The jury in the trial of Clinton Jencks does not include one single union member. It does not include one single Mexican-American. The prosecuting attorneys saw to that. They asked every prospective juror whether he was a union

member. They used peremptory challenges to eliminate the three [there were four] Mexican-Americans whose names were called." "Newspapers Convict Jencks before Trial; Press, Radio Refuse Mine-Mill Paid Ads," *The Union*, January 18, 1954.

9. According to the union's published trial reports, black juror Morrie B. White was "ignored by the other 11, left alone with segregated toilet and lunch rooms." "Special Report of the Trial of Brother Clinton Jencks," IUMMSW Jencks Defense Committee, 2, Box 62, Folder 1, Jencks Papers, University of Colorado. "This last point, indicating typical Texas racism, is on par with the treatment of a single Negro on the jury, Morie White, whose occupation was listed as elevator operator. When the court broke for recesses at lunch or at the end of the day, the white jurors trouped out to the elevator in a body. Five or ten minutes later, after almost everybody had left the courtroom and the corridor, White would make his way alone out of the jury chamber. When he went to the men's room, he had to go through the door labeled 'Colored.'" "Notes on the Jencks Trial," *Mine-Mill Staff Bulletin*, no. 53, February 9, 1954, 6, Box 62, Folder 1, Jencks Papers, University of Colorado.

10. In 1950, Grant County was 47 percent Mexican, but only 33 percent of voters and just 8.7 percent of jurors were Mexican. Lorence, *Suppression*, 14.

11. The lawyer was Carlos C. Cadena from San Antonio.

12. *Hernández v. Texas*, 347 U.S. 475 (1954). The defense challenge to that prohibition of women jurors also would do Jencks no good, Women were finally allowed to serve on Texas juries later in 1954 after Texas amended the state constitution on November 2, 1954.

13. After Texas amended its constitution in 1954 to include women on juries, the first women prepared to serve in El Paso in April 1955. Court observers were already familiar with the overrepresentation of El Paso's upper-crust on federal juries under Thomason and his predecessor, both of whom used Laurence Stevens as their jury commissioner. "Federal Court juries are virtually blue ribbon juries, carefully chosen, and some of the women who will serve here for the first time are expected to be socially prominent." "Women to Start Serving on Federal Juries in El Paso on April 4," *El Paso Herald-Post*, March 18, 1955. Two years later, a group of Permian Basin trial lawyers filed a complaint in Thomason's court critical of Thomason's employer-heavy jury panels and alleged a violation of the Seventh Amendment's right to trial by jury in civil cases. The jurors summoned to serve, the lawyers charged, mostly represented the employers' viewpoint and few workers were called. "Judge Defends His Court Officials," unknown publication of September 1957, Box 25, scrapbook p. 39, Thomason Papers.

14. Original Trial Transcript, 70.

15. The Supreme Court held, "Of course, we agree that the courts cannot 'ascertain the thought that has had no outward manifestation.' But courts and juries every day pass upon knowledge, belief and intent—the state of men's minds—having before them no more than evidence of their words and conduct, from which, in ordinary human experience, mental condition may be inferred. *See* 2 Wigmore, Evidence (3d ed.) §§ 244, 256 *et seq*. False swearing in signing the affidavit must, as in other cases

where mental state is in issue, be proved by the outward manifestations of state of mind. In the absence of such manifestations, which are as much "overt acts" as the act of joining the Communist Party, there can be no successful prosecution for false swearing." *American Communications Assn. v. Douds*, 339 U.S. 382, 411 (1950).

16. Original Trial Transcript, 72.

17. NLRB office manager Elsie Perryman, Bayard banker William James Upton, Silver City banker Don A. Wilson, and FBI Special Agent George F. Mesnig. Original Trial Transcript, 72, 116, 126, 133.

18. Original Trial Transcript, 215, 217.

19. Ibid., 198–210.

20. Jencks to Lorence, June 17, 1999, 9a, Lorence Papers; Art Leibson, "Court Hears Sensational Testimony," *El Paso Times*, January 13, 1954.

21. Art Leibson, "Court Hears Sensational Testimony," *El Paso Times*, January 13, 1954.

22. *American Communications Assn. v. Douds*, 339 U.S. 382 (1950).

23. In *Douds*, the court held, "This distinction is emphasized by the fact that members of those groups identified in § 9(h) are free to serve as union officers if at any time they renounce the allegiances which constituted a bar to signing the affidavit in the past. Past conduct, actual or threatened by their previous adherence to affiliations and beliefs mentioned in § 9(h), is not a bar to resumption of the position." *American Communications Assn. v. Douds*, 339 U.S. at 414.

24. Williams, "Yes, as I announced in my opening statement, from 1946 right on up to the filing of the instrument." Original Trial Transcript, 80–81, 85.

25. Ibid., 303, 309, 331, 347–48.

26. Ibid., 300.

27. Ibid., 371–72.

28. Ibid., 388.

29. Ibid., 388–90.

30. Ibid., 409.

31. Ibid., 409–19.

32. Ibid., 490–96, 498–507.

33. Ibid., 561–63, 564.

34. Ibid., 566–67, 568.

35. Art Leibson, "'I Am a Communist—And Proud of It,' Witness Testifies Jencks Told Him," *El Paso Times*, January 14, 1954; "Witnesses Charge Jencks Plotted with Commies to Control Unions," *El Paso Herald-Post*, January 14, 1954; "Former Pastor Here Says Jencks a Top Communist in New Mexico," *Albuquerque Journal*, January 14, 1954. It its editorial, the *Times* wrote, "The more we watch proceedings in the trial of Clinton Jencks in Federal District Court in El Paso, the more our respect for the investigative ability of the Federal Bureau of Investigation. . . . The FBI is one of the best safeguards to our lives and our freedoms." "FBI 'Delivers,'" *El Paso Times*, January 15, 1954.

36. FBI files note that the editor had formerly written favorable editorials and had correspondence with the director for some years. Hoover to Hooten, January 21, 1954, Jencks FBI File No. 122-232.

37. Art Leibson, "Defendant as A Red in 1950," *El Paso Times*, January 16, 1954.

38. Original Trial Transcript, 584–90.

39. Ibid., 591.

40. Ibid.

41. Ibid., 592–93.

42. Ibid., 598–99.

43. A news article noted that McTernan questioned Matusow for ten days in the *Flynn* case. "Informer Charges Accused Branded U.S. as Aggressor," *El Paso Herald-Post*, January 15, 1954. Other reports had Matusow on the stand a total of six days.

44. Original Trial Transcript, 606–13.

45. Ibid., 651–54.

46. Ibid., 658–61, 662.

47. Ibid., 667.

48. Ibid., 671, 673.

49. Ibid., 679, 680.

50. Witt: "So [Matusow's testimony] was most persuasive; he made a very good witness, a very persuasive kind of witness. He held up very well under cross-examination." Witt interview by Hoffman, 7.

51. Original Trial Transcript, 896–98.

52. *El Paso Herald-Post*, January 15, 1954.

53. *El Paso Times*, January 16, 1954.

54. In part of the trial that was not transcribed (Original Trial Transcript, 324), McTernan strenuously objected to Eckert's expertise and his testimony. Once again, the prosecution was attempting to prove Jencks's membership or affiliation by noting common policy positions between Jencks and the Party, what McTernan called parallelism. McTernan also accused the prosecutors of leaking Eckert's testimony to the prosecution-friendly *Herald-Post*. McTernan mentioned a morning edition reporting testimony that had not yet been heard. Mine-Mill Trial Bulletin, January 18, 1954, Box 62, Folder 1, Jencks Papers, University of Colorado.

55. "Judge Concedes a Point at T-H Trial of Jencks," *Daily Worker*, January 22, 1954.

56. Original Trial Transcript, 898–900, 906–9, 915–17, 920–23.

57. Ibid., 929, 932–34, 937–41, 963.

58. Ibid., 964–65, 968.

59. Ibid., 1117–26.

60. Ibid., 300.

61. Ibid., 1083–84, 1098, 1099. Broaddus:

"[Ford] said further that never, up until September of 1950, was Clinton E. Jencks taken from the State Board of the Communist Party of New Mexico. September of 1950, gentlemen [of the jury], five months after [the date of the affidavit]."

"Yet, until September of 1950, up until September 1950, he was never removed from the State Executive Board of the Communist Party, he was never disciplined."

"This man was never replaced on the State Executive Board. He was never disciplined for any Party defection up until September of 1950."

Referring to the 1949 affidavit dated October 15, 1949, the prosecutor said: "October of 1949. And he was never removed up to and through September of 1950."

Jencks "lived with it and schemed with it, gentlemen, from 1946, and continuing until April 28, 1950. At that time, he had never been replaced on the State Executive Board of the New Mexico Communist Party."

At the end of his summation, Broaddus stated, "He was never replaced on the State Executive Board of the Communist Party in New Mexico five months after he signed the affidavit."

62. Trial Transcript, 1179.

63. Ibid., 1185.

64. Ibid., 1113.

65. Ibid., 1104.

66. Ibid., 1061–63.

67. Ibid., 1067–68, 1069–70.

68. "Jury Finds Jencks Guilty," *El Paso Herald Post*, January 21, 1954.

69. Original Trial Transcript, 1127–29.

70. "Jury Finds Jencks Guilty," *El Paso Herald Post*, January 21, 1954. The *Herald-Post*'s extra edition may have gotten the bragging rights to the scoop, but it was the *El Paso Times* that first reached most home delivery readers the next morning with its banner headline, "Jencks Guilty, Gets 5 Years; Appeal Bond Set At $10,000." *El Paso Times*, January 22, 1954.

71. "Lawyers Plan to Appeal Conviction of Jencks," *El Paso Herald-Post*, January 22, 1954; "Jencks Is Found Guilty in El Paso Red Case," *Albuquerque Journal*, January 22, 1954; "Jencks' Lawyers Plan Appeal; Bond Posted," *Albuquerque Journal*, January 23, 1954.

72. *El Paso City Directory*, 1944, 383.

73. Jencks Defense Committee press release, January 21, 1954.

74. Jencks to Floyd Bostick, February 3, 1954, Box 302, Folder 302-2, Jencks Papers, University of Colorado.

75. "Jencks may Face State Prosecution," *Albuquerque Journal*, January 29, 1954.

76. "Jencks Appeal Hangs Fire in State Supreme Court," *Albuquerque Journal*, January 30, 1954.

CHAPTER 10

1. A detailed history of Matusow's background is in SAC NY to Director, May 15, 1953, Matusow FBI File No. 100-375988; Lichtman and Cohen, *Deadly Farce*, 20–24; Matusow, *False Witness*, 23; Caute, *Great Fear*, 133.

2. Matusow, *False Witness*, 33; New York FBI office memo, March 3, 1953, Matusow FBI File No. 100-375988.

3. Matusow testified before HUAC in executive session on November 27, 1951. *Hearing to Investigate Communist Activities*; Testimony of John J. and Martha N. Edmiston, *Strategy and Tactics of World Communism, Hearings*, 681–90, 671–90; Matusow, *False Witness*, 37; Lichtman and Cohen, *Deadly Farce*, 46–47.

4. *Communist Activities Among Youth Groups*, Hearings, 3314, 3323–24; *Subversive Control of Distributive, Processing, and Office Workers of America: Hearings*, February 13, 1952; Matusow, *False Witness*, 54, 64, 72, 88–92.

5. Institute of Pacific Relations, Hearings, 3823, 3829, 3831.

6. Matusow, *False Witness*, 60–64; Lichtman and Cohen, *Deadly Farce*, 65.

7. Lumet was then directing television drama. He later moved to film and accumulated impressive credits for highly regarded films, such as *Dog Day Afternoon*, *Serpico*, and *Network*, among others. In New York, Matusow made his allegations in the weekly newsletter, *Counterattack*. Matusow, *False Witness*, 108–9. When hired on by the newsletter, Matusow rose from selling its subscriptions in Ohio to being on the New York staff.

8. Sidney Lumet, Foundation Interviews. The blacklisting machinery in New York was operated by Aware, Inc., and the associated newsletter *Red Channels*. *Faulk v. Aware, Inc.*, 231 N.Y.S. 2d 270 (N.Y. Sup. Ct. 1962); Lichtman and Cohen, *Deadly Farce*, 63. Matusow claimed that he had helped lawyer Louis Nizer in his suit by telling Nizer to call ad man Frank Barton as a witness. Matusow, *False Witness*, 119–24.

9. Matusow, *False Witness*, 135, 149, 154–59; "Ex-Red Charges Union Heads Planned Korean War Strike" *El Paso Herald-Post*, October 9, 1952; Lichtman and Cohen, *Deadly Farce*, 67–68, 70–71.

10. Matusow, *False Witness*, 164, 167, 169; Lichtman and Cohen, *Deadly Farce*, 69–71.

11. Matusow, *False Witness*, 172–74; Lichtman and Cohen, *Deadly Farce*, 72.

12. Matusow, *False Witness*, 190–92.

13. Belmont to Ladd, June 9, 1953; SAC WFO to Director, June 17, 1953; Belmont to Ladd, June 22, 1953; all in Matusow FBI File No. 100-375988.

14. "Matusow Asks Divorce, $20,000 from His Wife," *Albuquerque Journal*, September 20, 1953.

15. New York Times to Hoover, October 1, 1953; Belmont to Ladd, October 6, 1953; both in Matusow FBI File No. 100-375988; Matusow FBI File No. 100-375988; Lichtman and Cohen, *Deadly Farce*, 82–83, 87–88.

16. Matusow, *False Witness*, 186; Belmont to Ladd, December 4, 1953, Matusow FBI File No. 100-375988.

17. Lichtman and Cohen, *Deadly Farce*, 92–93.

18. Baumgartner to Belmont, October 25, 1954, Matusow FBI File No. 100-375988; Lichtman and Cohen, *Deadly Farce*, 94.

19. Matusow, *False Witness*, 231; Baumgartner to Belmont, July 2, 1954; Oxnam to Brownell, October 19, 1954; both in Matusow FBI File No. 100-375988. The

Communist Party would later challenge this SACB proceeding in a case that reached the Supreme Court, which will be mentioned in a later chapter.

20. Lichtman and Cohen, *Deadly Farce*, 96–97. In an October HUAC hearing, Oxnam criticized the Department using Matusow. He testified that he "was astounded that Attorney General Herbert Brownell Jr. would 'rely on the testimony of a person like Harvey Matusow' in any legal proceeding." "Witness Admitted Lies, Oxnam Says," *New York Times*, October 19, 1954.

21. Testimony of Harvey M. Matusow, *Communist Activities Among Youth Groups, Hearings*, July 12, 1954, 5843, 5846, 5847; Matusow, *False Witness*, 232; Kahn, *Matusow Affair*, 12; Lichtman and Cohen, *Deadly Farce*, 95–97.

22. New Trial Transcript, 478.

23. "Clinton Jencks Ordered Back to Jail," *Silver City Daily Press*, June 23, 1954; "Mine-Mill Men Must Go to Jail," *El Paso Times*, June 24, 1954; "Mine, Mill Union Leaders Ordered to Serve Terms," *Albuquerque Journal*, June 24, 1954.

24. "Gov. Mechem Denies Pardon from Jail Term for Jencks," *Silver City Daily Press*, July 8, 1954; "Mine-Mill Sextette Back in Jail to Finish 90-Day Stay," *Silver City Enterprise*, July 15, 1954; "Mine, Mill Union Officials Back Behind the Bars," *Albuquerque Journal*, July 14, 1954.

25. Kahn, *Matusow Affair*, 23; Lichtman and Cohen, *Deadly Farce*, 101–3.

26. Kahn, *Matusow Affair*, 47–48, 53–54, 68–69; Lichtman and Cohen, *Deadly Farce*, 114–16.

27. Kahn, *Matusow Affair*, 93; Lichtman and Cohen, *Deadly Farce*, 115–17.

28. Lichtman and Cohen, *Deadly Farce*, 118–19.

CHAPTER 11

1. Stewart Alsop, "Matter of Fact, Legal Lying," *Medford* (Ore.) *Mail Tribune*, January 30, 1955; Kahn, *Matusow Affair*, 107–8.

2. "Attorney in El Paso for Filing," *El Paso Times*, January 28, 1955; "New Hearing Set for Jencks," *El Paso Herald-Post*, January 28, 1955; "Jencks Gets Hearing March 7," *El Paso Times*, January 29, 1955; "Red Informer Says He Lied at Trial," *New York Times*, January 29, 1955.

3. "Mine-Mill Union Opens Fight on U.S. Witnesses," *El Paso Herald-Post*, January 29, 1955; "Jencks' New Trial Bid Stirs Union Assembly Today," *Albuquerque Journal*, January 29, 1955; "Mine, Mill Men Blast Matusow," *El Paso Times*, January 30, 1955; "Mine-Mill Union Raps Matusow and Segregation," *Albuquerque Journal*, January 30, 1955;

4. Edward Ranzal, "Anti-Red Witness Confesses He Lied," *New York Times*, February 1, 1955.

5. Kahn, *Matusow Affair*, 120.

6. "Repentant Matusow," *New York Times*, February 6, 1955; Drew Pearson, "Ex-Red Matusow on Inside with McCarthy," *Denver Post*, February 4, 1955; Murray Kempton, "The Renegade," *New York Post*, February 4, 1955; "The Fruits of Falsehood," *Deseret*

News, February 4, 1955; "The Perjurer," *The New Mexican*, February 4, 1955; "The Matusow Case," *New York Herald Tribune*, February 4, 1955.

7. *El Paso Herald-Post*, February 4, 1955.

8. Steinbeck, "The Death of a Racket."

9. Kahn, *Matusow Affair*, 126, 142, 148.

10. Edward Ranzal, "'53 Matusow Note Cites 'Dishonesty,'" *New York Times*, February 11, 1955.

11. Marie Natvig claimed that FCC lawyers had prevented her from retracting her previous false testimony. "Witness Says She Lied," *New York Times*, February 11, 1955. The FCC later held her testimony to be "completely incredible." "FCC Testimony by Woman Voided," *New York Times*, February 18, 1955. Later, Lowell Watson said that he had lied about Lamb's Communist ties. "TV Owner's Case in F.C.C. Near End," *New York Times*, February 25, 1955; Kahn, *Matusow Affair*, 162.

12. "Matusow Sought Anti-Reds' Favor," *New York Times*, February 12, 1955.

13. "'False Witness,'" *New York Times*, February 13, 1955.

14. Edward Ranzal, "Matusow Admits Recantation Pays," *New York Times*, February 15, 1955.

15. Edward Ranzal, "Matusow Admits Faking Blacklists," *New York Times*, February 16, 1955.

16. "Matusow Admits Lie About Oxnam," *New York Times*, February 17, 1955.

17. Luther A. Huston, "Matusow Study Widened by U.S.," *New York Times*, February 18, 1955.

18. Kahn, *Matusow Affair*, 170–71; Russell Baker, "No Longer a Liar, Matusow Swears," *New York Times*, February 22, 1955.

19. Russell Baker, "Matusow Blames M'Carthy for Lies," *New York Times*, February 23, 1955; Don Irwin, "Matusow Accuses McCarthy," *New York Herald Tribune*, February 23, 1955; "M'Carthy Ties in 1952 Cited by Matusow," *Washington Post*, February 23, 1955.

20. Russell Baker, "M'Carthy Scores Matusow Queries," *New York Times*, February 24, 1955.

21. Russell Baker, "Matusow Admits Lies Against 244," *New York Times*, March 3, 1955.

22. *Strategy and Tactics of World Communism*, Hearings; Kahn, *Matusow Affair*, 170–71.

23. "Texas Court Hears Matusow This Week," *New York Times*, March 6, 1955; "Harvey Matusow To Jencks Action," *Albuquerque Journal*, March 6, 1955.

24. Russell Baker, "U.S. Jury Indicts a False Witness," *New York Times*, March 8, 1955.

25. House committees considered providing witnesses with greater protection when they appeared. Senate committees investigated the government's administration of its security program. C. P. Trussell, "Fair Inquiry Code Pressed in House," *New York Times*, March 7, 1955; Russell Baker, "Security Inquiry Called Red Issue," *New York Times*, March 9, 1955. Asst. Attorney General Tompkins had been in El

Paso to confer with his lawyers, but quickly returned to Washington to defend the government's controversial use of paid Communist informants and experts.

26. "Jencks Arrives for Hearing," *El Paso Times*, March 7, 1955.

27. Jencks, "Palomino," 76–77, Box 1, Folder 1, Jencks Papers, University of Colorado.

28. "Matusow Book Publisher Helped Lea," *El Paso Times*, March 10, 1955. Cameron later went to Alfred A. Knopf.

29. Matusow specified as false his testimony about his meeting with Jencks at the San Cristóbal Valley Ranch. He admitted that, contrary to his previous testimony, he and Jencks had not discussed any of the following issues: the Communist Party, the transfer of his CP membership to New Mexico, the Stockholm Peace Appeal being Communist, working with Communist Mexican miners to disrupt Korean war production, Jencks's Communist book collection, ANMA being under CP control.

30. Jencks, "Palomino," 78, Box 1, Folder 1, Jencks Papers, University of Colorado; "Matusow Considered Suicide in 1953 Letter to Sen. Joe McCarthy Reveals," *El Paso Times*, March 8, 1955; "Jury Hears Witnesses in Matusow Lie Probe," and "Two-Story Man Cross-Examined by U.S. Attorney," *El Paso Herald-Post*, March 8, 1955; "Quiz Mine-Mill Leaders in Matusow Lie Inquiry," *El Paso Herald-Post*, March 9, 1955; "Matusow Recants in Texas," *New York Times*, March 8, 1955; "Jury Studies Matusow," *New York Times*, March 9, 1955; "Matusow Says He Feared to Tell He Had Lied," *El Paso Times*, March 10, 1955; "Want to Learn If Sale of Book Switched Witness," *El Paso Herald-Post*, March 10, 1955; "Feared for Life, Matusow Testifies," *El Paso Herald-Post*, March 10, 1955.

31. New Trial Transcript, 26–48, 722–25. Bigbee repeated the same request at pp. 107 and 147.

32. "Matusow Shouts 'Lie' Under Fire in Court," *El Paso Herald-Post*, March 11, 1955.

33. New Trial Transcript, 686.

34. Ibid., 264–66, 291, 322, 337, 345, 644, 701; "Matusow Says Lies Are Ended," *Albuquerque Journal*, March 9, 1955. In its part of the hearing, the government produced a mixed record about Matusow's finances while in Taos. Most witnesses testified that Matusow was broke except for one who said that from one day to the next Matusow claimed to have been paid one thousand dollars and flashed a roll of bills. Testimony of Riley Alvin Taintor, New Trial Transcript, 731–37. Two witnesses were called regarding conversations they had with Jencks after his confrontation with Matusow in Salt Lake City. One witness, Ernest V. Weinert, said he overheard another Mine-Mill member named Graham Dolan confront Jencks over Matusow's testimony that day. Dolan told Jencks that he should not have talked to Matusow at all at San Cristóbal. Jencks replied that he did talk to Matusow and just "handed him a line." Testimony of Ernest V. Weinert, , New Trial Transcript, 531–34; "Matusow May Face Contempt Count as Jencks Hearing Concludes," *El Paso Times*, March 11, 1955; "U.S. To Call More Surprise Witnesses in Matusow Inquiry," *El Paso Herald-Post*, March 11, 1955.

35. Witt testimony, New Trial Transcript, 770–805.

36. Ibid., 815–18.

37. New Trial Transcript, 819–20, 823. On March 16, Matusow had a two-hour hearing with Thomason that changed nothing. Perhaps fearing the backlash from representing an unpopular client, the lead lawyer for Matusow took the stand to assure the court that he was never a Communist. Afterward, waiting to be taken to jail, Matusow said that he was "disappointed but not surprised . . . I have no ill will against the judge," he added. Thomason confirmed that he held Matusow in contempt, sentenced him to three years in prison, and set a bond of ten thousand dollars. "Matusow Gets Three Years," *El Paso Herald-Post*, March 16, 1955; "Judge Holds Matusow in Contempt," *El Paso Herald-Post*, March 12, 1955; "Matusow Actions Called Contempt by El Paso Judge, *Albuquerque Journal*, March 13, 1955; "Matusow is Held on Contempt Rule, *New York Times*, March 13, 1955; "Matusow Receives 3-Year Prison Term," *New York Times*, March 17, 1955. It would be one month before Matusow would make bond. Albert Kahn persuaded a wealthy, leftist Connecticut couple, Henry and Anita Parkhurst Wilcox, to make bond for Matusow. "N.Y. Woman Provided Matusow's $10,000 Bail," *New York Herald Tribune*, April 18, 1955.

38. New Trial Transcript, 824–25.

39. This news was reported even in the *Times of London*. "Mr. Matusow Charged," *Times of London*, March 13, 1955; "Mine-Mill Top Lawyer Disbarred in E.P. Court," *El Paso Herald-Post*, March 12, 1955.

40. New Trial Transcript, 819–20, 823–25; "New Trial for Jencks Denied," *El Paso Herald-Post*, March 12, 1955.

41. "The Jencks Case," *Daily Worker*, March 14, 1955.

42. "The Liar Lies—In Jail," *El Paso Herald Post*, March 17, 1955.

43. The editor also wrote, "Always loved and respected as a man and a public official, his already tall stature grew immensely when he gave the Communists and their stooges what was coming to them." E. M. Pooley, "Side-Bar Remarks," *El Paso Herald-Post*, March 18, 1955.

44. El Paso lawyer Albert Armendariz wrote, "Your demeanor and actions on the bench in the recent motion for new trial involving Clifton [sic] Jencks and your actions regarding his attorney, have been a source of pride and inspiration to everyone one of us who is relatively new in our profession. Armendariz to Thomason, March 25, 1955, Thomason Papers.

45. "Eastland Praises Judge," *New York Times*, March 17, 1955.

46. Jencks, "Palomino," 79, Box 1, Folder 1, Jencks Papers, University of Colorado.

47. "Matusow's Contempt," *Washington Post*, March 20, 1955.

48. The *Washington Post* editorial of February 28, 1955 noted: "The discovery that witnesses relied upon by the government in proceedings against American citizens have been guilty of cynical and repeated perjury ought to have aroused anger and concern in the Attorney General of the United States. Instead, it seems to have aroused in Herbert Brownell Jr. only irritation at the embarrassment inflicted on his department, and a petulant defense of the system which produced this perjury."

"U.S. Knew in 1952 Matusow Was Ill," *New York Times*, April 11, 1955; "Matusow Exposed Before Trial," *Stars and Stripes*, April 12, 1955.

49. Minutes of the meeting note: "The Attorney General called to the attention of the Cabinet the Jenks [sic] Case which had come up for re-trial in Texas because the original trial had been partially based on the evidence from Matusow. He stated that the Judge had now ruled that the original testimony of Matusow was true and that Matusow's recantation was false. He quoted at length the Judge's finding to the effect that the Matusow recantation had been motivated by a desire to publicize his book and by a Communist effort to discredit the US courts. The President commented that this finding tended to strengthen the Administration position in regard to the conduct of Employee Security cases and the question of confronting an employee with adverse witnesses." Minutes, Cabinet Meeting of March 18, 1955, Eisenhower Papers. The meeting also noted that the President was upset over the public statements of a member of his administration, former Washington Senator Harry P. Cain, whom he appointed to the Subversive Activities Control Board (SACB). Cain showed that Matusow was not the only one changing his colors. Cain was the same individual supported by Senator McCarthy in the 1952 Senate campaign. McCarthy had sent Matusow to Washington State to make outrageous charges against Cain's opponent, Henry Jackson. Jackson defeated Cain and then Cain went on the SACB. Until the time McCarthy came under assault in late 1954, Cain was his reliable ally and made his own controversial allegations. While serving on the SACB, however, Cain became a civil libertarian and pointed out excesses in the employee security program and in the attorney general's subversive list. On the day of the cabinet meeting, Cain had given a speech to a civil liberties group assailing those critical of witnesses who invoked the Fifth Amendment. "Cain Defends Use of 5th Amendment," *New York Times*, March 19, 1955.

50. *United States v. Flynn, et al.*, 130 F.Supp. 412 (S.D. NY, 1955).

51. Lichtman and Cohen, *Deadly Farce*, 139. Alfred Kahn expressed similar thoughts. Kahn said there were similarities in the New York and El Paso hearings. In both, the Justice Department was attempting to prove a conspiracy by Matusow and others, and both had grand juries feeding the lawyers evidence to be used at the hearing. "But there was one striking difference: the judge in New York was interested in upholding the law and the judge in El Paso was interested in upholding the authority of the government." Kahn, *Matusow Affair*, 198.

52. Edward Ranzal, "Matusow Lies Get 2 Reds New Trial," *New York Times*, April 23, 1955.

53. "New Trial," *New York Times*, April 24, 1955.

54. Alexander Feinberg, "U.S. Lays Perjury to Matusow Here," *New York Times*, July 14, 1955.

55. Press Release, U.S. Department of Justice, July 28, 1955; Petition, Herbert Brownell Jr. v. International Union of Mine, Mill and Smelter Workers, Subversive Activities Control Board, both in Box 1, Folder 35, Lorence Papers.

56. "Brownell Drops Informant Plan," *New York Times*, April 16, 1955.

CHAPTER 12

1. The appeal carried appeals court no. 15157 and the new trial was 15557. The court denied the motion to consolidate on April 22. "Appeals Court Refuses to Delay Jencks Hearing," *El Paso Times*, May 25, 1955.

2. "Judge Ben Cameron, 73, Dead," *New York Times*, April 4, 1964.

3. Lee, Shakely, and Brown, "Judge Warren Jones and the Supreme Court of Dixie," 211.

4. The *New York Times* reported: "Judge Ben F. Cameron . . . accused Chief Judge Elbert P. Tuttle of Atlanta of stacking the deck in hearings involving racial cases." "Feud Over Racial Cases Flares in U.S. Appeals Court in South," *New York Times*, July 31, 1963. It came known as the court-packing scandal, which rocked the Fifth Circuit Court to its core. In a school desegregation case, Cameron filed a long and contentious dissent in which he accused Tuttle, the court's then chief judge, of rigging the selection of judges to sit in racial cases in favor of the liberal "Four." In his study of twenty-five cases, Cameron found that "The Four" sat on twenty-two of them. Jones participated in the investigation to determine the facts behind Cameron's charge. Although Tuttle insisted that the assignment of The Four to twenty-two out of twenty-five racial cases happened by "pure chance," the clerk's office produced evidence to support Cameron. In his dissent, Cameron found the following: "A member of The Four was substituted for the resident Circuit Judge in each instance, and another member of The Four was substituted for the additional District Judge. The idea that the Chief Judge may thus gerrymander the United States Judges of a State in order to accomplish a desired result is, I think, entirely foreign to any just concept of the proper functioning of the judicial process." *Armstrong v. Board of Education of the City of Birmingham, Ala.*, 323 F.2d 333, 358 (5th Cir. 1963); Lee, "Judge Warren Jones and the Supreme Court of Dixie," 247, 248.

5. In *Douds* the Supreme Court wrote, "This distinction is emphasized by the fact that members of those groups identified in § 9(h) are free to serve as union officers if at any time they renounce the allegiances which constituted a bar to signing the affidavit in the past. Past conduct, actual or threatened by their previous adherence to affiliations and beliefs mentioned in § 9(h), is not a bar to resumption of the position." *American Communications Assn. v. Douds*, 339 U.S. 382, 414 (1950).

6. Government's Reply Brief, 41–43.

7. *Jencks v. United States*, 226 F.2d 540 (5th Cir. 1955), cert. granted; "Jailed Unionist Appeals, Cites Matusow Shift," *Washington Star*, May 24, 1955; "Union Leader's Appeal Heard by Court Here," *New Orleans Statesman*, May 25, 1955; "Court Ponders Jencks Appeal," *New Orleans Times Picayune*, May 25, 1955.

8. *Jencks v. United States*, 226 F.2d 553 (5th Cir. 1955), cert granted; "Appeals Court Upholds Jencks Conviction," *Albuquerque Journal*, October 27, 1955; "Judge in Torrid Statement Blasts Lies of Matusow," *Albuquerque Journal*, October 27, 1955;

9. Like McTernan, the Flynn case defense attorney, Harry Sacher, also approached Kahn about a recantation after he heard about Matusow's change of testimony. "Matusow's Book Drew Union Cash," *New York Times*, March 9, 1956.

10. *Matusow v. United States*, 229 F.2d 335 (5th Cir. 1956).

11. Travis was also indicted for having filed a false affidavit. Jencks later wrote about his forced resignation. "Mine-Mill Executive Board members told Jencks and Travis that, in asking for the resignations, they hoped to strengthen the Union's ability to fight off raids, to get government to let up on attacks against Mine-Mill, and to improve the chances of merger negotiations that were then under way with several other unions. The strategy did not work. Harrassment [sic] intensified." Jencks, "Jencks vs. U.S.," 4, Wood Collection.

12. Jencks, "Palomino," 83–83, 86–87, Box 1, Folder 1, Jencks Papers, University of Colorado.

13. "High Court Agrees to Jencks Plea," *New York Herald Tribune*, March 5, 1956; "Convicted Labor Man Wins Court Hearing," *Washington Post*, March 8, 1956.

CHAPTER 13

1. Lichtman, *Supreme Court*, 64.

2. *Yates, Steinberg, Stack, et al. v. United States* (whether evidence in Smith Act prosecution was sufficient for advocating and organizing government overthrow); *Schneiderman v. United States* (same as *Yates* above); *Richmond* and *Connelly v. United States* (same as *Yates* above); *Yates v. United States* (whether *Yates* could be punished multiple times for refusing to answer questions as a witness while on trial); *Mesarosh* [Nelson] *v. United States* (whether case should be remanded or reversed and remanded for new trial because of false testimony by government witness in Smith Act prosecution); *Scales v. United States* (Smith Act prosecution, Solicitor confessed error); *Lightfoot v. United States* (Smith Act prosecution, Solicitor confessed error); *Jencks v. United States; Rowaldt v. Perfetto* (deportation case, whether past CP membership was too ephemeral to show affiliation); *Amalgamated Meat Cutters & Butcher Workmen of North America v. National Labor Relations Board* (whether a union could be prosecuted for a false non-Communist affidavit); *Kremen v. United States* (whether seizure of entire contents of cabin where Smith Act fugitives hid was unreasonable); *Konigsberg v. State Bar of California* (whether earlier CP membership was proper basis for denying applicant a bar license for not having good moral character); *Schware v. Bar Examiners of New Mexico* (whether applicant was denied due process in refusal to find good moral character to a former CP member who otherwise established good character); *Sweezy v. New Hampshire* (whether Sweezy, who refused to answer questions, was denied due process in investigation to find subversives if the inquiry was not pertinent to any legislative activity); *Service v. Dulles* (whether Service was improperly discharged from his employment for being a security risk); *United States v. Witkovich* (whether statute giving a state ttorney general power to inquire into any matter to determine location of individual who had overstayed an order of deportation was overbroad).

3. Lichtman, *Supreme Court*, 78, 88.

4. Warren said, "I have decided to reverse on Matusow's evidence. On the act, I would sustain the registration provisions and strike down all of the personal sanctions

against party officers and members. I would reserve the Fifth Amendment question."
Dickson, ed., *Supreme Court in Conference*, 294.

5. 351 U.S. 115 at 124–25.

6. 352 U.S. 1 at 9, 14.

7. Rankin to Lindsay, September 11, 1956, Box 3, Folder 5, Lindsay Papers.

8. Oral argument transcript, part 1, p. 4.

9. Ibid., part 1, pp. 7, 9.

10. Ibid., part 2, p. 9. McTernan argued, "I think that the importance of the witness' testimony to the prosecution is an extremely important element. I concede, Mr. Justice Frankfurter, that our case, here, for the production of the record at the trial does not turn upon a showing of contradiction. It turns upon these other policy considerations, to which I think we must add the fact that our effort to show a contradiction was frustrated [because Matusow said he couldn't remember]."

11. *American Communications Association v. Douds*, 339 U.S. 382 (1950); Oral argument transcript, part 2, pp. 17–19.

12. To McTernan, writing to Jencks the week after the argument, the need for inconsistency raised by Lindsay was a dead issue. According to McTernan, the solicitor general had conceded the week before in the Lightfoot case that the reports should be produced even without any inconsistency. McTernan to Jencks, October 25, 1956, Box 1, Folder "C.J. Misc. Mat," Kahn Papers, and Box 2, Folder 49, Lorence Papers.

13. Oral argument transcript, part 2, p. 30.

14. Ibid., 47.

15. Ibid., 53.

16. Ibid., 63.

17. As part of the post-argument process, Earl Warren's clerk noted in a memo to Warren that the government had filed copies of the reports in a sealed envelope. The clerk suggested that it would be "most unwise" for the court to read the reports. There is no indication that they did so. Supplemental Memo to Earl Warren, Box 2, Folder 49, Lorence Papers.

18. From notes taken by Justice Douglas, we know how the Justices saw the case as they considered their approaches. Dickson, ed., *The Supreme Court in Conference*, 555.

19. Ibid., 555–57. Clark followed up on that conference by submitting a detailed twenty-two-page memorandum on November 27 making his case for the secrecy of FBI records. Clark, Memorandum to the Conference, November 27, 1957, Clark Papers.

20. At that March conference a headcount was taken, and the senior judge in a group would determine who would write the opinion. Warren led the discussion: "I reverse." The most compelling case for error was that Thomason "refused to examine Matusow's reports. That was error." Warren again expressed his poor opinion of Thomason: "The court should have resolved [the conflict between the testimony and the reports.] I do not think that the case should go back to the district court on this point, as the district judge was prejudiced." Warren also found the instructions erroneous. Black only said, "I reverse." Frankfurter found the membership instruction defective. As for the reports, Frankfurter again opposed a trial court's private

viewing, a process that excluded defense counsel and was the equivalent of an ex parte conversation between the prosecution and the court. Douglas: "I reverse." Burton would reverse but only to permit the court's examination of the reports. He found the instructions "dubious." Clark said that only the court should see the reports and that he approved of the instructions. Harlan would reverse on both reports and instructions. Brennan said that if a witness admitted to making a report, the defense should have it, not just the court. Inconsistency should not be the test. If the government refused to produce a report, the case should be dismissed. Dickson, ed., *The Supreme Court in Conference*, 558.

21. Perhaps Brennan was responding to concerns about the jury instruction section in his May 6 draft. On May 9, Douglas wrote to Brennan outlining his reservations about the draft's treatment of the affiliation instruction. To Douglas, a loose definition of affiliation would ensnare in those who shared legitimate views with Communists, for example, views on civil rights, labor rights, and other domestic issues. Douglas to Brennan, May 9, 1957, Brennan Papers. Harlan indicated complete agreement with the May 6 draft and its treatment of the jury instructions. Harlan to Brennan, May 10, 1957, Brennan Papers. When Brennan circulated his May 13 draft that eliminated ruling on the instructions, Douglas quickly agreed—as did Warren, nine days later. Douglas to Brennan, May 14, 1957, and Warren to Brennan, May 22, 1957, both in Brennan Papers. It could well be that when Brennan dropped the instructions in the May 13 draft, he lost Harlan. He lost Harlan who, like Burton and Frankfurter, wanted to rule on the instructions, but he also lost Harlan as to whether the refusal to produce the reports required a new trial or only examination by the trial court. Harlan signed on with Burton that the matter was for the trial court to determine.

22. The majority and the Clark dissent read *Gordon v. United States* differently. Brennan wrote that *Gordon* did not require inconsistency, and Clark in his dissent insisted that *Jencks* left *Gordon* unresolved and a future source of confusion. The problem with *Gordon* was that Jackson's opinion in *Gordon* was unclear in citing an inconsistency in one part of the opinion and not mentioning the need for inconsistency in another part. 344 U.S. at 418 and 420.

23. Brennan wrote, "The Government can invoke its evidentiary privileges only at the price of letting the defendant go free. The rationale of the criminal cases is that, since the Government which prosecutes an accused also has the duty to see that justice is done, it is unconscionable to allow it to undertake prosecution and then invoke its governmental privileges to deprive the accused of anything which might be material to his defense." 353 U.S. at 671.

24. As for the affiliation instruction, they wrote: "This instruction allowed the jury to convict petitioner on the basis of acts of intermittent cooperation. It did not require a continuing course of conduct "on a fairly permanent basis" "that could not be abruptly ended without giving at least reasonable cause for the charge of a breach of good faith." 353 U.S. at 679–80.

25. 353 U.S. at 679.

26. 353 U.S. at 681–82. It was unlikely that Clark had Lord Byron's poetry in mind when he used the term "Roman holiday" to make his point. Rather, Clark probably meant that criminals would be frolicking in FBI files, a reference to the 1953 film of that name written by prominent Hollywood Ten member Dalton Trumbo. Among those repeating Clark's characterization was *Time* magazine. *Time*, June 17, 1957, 20.

27. Lichtman, *Supreme Court*, 92, 105. In private notes to Brennan, Frankfurter referred to Clark's misleading dissent. In the most incisive and penetrating review of the Jencks decision, I. F. Stone wrote, "And the press has taken more seriously than the facts warrant Mr. Justice Clark's almost hysterical protest that the Court has opened FBI files to criminals. I. F. Stone, "The Jencks Decision Reopens the Matusow Case," *I. F. Stone's Weekly* 5, no. 23 (June 10, 1957): 1.

28. "Clark Has Regret on Loyalty Lists," *New York Times*, March 9, 1961; "Revised Law," Editorial, *Oakland Tribune*, March 16, 1961.

29. *New York Times*, June 4, 1957; *El Paso Herald-Post*, June 4, 1957; *Washington News*, June 13, 1957; "The Supreme Court, Direction Disputed" and "The Jencks Case," *Time*, June 17, 1957.

30. Luther A. Huston, "U.S. Aides Study F.B.I. Data Ruling," *New York Times*, June 5, 1957.

31. "Judge Hits Jencks Case Reversal," *El Paso Times*, June 7, 1957. Thomason's doomsday declarations, of course, were absurd. Conviction rates in federal court, even after liberal Warren-era decisions, remain extraordinarily high. In following the law, the Justice Department has no trouble getting convictions.

32. *I. F. Stone's Weekly*, June 24, 1957.

33. The cases of *Watkins* and *Sweezy* involved contempt for refusal to answer questions. *Watkins* involved HUAC, and the court held that a legislative committee must have a legislative purpose to pursue examination of witness. Clark was the sole dissenter. *Watkins v. United States*, 354 U.S. 178 (1957). Sweezy was called before a one-man committee of the New Hampshire legislature that delegated the hearing to its state attorney general. The court found the process had violated Sweezy's First Amendment rights. *Sweezy v. New Hampshire*, 354 U.S. 234 (1957). The fourth case was that of John Stewart Service, the foreign service officer and China expert who was fired from his State Department position on loyalty charges after Service was tied to the controversial *Amerasia* case by McCarthy. In a unanimous opinion, the court ordered Service reinstated after finding that State had not followed its own procedures. *Service v. Dulles*, 354 U.S. 363 (1957).

34. *Yates v. United States*, 354 U.S. 298 (1957).

35. Lichtman, *Supreme Court*, 91, 105.

36. Journal of the Senate, June 24, 1957, 85th Cong., 1st Sess., 339. The President also addressed the decision in at least two press conferences. Two days before the hearing, President Eisenhower addressed the Supreme Court controversy at a press conference. He said, "I still believe that the United States respects the Supreme Court and looks to it as one of the great stabilizing influences in this country to keep us from going from one extreme to the other; and possibly in their latest series

of decisions there are some that each of us has very great trouble understanding." "Transcript of the President's News Conference on Foreign and Domestic Affairs," *New York Times*, June 27, 1957. At his July press conference, some took the President's remarks as being critical of the Jencks decision, although Eisenhower only said the administration opposed the "widespread opening of the F.B.I. files." "Transcript of President's News Conference on Foreign and Domestic Affairs," *New York Times*, July 18, 1957; Editorial, *Atlanta Journal*, July 18, 1957

37. The cabinet meeting agenda noted, "The recent Supreme Court decisions, especially in the Jenks [*sic*], Watkins, Service and California Communists cases have evoked comments, questions, and controversy." The meeting minutes noted, "In regard to the Jenks [*sic*] case, Mr. Brownell stated that there is presently much confusion on the extent to which files have to be opened up prior to testimony by a Government witness. He reported that the Justice Department will testify in favor of legislation to establish a 'reasonable interpretation' on the extent of opening files." Cabinet Meeting of June 28, 1957, Eisenhower Papers.

38. "Law Enforcement 'Crisis,'" *Washington Star*, July 23, 1957.

39. Testimony of Attorney General Herbert Brownell Jr., *Hearing, Subcommittee on Improvements in the Federal Criminal Code of the Committee on the Judiciary*; Jay Walz, "Bill to Protect F.B.I. File Voted by Senate Group," *New York Times*, June 29, 1957.

40. *Establishing Procedures for the Production of Government Records*, Senate Report No. 569; *Establishing Procedures for the Production of Certain Government Records*, House Report No. 700.

41. Draft of S-2377 was criticized by Wayne Morse, Joseph Clark Jr. of Pennsylvania, and John W. Bricker of Ohio as being "too harsh." In compromise, the government must turn everything relevant, only then give it to court if something must be excised. Sanction is to strike testimony, declare mistrial, or "take such other action as the court deems appropriate." The liberal senators also wanted pretrial disclosure. Anthony Lewis, *New York Times*, August 13, 1957.

42. Other than the Jencks Act, the main court-curbing legislation was postponed until the second session of the 85th Congress, when Johnson once again saved the day for the Supreme Court. Caro, *The Years of Lyndon Johnson: Master of the Senate*, 996–98, 1030–33.

43. Anthony Lewis, "Jencks Case Decision: Congress Weighs Move; Justice Department and F.B.I. Are Looking for Legislative Help Two Reasons Principle Accepted Hoffa Case Cited," *New York Times*, August 18, 1957.

44. *Congressional Record*, August 27, 1957, 85th Cong., 1st Sess., 14417.

45. William S. White, "Senate Votes Rights Bill and Sends it to President; Thurmond Talks 24 Hours" and "Senate Approves Curb on F.B.I. File," *New York Times*, August 30, 1957.

46. John D. Morris, "Congress Closes as House Passes Aid and F.B.I. Bills," *New York Times*, August 31, 1957. On the day it became obvious that the Jencks bill would pass, Frankfurter wrote a note to Brennan expressing regret that he might have been at fault for the controversy caused by Clark's dissent in the Jencks case. He wrote, "The

fact is that I very largely blame myself for all the dust that the case kicked up. I firmly believe that if I had not allowed my good-colleague xx to suppress my good sense the rumpus would have been avoided. For if I had wisdom xxx, I would have written a short concurrence with your opinion sticking my pen into Tom's [Clark] hot air and puncturing his balloon, by stating the exact narrow holding of the decision and exposing the non-holding. The upshot of it would have been that in order to have a Court opinion you, like a sensible lad, would yourself have added to substance of this indirect refutation of Tom, would have failed—or, rather not retained Tom's adherence, and Brownell & Co., largely Bill Rogers and Olney, would not have made themselves the enslaved tools of Edgar Hoover." Frankfurter to Brennan, August 29, 1957, Brennan Papers.

47. Section 3500, Title 18, *United States Code*, which is incorporated in Rule 26.2 of the Federal Rules of Criminal procedure, provides:

(a) In any criminal prosecution brought by the United States, no statement or report in the possession of the United States which was made by a Government witness or prospective Government witness (other than the defendant) to an agent of the Government shall be the subject of subpoena, discovery, or inspection until said witness has testified on direct examination in the trial of the case.

(b) After a witness called by the United States has testified on direct examination, the court shall, on motion of the defendant, order the United States to produce any statement (as hereinafter defined) of the witness in the possession of the United States which relates to the subject matter as to which the witness has testified. If the entire contents of any such statement relate to the subject matter of the testimony of the witness, the court shall order it to be delivered directly to the defendant for his examination and use.

(c) If the United States claims that any statement ordered to be produced under this section contains matter which does not relate to the subject matter of the testimony of the witness, the court shall order the United States to deliver such statement for the inspection of the court in camera. Upon such delivery the court shall excise the portions of such statement which do not relate to the subject matter of the testimony of the witness. With such material excised, the court shall then direct delivery of such statement to the defendant for his use. If, pursuant to such procedure, any portion of such statement is withheld from the defendant and the defendant objects to such withholding, and the trial is continued to an adjudication of the guilt of the defendant, the entire text of such statement shall be preserved by the United States and, in the event the defendant appeals, shall be made available to the appellate court for the purpose of determining the correctness of the ruling of the trial judge. Whenever any statement is delivered to a defendant pursuant to this section, the court in its discretion, upon application of said defendant, may recess proceedings in the trial for such time as it may determine to be reasonably required for the examination of such statement by said defendant and his preparation for its use in the trial.

(d) If the United States elects not to comply with an order of the court under paragraph (b) or (c) hereof to deliver to the defendant any such statement, or such portion thereof as the court may direct, the court shall strike from the record the testimony of the witness, and the trial shall proceed unless the court in its discretion shall determine that the interests of justice require that a mistrial be declared.

(e) The term "statement," as used in subsections (b), (c), and (d) of this section in relation to any witness called by the United States, means—

(1) a written statement made by said witness to an agent of the Government and signed or otherwise adopted or approved by him or;

(2) a stenographic, mechanical, electrical, or other recording, or a transcription thereof, which is a substantially verbatim recital of an oral statement made by said witness and recorded contemporaneously with the making of such oral statement; or

(3) a statement, however taken or recorded, or a transcription thereof, if any, made by said witness to a grand jury.

Pub. L. 85-269, Sept. 2, 1957, 71 Stat. 595.

48. Address of J. Edgar Hoover, Proceedings of 39th National Convention of the American Legion, September 16–19, 1957; House Document No. 303, 85th Cong., Second Sess.

49. Jack Steele, "U.S. Won't Attempt a New Jencks Trial," *New York Telegram & Sun*, September 13, 1957.

50. "U.S. Drops Case Against Jencks," *New York Times*, January 1, 1958; Anthony Lewis, "U.S. Aides Dispute Theory on Jencks," *New York Times*, January 2, 1958; "U.S. Decides to Drop Case Against Jencks," *Washington Post*, January 1, 1958; "U.S. Drops Red Case to Guard FBI Files," *Detroit News*, January 1, 1958.

51. Steve Murdock, "Jencks Talks about the Meaning of His Case," *The Worker*, January 26, 1958.

52. "Jencks Is Happy He's a Free Man," *Oakland Tribune*, January 1, 1958; "U.S. Drops Red Case to Guard FBI Files," *Detroit News*, January 1, 1958.

CHAPTER 14

1. An El Paso editor wrote, "Jencks was spared a prison term by a Supreme Court decision which found his conviction in U.S. District Court in El Paso technically faulty because his attorneys had not been permitted to look into secret Federal Bureau of Investigation files. *** He never was cleared but the Justice Department chose to let him go, rather than open the files." The editor went on to complain that such a man should not be allowed to teach. "Jencks Case Epilogue," *El Paso Herald-Post*, May 15, 1959.

2. I. F. Stone. "The Jencks Decision Reopens the Matusow Case." *I. F. Stone's Weekly* 5, no. 23 (June 10, 1957): 4.

3. The then Yeshiva University professor Ellen Schrecker obtained the release of many Jencks FBI files. Many of those files are in the Jencks Papers at the University

of Colorado. Lorence to Legislative Archives, September 17, 2009, Box 1, Folder 24, Lorence Papers. In addition to the Schrecker FOIA requests, this author made independent requests and received thousands of pages of Jencks, Matusow, and other files.

4. Jencks to Lorence, June 17, 1999, Jencks-Lorence Correspondence, Lorence Papers; Mine-Mill Union, "Portrait of a Labor Organizer," 4–6, Box 1, Folder 5, Lorence Papers.

5. File on Clinton Jencks and Hermoine Heidbrink Jencks, St. Louis, Jencks FBI File No. 100-9150. A witness in a HUAC executive session, private investigator Fred W. Bender, identified Jencks among those active in the St. Louis Communist Party in October 1940. HUAC list of Communist Party members in Colorado, November 18, 1953, Box 1, Folder 30, Lorence Papers.

6. Jencks to Lorence, June 17, 1999, Jencks-Lorence Correspondence, Lorence Papers; FBI reports, St. Louis, Jencks File No. 100-9150, January 17 and September 15, 1941.

7. Jencks to Lorence, June 17, 1999, Jencks-Lorence Correspondence, Lorence Papers; FBI report, St. Louis, Jencks File No. 100-9150, June 6, 1942.

8. FBI Reports, Denver, Jencks File No. 100-39680, October 9 and 16, 1946.

9. FBI Report, Denver, Jencks File No. 100-39680, October 9, 1946. Bureau headquarters denied the security index card, and the agent withdrew his request once the Jencks family left Denver for Grant County, New Mexico, in April 1947. Denver to Director, Jencks File No. 100-39680, October 16, 1946 and May 26, 1947.

10. El Paso to Director, Jencks File No. 100-39680, July 9, 1947.

11. FBI Report, El Paso, July 9, 1947; El Paso to Director, September 6, 1947; Director to El Paso, October 24, 1947; DETCOM and COMSAB designations in El Paso to Director, November 2, 1949; all in Jencks File No. 100-39680. Virginia was also placed on the Security Index. El Paso to Director, June 8 and September 19, 1949, Jencks FBI File No. 100-39680.

12. In addition to putting Jencks on the Security Index, the bureau also designated Jencks as a "key figure," as he was on the executive committee. El Paso to Director, August 5, 1949.

13. Original Trial Transcript, 133.

14. Jencks to Lorence, June 17, 1999, Jencks-Lorence correspondence, Lorence Papers.

15. Jencks mentioned his resignation to James Lorence, writing, "I sat down and wrote a letter resigning from the Communist Party and ending any affiliation with that party. My affidavits were truthful and honest. Then I went on with my work as President of Local 890 and International Representative of the Min, Mill and Smelter Workers Union." Jencks to Lorence, June 19, 1999, 9a, Jencks-Lorence Correspondence folder, Lorence Papers. Although Jencks submitted his written resignation to the Party, it was never mentioned at trial by the defense. With Jencks not taking the stand or presenting any evidence, perhaps there was no vehicle to introduce the document. It could also be that Jencks had lost his copy of the letter.

His stepdaughter Linda recalled accidentally finding the resignation in a book. Virginia Jencks took the letter and said no more. Linda Halley Rageh to Lorence, email, May 17, 2010, Box 1, Folder 22, Lorence Papers. In an interview by Patricia Burch-Vaughn, Jencks repeated his assertion that he was no longer a Party member when he signed the affidavit. "I answered this question truthfully, when I filed the non-Communist Affidavit required of elected union officers under the Taft-Hartley Act. . . . United States government representatives knew my affidavit was truthful when they were forced to resort to the use of a paid professional liar in their attempt to remove me from the job I had been elected to do." Jencks interview by Patricia Burch-Vaughn, c. March 1987, Box 2, Folder 4, Burch-Vaughn Papers, also in Box 2, Folder 10, Lorence Papers. In his 1959 HUAC testimony, Jencks said he that he was not then a CP member nor was he a non-member still under Party discipline. He meant that when he resigned, he did so completely and did not remain affiliated in any way. Testimony of Clinton Edward Jencks, July 22, 1959, House Report No. 1251 (86th Cong.), annual report for 1959.

16. El Paso FBI reports (SA J. Phillip Claridge), September 16, 1948, April 19 and 22, May 27, June 14 and 17, August 2, September 22, 1949, Jencks FBI File No. 122-232.

17. Albuquerque FBI reports, January 19 and 31, 1950, Jencks File No. 122-232.

18. Director to Albuquerque, February 27, 1950, Jencks File No. 122-232.

19. On December 2, 1949, in anticipation of the San Lorenzo meeting, Ford attended a meeting at the Albuquerque home of Party chair DiSanti. DiSanti told Ford that the coming San Lorenzo meeting was needed "because Clinton Jencks was no longer in the Party, since he resigned in order that he could sign the non-Communist affidavit and comply with the provisions of the Taft-Hartley Act." The resignation, he said, was necessary so Jencks could function for his union and "carry out his union affairs." Albuquerque FBI memo, December 22, 1949, Jencks File No. 122-232 and File No. 66-159-112.

20. March 31, 1950. Given Ford's information, the Albuquerque case agent changed Jencks's Security Index Card noting, "Subject resigned from CP in October 1949 to sign non-Communist affidavit with N.L.R.B." He was no longer listed as a member of any suspect group but was still designated for DETCOM and COMSAB treatment. Albuquerque FBI report, March 31, 1950, Jencks File No. 100-39680.

21. April 5, 1950, some three weeks before the affidavit in question was signed. "There is no information concerning any activity whatsoever on the part of Jencks in connection with the Communist Party since resignation in October 1949, except the allegation made by this Informant [Ford] to the effect that he resigned from the party in order that he could execute the non-Communist affidavit. Albuquerque FBI report, April 5, 1950, Case No. 122-232; April 17, 1950 [Eleven days before the April 28 affidavit]. Headquarters admonished the agent to continue his investigation, and the agent responded by requesting that he be allowed to interview Jencks to make a case through that path, but the bureau refused to grant permission. Director to FBI, April 17, 1950; Albuquerque to Director, May 18, 1950; Director to Albuquerque, May 24, 1950.; all in Jencks File No. 122-232.

22. May 10, 1950 (twelve days after Jencks signed the affidavit on April 28). The Albuquerque case agent again advised the bureau that Jencks resigned from the Party in October 1949 so that he could sign the non-Communist affidavit. Where Ford previously said that Jencks resigned to carry out his union duties, now the agent added that Jencks would not be given Party assignments but was to follow Communist Party policy in his union work. Albuquerque FBI report, May 10, 1950, Case No. 100-39680.

23. June 20, 1950. Given the lack of a case, the bureau advised the case agent to put the file in an inactive status and keep an eye on developments, as the statute of limitations had not expired. Director to Albuquerque, June 20, 1950, Jencks File No. 122-232.

24. Albuquerque FBI report, June 5, 1950. Jencks File No. 122-232.

25. Albuquerque FBI report, June 22, 1950; Director to Assistant Attorney General McInerney, June 28, 1950; both in Jencks File No. 122-232.

26. Cleveland to Belmont, January 8, 1952; Albuquerque to Director, January 2, 1952; both in Jencks File No. 122-232.

27. The Solicitor's office is proud of its special character and places importance on its duty of candor. It also continues to regret instances when it has failed in that obligation, most famously in the World War II Japanese internment cases when it withheld from the court an internal government report concluding that Japanese Americans were not security risks. Neal Katyal, "Solicitor General," 3027; "Confession of Error: The Solicitor General's Mistakes During the Japanese-American Internment Cases," www.justice.gov/opa/blog/confession-error-solicitor-generals-mistakes -during-japanese-american-internment-cases. The solicitor general in the Obama Administration described the office's tradition of candor in an interview: "One of those principles is an *unflinching duty of candor* to the Court, so we've had a couple of episodes where we've made mistakes and had to correct them with the Court. *** We are going to litigate respectfully and without any exaggeration, and certainly *with an obligation to disclose adverse factual information.* All of that long pre-dated me, and these principles help the office maintain its credibility. And this credibility is very important over time in the executive branch's relationship with the Court, *because it allows the Court to rely with confidence on what we say*" (emphasis added). Alexandra Gutierrez, SCOTUSblog, June 30, 2016. www.scotusblog.com/2016/06 /as-obama-term-winds-down-solicitor-general-don-verrilli-makes-his-exit/.

28. Brief for the United States, 10, Jencks Supreme Court Briefs.

29. Sizoo to Belmont, October 3, 1956, Jencks File No. 122-232.

30. Director to Assistant Attorney General Tompkins, October 4, 1956, Jencks File No. 122-232.

31. Director to Assistant Attorney General Tompkins, October 4, 1956; Belmont to Sizoo, October 4, 1956; both in Jencks File No. 122-232. Sizoo wrote about Ford's testimony that he was unaware whether Jencks had resigned or been replaced.

32. Oral argument transcript.

33. Justice Brennan writing for the majority: "The Government bridged the gap between October 15, 1949, and July or August 1950 with the testimony of Ford that,

during that period, the Party took no disciplinary action against the petitioner for defection or deviation, and did not replace the petitioner in the Party office which Ford testified the petitioner held as a member of the Party State Board. 353 US at 660. *** Ford testified that, between August 1949 and September 1950, when Ford ceased his activities with the New Mexico Party, there was no disciplinary action taken against the petitioner and, to his knowledge, the petitioner was not replaced in his position on the State Board of the Communist Party." 353 US at 662.

CHAPTER 15

1. Matusow, *False Witness*, 27; FBI report, New York to Salt Lake City, August 10, 1953, Jencks File No. 122-232 referring to New York's file on Matusow, File No. 100-94014.

2. Albuquerque FBI report, August 22, 1950, Jencks File No. 100-39680. Although Matusow only worked twenty-five days for the New York office—where agents made derogatory comments about his personality—the Albuquerque case agent, who had just met the man, noted that Matusow was "an informant of known reliability."

3. Albuquerque FBI report, October 20, 1950, Jencks File No. 100-39680.

4. FBI report, New York to Salt Lake City, August 10, 1953, Jencks File No. 122-232, referring to the New York's file on Matusow, File No. 100-94014. The bureau instructed San Antonio and New York offices to spend no time or effort using Matusow's services, nor should they "encourage him to act in a confidential capacity and to accept only such information as he might volunteer." FBI report, New York to Salt Lake City, August 10, 1953, File Nos. 122-232 and 100-94014; Matusow, *False Witness*, 33–35.

5. With respect to his work with Mexican miners, Matusow wrote, "He [Jencks] told of his trip to Mexico in relation to the mine union and displayed a lapel pin which designated his membership in the Mexican Miners Union. He spoke of the need for cooperation among the trade unions in an effort to prevent war which is being perpetrated by American capitalists." Statement of Harvey Matusow, December 29, 1951, in Cincinnati FBI report, January 9, 1952, Jencks File No. 122-232.

6. Ibid.

7. New York to Salt Lake City, August 10, 1953, Jencks File No. 122-232. Another bureau warning to Matusow in SAC NY to Director, December 3, 1952, Matusow FBI File No. 100-375988. Also, SAC NY to Director, April 24, 1953, Matusow FBI File No. 100-375988, in which New York warned other offices to maintain distance from Matusow and receive only information "of current value," reiterating that "Matusow has been considered as unstable and unreliable in the past and has made irresponsible statements for which he has been reprimanded. He has been evaluated as vain, egotistical, self-centered and inclined to 'blow up' his CP background in order to make an impression."

8. The FBI's Nichols noted, "Radio station looking to hire Matusow, and Nichols told friend of radio station to watch out for Matusow as he had made 'wild statements which he had not been able to back up.'" Nichols to Tolson, June 26, 1953; Newspapers

reported Matusow was ready to assist in Smith Act prosecution. Hoover warned Olney, "You are, of course, familiar with certain difficulties that arose in connection with his testimony." Hoover to Assistant Attorney General Warren Olney III, August 19, 1953; both in Matusow FBI File No. 100-375988.

9. Hoover to Assistant Attorney General Olney, October 9, 1953; Belmont to Ladd, October 8, 1953; both in Matusow FBI File No. 100-375988.

10. John and Martha Edmiston, affidavit, Matthews Papers.

11. Nichols to Tolson, May 13, 1953, Matusow FBI File No. 100-375988.

12. Hoover to SAC WFO [Washington Field Office], December 11, 1953, Matusow FBI File No. 100-375988.

13. Francis C. Broaddus Jr., interview with author, 13. Broaddus was interviewed by the FBI in February 1955 and said that he did not handle Matusow's grand jury appearance. In preparing for trial, the attorneys held four meetings, perhaps at U.S. attorney Charles Herring's hotel room. Present were Herring, Williams, Alderman, and Broaddus. To Broaddus, Matusow talked a lot, and they had trouble pinning him down. "Broaddus described Matusow as an untrustworthy, unpredictable liar and a person who had to have an audience so that he could impress others with his importance. Nevertheless, Broaddus said that he did not believe that the things Matusow had testified to were false because they conformed in general to other testimony in the case, but that it was possible that Matusow might have elaborated or exaggerated the facts." Hoover to Tompkins, February 21, 1955, Matusow FBI File No. 100-375988. This last statement by Broaddus was inaccurate. Matusow was the only witness who testified about Jencks's post-affidavit activities, and his testimony about conversations with Jencks at the San Cristóbal Valley Ranch was uncorroborated.

14. Gallup reported that as the Jencks trial began, Hoover had a 78 percent favorable rating and only 2 percent of Americans disapproved of his performance. "Public Gives Overwhelming Vote of Confidence to J. Edgar Hoover," *Public Opinion News Service*, December 25, 1953.

15. Charles Brown to Hoover, January 22, 1954, Jencks File No. 122-232.

16. Charles Brown to Hoover, January 26, 1954, Jencks File No. 122-232.

17. Thomason to Charles W. Brown, January 26, 1954, Jencks File No. 122-232.

18. Charles F. Herring to Hoover, January 29, 1954; Hoover to Herring, February 3, 1954; Alderman to Hoover, February 15, 1954; all in Jencks File No. 122-232.

19. Charles F. Herring to Harvey Matusow, February 5, 1954, Matusow, *False Witness*, 201.

20. Belmont to Boardman, January 25, 1955, Jencks File No. 122-232.

21. Victor P. Keay, Inspector-in-Charge, FBI Internal Security/Liaison Sections, Domestic Intelligence Division.

22. Keay to Belmont, January 28, 1955, Jencks File No. 122-232.

23. El Paso FBI to Director, Teletype, January 28, 1955, Jencks File No. 122-232.

24. Boardman to Director, February 4, 1955, Jencks File No. 100-39680.

25. The FBI developed a record noting instances in which the bureau had warned Justice about Matusow's unreliability in the Flynn case. In a meeting on the Matusow

scandal between the special agent in charge of the New York office and U.S. attorney J. Edward Lumbard on February 19, 1955, the FBI detailed several instances when Justice was warned. Lumbard admitted that his office had received the warnings. FBI told the U.S. attorney's office, "The fact that Matusow had probably committed perjury in the nineteen fifty-two trial was also known to U.S. Attorney's office at that time, also to Lumbard. It was also called to Mr. Lumbard's attention that the Bureau in Washington had called the Department's attention to this man's character on various occasions." Teletype, New York to Director, February 20, 1955, Matusow FBI File No. 100-375988. This seemed to be a recurring problem. In October 1956, the then U.S. attorney Paul W. Williams was quoted in New York newspapers as saying in his summation in Matusow's perjury trial that the Justice lawyers were unaware of Matusow's unreliability when the FBI produced Matusow as a witness. Hoover and others immediately reminded Williams and the publications that the FBI had warned Justice about Matusow in 1952 in the Cincinnati report. Hoover complained to the attorney general, who responded with a contrite reply that the FBI had warned Justice about Matusow in 1952. Hoover to Williams, October 3, 1956; Hoover to Attorney General, October 3, 1956; both in FBI File No. 62-49765-367.

26. With news of Matusow's recantation affidavit, the bureau immediately issued a directive to its field offices across the nation to find every copy of a Matusow report and retype the pages mentioning Matusow to change him from "a previously reliable informant" to one "of known unreliability." It was a massive undertaking.

27. An example of its practices is found in a memo written by Asst. FBI Director L. B. Nichols. Nichols wrote, "The Matusow incident is getting out of control more and more . . . I feel that we have now arrived at the point where we have got to start some publicity along the affirmative lines." Nichols noted that he had called anti-Communist columnist David Lawrence and asked whether he saw a difference between the [J. Robert] Oppenheimer and Matusow cases. Nichols succeeded in having Lawrence pen a favorable column in the *Washington Star* that day. Nichols suggested that the contacts be oral "with the view of building up the backfire." He asked for approval of the plan. In a handwritten note, Hoover agreed, adding that the Justice Department was incapable of launching a defense and opposed helping HUAC. Nichols to Tolson, February 8, 1955, Matusow FBI File No. 100-375988.

28. FBI Denver teletype to Director and El Paso, March 2, 1955, Jencks File No. 122-232.

29. Belmont to Boardman, March 3 or 8, 1955, Jencks File No. 100-39680. Upon review, the bureau determined that the memo of August 28 was never sent to headquarters and was only attached to another memo sent to Chicago, so the bureau had been unaware of the discrepancy.

30. Belmont to Boardman, March 3 or 8, 1955, Jencks File No. 100-39680. The bureau had already been embarrassed with the revelation of one of its black bag jobs, an illegal wiretap in the high profile Coplon case. It would in the future doctor its records and avoid, at all costs, a repetition of any disclosures that harmed the bureau's image. *Coplon v. United States*, 185 F.2d 629 (2nd Cir. 1950); Schrecker, *Many Are the Crimes*, 222–23.

31. Hoover to Staff, March 1, 1955, Matusow FBI File No. 100-375988.

32. The *Denver Post*, February 8, 1955.

33. Brief on Ex-Communists as Witnesses, FBI File No. 100-418105-12. This was a detailed eighty-six-page report prepared by the Justice Department in February 1955 and later supplemented. See also, Attorney General to Hoover, February 25, 1955, Matusow FBI File No. 100-375988; "Attorney General Says: Reds Are Trying to Wreck Informant System of FBI," *U.S. News & World Report*, April 1, 1955, 68.

34. Senate Judiciary Committee Chair James O. Eastland took to the Senate floor to commend Thomason, and in a letter, Hoover promptly thanked Eastland for supporting Thomason and for the work his Senate subcommittee performed. Hoover to Eastland, March 7, 1955; Hoover to Eastland, March 17, 1955; both in Jencks File No. 100-39680.

35. Hoover to Thomason, March 31, 1955, Thomason Papers. "Judge Medina" referred to U.S. district judge Harold R. Medina, who presided in the Smith Act Dennis case.

36. Cameron to Hoover, June 13, 1957; Belmont to Boardman, June 18, 1957; Hoover to Cameron, June 19, 1957; all in Jencks File No. 122-232.

37. Oral argument transcript, 51.

CHAPTER 16

1. Lorence, *Suppression*, 110, 113–14.

2. Biberman, "Report on 'Salt of the Earth,'" July 16, 1954, Box 2, Folder 37, Lorence Papers. It was not only Metzger in opposition but also Father Rahm, the active El Paso Jesuit. Alfredo C. Montoya questionnaire, Box 2, Folder 16, Lorence Papers.

3. Lorence, *Suppression*, 120–27, 136, 140–43; Lorence, "Salt and Free Expression," 422–25, 427.

4. Peary, *Cult Movies 2*, 137; Rosaura Revueltas interview by Rosenfelt et al., August 1, 1975, Box 2, Folder 71, Lorence Papers; Lorence, *Suppression*, 153–54, 171–77; Lorence, "Salt and Free Expression."

5. Mine-Mill accepted Jencks's resignation effective June 1, 1956, promised to continue supporting his defense, and paid for his moving expenses to the Bay Area. John Clark to Clinton Jencks, March 28, 1956, Box 61, Folder 12, Jencks Papers, University of Colorado. The reasons for obtaining the Jencks and Travis resignations became apparent a week after John Clark's letter to Jencks: on April 6, Mine-Mill and the Steelworkers held exploratory merger talks. Note, April 6, 1956, Box 1, Folder 43, Lorence Papers.

6. Jencks, "What Has Happened to Clint Jencks Since the U.S. Supreme Court Victory," Box 1, Folder 2, Jencks Papers, University of Colorado.

7. Local 890 members had long reported on visits by FBI agents inquiring about Jencks and telling them that Jencks was a CP member. Box 27, Folder 16, Jencks Papers, University of Colorado.

8. Jencks, "Palomino," 84–97, Box 1, Folder 1, Jencks Papers, University of Colorado.

9. Linda Rageh to James Lorence, May 22, 2010, Box 1, Folder 22, Lorence Papers; Jencks, "Palomino," 96, Box 1, Folder 1, Jencks Papers, University of Colorado.

10. "Clinton Jencks—who refused to say under oath if he was a Communist and whose name is the key word of a legal principle which opened FBI files to the Reds—is on his way to a job teaching American youngsters about economics." Neil McNeil, "Foundation to Back Jencks as Teacher," *Washington Daily News*, May 13, 1957; "Fellowship Winner to Face Probe," *Oakland Tribune*, May 13, 1959; "Another Subpoena for Jencks," *San Francisco Chronicle*, June 19, 1959.

11. *Testimony of Clinton Edward Jencks, Hearings, Committee on Un-American Activities*, 1087–88.

12. Ibid., 1091.

13. Ed Edstrom, "Deny Vindication in Jencks' Case," *New York Journal-American*, July 23, 1959.

14. *Testimony of Clinton Edward Jencks, Hearings, Committee on Un-American Activities*, 1085–86.

15. The bureau's San Francisco office noted that Jencks had not been active in the party for years and requested permission to remove him from the DETCOM and Key Figure lists. Headquarters approved removing the Key Figure designation given that Jencks had held no party office nor attended any meetings for more than a decade; nevertheless it retained his DETCOM tab. San Francisco to Director, February 14, 1957; Director to San Francisco, March 6, 1957; both in FBI File No. 1358252. The explanation was that Jencks was kept on the Security Index not because he was danger but because he was a "cause celebre" and continued being involved in leftist groups. Director to San Francisco, May 25, 1960, Jencks File No. 100-39680.

16. Jencks, "Palomino," 97, Box 1, Folder 1, Jencks Papers, University of Colorado.

17. Ibid., 98.

18. Linda Rageh to James Lorence, May 17, 2010, 3; Linda Rageh to James Lorence, May 28, 2010; both in Box 1, Folder 22, Lorence Papers.

19. Jencks, "Palomino," 116, Box 1, Folder 1, Jencks Papers, University of Colorado.

20. Ibid., 120–22.

21. He joined Jarrico and others in complaining about hardline repression in Czechoslovakia. Ceplair, *The Marxist*, 230.

22. "Clinton Edward Jencks," *San Diego Union*, January 4, 2006.

23. 40th Year Anniversary of the Empire Zinc Strike, Box 1, Folder 32, Lorence Papers. Virginia's wish for her ashes was fulfilled, but her daughter Linda decided to remove the remains when no burial marker was placed at Bayard. She reburied the ashes at her Berkeley home. Heather Wood, interview by author, October 20, 2017.

24. Obituary, *San Francisco Examiner*, September 23, 1979. The Arkansas-born Ford began his career in Mesa, Arizona while he was a student at Arizona State University and only nineteen years old. He went to Salt Lake City, where he joined the Communist Party, and then to Albuquerque where, in addition to his ministry, he was head of the NAACP and active in the 1948 Wallace campaign. "Witness Testifies Jencks Directed N.M. Commie Drive," *El Paso Herald-Post*, January 13, 1954.

25. Douglas Martin, "Harvey Matusow, 75, an Anti-Communist Informer, Dies," *New York Times*, February 4, 2002; Lichtman and Cohen, *Deadly Farce*, 155–60; Kahn, *Matusow Affair*, 265–66. A blog has biographical material. John May, "Harvey Matusow: A Life in Five Posts." Matusow's papers are archived at the University of Sussex.

CHAPTER 17

1. "No incident of espionage by Japanese-Americans was ever uncovered." Maggie Jones, "Aiko Herzig Yoshinaga: From Deep in the Archives She Brought Justice for Japanese Americans," *New York Times Magazine*, December 30, 2018, 51, 52.

2. Provision by provision, the Supreme Court invalidated the Subversive Activities Control Act that punished aspects of CP membership. The court held that the law "quite literally establish[ed] guilt by association alone, without any need to establish that an individual's association [posed] the threat feared by the Government proscribing it. The inhibiting effect on the exercise of First Amendment rights [was] clear." *United States v. Robel*, 389 U.S. 258, 265 (1967).

3. Isserman and Schrecker, "Dangerous Tendency," 159.

4. Powers, "The Plot Thickens"; Isserman and Schrecker, "Dangerous Tendency," 168–69.

5. Powers, "The Plot Thickens," 54.

6. Hodges, "Making and Unmaking," 12. Among HUAC's southerners were Martin Dies of Texas, Johns S. Wood of Georgia, John E. Rankin of Mississippi, J. Hardin Peterson of Florida, and Herbert C. Bonner of North Carolina, with James O. Eastland of Mississippi on the Senate subcommittee.

7. Regarding the foreign connection, in 1947 Attorney General Tom C. Clark ran a study of 4,984 CP members. He found that 78 percent were foreign born and 56 percent were born in Russia. Caute, *Great Fear*, 225; Philip Roth, *I Married a Communist*, 274.

8. The FBI's use of illegal wiretaps and microphones ("bugs") went back at least to the 1920s. See "Microphone: Policy Brief," 1966, part 12 of 30, FBI Records: The Vault, Surreptitious Entries (Black Bag Jobs). https://vault.fbi.gov/Surreptitious%20 Entries%20(Black%20Bag%20Jobs)%20. At times, the FBI informed some attorneys general of the practices. After Hoover's black bag jobs were exposed in the 1970s, the FBI investigated and documented "technical surveillance" occurrences, renaming them "surreptitious entries or black bag jobs."

9. Judge R. E. Thomason, "Judge Thomason Recalls, Jencks Case Caused Law to Be Rewritten," *El Paso Times*, January 28, 1956.

10. Witt interview with Hoffman, 13.

11. Original Trial Transcript, 193, 195.

12. Prosecutor Broaddus recently stated that he was not involved in preparing Ford and Matusow and was unaware of Jencks's Party resignation. Interview of Francis C. Broaddus Jr., in Hoover to Tompkins, February 21, 1955, Matusow FBI File No. 100-375988; Broaddus interviews with author, October 27, 2016, p. 13, and September 27, 2018.

13. The FBI noted that Alderman had the reports and should have questioned Ford about his expected testimony. Sizoo wrote, "Ford was interviewed by a Department Attorney [Alderman] in Los Angeles, California, prior to his testimony in this case. The Department, at that time, had copies of the Bureau reports and should have been able to question Ford regarding any differences in the information he expected to testify to and the information in these reports. The trial attorney apparently made no attempt to clarify Ford's answer to this particular question despite the information in the FBI reports." Sizoo to Belmont, October 4, 1956, Jencks File No. 122-232.

14. Isserman and Schrecker, "Dangerous Tendency," 165; Paul Jarrico, Q & A of January 19, 1989, Box 2, Folder 70, Lorence Papers. Jarrico later insisted that the U.S. Communist Party should have cut ties with the Kremlin and should have been a political party in the American tradition. Americans would not buy into communism that would not give them the same civil liberties they had under capitalism. Ceplair, *The Marxist*, 169, 170. The Communist Party under Browder had become more liberal and American. When the accommodating Party leadership was overthrown in 1958 by William Z. Foster with a return to its old hardline, many members left the party, including Jarrico. Others had left when the Soviets invaded Hungary in 1956. Dalton Trumbo also described the American CP's ties to the Kremlin in the same terms. How "stupid" it had been, Trumbo wrote. The party's "most glaring stupidity, which was its thralldom to the Soviet Union, and the mystique that arose therefrom." Ceplair and Trumbo, *Dalton Trumbo*, 322.

15. Isserman and Schrecker, "Dangerous Tendency," 165.

16. Jencks to Lorence, June 17, 1999, Lorence Papers. Less than a year after admitting to Lorence that he had joined the Young Communist League in 1937, Jencks asked Lorence to omit mention of that fact. Jencks to Lorence, March 30, 2000, Jencks-Lorence correspondence folder, Lorence Papers. Jencks was even discrete with his granddaughter Heather Wood, who asked him whether he had been "a card-carrying member of the Communist Party." He neither affirmed or denied it. Heather Wood to James Lorence, undated note, Box 1, Folder 22, Lorence Papers.

17. Jencks to Lorence, June 17, 1999, Lorence Papers, 4a.

18. Witt interview with Hoffman, 2–3. Witt added, "The [EZ] strike had racial overtones because most of the workers were Chicanos. Jencks' wife also was very active and very combative and very aggressive. They both were. Would be constantly engaged in debates of one kind or another with the Anglos, as they're called down there, about racial questions, about the strike, and that kind of thing. So he was quite a well-known personality in the area, and we all felt—he felt of course—the union felt and I felt that his indictment was an outcome mainly of that strike and of his activities otherwise because he and his wife were in on everything that today we would call left. Now, they were not open Communists, or as far as anybody knew, even though that was the issue in the case, concealed Communists. They were open left wingers. They were on that side of every issue which was current at the time. So they, particularly Clint himself, stood out." On the other hand Jencks's sister, Rosemary Hathaway, always saw Clinton as modest and reluctant to speak of himself.

He was not a braggart and never talked about his war record, for example. Interview of Rosemary Hathaway, December 3, 1909, Box 2, Folder 73, Lorence Papers.

19. Virginia heard that locally "a lot of negative feelings arose from the showing of the film," such as Chacón getting too much attention. Undated letter, Virginia Jencks to Michael Wilson, Folder 7, Box 45, Wilson Papers. Lorenzo Tórrez, a CP member and an important figure in Local 890 along with his wife, Anita, tried to enlist Jencks for help on a Party project when Jencks was an academic in San Diego and no longer a member. Tórrez noted that it was African Americans Bill Taylor and Frances Williams who steered Wilson and Biberman to focus the film on the Mexican miners. Tórrez seemed to be close and friendly with Jencks, and so his angry, handwritten note might have been written during a temporary breach between the men. Torres wrote, "On hind sight, increased experience as well as the information available, I must concluded [sic] that Jencks was and is basically an opportunist. He worked himself into a box, because he never was a member of the working class and never had expectation of living as one." Box 7, Folders 14 and 17, Lorenzo Tórrez Papers.

20. Virginia Jencks Chambers interview by Albert Kahn, March 13, 1977, Box 1, Folder 9, Lorence Papers.

21. Linda Rageh felt that she had lost a federal job in Berkeley soon after two FBI agents asked neighbors about her. Rageh to James Lorence, May 17, 2010, Box 1, Folder 22, Lorence Papers.

22. Heather Wood to Lorence, Box 1, Folder 22, Lorence Papers.

23. Daughter Linda Rageh said Jencks was a "philanderer," was vengeful toward Virginia, and failed to make his twenty-five-dollar alimony payments. Linda Rageh to James Lorence, May 17, 2010, 3, Box 1, Folder 22, Lorence Papers. Clinton's sister Rosemary Hathaway told Lorence, "Clint was always a charmer who was attractive to and by women. He was something of a womanizer." Rosemary Hathaway interview by James Lorence, December 3, 2009, Box 2, Folder 79, Lorence Papers.

24. To Virginia, Clinton always turned the other cheek. After their new car was shot up during the filming of *Salt of the Earth*, Jencks told her, "Never mind. The insurance will cover it." The company did cover it, and then it cancelled the policy. Undated note, Virginia Jencks to Michael Wilson, Box 45, Folder 7, Wilson Papers.

25. Whether the women returned to the "old way" is a complicated question addressed in detail by Deborah Silverton Rosenfelt. Rosenfelt noted that in times of crisis, women sometimes assumed positions of equality but later "went back to the old way" after the crisis passed. Women were out of Local 890 in 1966. Rosenfelt visited Grant County in 1975 and did not find it to be a feminist outpost. She interviewed five of the women strikers, and two found their marriages "more egalitarian" post-strike. The auxiliary had fallen by the wayside. Virginia Chacón: "We're still back in the old way. Not the new way. . . . We went back to the old way. And it's still in existence." Rosenfelt concluded that the "feminist struggle may be the longest one of all." Wilson and Rosenfelt, Commentary, *Salt of the Earth*, 135–46.

26. Among those inspired was Primo Cabello, member of Los Angeles Mine-Mill Local 700, who wrote a corrido in Spanish commemorating the EZ strike. "Corrido

of Empire Zinc," Wood Collection. It reads in part, "But the strike is not over/for the brave women/in beating the scabs/are winning on all fronts."

27. In *Brady v. Maryland*, 373 U.S. 83 (1963), the Supreme Court found suppression of exculpatory evidence by the prosecution to constitute a deprivation of due process.

28. The interviewer asked Clark whether he thought the Hiss case, prosecuted when Clark was attorney general, was a miscarriage of justice. Clark responded, "Well, I did not at the time. But now I think it was. I think that, while Mr. Hiss might have been a little bit over-anxious in his activities at the time, it was largely caused by the atmosphere, the climate, with reference to communism then prevalent. The Russians were our Allies, and he possibly thought that if he did do what they said he did, that he thought he was doing no wrong. Of course, I think some of the Communist reports that the FBI made on other cases were just fantastic. It's just unbelievable that some of the things happened that were reported in various Communist investigations. They must have happened or they wouldn't have reported them, but I think the Communist scare was highly exaggerated." Interview of Clark interview by Hess, October 17, 1972, 187, 192, 193.

BIBLIOGRAPHY

ARCHIVAL SOURCES

Bancroft Library Photographic Collection. University of California at Berkeley.

Biberman, Herbert, and Gale Sondergaard Papers. Wisconsin Historical Society, Archives and Manuscript Division, Madison.

Board of Inquiry on the Labor Disputes Involving the Non-ferrous Metals Industry Documents, 1951, Collection No. 5075 and Records on Microfilm, No. 5412 mf., Cornell University Library, Kheel Center for Labor-Management Documentation and Archives, Ithaca, N.Y.

Brennan, William J., Jr. Papers. Library of Congress, Manuscript Division, Washington, D.C.

Burch-Vaughn, Patricia. Personal Papers. Clinton E. Jencks materials.

Cargill, Jack. Collection. Western New Mexico University, Special Collections, Silver City.

Chacón, Juan, Collection, Western New Mexico University, Special Collections, Silver City.

Clark, Tom C. Oral History. Truman Library and Museum, Independence, Mo.

Clark, Tom C. Papers, Box A51, Folder 2. University of Texas at Austin, Tarlton Law Library, Special Collections.

Communist Party USA. Records. Library of Congress, Manuscript Division, Washington, D.C.

Eisenhower, Dwight D. Papers. Dwight D. Eisenhower Presidential Library, Abilene, Kan.

FBI File No. 100-358086. FBI Custodial Detention and Security Index Program, The Vault, FBI online archive, https://vault.fbi.gov/.

Federal Bureau of Investigation. Records. U.S. National Archives and Records Administration, Washington, D.C.

Immigration and Customs Enforcement and related agencies. Records. U.S. National Archives and Records Administration, Washington, D.C.

Independent Productions Corporation Papers. Wisconsin Historical Society, Archives and Manuscript Division, Madison.

Jarrico, Paul. Collection. Columbia University, Rare Book & Manuscript Library, New York. (This collection was not consulted and is being processed at this date.)

Jencks, Clinton E. File Nos. 100-9150, 122-232, 100-39680. Federal Bureau of Investigation, U.S. Department of Justice, Washington, D.C.

Jencks, Clinton E. Papers, MSS-137. Arizona State University Libraries, Chicano Research Collection, Phoenix.

Jencks, Clinton E. Papers. University of Colorado at Boulder Library, Special Collections, Boulder.

Jones, Marvin. Oral History. Truman Library and Museum, Independence, Mo.

Kahn, Albert. Papers. Wisconsin Historical Society, Archives and Manuscript Division, Madison.

Lazar, Ernie. FOIA Collection. Online archive, https://archive.org/details/ernie1241_fbiinformants&tab=about.

Lindsay, John Vliet. Papers, MS 592. Yale University Library, Manuscripts and Archives, New Haven, Conn.

Lorence, James J. Personal papers.

Matthews, J. B. Papers. Duke University, Rubenstein Rare Book and Manuscript Library, Durham, N.C.

Matusow, Harvey Marshall. File Nos. 100-375988 and 100-94014. Federal Bureau of Investigation, U.S. Department of Justice, Washington, D.C.

Meiklejohn Civil Liberties Institute Archives. University of California at Berkeley.

Los Mineros Photographs, MP SPC 186. Arizona State University Libraries, Chicano Research Collection, Phoenix.

Montoya, Alfredo Chávez. Papers, 1930–95, MSS 676 BC. University of New Mexico, Center for Southwest Research, Albuquerque.

New York University Library, Tamiment Library and Robert F. Wagner Labor Archives, New York.

Oral Argument transcripts and audio, *Jencks v. United States.* Oyez, Legal Information Institute Supreme Court Resources, www.oyez.org.

Silver City Daily Press Collection. Western New Mexico University, Special Collections, Silver City.

Silver City Enterprise, Empire Zinc Strike Collection. Silver City Public Library, Silver City, N.Mex.

Thomason, R. E. Papers, MS 140. University of Texas at El Paso Library, Special Collections.

Tórrez, Lorenzo. Papers, 1959–2000, MS 384. New Mexico State University Library, Archives and Special Collections, Las Cruces.

Truman, Harry S. Correspondence and daily appointments. Truman Library and Museum, Independence, Mo.

U.S. Court of Appeals for the Fifth Circuit. Records. *United States v. Jencks* and *United States v. Matusow*. National Archives and Records Administration, Fort Worth Federal Records Center, Fort Worth, Tex.

U.S. Department of Justice legal divisions. Records. U.S. National Archives and Records Administration, Washington, D.C.

U.S. District Court for the Western District of Texas. Records. *United States v. Jencks*. National Archives and Records Administration, Fort Worth Federal Records Center, Fort Worth, Tex.

United Steelworkers of America and Labor Oral History Collection, HCLA 1684. Pennsylvania State University Libraries, Special Collections, University Park.

Warren, Earl. Papers. Library of Congress, Manuscript Division, Washington, D.C.

Western Federation of Miners and International Union of Mine, Mill, and Smelter Workers. Archives. University of Colorado at Boulder Library, Special Collections, Boulder.

Western Federation of Miners and International Mine, Mill and Smelter Workers, 1893–1955. Collection No. 5268. Cornell University Library, Kheel Center for Labor-Management Documentation and Archives, Ithaca, N.Y.

Wilson, Michael. Papers, 1942–77, PASC 52. Young Research Library, Special Collections. University of California at Los Angeles.

Wood, Heather. Collection. Berkeley, Calif.

MEMOIRS AND DIARIES

Abt, John J., with Michael Myerson. *Advocate and Activist: Memoirs of an American Communist Lawyer*. Urbana: University of Illinois Press, 1993.

Biberman, Herbert. *Salt of the Earth: The Story of a Film*. Boston: Beacon Press, 1965.

Chambers, Whittaker. *Witness*. Washington, D.C.: Regnery History, 2014.

Healey, Dorothy, and Maurice Isserman. *Dorothy Healey Remembers: A Life in the American Communist Party*. New York: Oxford University Press, 1990.

Jarrico, Paul, and Herbert J. Biberman. "Breaking Ground." *California Quarterly* 2, no. 4 (Summer 1953): 60–63.

Kahn, Albert E. *The Matusow Affair: Memoir of a National Scandal*. Mt. Kisco, N.Y.: Moyer Bell, 1987.

Matusow, Harvey. *False Witness*. New York: Cameron and Kahn, 1955.

Revueltas, Rosaura. "Reflections on a Journey." *California Quarterly* 2, no. 4 (Summer 1953): 64–65. Reprinted in *Salt of the Earth*. Edited by Michael Wilson and Deborah Silverton Rosenfelt, 174–76. New York: Feminist Press, 1978.

Smith, Craig. *Sing My Whole Life Song: Jenny Vincent's Life in Folk Music and Activism*. Albuquerque: University of New Mexico Press, 2007.

UNITED STATES COURT RECORDS

Jencks New Trial Motion Appeal Record. *Jencks v. United States, No. 15557*, U.S. Court of Appeals for the 5th Circuit, 7RA-361, RG 276, National Archives and Record Administration, Fort Worth.

Jencks Original Trial Transcript. *Jencks v. United States. U.S. Supreme Court Transcript of Record with Supporting Pleadings*, n.p. Gale Primary Sources, The Making of Modern Law, n.d. [Supreme Court Case No. 23, October Term, 1956.] [Index at pp. i-v.]

Jencks Pretrial Transcript. *United States v. Clinton E. Jencks, No. 54013*, U.S. District Court for the Western District of Texas, No. 7RA-361, RG21, National Archives and Record Administration, Fort Worth.

Jencks Supreme Court Briefs. *Jencks v. United States, U.S. Supreme Court Transcript of Record with Supporting Pleadings*, n.p., Gale Primary Sources, The Making of Modern Law, n.d. [Supreme Court Case No. 23, October Term, 1956.]

Jencks Trial Appeal Record. *Jencks v. United States, No. 15157*, U.S. Court of Appeals for the 5th Circuit, No. 7RA-361, RG 276, National Archives and Records Administration, Fort Worth.

NEW MEXICO STATE COURT RECORDS

Jencks, et al. v. Goforth, Sheriff, No. 5587, New Mexico Supreme Court. Court opinion at 261 P.2d 655, September 25, 1953. [Habeas corpus case filed by Jencks, et al.]

Local 890, IUMMSW, et al. v. New Jersey Zinc Co., New Mexico Supreme Court No. 5579, also No. 12812, Grant County, New Mexico, District Court. Filed June 12, 1951. [The original injunction case and not appealed by the union. The transcript cited refers to the record in this file.]

New Jersey Zinc Co. v. Local 890 of IUMMSW, et al., No. 5626, New Mexico Supreme Court. Opinion at 262 P.2d 648, September 25, 1953. [Civil contempt case filed by New Jersey Zinc.]

New Jersey Zinc v. Local 890 IUMMSW, et al., No. 5653 New Mexico Supreme Court. Court opinion at 262 P.2d 654, September 25, 1953. [A related contempt case against union, Jencks, et al.]

COURT CASES CITED

Abrams v. United States, 250 U.S. 616 (1919).

Amalgamated Meat Cutters v. NLRB, 352 U.S. 153 (1956).

American Communications Assn. v. Douds, 339 U.S. 382 (1950).

American Smelting & Refining Company v. N.L.R.B., 128 F.2d 345 (5th Cir. 1942).

Communist Party of the United States v. Subversive Activities Control Board, 351 U.S. 115 (1956).

Debs v. United States, 249 U.S. 211 (1919).

Dennis v. United States, 341 U.S. 494 (1951).

Griggs v. Duke Power Co., 401 U.S. 424 (1971).

Hernández v. Texas, 347 U.S. 475 (1954).

Hirabayashi v. United States, 320 U.S. 81 (1943).

Hohri v. United States, 782 F.2d 227, 234 (DC Cir. 1986), rehearing denied in 793 F.2d 304, vacated and remanded by the Supreme Court in 482 U.S. 64 (1987).

Jencks, et al. v. Goforth, Sheriff, 261 P.2d 655 (NM Sup. Ct. 1953).

Jencks v. United States, 226 F.2d 540 (5th Cir. 1955), Cert. granted.

Jencks v. United States, 226 F.2d 553 (5th Cir. 1955), Cert. granted.

Jencks v. Unites States, 353 U.S. 657 (1957).

Konigsberg v. State Bar of California, 353 U.S. 252 (1957).

Kremen v. United States, 353 U.S. 346 (1957).

Lightfoot v. United States, 355 U.S. 2 (1957).

Korematsu v. United States, 323 U.S. 214 (1944).

Matusow v. United States, 229 F.2d 335 (5th Cir. 1956).

Mesarosh [Nelson] v. United States, 352 U.S. 1 (1956).

National Labor Relations Board v. Nevada Consolidated Copper Corporation, 316 U.S. 105 (1942).

Nevada Consolidated Copper Corporation v. National Labor Relations Board, 122 F.2d 587 (10th Cir. 1941), cert. granted.

New Jersey Zinc Co. v. Local 890 of International Union of Mine, Mill & Smelter Workers et al., 261 P.2d 648 (NM Sup. Ct. 1953).

New Jersey Zinc Company v. Local 890 Of International Union of Mine, Mill and Smelter Workers, et al., International Union of Mine, Mill and Smelter Workers, et al, and Clinton E. Jencks, et al., 261 P.2d 654 (NM Sup. Ct. 1953).

Richmond and Connelly v. United States, 354 U.S. 298 (1957).

Rowaldt v. Perfetto, 355 U.S. 115 (1957).

Scales v. United States, 355 U.S. 1 (1957).

Schenck v. United States, 249 U.S. 47 (1919).

Schneiderman v. United States, 354 U.S. 298 (1957).

Schware v. Bar Examiners of New Mexico, 353 U.S. 232 (1957).

Service v. Dulles, 354 U.S. 363 (1957).

Stanford v. Texas, 379 U.S. 476 (1965).

Sweezy v. New Hampshire, 354 U.S. 234 (1957).

United States v. Dennis, et al., 341 U.S. 494 (1951).

United States v. Flynn, et al., 216 F.2d 354 (2d Cir. 1954).

United States v. Matusow, 244 F.2d 532 (2d Cir. 1957), cert. denied.

United States v. Robel, 389 U.S. 258, 265 (1967).

United States v. Witkovich, 353 U.S. 194 (1957).

Yates v. United States, 355 U.S. 66 (1957).

Yates v. United States, 356 U.S. 298 (1957).

NATIONAL LABOR RELATIONS BOARD DECISIONS

In the Matter of American Smelting & Refining Company and International Union of Mine, Mill and Smelter Workers, Local 509. NLRB Decisions, 34:968, August 26, 1941.

In the Matter of Kennecott Copper Corporation Nevada Consolidated Copper Corporation. NLRB Decisions, 40:986, April 29, 1942.

In the Matter of Nevada Consolidated Copper Corporation and International Union of Mine, Mill and Smelter Workers. NLRB Decisions, 26:1182, August 24, 1940.

STATUTES AND EXECUTIVE ORDERS

Act to Prevent Pernicious Political Activities of 1939 (Hatch Act), Title 5, *United States Code,* Sections 101, et seq.

Alien Registration Act of 1940 (Smith Act), Title 8, *United States Code,* Section 451 and Title 18, *United States Code,* Section 2385.

Communist Control Act of 1954, Title 50, *United States Code,* Sections 781 and 841, et seq.

Emergency Detention Act of 1950, Title II of the Internal Security Act of 1950. See: Subversive Activities Control Act.

Emergency Quota Law of 1921, 42 *Stat.* 5, May 19, 1921.

Espionage Act of 1917, Title 18, *United States Code,* Sections 792, et seq.

Executive Order 8802, 6 F.R. 3109, June 27, 1941.

Executive Order 9066, F.R. 1407, February 19, 1942, and related military proclamations.

Executive Order 9102, F.R. 2165, March 20, 1942.

Executive Order 9806, 11 F.R. 13863, November 25, 1946.

Executive Order 9835, 12 F.R. 1935, March 25, 1947.

Executive Order 10450, 18 F.R. 2489, April 27, 1953.

Fair Labor Standards Act of 1938, Title 29, *United States Code,* Sections 201, et seq.

Final Report, Japanese Evacuation from the West Coast, 1942. Washington, D.C.: Government Printing Office [GPO], 1943.

Foreign Agents Registration Act of 1938, Title 22, *United States Code,* Sections 611, et seq.

Immigration and Nationality of Act of 1952 (McCarran-Walter Act), Title 8, *United States Code,* Section 1101, et seq.

Immigration Act of 1903 (Anarchist Exclusion Act), 32 *Stat.* 1213, 1214, March 3, 1903.

Immigration Act of 1917, 39 *Stat.* 874, February 5, 1917.

Internal Security Act of 1950 (McCarran Act), 64 *Stat.* 987, September 22, 1950. Title 50, *United States Code,* Section 781, et seq.

Jencks Act, Title 18, *United States Code,* Section 3500.

Labor-Management Relations Act of 1947 (Taft-Hartley Act), Title 29, *United States Code,* Sections 401, et seq.

National Labor Relations Act of 1935 (Wagner Act), Title 29, *United States Code,* Sections 151, et seq. (Provision for non-Communist affidavit is Section 9(h) of the Act.)

Norris-LaGuardia Act of 1932, (Anti-Injunction Act), Title 29, *United States Code,* Sections 101, et seq.

Public Information Act of 1966, (Freedom of Information Act), Title 5, *United States Code,* Sections 552, et seq.

Subversive Activities Control Act of 1950, Title I of the Internal Security Act of 1950. See: Emergency Detention Act.

Texas Communist Control Act, Article 6889-3, Texas Revised Civil Statutes.
Texas Sedition Act, Chapter 557, Texas Government Code.

CONGRESSIONAL HEARINGS AND REPORTS

Charges of Illegal Practices of the Department of Justice: Hearings before the United States Senate Committee on the Judiciary. 66th Congress, Third Session, January 19, 25, 27, February 1, March 3, 1921. Washington, D.C: GPO, 1921.

Communist Activities Among Youth Groups (Based on Testimony of Harvey M. Matusow), Part 2: Hearings before the Committee on Un-American Activities, House of Representatives. 83rd Congress, Second Session, July 12, 1954. Washington, D.C.: GPO, 1954.

Communist Domination of Union Officials in Vital Defense Industry—International Union of Mine, Mill, and Smelter Workers: Senate Judiciary Committee, Subcommittee on Internal Security. 82nd Congress, Second Session. Washington, D.C.: GPO, 1952.

Communist Infiltration of the Motion Picture Industry: Hearings before the Committee on Un-American Activities, House of Representatives. 80th Congress, First Session. Washington, D.C.: GPO, 1947.

Communist Infiltration of Hollywood Motion-Picture Industry, Part 1: Hearings before the Committee on Un-American Activities. 82nd Congress, First Session. Washington, D.C.: GPO, 1951.

Establishing Procedures for the Production of Certain Government Records in Federal Criminal Cases. House Report No. 700. 85th Congress, First Session. Washington, D.C.: GPO, 1957.

Establishing Procedures for the Production of Government Records in Criminal Cases in United States Courts. Senate Report No. 569. In Senate Reports, vol. 3, Miscellaneous Reports on Public Bills. 85th Congress, First Session. Washington D.C.: GPO, 1957.

Final Report of the Select Committee (Church Committee) to Study Governmental Operations with Respect to Intelligence Activities, United States Senate. Vol. 2, Intelligence Activities and the Rights of Americans; Vol. 3, Supplementary Detailed Staff Reports on Intelligence Activities and the Rights of Americans. Washington, D.C.: GPO, 1976.

Hearing, Subcommittee on Improvements in the Federal Criminal Code of the Committee on the Judiciary. U.S. Senate, June 28, 1957. Report of Proceedings, vol. 1. Washington, D.C.: Ward & Paul, 1957.

Hearing to Investigate Communist Activities. Focuses on Communist Party membership and activities in New York City and Puerto Rico, Communist youth groups and summer camps, and distribution of communist propaganda, Committee on Un-American Activities, House of Representatives. 82nd Congress, Executive Session, November 27, 1951. HRG-1951-UAH-0066.

Hearings, Committee on Un-American Activities, House of Representatives. 80th Congress, First Session, February 27, July 23, 24, and 25, 1947. Washington, D.C.: GPO, 1947.

Hearings Regarding Communism in the United States Government, Part 2, Committee on Un-American Activities, House of Representatives. 81st Congress, Second Session, August 28 and 31, September 1 and 15, 1950. Washington, D.C.: GPO, 1950.

Hearings Regarding the Communist Infiltration of the Motion Picture Industry, Committee on Un-American Activities, House of Representatives. 80th Congress, First Session, October 1947. Washington, D.C.: GPO, 1947.

Institute of Pacific Relations: Report of the Senate Judiciary Committee, Subcommittee on Internal Security. 82nd Congress, Second Session, part 9, March 13, 1952. Washington: GPO, 1952.

Interim Report on Hearings Regarding Communist Espionage in the United States Government. PL 601, House Un-American Activities Committee. 88th Congress, Second Session, August 28, 1948. Washington, D.C.: GPO, 1948.

Interlocking Subversion in Government Departments, Hearing before the Subcommittee to Investigate the Administration of the Internal Security Act and Other Internal Security Laws of the Committee on the Judiciary, United States Senate. 83rd Congress, First Session [84th Congress, First Session], part 10, May 26, 1953. Washington, D.C.: GPO, 1953.

Internal Security Act of 1950, as Amended, and Communist Control Act of 1954: Committee on Internal Security, House of Representatives. 91st Congress, First Session. Washington, D.C.: GPO, 1969.

Investigation of Communist Activities in Los Angeles, Calif., Area, Part 10: Hearing, Committee on Un-American Activities, House of Representatives. 84th Congress, Second Session, April 20 and 21, 1956. Washington, D.C.: GPO, 1956.

Investigation of Communist Activities in the Rocky Mountain Area, Parts 1 and 2: Hearings, Committee on Un-American Activities, House of Representatives. 84th Congress, Second Session, May 15–18, 1956. Washington, D.C.: GPO, 1956.

Legislative History of Taft Hartley Act. Vol. 1. Washington, D.C.: GPO, 1948.

Matters Relating to the Labor-Management Relations Act of 1947: Hearings of the Committee on Education and Labor, House of Representatives. 83rd Congress, First Session, March 16–20, 1953. Washington, D.C.: GPO, 1953.

Report on the National Lawyers Guild: Legal Bulwark of the Communist Party. House Report No. 3123, House Un-American Activities Committee. 81st Congress, Second Session. Washington, D.C.: Committee on Un-American Activities, House of Representatives, September 21, 1950.

Security—Government Printing Office: Hearings of the Permanent Subcommittee on Investigations of the Senate Committee on Government Operations. 83rd Congress, First Session, August 17 and 18, 1953. Washington, D.C.: GPO, 1953.

Strategy and Tactics of World Communism, the Significance of the Matusow Case: Hearings before the Subcommittee to Investigate the Administration of the Internal Security Act and other Internal Security Laws, Senate Judiciary Committee. 84th Congress, First Session, part 8, March 9, 1955. Washington, D.C.: GPO, 1955.

Subversive Control of Distributive, Processing, and Office Workers of America: Hearings before the Subcommittee on Internal Security, Senate Judiciary Committee. 82nd Congress, First and Second Sessions. Washington, D.C.: GPO, 1952.

Subversive Infiltration of Radio, Television and Entertainment Industry: Hearings, Senate Judiciary Committee, Subcommittee on Internal Security. 82nd Congress, Second Session, part 9, March 20, 1952. Washington: GPO, 1952.

Testimony of Clinton Edward Jencks. Hearings, Committee on Un-American Activities, House of Representatives. 86th Congress, First Session, July 22, 1959. Washington, D.C.: GPO, 1959.

Violations of Free Speech and Rights of Labor: Digest of Report of the Committee on Education and Labor Pursuant to S. Res. 246. 74th Congress. Washington, D.C.: GPO, 1939.

DIRECTORIES

Colorado Springs City Directories.
El Paso City Directory, 1944. El Paso, Tex.: Hudspeth Directory, Co., 1944.

INTERVIEWS

Broaddus, Francis C. "Skip" Jr. Interviews with author by telephone, October 27, 2016, and by correspondence, September 27, 2018.

Brownell, Herbert. Interviews. Dwight D. Eisenhower Presidential Library, Abilene, Kan.

Clark, Tom C. Interviews by Jerry N. Hess, October 17, 1972 and February 8, 1973, Harry S. Truman Presidential Library, Independence, Mo.

Flores, Arthur V. *Salt of the Earth* Recovery Project interview, May 4, 2018. https:// saltoftheearthrecoveryproject.wordpress.com/2018/05/04/art-flores/.

———. Written interview by author, August 10, 2018.

Hathaway, Rosemary. Interview by James J. Lorence, December 30, 2009.

Humble, Terrence. Interview with author, Bayard, N.Mex., February 27, 2017.

Jarrico, Paul. Interview, UCLA Oral History Collection, March 13, 1990.

Jarrico, Sylvia. Interview, UCLA Oral History Collection, February 2, 1975.

Jencks, Muriel Sobelman. Telephone interviews with author, October 12, 2016 and January 23, 2017.

Lumet, Sidney. Foundation Interviews, Part Four, October 28, 1999. https://interviews .televisionacademy.com/interviews/sidney-lume.

Margolis, Ben. Interview, UCLA Oral History Collection, September 13, 1984.

Silex, Humberto. Interviews by author, September 9, 21, 23, and 28, 1991 and May 23, 1993. Transcripts and video archived with Special Collections at the University of Texas at El Paso Library.

———. Interview by Oscar J. Martinez and Art Sadin, April 28, 1978. "Interview no. 505," Institute of Oral History, University of Texas at El Paso.

Tórrez, Anita. Interview with author, Tucson, Ariz., October 11, 2016.

Witt, Nathan. Interview by Judith H. Byne of Cornell University, February 17, 1969.

———. Interview by Alice Hoffman of Pennsylvania State University, July 11, 1974.

———. Interview by Phil Stebbins of Pennsylvania State University, December 22, 1969.

Wood, Heather. Interview with author, Berkeley, Calif., October 17, 2016.

BOOKS

Acuña, Rodolfo F. *Corridors of Migration: The Odyssey of Mexican Laborers, 1600–1933*. Tucson: University of Arizona Press, 2007.

Albro, Ward S. *To Die on Your Feet: The Life, Times, and Writings of Práxedis G. Guerrero*. Fort Worth: Texas Christian University Press, 1996.

Alexander, Charles C. *The Ku Klux Klan in the Southwest*. Lexington: University of Kentucky Press, 1965.

Andrews, Gregg. *Shoulder to Shoulder? The American Federation of Labor, the United States, and the Mexican Revolution, 1910–1924*. Berkeley: University of California Press, 1991.

Baker, Ellen R. *On Strike and on Film: American Families and Blacklisted Filmmakers in Cold War America*. Chapel Hill: University of North Carolina Press, 2007.

Bentley, Eric, ed. *Thirty Years of Treason: Excerpts from Hearings before the House Committee on Un-American Activities, 1938–1968*. New York: Thunder's Mouth Press, Nation Books, 2002.

Berman, David R. *Radicalism in the Mountain West, 1890–1920*. Boulder: University Press of Colorado, 2007.

Bicknell, Thomas William. *The History of the State of Rhode Island and Providence Plantations*. New York: American Historical Society, 1920.

Brown, Ralph S. *Loyalty and Security: Employment Tests in the United States*. New Haven: Yale University Press, 1958.

Browne, William B., comp. *Genealogy of the Jenks Family of America*. Concord, New Hamp.: Rumford Press, 1952.

Cargill, Jack. "Empire and Opposition: Class, Ethnicity and Ideology in Mine-Mill Union of Grant County, New Mexico." Master's thesis, University of New Mexico, 1979.

Carleton, Don E. *Red Scare: Right-Wing Hysteria, Fifties Fanaticism, and Their Legacy in Texas*. Austin: University of Texas Press, 2014.

Caro, Robert A. *The Years of Lyndon Johnson: Master of the Senate*. New York: Vintage Books, 2003.

Caute, David. *The Great Fear: The Anti-Communist Purge Under Truman and Eisenhower*. New York: Simon and Schuster, 1978.

Ceplair, Larry. *The Marxist and the Movies, A Biography of Paul Jarrico*. Lexington: University Press of Kentucky, 2007.

———, and Steven Englund. *The Inquisition in Hollywood: Politics in the Film Community, 1930-60*. Urbana: University of Illinois Press, 2003.

———, and Christopher Trumbo. *Dalton Trumbo, Blacklisted Hollywood Radical*. Lexington: University Press of Kentucky, 2015.

Chapin, Orange. *The Chapin Genealogy: Descendants of Dea. Samuel Chapin*. Northampton, Mass.: Metcalf, 1869.

Cleary, Helen Clarke Jenks. *Jenks Genealogy with Allied Families*. Ypsilanti, Mich.: Helen Clarke Jenks Cleary, 1937.

Cook, Bruce. *Trumbo*. New York: Grand Central Publishing, 2015.

Crossman, Richard H., ed. *The God That Failed*. New York: Columbia University Press, 2001.

Deutsch, Sarah. *No Separate Refuge, Culture, Class, and Gender on an Anglo-Hispanic Frontier in the American Southwest*. New York: Oxford University Press, 1987.

Dickson, Del, ed. *The Supreme Court in Conference, 1940–1985*. New York: Oxford University Press, 2001.

Emerson, Edward Waldo. *Henry Thoreau as Remembered by a Young Friend*. Boston: Houghton Mifflin, 1917.

Fariello, Griffin. *Red Scare: Memories of the American Inquisition, An Oral History*. New York: W. W. Norton, 1995.

García, Mario T. *Mexican Americans*. New Haven: Yale University Press, 1989.

Gómez-Quiñones, Juan. *Mexican American Labor, 1790–1990*. Albuquerque: University of New Mexico, 1994.

Griffith, Robert. *The Politics of Fear: Joseph R. McCarthy and the Senate*. Lexington: University Press of Kentucky, 1970.

Gutiérrez, David G. *Walls and Mirrors: Mexican Americans, Mexican Immigrants, and the Politics of Ethnicity*. Berkeley: University of California Press, 1995.

Hart, John Mason. *Anarchism and the Mexican Working Class, 1860–1931*. Austin: University of Texas Press, 1978.

———. *Revolutionary Mexico, The Coming and Process of the Mexican Revolution*. Berkeley: University of California Press, 1989.

Haynes, John Earl, and Harvey Klehr. *Venona: Decoding Soviet Espionage in America*. New Haven: Yale University Press, 2000.

Hodges, Robert C. "The Making and Unmaking of Salt of the Earth: A Cautionary Tale." Ph.D. diss., University of Kentucky, 1997.

Hudson, Kent. "Mine-Mill: The Voices from the Mountains." Ph.D. diss., Union Institute and University, 1979.

Huggard, Christopher J., and Terrence M. Humble. *Santa Rita Del Cobre: A Copper Mining Community in New Mexico*. Boulder: University Press of Colorado, 2012.

Irons, Peter. *Justice at War: The Story of the Japanese American Internment Cases*. New York: Oxford University Press, 1983.

Jensen, Vernon H. *Heritage of Conflict, Labor Relations in the Nonferrous Metals Industry up to 1930*. Ithaca: Cornell University Press, 1950.

———. *Nonferrous Metals Industry Unionism, 1932–1954*. Ithaca: Cornell University Press, 1954.

Jones, Jacqueline. *Soldiers of Love: Northern Teachers and Georgia Blacks, 1865–1873*. Chapel Hill: University of North Carolina Press, 1980.

Kessell, John L. *Kiva, Cross and Crown: the Pecos Indians and New Mexico 1540–1840*. Washington, D.C.: National Park Service, 1979.

Kessler, Lauren. *Clever Girl: Elizabeth Bentley, the Spy Who Ushered in the McCarthy Era*. New York: Harper Collins Publishers, 2003.

Kluger, James R. *The Clifton-Morenci Strike: Labor Difficulty in Arizona, 1915–1916.* Tucson: University of Arizona Press, 1970.

Lay, Shawn. *War, Revolution and the Ku Klux Klan.* El Paso: Texas Western Press, 1985.

Lichtman, Robert M. *The Supreme Court and McCarthy-Era Repression, One Hundred Decisions.* Urbana: University of Illinois Press, 2015.

———, and Ronald D. Cohen. *Deadly Farce: Harvey Matusow and the Informer System in the McCarthy Era.* Urbana: University of Illinois Press, 2004.

Lorence, James J. *Palomino: Clinton Jencks and Mexican-American Unionism in the American Southwest.* Urbana: University of Illinois Press, 2013.

———. *The Suppression of Salt of the Earth: How Hollywood, Big Labor, and Politicians Blacklisted a Movie in Cold War America.* Albuquerque: University of New Mexico Press, 1999.

Lundwall, Helen, and Terrence Humble. *Copper Mining in Santa Rita, New Mexico, 1801–1838.* Santa Fe: Sunstone Press, 2012.

Martinelli, Phylis Cancilla. *Undermining Race: Ethnic Identities in Arizona Copper Camps, 1880–1920.* Tucson: University of Arizona Press, 2009.

McWilliams, Carey. *North from Mexico: The Spanish Speaking People of the United States.* New York: Praeger Publishers, 1990.

———. *Witch Hunt, The Revival of Heresy.* Boston: Little, Brown, 1950.

Mellinger, Philip J. *Race and Labor in Western Copper: The Fight for Equality, 1896–1918.* Tucson: University of Arizona Press, 1995.

Morgan, Ted. *Reds: McCarthyism in Twentieth-Century America.* New York: Random House, 2004.

Murphy, Walter F. *Congress and the Court.* New Orleans: Quid Pro Quo Books, 2014.

Nelson, Steve. *The 13th Juror.* New York: Masses & Mainstream, 1955.

Powers, Richard Gid. *Secrecy and Power: The Life of J. Edgar Hoover.* New York: The Free Press, 1987.

Raat, W. Dirk. *Revoltosos: Mexico's Rebels in the United States, 1903/1923.* College Station: Texas A&M University Press, 1981.

Romerstein, Herbert, and Eric Breindel. *The Venona Secrets: The Definitive Exposé of Soviet Espionage in America.* Washington, D.C.: Regnery History, 2000.

Rosenblum, Jonathan D. *Copper Crucible: How the Arizona Miners' Strike of 1983 Recast Labor-Management Relations in America.* Ithaca: Cornell University Press, 1998.

Roth, Philip. *I Married a Communist.* New York: Vintage Books, 1998.

Rovere, Richard H. *Senator Joe McCarthy.* New York: Harcourt, Brace and Company, 1959.

Sabin, Arthur J. *In Calmer Times, The Supreme Court and Red Monday.* Philadelphia: University of Pennsylvania Press, 1999.

Saxman, Christopher, and Terry Humble. *Relics of the Underground Metal Miners: A Pictorial History of the Central Mining District, Grant County, New Mexico.* Hanover, N. Mex.: Arch Publishing, 2018.

Schrecker, Ellen. *The Age of McCarthyism: a Brief History with Documents.* Boston: Bedford Books, 1994.

————. *Many are the Crimes: McCarthyism in America*. Boston: Little, Brown and Company, 1998.

Schrecker, Ellen, editor. *Cold War Triumphalism: The Misuse of History After the Fall of Communism*. New York: New Press, 2004.

Shapleigh, Eliot. *Texas on the Brink: How Texas Ranks among the 50 States*, n.p., 2005.

Shideler, Harry W. *History of the Shideler Family*. Girard, Kan.: Harry W. Shideler, 1931.

Smith, Robert Samuel. *Race, Labor, and Civil Rights: Griggs versus Duke Power and the Struggle for Equal Employment Opportunity*. Baton Rouge: Louisiana State University Press, 2008.

Sonnichsen, C. L. *Pass of the North II, 1918–1980*. El Paso: Texas Western Press, 1980.

Stouffer, Samuel A. *Communism, Conformity and Civil Liberties: A Cross-section of the Nation Speaks Its Mind*. New York: Doubleday, 1955.

Theoharis, Athan. *Chasing Spies: How the FBI Failed in Counterintelligence But Promoted the Politics of McCarthyism in the Cold War Years*. Chicago: Ivan R. Dee, 2002.

————. *Seeds of Repression: Harry S. Truman and the Origins of McCarthyism*. Chicago: Quadrangle Books, 1971

Thomason, Robert Ewing. *Thomason, the Autobiography of a Federal Judge*. Edited by Joseph M. Ray. El Paso: Texas Western Press, 1971.

Vargas, Zaragosa. *Labor Rights Are Civil Rights: Mexican American Workers in Twentieth-Century America*. Princeton: Princeton University Press, 2004.

Von Hoffman, Nicholas. *Citizen Cohn: The Life and Times of Roy Cohn*. New York: Doubleday, 1988.

Weiner, Tim. *Enemies: A History of the FBI*. New York: Random House, 2012.

Weinstein, Allen. *Perjury: The Hiss-Chambers Case*. New York: Alfred A. Knopf, 1978.

Weisbrode, Kenneth. *The Year of Indecision, 1946: A Tour Through the Crucible of Harry Truman's America*. New York: Viking, 2016.

Wilson, Michael. *Salt of the Earth*. Screenplay. New York: Feminist Press, 1978.

Wilson, Michael, and Deborah Rosenfelt. *Salt of the Earth*. New York: Feminist Press, 1993.

Ybarra, Bob. *My Demons Were Real: Constitutional Lawyer Joseph Calamia's Journey*. Houston: Arte Público Press, 2010.

BOOK CHAPTERS AND ARTICLES

"The Aftermath of the Jencks Case." *Stanford Law Review* 11, no. 2 (March 1959): 297–337.

Baker, Ellen. "'I Hate to Be Calling Her a Wife Now': Women and Men in the *Salt of the Earth* Strike, 1950–1952." In *Mining Women: Gender in the Development of a Global Industry, 1670 to the Present*, edited by Jaclyn J. Gier, and Laurie Mercier, 213–32. New York: Palgrave MacMillan, 2006.

Balthaser, Benjamin. "Cold War Re-Visions: Representation and Resistance in the Unseen Salt of the Earth." *American Quarterly* 60, no. 2 (June 2008): 347–71.

Burns, James MacGregor. "A New House for the Labor Board." *The Journal of Politics* 3, no. 4 (November 1941): 486–508.

Cargill, Jack. "Empire and Opposition: The 'Salt of the Earth' Strike." In *Labor in New Mexico: Unions, Strikes and Social History since 1881,* edited by Robert Kern, 183–267. Albuquerque: University of New Mexico Press, 1983.

Caulfield, Norman. "Wobblies and Mexican Workers in Mining and Petroleum, 1905–1924." *International Review of Social History* 40 (1995): 51–76.

Ceplair, Larry. "The Film Industry's Battle against Left-Wing Influences, from the Russian Revolution to the Blacklist." *Film History: An International Journal* 20, no. 4 (2008): 399–411.

Chacón, Justin Akers. "Magonismo and the Roots of Revolutionary Internationalism." *International Socialist Review,* no. 101 (Summer 2016). http://isreview.org /issue/101/magonismo-and-roots-revolutionary-internationalism

Cotter, Cornelius P., and J. Malcolm Smith. "An American Paradox: The Emergency Detention Act of 1950." *Journal of Politics* 19, no. 1 (February 1957): 20–33.

Devinatz, Victor G. "Red Unionism During the Depression and Under McCarthyism: Reflections on Mine-Mill, the Workers Unity League, and the Minneapolis Teamsters." *American Communist History* 13, nos. 2–3 (2014): 189–98.

Dinwoodie, D. H. "The Rise of Mine-Mill Union in Southwestern Copper." In *American Labor in the Southwest,* edited by James C. Foster, 19–56. Tucson: University of Arizona Press, 1982.

Douglas, William O. "The Black Silence of Fear." *New York Times Magazine,* January 13, 1952.

Foster, James C. "The Western Wobblies." In *American Labor in the Southwest,* edited by James C. Foster, 59–64. Tucson: University of Arizona Press, 1982.

Gilbert, Jess. "Eastern Urban Liberals and Midwestern Agrarian Intellectuals: Two Group Portraits of Progressives in the New Deal Department of Agriculture." *Agricultural History* 74, no. 2 (Spring 2000): 162–80.

Gonzales, Michael J. "U.S. Copper Companies, the Mine Workers' Movement, and the Mexican Revolution, 1910–1920." *Hispanic American Historical Review* 76, no. 3 (August 1996): 503–34.

Gutiérrez, Édgar O. "Santa Rita del Cobre, un mineral en el siglo XIX." *Actas del Cuarto Congreso Internacional de Historia Regional Comparada,* Universidad Autónoma de Ciudad Juárez, 1997, 389–98.

Heyman, Josiah. "The Oral History of the Mexican American Community of Douglas, Arizona, 1901–1942." *Journal of the Southwest* 35, no. 2 (Summer 1993), 186–206.

Huggard, Christopher J. "Copper Mining in Grant County, 1900–1945." In *Essays in Twentieth-Century New Mexico History,* edited by Judith Boyce DeMark, 43–61. Albuquerque: University of New Mexico Press, 1994.

Irons, Peter. "How Solicitor General Fahy Misled the Supreme Court in the Japanese-American Internment Cases: A Reply to Charles Sheehan." *American Journal of Legal History* 55 (2015): 298, 312.

Katyal, Neal Kumar. "The Solicitor General and Confession of Error." *Fordham Law Review* 81 (2013): 3027.

Kern, Robert. "Organized Labor: Race, Radicalism, and Gender." In *Essays in Twentieth-Century New Mexico History*, Edited by Judith Boyce DeMark, 149–67. Albuquerque: University of New Mexico Press, 1994.

Isserman, Maurice, and Ellen Schrecker. "'Papers of a Dangerous Tendency': From Major Andre's Boot to the VENONA Files." In *Cold War Triumphalism, The Misuse of History After the Fall of Communism*, edited by Ellen Schrecker, 149–73. New York: New Press, 2004.

"The Jencks Legislation: Problems in Prospect." *Yale Law Journal* 67, no. 4 (February 1958): 674–99.

Lay, Shawn. "Imperial Outpost on the Border: El Paso's Frontier Klan No. 100." In *The Invisible Empire in the West*, edited by Shawn Lay, 67–95. Urbana: University of Illinois Press, 1992.

Lee, Allison Herren, William W. Shakely, and J. Robert Brown Jr. "Judge Warren L. Jones and the Supreme Court of Dixie." *Louisiana Law Review* 59 (Fall 1998): 209–52.

Lichtman, Robert M. "Louis Budenz, the FBI, and the 'List of 400 Concealed Communists': An Extended Tale of McCarthy-Era Informing." *American Communist History* 3, no. 1 (2004): 25–54 .

Lorence, James J. "Clinton Jencks, The Wartime Generation, and Mine-Mill Social Activism in the Southwest, 1945–1950." Unpublished. Expanded version of a paper presented at the North American Labor History Conference, Detroit, October 22, 1999. Expanded for the seminar "Labor and the Cold War," Center for Recent United States History, University of Iowa, Iowa City, February 19, 2000.

———. "Mexican American Workers, Clinton Jencks and Mine-Mill Social Activism in the Southwest, 1945–1952." In *Labor's Cold War: Local Politics in a Global Context*, edited by Shelton Stromquist, 204–25. Urbana: University of Illinois Press, 2008.

———. "Mining Salt of the Earth." *Wisconsin Magazine of History* 85, no. 2 (Winter 2001–2): 28–43.

———. "*Salt of the Earth* and Free Expression: Mine-Mill Union and the Movies in the Rocky Mountain West." *New Mexico Historical Review* 76, no. 4 (October 2001): 414–30.

———. "The Suppression of 'Salt of the Earth' in Midwest America: The Underside of the Cold War Culture in Detroit and Chicago." *Film History* 10, no. 3, "The Cold War and the Movies" (1998): 346–58.

Margolin, Robert J. "Comment, Constitutional Law: Due Process and Right of Confrontation: Jencks Act." *Michigan Law Review* 58, no. 6 (April 1960): 888–904.

Marin, Christine. "The Union, Community Organizing, and Civil Liberties: Clinton Jencks, *Salt of the Earth*, and Arizona Copper in the 1950s." *Mining History Journal* 7 (2000): 64–70.

Marion, J. Hardin III. Case Comment. "The Jencks Case." *Washington and Lee Law Review* 15, no. 1 (1958): 88–99.

Mellinger, Phil. "How the IWW Lost Its Western Heartland: Western Labor History Revisited." *Western Historical Quarterly* 27, no. 3 (Autumn 1996): 303–24.

————, "'The Men Have Become Organizers': Labor Conflict and Unionization in the Mexican Mining Communities of Arizona, 1900–1915." *Western Historical Quarterly* 23, no. 3 (August 1992): 323–47.

Monroy, Douglas. "Fence Cutters, Sedicioso, And First-Class Citizens: Mexican Radicalism in America." In *The Immigrant Left in the United States*, edited by Paul Buhle and Dan Georgakas, 11–44. Albany: State University of New York Press, 1996.

Moreno, Luis H. "Mexican American Working-Class Activism." *Journal of American Ethnic History* 34, no. 1 (Fall 2014): 101–4.

Murdock, Abe. "NLRA. Should the Act Be Amended?" *Virginia Law Review* 27, no. 5 (March 1941): 633–63.

Nelson, Lawrence J. "The Art of the Possible: Another Look at the 'Purge' of the AAA Liberals in 1935." *Agricultural History* 57, no. 4 (October 1983): 416–35.

Packer, Herbert L. "A Tale of Two Typewriters." *Stanford Law Review* 10, no. 3 (May 1958): 409–40.

Peary, Danny. "Salt of the Earth." In *Cult Movies 2*, 135–38. New York: Dell, 1983.

Powers, Thomas. "The Plot Thickens." *New York Review of Books* 47, no. 8 (May 11, 2000):53—60

"Salt of the Earth," *California Quarterly* 2, no. 4 (Summer 1953).

Schrecker, Ellen W. "Archival Sources for the Study of McCarthyism." *The Journal of American History* 75, no. 1 (June 1988): 197–208.

————. "Soviet Espionage in America: An Oft-Told Tale." *Reviews in American History* 38, no. 2 (June 2010): 355–61.

Steece, Arvel M. "Congregationalism and Pacifism." *Washington Gladden Society*, undated. http://washingtongladdensociety.org/documents/pacifism.pdf

Steinbeck, John. "The Death of a Racket," *Saturday Review* 38, no. 14 (April 2, 1955): 26.

Taslitz, Andrew E. "Stories of Fourth Amendment Disrespect: From Elian to the Internment." *Fordham Law Review* 70, no. 6 (2002): 2257–2359.

Theoharis, Athan. "The FBI and the American Legion Contact Program, 1940–1966." *Political Science Quarterly* 100, no. 2 (Summer 1985): 271–86.

————. "A Lawless Agency: The FBI and the 'Hollywood Ten.'" *Rhetoric & Public Affairs* 2, no. 3 (Fall 1999): 415–30.

————. "Venona: Decoding Soviet Espionage in America by John Earl Haynes and Harvey Klehr." *American Historical Review* 106, no. 1 (February 2001): 209–10

Weinberg, Carl R. "'Salt of the Earth': Labor, Film, and the Cold War." *OAH Magazine of History* 24, no. 4, "The Cold War Revisited" (October 2010): 42–45.

Williams, Heather E. "Justice Unbalanced: Clinton Jencks—The Man—The Act." *Champion* (July 2005): 12.

Wilson, Michael. "Salt of the Earth." *California Quarterly* 2, no. 4 (Summer 1953): 3–59.

Yates, W. Ross. "Samuel Wetherill, Joseph Wharton, and the Founding of the American Zinc Industry." *Pennsylvania Magazine of History and Biography* 98, no. 4 (October 1974): 469–514.

Zarnow, Leandra. "Braving Jim Crow to Save Willie McGee: Bella Abzug, the Legal Left, and Civil Rights Innovation, 1948–1951." *Law & Social Inquiry* 33, no. 4 (Fall 2008): 1003–41.

FILM, VIDEO, AND OTHER SOURCES

Committee on Un-American Activities. Directed by Robert Carl Cohen, 1962. YouTube video, 43:52, posted by "radicalfilms," April 8, 2007. www.youtube.com /watch?v=U1Z5aYU6xoo.

A Crime to Fit the Punishment. Directed by Barbara A. Moss and Stephen Mack. Produced by Barbara A. Moss. 1982. Chicano Research Center collection, County of Los Angeles Public Library, Los Angeles. https://archive.org/details/clcop_000371.

"The Hollywood Blacklist." *Mysteries and Scandals*, season 2, episode 13, directed by Joel K. Rodgers and Liz Flynn, aired May 31, 1999. "Blacklist Hollywood 10 Mysteries and Scandals," YouTube video, 42:05. Posted by "Bob Daugherty," October 21, 2016. www.youtube.com/watch?v=HEvWDLXd4CQ.

Hollywood on Trial. Directed by David Helpern. Cinema Associates, 1976. "'Hollywood on Trial'—Dir. David Halpern. 1976," YouTube video, 1:42:04. Posted by "Adam Teoman," April 15, 2015. www.youtube.com/watch?v=KxFMsZGLleQ

The Hollywood Ten. Directed by John Berry. Ironweed Films, 1950. "The Hollywood Ten (1950)," YouTube video, 15:01, posted by "Mathew Hormann," January 9, 2011. https://www.youtube.com/watch?v=taancRcLQ80&t=3s.

May, John. "Harvey Matusow: A Life in Five Posts." *The Generalist* (blog), April 21, 2008. https://hqinfo.blogspot.com/2008/04/harvey-matusow-life-in-five-posts.html.

One of the Hollywood Ten. Directed by Karl Francis. Bloom Street Productions, 2000.

Salt of the Earth. Directed by Herbert J. Biberman. Independent Productions and International Union of Mine, Mill & Smelter Workers, 1954. www.youtube.com /watch?v=i9oY4rmDaWw.

ACKNOWLEDGMENTS

NO CASE OR STATUTE IS INVOKED BY NAME in the federal courts more than *Jencks v. United States* or the Jencks Act, laws obligating the prosecution to provide witness statements to defendants. Despite its use in every criminal trial, few of us are familiar with the story behind the case. Matusow's role in *Jencks* became a national scandal for the prosecution, and this book now reveals the government's misrepresentations to the Supreme Court. So far as we can tell, it is the only Texas prosecution under federal or state Communist control statutes.

In telling the Jencks story, I am indebted to scores of individuals whose work forms this book's foundation. They are the authors, journalists, researchers, and archivists of the primary materials, articles, books, oral histories, and finding aids we gather and synthesize—and hopefully present to readers as a coherent story.

This book is about the lives of Clinton and Virginia Jencks, the men and women of Mine-Mill Local 890, and their work during the red scare of the 1940s and '50s. They are the primary sources for what is written here. Clinton and Virginia Jencks left a magnificent record, much of which is found in Special Collections at the University of Colorado Library. Clinton Jencks himself spent a year organizing this archival gem, which includes records of the Western Federation of Miners, Mine-Mill, and Jencks's own papers.

The now deceased historian James J. Lorence spent much of his life collecting material and writing about leftists, labor organizers, radical film, and Clinton Jencks. His personal papers, as well as his books and articles, were invaluable. His widow, Donna Lorence, generously gave me access to those files. Historian Patricia Burch Vaughn provided her Jencks collection and her thoughts on some of the issues involved. Grant County historian and author Terrence Humble has been a wonderful resource and a good friend, always willing to respond to questions about the mines and personalities in Grant County. Jack Cargill donated his important Mine-Mill research materials to Western New Mexico University. Alfredo Chávez Montoya, deceased, a committed union man, left his important collection to the University of New Mexico. He amassed a comprehensive record of Mine-Mill during the time he and Jencks were active in the union. Historian Ellen Schrecker's impressive body of work on anticommunism and the FBI files she accumulated in years of fighting and litigating are crucial to the Jencks story. From Clinton's granddaughter Heather Wood, I learned about the personal side of the Jencks family, and she kindly shared her collection.

I am grateful to many who have studied anticommunism and Communists, including the following individuals, whose work was important to understanding the story of Clinton Jencks: Ellen R. Baker, David Caute, Larry Ceplair, Ronald D. Cohen, Robert M. Lichtman, Ted Morgan, Athan Theoharis, and Zaragosa Vargas; and also those who helped to navigate important archival resources, including David Hays (Special Collections, University of Colorado Libraries), Andrea Jáquez (Western New Mexico University Library), and Claudia Rivers (Special Collections, University of Texas at El Paso Library). I thank the following individuals who gave their time for interviews or for reviewing and helping to improve the manuscript: Francis C. Broaddus Jr., Jamie Bronstein, Mark Cioc-Ortega, Ronald D. Cohen, Arthur Flores, Humberto Silex (deceased), Judge Thomas A. Spieczny, and Anita Tórrez.

Finally, I appreciate the University of Oklahoma Press and J. Kent Calder for undertaking this project, Steven Baker and Maura McAndrew for their assistance in editing the manuscript, and Michael E. Tigar for his foreword. Thanks always to my wife, Mary Hull, for her constant support and input.

Raymond Caballero
Portland, Oregon, 2019

INDEX

Abraham Lincoln Brigade, 21, 41, 169, 274n15

Abt, John, 25, 52, 101, 241n26, 242n26; and Ware Group, 52, 100–101, 242n36

Acosta, Rodolfo, 78

A.F. of L. *See* American Federation of Labor (A.F. of L.)

Alderman, Joseph J., 88, 97, 144, 182–84, 240n14; and Ford, J. W., 173, 200–201; and Jencks trial, 111–12, 120; and Matusow, 266n13

Allen, Woody, 126

Alsop, Stewart, 133

Alvey, Brandon, 139. *See* Jencks case (district court proceedings)

American Federation of Labor (A.F. of L.), 17, 49, 67; and Hollywood, 76–77; and Thomason, R. E., 96, 239n11; and Witt, Nathan, 100

American Legion, 164; and Hollywood, 76, 188

ANMA. *See* Asociación Nacional Mexicana Americana

anticommunism, anti-Communist movement: antisemitism, racism, and xenophobia of, 196–98; history of, 25–30; and Hoover, J. Edgar, 26–28, 165; and immigration, 198; methods of, 32, 36–41; red scare hysteria of, 7, 25–26, 37, 206–7; repression by, 25–41, 237n22. *See also* Hoover, J. Edgar; McCarran Act; McCarthy, Joseph; Smith Act

Asociación Nacional Mexicana Americana, 23, 48, 67, 113, 115, 223n32

attorneys. *See* Jencks prosecutors; Jencks defense lawyers

Army-McCarthy hearings, 129, 134–35

Bear Mountain Lodge, 78, 81

Belmont, Alan H., 182–85

Benjamin, Richard, 84

Bentley, Arvilla (wife of Harvey Matusow), 128

Bentley, Elizabeth, 126, 137, 215n1

Berresford, Richard B., 86–88

Biberman, Herbert, 71–74, 83–84; and contempt sentence, 218n36; and Hollywood Ten, 218nn33–34

Biberman, Sonja Dahl, 77

Biddle, Francis, 40

Bigbee, Harry L., 139–40, 251n31

Bioff, William Morris, 74–75; corruption history of, 232–33n21

Bird, Florence "Chickie" (Jencks's third wife), 192

Black, Hugo, 156–57, 159, 198, 256n20

Boardman, Leland V., 184

Bogart, Humphrey, 34, 218n35

Bostick, Floyd, 84

Brennan, William J., Jr., 152, 154, 157–60, 256n20, 257nn21–23

Brewer, Roy: and Hollywood, 74–76; and Salt of the Earth, 76–77, 78, 80, 188, 199, 233n27

Broaddus, Francis C., Jr., 97, 113, 129, 246n61, 270n12; and Matusow, 266n13

Brooks, Clay Martin, 112–13

Browder, Earl, 31, 168, 271n14

Browne, George E., 74–75, 232n21

Brown v. Board of Education, 96, 108, 152

Brownell, Herbert Jr., 259n37; and Lindsay, John, 154; and Matusow, 201, 249n20, 252n48; and witness scandal, 137, 143, 163, 179

Budenz, Louis, 38, 88, 118, 126, 137–38

Burns, William J., 28

Burton, Harold Hitz, 158–60, 256n20, 257n21

Burttram, Julian H. (special agent), 140, 179, 184–85

Cameron, Angus, 131, 139,

Cameron, Benjamin Franklin, 145–46;
and panel assignment controversy, 146, 254n4; and Jencks case, 147–49, 161, 186

Cameron and Kahn, 131, 136, 140, 149

Cammer, Harold I., 100, 242n31

Catholic Church, 30, 76

Central Protective Committee, 82

Chacón, Juan, 48, 87, 149, 206; and Salt of the Earth, 78, 204, 236n7

Chacón, Virginia, 54, 58, 188, 206, 226n35, 272n25

Chambers, Whittaker, 211n13; and Hiss, Alger, 124, 218n38; and House Un-American Activities Committee, 47; and Ware Group, testimony of, 52, 100–101, 242n36

Charney, George Blake, 144

Chávez, Aurora, 58

CIO. See Congress of Industrial Organizations (CIO)

Claridge, J. Phillip (special agent), 87, 171, 173–74

Clark, John, 45–47, 53, 268n5

Clark, Tom C., 207, 270n7; and Communist cases, 36, 273n28; Frankfurter criticism of, 258n27, 259–60n46; and Hoover, J. Edgar, 35, 219n40, 220n63; and Jencks case, 158–61, 163, 199, 256n19, 256n20, 257n22, 258nn26–27; and Parnell, Thomas J., case, 218n38

Cohen, Ronald D., 143

Cohn, Roy, 40; and Flynn case, 98, 126, 131, 134, 136, 143–44

Communist Party of the United States: history of, 25–32; relation to Soviet party of, 25

Communist Party v. SACB, 153

Communists: activism of, 197–98; Soviet collusion of, 25, 197; threat to social and economic order of, 197

Conference of Studio Unions (CSU), 75–76

Congress of Industrial Organizations (CIO), 17; 1948 and presidential campaign, 46, 48, 222n22; and anti-Communist affidavit, 45, 121; and film local, 77; and Mine-Mill expulsion from, 49–51, 118; and Witt, Nathan, 100, 239n11

Coolidge, Calvin, 28

Crouch, Paul, 88, 137–38, 153

CSU. *See* Conference of Studio Unions (CSU)

Currie, James Edward, 110

Cvetic, Matthew, 38

Daugherty, Harry M., 28

Debs, Eugene V., 13, 28, 216n10

Dennis, Eugene, 36

Dennis v. United States, 268n35; Douglas, William O., dissent in, 37; and Smith Act prosecutions, 38, 118,

Dewey, Thomas E., 46, 48, 152

Dimock, Edward J., 135; and Flynn motion for new trial, 136–37, 143–44, 149

DiSanti, Joseph R., 111, 115, 170, 172, 263n19

Distributive, Processing and Office Workers of America (DPOWA), 89–91

Dmytryk, Edward, 35, 218n33, 218n36, 231n4, 233n27

Douglas, William O., 153; and Dennis dissent, 37; and Jencks case, 155, 158–59, 256n18, 256n21, 257n21

Eastland, James O., 38, 137, 142, 153, 268n34, 270n6. *See also* Senate Internal Security Subcommittee

Eckert, Kenneth, 45–47, 49, 66, 222n20; and Jencks trial, 118–19, 246n54

Edmiston, John and Martha, 125, 180–81

Eisenhower cabinet: and *Jencks* decision, 162–63, 259n37; Matusow discussion in, 138, 143, 185, 253n49

Elfers, E. B., 89, 97, 106, 120, 139, 165,

Empire Zinc Co. and mine, 42, 50. *See also* Empire Zinc Strike; New Jersey Zinc

Empire Zinc strike, 51–69; assessment of, 68–69; bargaining committee arrest in, 65; discrimination issues in, 54, 60; injunctions in, 60, 64; Mine-Mill headquarter's concern over, 55; peace bonds in, 62; settlement of, 64; start of, 52–53; strikebreakers in, 57; union demands in, 53–54; violence in, 61, 62; women pickets, arrest of, 58–59; women pickets in, 58, 61

EZ. *See* Empire Zinc Co. and mine

False Witness. See Matusow, Harvey Marshall

Fatima secret, 4

Federal Bureau of Investigation: and Communist control, 4, 26; Custodial Detention Program, 35, 40–41, 169; harassment by, 40, 167, 189–90, 197; and Hollywood, 32–33, 76; illegal activity of, 28, 32, 36, 164, 185, 198; and Jencks, 87, 111, 114, 168–74; loyalty and security investigations of, 44; and Matusow, 115–16, 125, 128, 134, 178–85; and red scare, 29; and secrecy of files, 158–65; Security Index of, 52, 169

Fierro Riot, 48,

Flynn, Elizabeth Gurley, 38, 98, 126, 241n20

Foley, William, 183

Ford, Jerry W.: career and death of, 193; FBI statements of, 116–17, 147; and Jencks Party resignation, 121, 167–81; testimony of, 107, 111–12, 120

Foy, Franey, 82
Foy, Tom, 56, 58, 62, 82
Frank, Jerome, 99, 241n26
Frankfurter, Felix, 99, 153; and Jencks
    argument, 155–57, 159–60; and
    Jencks decision, 256n20, 257n21,
    258n27, 259n46
Freedom of Information Act (FOIA),
    168, 210n4
Freedmen's Bureau (Bureau of Refugees,
    Freedmen, and Abandoned Lands),
    11, 197

Geer, Will, 78, 234n34
Goforth, Leslie, 56, 57–68
Grant County Mine-Mill locals:
    amalgamation of into Local 890,
    54; and Empire Zinc Hanover local
    604, 42; and Hurley local 69, 22,
    42; and Santa Rita local 63, 22, 42;
    and Vanadium local 530, 42
Grant County, N.Mex.: history of,
    19–20; dual wage system in, 19–21;
    segregation in, 20, 212n6

Hannett, A. T., 139
Harding, Warren G., 28, 216n9
Harlan, John Marshall, 155, 158–60,
    256n20, 257n21
Harris, David H., 139–41
Heidbrink, Hermoine (Jencks's first
    wife), 14
Herblock cartoon, 135
Hernández v. Texas, 108, 244n12
Herring, Charles F., 97, 113, 118,
    181–82, 201, 266n13
Hiss, Alger, 67, 124, 242n36, 273n28;
    and Ware Group, 47, 101, 218n38
Hohri v. United States, 6, 209nn4–5
Hollywood: and blacklist, 34–35
    71–72; film content control of,
    231n1, 231nn3–4; and Hollywood

Ten, 32–35, 218n33; Hoover, J.
    Edgar, interest in, 32–33; House
    Un-American Activities Committee
    and, 32–35; studio oligopoly in, 70
Holmgren, Rodney, 90, 103, 243n45
Hoover, J. Edgar, 26, 38; and anti-
    Communist leadership, 7, 38;
    commendation letters of, 114; and
    Communist threat, 29; and FBI
    illegal activities, 28, 35, 219n40,
    219n45; and Hollywood, 32–33; and
    Jencks Act and case, 164–65, 175;
    and Matusow, 128, 179, 184–85; and
    Palmer raids, 27, 216n8, 217n13;
    public popularity of, 4, 114, 182, 184,
    266n14; and public relations, 179,
    246n36; and security and detention
    programs, 35, 40–41, 220n63;
    and Smith Act, 36; suggestion
    of Matusow perjury by, 180–81,
    184, 201, 265n8, 266n25; and
    Thomason, 186, 199, 268nn34–35
Hopper, Hedda, 76
House Un-American Activities
    Committee (HUAC): and anti-
    Communist methods, 32, 267n27;
    and Chambers, Whittaker, 47,
    52, 100, 242n36; creation of, 7;
    and Hollywood, 32–35, 71–71, 76,
    218n31, 218n33, 234n34; Jencks
    and, 190, 262n5, 262n15; and
    Matusow, 125–26, 130, 135, 180–81,
    248n3, 249n20; and McTernan,
    John, 98; and Parnell, Thomas
    J., 33–35, 218n38; and southern
    segregationists, 197, 270n6
HUAC. See House Un-American
    Activities Committee (HUAC)
Hughes, Howard, 72, 84

IATSE. See International Alliance of
    Theatrical Stage Employees (IATSE)

Independent Production Company, 71–72, 74, 232n8; and distribution and showing of *Salt of the Earth*, 188–89; and filming *Salt of the Earth*, 77, 80; and obstruction of *Salt of the Earth*, 76–85

Internal Security Act of 1950. *See* McCarran Act

International Alliance of Theatrical Stage Employees, 74; and Brewer, Roy, 75–77; corruption history of, 74–75, 232n21

International Union of Mine, Mill, and Smelter Workers. *See* Mine-Mill Union

IPC. *See* Independent Production Company

Jackson, Donald, 81–82, 84, 236n7

Jackson, Henry M., 137, 139, 253n49

Japanese internment, 35, 41, 202, 270n1; logic behind, 196; and Ringle report, 5–7, 264n27; Supreme Court approval of, 5–6; Warren, Earl, views of, 152

Jarrico, Paul, 71–72; and communism, 202, 212n23, 271n14; and Hollywood film content, 231n1; and Jencks, 204, 232n11; and *Salt of the Earth*, 74–77, 80, 234n37

Jarrico, Sylvia Gussin, 72–73

Jefferson School bookstore, 126

Jencks, Clinton Edward: activism of, 12–13; Anglo community antipathy toward, 44, 83–84; anti-Fascism of, 14; Arizona residence of, 149–50; arrest of, 57, 87; attacks against, 49, 62, 83–84, 235n48; blacklisting of, 149–50, 189–90; British coal miners study by, 192; California Bay Area employment problems of, 189–90; California Bay Area residence of, 189; character of,

204–5; childhood of, 10, 11–12; college years of, 13; commitment to poor and discriminated of, 12, 206; Communist Party membership of, 13, 31, 202–3; Communist Party resignation of, 49, 170–76, 200–201, 262n15, 263nn19–21; contempt sentence of, 60, 64–65, 123, 130, 229nn64–65; death of, 193; Denver residence of, 16–17, 168; divorce of, 192; and Empire Zinc strike, 51–65, 68–69; family history of, 10–11; Federal Bureau of Investigation file of, 168–70; and Federal Bureau of Investigation security lists, 169, 191, 262n9, 262nn11–12, 263n20, 269n15; and Grant County Mine-Mill locals, 42–48; Grant County residence of, 42, 89, 123; and House Un-American Activities Committee, 190–91; indictment of, 87–88, 236n3; and Jarrico, Paul, 72; Jencks defense committee, 123; and Lorence, James J., 17, 170, 203, 223n34; and marriage to Bird, Florence "Chickie," 197; and marriage to Heidbrink, Hermoine, 14; and marriage to Sobelman-Brodshatzer, Muriel, 193; and marriage to Derr, Virginia, 14; and Matusow, Harvey, 66–68, 88; and McCarran Committee, 65–68; and Mexican discrimination, 43–44, 48–49, 213nn11–12, 222n16; and Mexican miners, 42; military decorations of, 15–16, 212n20; military service of, 14–16; and Mine-Mill Conventions, 49, 52; and Mine-Mill union, 17; Mine-Mill union termination of, 149, 268n5; morals and ethics of, 10,12, 205; and new trial hearing, 138–41; and NLRB non-Communist affidavit,

Jencks, Clinton Edward (*continued*)
49, 51; religious views of, 211n10;
Roosevelt, Franklin and Eleanor,
meeting with, 14; and *Salt of the
Earth*, 72, 78–85; and San Cristóbal
Valley Ranch, 52, 68, 72, 115; and
San Diego State University, 192;
St. Louis residence of, 14; and
University of California at Berkeley,
190–92; and University of Colorado
(Boulder), 13, 31; as victim of
McCarthyism, 8, 26; and Wallace–
Progressive Party campaign, 47–48;
and Woodrow Wilson Fellowship,
190–91; and Young Communist
League, 13, 168, 271n16. *See also
entries under* Jencks case
Jencks, Clinton Michael (Jencks's son),
15, 87, 193
Jencks, Dewitt Clinton (Jencks's
grandfather), 11
Jencks, Horace Ebenezer (Jencks's
father), 10–11, 13, 211n7
Jencks, Leavens (Jencks's great-
grandfather), 11
Jencks, Ruth Shideler (Jencks's
mother), 10–11
Jencks, Virginia Derr (Jencks's second
wife), 14, 205; arrest of, 59; assaults
on, 62; burial of, 193; Clinton
Jencks's divorce from, 192–93; and
Clinton Jencks case, 123, 166; and
Clinton Jencks Party resignation,
49, 262n15; Communist Party
activities of, 111, 168, 170; death of,
252; and Empire Zinc Strike, 58,
226n35; and FBI security index, 52,
262n11; and Ladies' Auxiliary, 54;
legacy of, 205–6; and marriage to
Jencks, 14; and marriage to Thomas
Chambers, 193; and *Salt of the
Earth*, 72, 78, 232n11, 272n19; union
work of, 43

Jencks Act, 8; congressional response
to *Jencks* decision, 161–62; Hoover,
J. Edgar, reaction to, 164–65;
importance of, 206; passage of,
162–65; statute explained, 164,
260n47
Jencks case (district court proceedings),
187–92; Broaddus summation, 120,
246n61; indictment, 87, 236n3;
indictment dismissal, 165–66; jury
instructions, 122; jury selection,
105–8; Matusow confessional
affidavit and, 131–34; McTernan
summation, 120–21; motion for
new trial, 134; motion for new trial
hearing, 138–41; pretrial motions,
89, 102–4; sentencing, 122;
testimony of Brooks, Clay Martin,
112–13; testimony of Currie, James
Edward, 110; testimony of Eckert,
Kenneth, 118, 119; testimony of
Ford, Rev. J. W., 111–12; testimony of
Knott, George, in 113; testimony of
Matusow, Harvey Marshall, 115–17;
testimony of Peterson, James E., 113;
testimony of Terrazas, Jesus, 113,
119; testimony of Thompson, John
P., 119; verdict, 122; Williams trial
summation, 121–22
Jencks case (U.S. Court of Appeals),
145–50; court scandal, 254n4;
decision, 147–49; and judges,
145–46
Jencks case (U.S. Supreme Court),
151–62; Brennan opinion, 158–60;
Clark dissent, 160–61; concurring
opinion, 160; drafting decision,
158–60, 257nn21–24; Eisenhower
comments on, 258–59nn36–37;
Frankfurter comment on Clark
dissent, 259–60n46; Friday
conferences, 157–58, 256n20;
importance of, 206; justices on

case, 152, 155; Lindsay argument, 156–57; Lindsay's misrepresentation to Court, 176–77; McTernan oral argument, 155–56, 256n10; reaction to decision, 161; Solicitor General's Office conduct, 173–74; Thomason reaction to decision, 161–62

Jencks defense lawyers. See Bigbee, Harry L.; Elfers, E. B.; Hannett, A. T.; McTernan, John T.; Witt, Nathan

Jencks prosecutors, 200–202. See Alderman, Joseph J.; Alvey, Brandon; Broaddus, Francis C., Jr.; Harris, David H.; Herring, Charles F.; Pine, Robert S.; Williams, Holvey

Jencks v. United States. See entries under Jencks case

Jenks, Joseph (immigrant progenitor), 10–11

Jenks, Joseph, III (Rhode Island governor), 11

Jenks, Joseph, Jr. (Rhode Island settler), 11

Johnson, Hubert Herndon, 122–23

Johnson, Lyndon B., 96–97, 163, 168, 240n12

Johnson, Manning, 153

Johnson's Super Market, 126

Jones, Warren Leroy, 145–46, 149, 254n4

Kahn, Alfred, 130–36, 140, 149, 252n37, 253n51, 254n9. See also Cameron and Kahn

Keating, Kenneth, 162

Keay, Victor P., 183

Keener, George H., 87

Kelley, Esther (Jencks's great-grandmother, wife of Leavens Jencks), 11

King, Martin Luther, Jr., 198

Knott, George, 113

Korean Conflict, 69, 88, 113–19, 125, 179

Korematsu, Fred, 196

Korematsu v. United States, 5, 209n3

Ladies Auxiliary Local, 43, 54, 58

Lamb, Ted, 136

Lardner, Ring, Jr., 35, 218n33, 219n38

Larson, Orville, 18,

Lazarus, Simon M., 71, 76–77, 234n34

Lattimore, Owen, 126

Lea, Tom, Jr., 139

Lea, Tom, Sr., 94–95, 238n4

Lett, Earl, 82–84, 110, 235nn48–49, 235n53

Lichtman, Robert M., 143, 162, 217n25

Lindsay, John V.: misrepresentation to Supreme Court, 174, 176–77; Supreme Court argument of, 9, 154, 156–57, 174

Local 890. See Grant County Mine-Mill locals

Lorence, James J., 17, 170, 203, 233n39, 262n15, 271n16

Lumbard, J. Edward, 136, 267n25

Lumet, Sidney, 126, 137, 248n7, 248n8

Mansfield, Mike J., 137

Margolis, Ben, 97–99, 154, 162, 240n17

Marshall, A. W., 58–60, 64–65, 227n49, 228n64

Mata, Arturo, 214n20, 215n29

Matthews, J. B., 38, 66

Matusow, Harvey Marshall: and 1952 campaign, 126–28, 137; blacklisting activities of, 126; cabinet discussion of, 253n49; career of, 193–94; and Communist Party, 124–25; death of, 194; and Dimock, Edward J., 143–44; and Edmiston, John and Martha, 125, 181; El Paso contempt case and appeal, 141, 148–49, 252n37; FBI

Matusow, Harvey Marshall (*continued*)
files of, 179–81, 265n2, 265nn4–8,
266n25, 267nn26–27; FBI
informant, 125; FBI warnings about,
184, 265n2, 265n4, 265nn7–8,
267nn25–27; and Flynn case
motion for new trial, 136–37,
142–43; and Hoover, J. Edgar,
suggestion of perjury, 180, 184;
and House Un-American Activities
Commission, 125, 130, 248n3;
imprisonment of, 193–94; and
Jencks indictment, 88; Jencks trial
testimony of, 115–17; and Latimore,
Owen, 126; and Lumet, Sydney,
126, 248nn7–8; and McCarthy,
Joseph, 126–27, 230n76; and
motion for new trial hearing (El
Paso), 139–42; and motion for new
trial hearing (New York), 136–37;
and Ohio Un-American Activities
Commission, 181; and Oxnam, G.
Bromley, 129–30, 136–37, 248n19;
perjury affidavit and *False Witness*
of, 131–34; personal history, 124–25;
and professional anticommunist
witnesses, 38, 124, 125–27; and
prosecutors, 201; recantation
controversy of, 142–44; and San
Cristóbal Valley Ranch, 66–68,
115–16, 125, 169, 184, 251n29,
251n34; and Senate Subcommittee
on Internal Security, 66–68, 127,
137–38; and Stone, I. F., 167–68; and
Texas Industrial Commission, 91;
and Thomason ruling, 142–43
McCarran, Patrick A., 65–68, 127.
See Senate Internal Security
Subcommittee
McCarran Act (Internal Security
Act of 1950), 52, 198; Emergency
Detention Act, 32; Subversive
Activities Control Board, 153

McCarthy, Joseph R.: and 1952
campaign, 127, 136–37, 253n49; and
anticommunism, 3, 7, 26, 222n22;
and Army-McCarthy hearings, 129,
13; censure of, 131; and Communist
lists, 196, 220nn58–59; and failure
to find Communist spies, 197; and
Matusow, 38, 127–28, 136–37, 139,
230n76; and McTernan, John, 98;
personal history of, 39–40; and
repressive methods, 26, 35, 133,
193, 201; and Supreme Court, 153;
Wheeling speech of, 39–40
McCarthyism. *See* anticommunism,
anti-Communist movement
McClendon, Sarah, 91
McTernan, John T.: and Flynn case,
241n20, 246n43; and Jencks
appeal, 145–48; and Jencks case
dismissal, 166; and Jencks pretrial
matters, 89, 102–3; and Jencks trial,
109–19, 243n5, 246n54; Jencks trial
summation of, 120–21; and Jencks
Supreme Court case, 154–56, 256n10;
and Margolis, Ben, 98; and Matusow
recantation, 130; and motion for
new trial, 130; and Nelson-Mesarosh
cases, 240n19; personal history of,
97–99, 240n17, 242n30
Mechem, Edwin L., 62
Mesarosh, Stjepan. *See* Nelson, Steve
Metzger, Bishop Sydney M., 188,
268n2
Mexican Americans: discrimination
against, 18–21, 22–23, 212n6, 213n8,
215n29; and dual wage system, 20,
213nn10–12, 215n26; labor history
of, 21–23, 214n13, 214n16; and
view that labor rights included civil
rights, 23
Mine-Mill Union: and 1948 election,
46–48; archive of, 193; activism of,
48, 198; and CIO, 45–46, 49–51;

and Communists, 66, 68, 80, 113, 118, 144, 227n47; and Empire Zinc strike, 53, 55, 60–61, 64, 84; and Grant County locals, 22–23, 51; history of, 17, 214n13, 214n20; and Jencks, 16–18, 42, 88, 123, 139; and Jencks resignation, 149; and Jencks trial, 103, 110; and Matusow, 131, 134, 140–41; and non-Communist affidavit, 45, 49, 170; and *Salt of the Earth*, 77, 86; Texas investigation of, 89–90

Montoya, Alfredo C., 43, 48, 111
Montoya, Cipriano, 56, 225n21
Morris (banker, Sunday school superintendent), 12
Mundt Bill, 172
Mundt, Karl E., 68

National Labor Relations Act (Wagner Act), 22, 99, 238n6, 239n12
National Labor Relations Board (NLRB): creation of, 22; and Empire Zinc strike, 61, 64; and McTernan, John T., 98, 242n30; and Mine-Mill affidavit boycott, 45–46; non-Communist affidavit of, 45–46, 51, 87, 236n3; and Witt, Nathan, 99–100, 242n30
National Lawyers Guild, 33, 217n27; and FBI, 35–36; and McTernan, John T., 97–98; and Witt, Nathan, 97
Natvig, Marie, 138, 250n11
Nelson, Steve (aka Mesarosh, Stjepan): and Mesarosh case, 154–55, 174; and Nelson case, 98, 153, 240n19
Nevada Consolidated Copper Co., 22–23
New Jersey Zinc Co., 53
New York Times, 161, 194; and Empire Zinc strike, 59; Matusow allegations against, 67, 128–29, 133, 136, 139, 178, 180, 184

Nixon, Richard M.: and Hiss, Alger, 101, 242n36; and Taft-Hartley, 240n12

Ohio Un-American Activities Commission, 125–26, 181
O'Mahoney, Joseph C., 163
Oxnam, G. Bromley, 129–30, 136–37, 149, 249n20

Palmer, A. Mitchell, 27, 216n8
Palmer Raids, 27–29, 216n8, 217n13
Pathé Labs, 77, 81, 84
Phelps Dodge Refinery, 62, 123, 231n86
Philbrick, Herbert, 4
Pidgeon, Walter, 80
Pine, Robert S., 165
Popular Front, 30–31
Pressman, Lee: and Agriculture Department, 25, 241n26; and CIO, 222n22; and Communist Party, 52; and steelworkers, 100; and Ware Group, 47, 52, 100–101, 242n36
Progressive Party, 46, 48, 171, 223n29
Provencio, B. G., 48

Rageh, Linda Halley (Jencks's adopted daughter), 14–15, 190, 204, 272n21, 272n23; and Empire Zinc strike, 59, 62; and Jencks's Party resignation, 49, 263n15; and Virginia's burial, 193, 269n23
Rankin, J. Lee (solicitor general), 154, 174–76
Reagan, Ronald, 71, 231n3
red scares. *See* anticommunism
Revueltas, Rosaura, 78, 81–82, 96, 233n33
Riesel, Victor, 80
Ringle report, 5–6, 196, 209n5
Roach, Joe, 83
Roos, Alfred, 78, 80, 83–84, 234n36

Roosevelt, Franklin D.: admonition against unreasoning fear, 5, 206, 209n1; first inaugural address, 4–5; and Hiss, Alger, 100–101; and Japanese internment, 5–6; and Jencks, 14; and labor, 22; and New Deal, 29–30, 241n26; and Thomason, 95
Roth, Philip, 198

SACB. See Subversive Activities Control Board (SACB)
Sacher, Harry, 133–34, 254n9
Salt of the Earth, 70–85; blacklisted cast members in, 234n34; criticism of, 80–82, 102; and Jencks, 3; and Jencks prosecution, 87, 236n7; legacy of, 206; Mexicans portrayal in, 233n32; production and distribution problems of, 76, 188; violence in, 88, 110, 272n23. See also Biberman, Herbert; Brewer, Roy; IPC; Jarrico, Paul; Jencks, Clinton; Jencks, Virginia; Revueltas, Rosaura; Wilson, Michael
San Cristóbal Valley Ranch: Jencks or Jarrico at, 52, 72; and Jencks trial, 92, 102, 169, 184; Matusow at, 66, 68, 115–16, 121, 125, 179, 251n29
Santa Rita, N.Mex., 20, 22, 42, 54, 83, 205, 212n6. See Grant County, N.Mex.
Schrecker, Ellen, 8, 26, 88, 202
Scott, Adrian, 71, 77, 218n33
Senate Internal Security Subcommittee (SISS), 32; and Eastland Subcommittee, 137, 142, 197; and McCarran Subcommittee, 65–69, 101, 126. See also Eastland, James O.; McCarran, Patrick A.
Sheen, Bishop Fulton J., 4
Shepperd, John Ben, 89–91, 129

Shideler, Ruth (Jencks's mother), 10–11; marriage of, 11; morals and ethics of, 11; religiosity of, 11
Shivers, Alan, 89, 91, 102, 237n22
SISS. See Senate Internal Security Subcommittee (SISS)
Smercke, Fr. Francis, 83
Smith Act, 32; Dennis (New York) case under, 118; Flynn (New York) case under, 98, 116, 126, 184; immigration aspects of, 198; Mesarosh (Pennsylvania) case under, 98, 154, 240n19; prosecutions under, 36–37, 38; Yates (California) case under, 98, 154, 162, 255n2
Smith, Howard W., 36, 38, 96, 100, 152–53; and Thomason, R. E., 238, 239n11
Sobelman-Brodshatzer, Muriel (Jencks's fourth wife), 193
Sondergaard, Gale, 71–72, 233n32, 234n34
Sorrell, Herbert, 75
Spanish Civil War, 13, 30
Stalin, Joseph, 4; and Communist Party policies, 30; Hitler-Stalin Pact, 14, 31, 35, 211n16, 217n25; repressive measures of, 202, 217n24
Steinbeck, John, 135
Stevens, Laurence E., 103, 244
Stone, Harlan Fiske, 28
Stone, I. F., 162, 167; and Clark dissent, 258n27
Subversive Activities Control Board (SACB), 52, 129, 131, 144, 181; invalidation of, 270n2

Taft-Hartley Act: antilabor measure of, 44, 239n12; attempted repeal of, 47, 49, 223n33; non-Communist affidavit of, 45, 47, 171; passage of, 44–45; and Thomason, 96, 239n12; Truman veto of, 44, 46, 239n12

Taylor, Robert, 34
Terrazas, Jesus, 113–14, 119
Texas Industrial Commission, 91, 129
Thomas, J. Parnell, 33, 35; fraud
    conviction of, 218n38
Thomason, Robert Ewing:
    anti-Communist bias of, 96;
    congressional voting record of,
    96, 238nn6–7, 239nn10–12;
    criticism of, 142, 168, 199–200;
    desegregation orders of, 96; Hoover,
    J. Edgar, praise by, 186, 268n34;
    and Jencks case appeal, 147–48;
    and Jencks case dismissal, 165–66;
    and Jencks case motion for new
    trial, 134, 139–42, 148–49, 184–86;
    and Jencks case pretrial, 87, 89,
    102–4; and Jencks case trial, 105–23;
    Jencks decision assessment of, 167,
    199–200; and Ku Klux Klan, 238n4;
    and Matusow, Harvey, contempt
    case, 141; and Matusow controversy,
    142–44; personal history, 93–96;
    praise for, 142, 148, 181, 238n1,
    238n5; praise of FBI by, 182; reaction
    to Jencks decision of, 161; Revueltas
    deportation and, 82; Smith, Howard
    W., and, 239n11; Warren, opinion of,
    157–58, 200, 256n20; and witness
    statements, 116, 140, 155, 173; and
    Witt, Nathan, 141, 200. See Jencks
    case (district court proceedings)
Thompson, John P., 119
Thurmond, Strom, 46, 48, 164
Time Magazine: and Chambers,
    Whittaker, 100; and Empire Zinc
    strike, 59; Jencks case in, 190,
    258n26; Matusow allegations
    against, 128–29, 133, 136, 178; and
    Salt of the Earth, 85
Tompkins, William F., 139, 250n25
Tórrez, Anita, 18, 43, 206, 226n33,
    272n19

Tórrez, Lorenzo, 18, 43, 53, 214n20,
    215n30, 224n20, 272n19
Trachtenberg, Alexander, 126, 131, 136,
    143–44
Travis, Maurice: Communist Party
    membership of, 17, 45, 49, 112; and
    Empire Zinc strike, 55, 61, 224n20,
    226n36; and McCarran Committee,
    66; Mine-Mill resignation of, 149,
    268n5
Truman, Harry S.: 1948 campaign
    of, 46–48, 100; executive orders
    of, 44; and Herring, Charles, 97;
    and McCarthy, Joseph, 39, 220n59;
    and Taft-Hartley, 48–49, 223n33,
    239n12; and Thomason, R. E., 93;
    vetoes of, 44, 52, 96, 239n12; and
    Warren, Earl, 152
Tuttle, Elbert Parr, 145–46, 149; panel
    assignment controversy, 146, 254n4

United States Solicitor General's Office,
    173–74; duty of candor of, 5–7, 154,
    176, 187, 209n5, 264n27
United States v. Flynn: and Matusow,
    116, 126, 131, 136, 183, 201, 266n25;
    and McTernan, 98, 116, 241n20,
    246n43, 254n9; motion for new
    trial in, 132–34, 143–44; and Smith
    Act cases, 38. See also Cohn, Roy;
    Dimock, Edward J.; McTernan,
    John T.

Vincent, Craig, 48; and Jencks trial,
    91, 102; and Matusow, 52, 66, 68,
    115, 125
Vincent, Jenny Wells, 52, 66, 68, 91,
    115, 125
Vinson, Fred M., 151–52
Vishinsky, Andrei, 37, 86, 126

Waldorf Declaration, 34, 76
Wallace, Henry A.: and 1948 election,

Wallace, Henry A. (*continued*)
   46–48, 223n29; and Roosevelt
   cabinet, 46, 241n26. *See also*
   Progressive Party
Walter, Francis E., 135, 161, 190
Ware (Harold) Group, 52, 100–101,
   242n36. *See also* Abt, John;
   Chambers, Whittaker; Hiss, Alger;
   Pressman, Lee; Witt, Nathan
Warner, Harry, 74
Warner, Jack, 34
Warner Brothers Studios., 74–75
Warren, Earl, 48; as governor and
   justice, 151–53; and Jencks case,
   154–59; and Thomason, R. E.,
   opinion of, 157–58, 200, 256n20
Watkins, Arthur V., 66–68
Western Federation of Miners, 17,
   21–22, 193, 215n29
White, Morrie B., 107–8, 244n9
Williams, Henrietta, 73
Williams, Holvey, 184; and *Jencks* case
   appeal, 145, 173; and *Jencks* case
   trial, 97, 108–20, 266n13; and
   Jencks case summation, 121–23

Wilson, Michael, 73–74, 77, 78–80,
   232n16, 233n32, 234n34
Wilson, Zelma Gussin, 73
Wine, Russell, 139
Witt, Nathan: and Chambers,
   Whittaker, 47–48, 101, 242n36; and
   Empire Zinc strike, 61; and motion
   for new trial hearing, 139–42;
   and *Jencks* case trial, 89, 117; and
   Jencks, opinion of, 204, 271n18; and
   Matusow, 130–31, 149, 246n50; and
   Mexicans, opinion of, 18; personal
   history of, 97–101; and Senate
   Internal Security Subcommittee,
   66–67; and Thomason, R. E., 186,
   200; and Ware Group, 47–48, 101
Wood, Heather (granddaughter),
   204–5, 269, 271n16

Yarborough, Ralph, 89, 91
Yates v. United States, 154, 162
Yeagley, J. Walter, 176
Young Communist League, 13, 168,
   271n16

CPSIA information can be obtained
at www.ICGtesting.com
Printed in the USA
LVHW090557080819
626952LV00001B/34/P